Washington, Somoza, and the Sandinistas

State and Regime in U.S. Policy Toward Nicaragua, 1969–1981

MORRIS H. MORLEY
Macquarie University

CAMBRIDGE
UNIVERSITY PRESS

✧ **W9-ADK-066**

Published by the Press Syndicate of the University of Cambridge
The Pitt Building, Trumpington Street, Cambridge CB2 1RP
40 West 20th Street, New York, NY 10011-4211, USA
10 Stamford Road, Oakleigh, Melbourne 3166, Australia

First published 1994

Printed in the United States of America

Library of Congress Cataloging-in-Publication Data
Morley, Morris H.
Washington, Somoza, and the Sandinistas : state and regime in U.S.
policy toward Nicaragua, 1969–1981 / Morris H. Morley.
p. cm.
Includes bibliographical references (p.) and index.
ISBN 0-521-45081-0
1. United States – Foreign relations – Nicaragua.   2. Nicaragua –
Foreign relations – United States.   3. Nicaragua – Politics and
government – 1937–1979.   4. Nicaragua – Politics and
government – 1979–1990.   5. Somoza, Anastasio, 1925–1980.   I. Title.
E183.8.N5M67   1994
327.7307285 – dc20   93-34540
                                              CIP

A catalog record for this book is available from the British Library.

ISBN 0-521-45081-0 hardback

For Carmel and Rodney

Contents

vii

Acknowledgments

I wish to express my appreciation to the archivists at the Jimmy Carter Library, the Gerald R. Ford Library, and the Nixon Presidential Materials Staff; to Mrs. Olga Luck of the State Department's Office of Freedom of Information, Privacy and Classification Review; to Charles Kennedy, in charge of the Foreign Affairs Oral History Program at Georgetown University; and to Peter Kornbluh at the National Security Archive for their help in locating materials.

Special thanks are due to Helma Neumann, Maureen Moseley, and Sue Folwell for the skill and care with which they typed various drafts of this manuscript. The final manuscript benefited from discussions with my good mate and longtime collaborator, James Petras. Another old and generous friend, Michael Clarke, made sure I took time out during my visits to Washington, D.C., to shoot some pool and smell the roses.

The research for this book was facilitated by grants from Macquarie University and the Australian Research Council.

1

Introduction: Permanent and transitory interests in U.S. foreign policy

Interpreting U.S. foreign policy toward the Third World: State versus regime

The practice of contemporary U.S. policy toward Latin America is shaped by three broad-based concerns: support for open economies and development strategies that accord private foreign banking and investment capital a key role; support for regimes prepared to align themselves with efforts to contain, and even roll back, the forces of national and social revolution; and a determination to safeguard America's strategic and "national security" interests in conformity with regional and global goals. Throughout the 1950s, 1960s, and 1970s, Washington policymakers pursued these inter-related political, economic, and strategic objectives in association with, or through, an assortment of military or military-controlled governments that dominated the political landscape of the region.

Toward the end of the 1970s, however, the United States was forced to come to terms with an emerging new reality: dictatorships that had lost their capacity to enforce controls over their populations – that is, had experienced a widespread erosion of political legitimacy; the collapse of the dominant economic model as it became increasingly incapable of responding to min-imal class-based socioeconomic demands; and the appearance of mass-based, polyclass movements demanding a return to civilian rule. These developments forced the Carter, and subsequently Reagan, administrations to rethink the relationship between current strategies and broader policy objectives in the hemisphere. The principal dilemma confronting the White House was whether, and in what circumstances, it should withdraw support from disintegrating allies and throw its influence behind the forces pushing for a return to electoral politics.

Why the United States shifts policy track and starts advocating a transfer of political power to elected civilians after decades-long support for autocratic or authoritarian Third World allies is one of the central questions addressed by this study.

Historically, the possibility of a regime change leading to the demise of a longstanding Third World client has produced aggressive efforts by Washington to coopt and shape the political transition in a manner that limits losses and maximizes advantages. In these circumstances, two vital inter-related issues have preoccupied American policymakers: the nature of the opposition movement and the survival of the key institutions that define the state structure.

For successive U.S. administrations, what segment of the anti-regime force is dominant, and therefore most likely to direct the process of political and economic change in the event of a transition, has been a critical factor influencing the policy debate. The hegemony of conservative and/or moderate civilian forces implies limited socioeconomic reforms and accommodation with the existing state and class structure; a guerrilla-dominated movement conjures up images of far-reaching shifts in the distribution of political and class power, restructuring of the capitalist economy, and transformation of the state, especially the armed forces and the civil bureaucracy. In other words, Washington differentiates between those groups in nationalist, anti-dictatorial movements likely to pursue programs that do not challenge U.S. permanent interests, including historic linkages with collaborator groups in the economy, state, and society, and those anti-regime elements that, at least potentially, prefigure the shift of a whole geographic territory out of the American sphere of influence. Hence, the consistent pattern in U.S. policy when confronted by these situations: intervention in support of forces pushing for a regime change that have revealed a preparedness to accommodate basic American concerns, and active efforts to eliminate or marginalize the power of forces perceived to have the most radical implications for those concerns in the post-transition period.

In analyzing Third World political systems, Washington recognizes two levels of reality: the strategic and tactical or the state and regime. The state represents the permanent interests of class power and international alignments: the defense of capitalism and ties to Western markets and linkages to the U.S. hegemonic bloc. It is not based on or constructed by transitory public opinion or electoral processes – nor does it usually depend on political parties or personalities. The institutions or components of the state are products of long-term, large-scale processes – the interaction of dominant classes and the interrelation between classes, the permanent civil and military bureaucracy, the judiciary, and those institutions that control the economic levers of the accumulation process. The regime represents the day-to-day policy decisions at the executive military/civilian level that can modify or negotiate the operations of the permanent interests but never challenge them without evoking a crisis. Regimes are the elected or self-appointed policymakers, subject to renewal or replacement, operating within the context of the state and class framework. This study targets the state rather than the regime precisely because Washington's permanent (strategic) interests in Third World societies are vested in the composition, collaboration, ideology, and resources (especially coercive power) of the state. In a crisis or period of political upheaval, the regime may be expendable; the state is not.

American foreign policy toward the Third World focuses on the notion of violence as the ultimate arbiter of power and guarantor of basic U.S. interests – political, economic, and strategic. Hence, the composition of, and control over, the armed forces and police is a more basic concern to the White House and State Department than who dominates the executive and legislative branches of government. Of course, U.S. policymakers are aware that hostile regimes can provoke a crisis by challenging the state, even leading to political cleavages within the state, and thus try to support regime changes congruent with the state. The level of Washington's concern over challenges to the state is incomparably greater than over changes in regime. The state/regime distinction is crucial in deciphering why the U.S. opposes Third World "revolution" and on occasion tolerates Third World "reform." Revolutions challenge the state; reforms operate through changes in the regime based on the preexisting state.

American policymakers' preoccupation with the survival of the coercive institutions has manifested itself most strongly in cases where the political challenge to an allied incumbent includes a significant radical nationalist and/or anti-capitalist component. These occasions provide the most graphic illustration of Washington's order of priorities: Ensuring the survival of the state takes precedence over the fate of a longtime friendly client. The possible alternative is not one the White House wishes to contemplate: a restructured armed forces and a new chain of command with no prior allegiances to, or linkages with, its counterparts in the United States. In the event Washington deems the new regime hostile to U.S. permanent interests and pursues a policy of confrontation and destabilization, the absence of a collaborator armed forces is a powerful obstacle, as the Cuban Revolution showed, to the achievement of the fundamental strategic objective.

However, this state/regime distinction is no less relevant to elected civilian governments than to client dictators such as Batista in Cuba or Somoza in Nicaragua. As the cases of Goulart in Brazil and Allende in Chile make abundantly clear, both Democratic and Republican administrations have pursued similar confrontationist policies where changes of regime via the ballot box have not been congruent or "compatible" with the preexisting state. Where these regimes have attempted to restructure the state apparatus and state-class relations as part of a new socioeconomic project, Washington has actively intervened and promoted a period of "instability" and "conflict" between the regime and state – which the latter has invariably won, usually overthrowing the regime, on occasion forcing a modification in its behavior.

The critical factor explaining U.S. shifts in support for a particular Third World regime – its preparedness to jettison a longstanding client ruler – is fundamental opposition to the appearance of democratic mass social movements from below wanting to change the regime and the state. United States support for, and promotion of, changes from military/dictatorial to electoral/civilian regimes is precipitated by fear and hostility toward those movements that manifest anti-regime and anti-state objectives. The policy shift is designed to preempt and divide these movements by coopting the bourgeois civilian opposition and grafting a regime composed primarily of these forces onto the existing state structure. What typically follows this kind of political transition is efforts to divide and demobilize the democratic mass social movement (the perceived threat to U.S. permanent interests) through a combination of clientele relations and repression.

The basic hypothesis of this study is that Washington's policy toward the Third World has always operated within a state-regime framework, supporting and defending by all means at its disposal client-states while retaining a flexible tactical position regarding regimes. This two-track approach reveals both U.S. rigidity about changes in state structures and flexibility in relation to regime changes. Writers who conflate these essentially different phenomena have been mistaken about the options and choices open to American policymakers. Liberal critics who associate U.S. policy exclusively with dictatorships fail to explain the accommodation to electoral transitions, indeed Washington's pronounced shift toward a preference for Third World civilian governments since the late 1970s. Likewise, conservative writers who criticize the White House for dumping right-wing military regimes fail to recognize the deeper structural continuities that preoccupy U.S. policymakers – they confuse regime with state.

Nor are explanations of policy shifts toward dictatorial or electoral regimes with reference to bureaucratic infighting (for example, National Security Council vs. State Department), particular parties in power (Democrats are supposedly more disposed to electoral regimes, Republicans to military rulers), or influential policymakers (for example, Kissinger, Brzezinski, Vance) very convincing. American policy operates along multiple tracks to provide maximum flexibility and leverage in confronting rapidly evolving situations. The use of various policy instruments does not indicate a contradictory approach due to bureaucratic or personal rivalries, but must be viewed as

part of a complementary and coherent strategy within which individual policymakers or agencies predominate at any particular moment depending on
the level and scope of the conflict in the target country. Operationally, executive branch foreign policy agencies share a common perspective – a
consensus over policy goals. Within this larger framework one finds a combination of overlapping responsibilities and bureaucratic conflicts rooted in
functional responsibilities and particular agency interests. In specific instances where Washington has spurred regime changes, the supposedly con-
flicting executive branch agencies have cooperated and pursued
complementary policies. Moreover, both Democratic and Republic administrations have pursued policies promoting cooperation with civilian or military regimes and, at different times, have supported regime changes from
electoral to military and vice versa.

In light of the preparedness on the part of U.S. governments to accommodate and support autocratic Third World governments over extended
time periods in the absence of challenges to the regime or state (for example,
Batista's Cuba, Somoza's Nicaragua, the Shah's Iran, Marcos's Philippines,
Pinochet's Chile), an abrupt policy change toward such clients cannot be
explained in terms of any White House commitment to promoting or imposing democratic values, but only in relation to permanent interests. U.S.
policymakers interpret a change from dictatorship to democratic regime,
first and foremost, as a mechanism for preserving the state (the most important safeguard of these interests), not as a mode of promoting democ-
ratization and the values that accompany it.*

The transition from a military dictatorship to an elected regime in Chile
in December 1989 is particularly instructive in this regard. Having supported the Pinochet armed forces coup that overthrew the democratic socialist government of Salvador Allende in September 1973, and hailed the
free-market, export-oriented economic model implemented by the generals,
a decade of brutal authoritarian rule did not induce even the Carter administration (which opposed bilateral and multilateral aid to the dictatorship on
human rights grounds) to push for a return to civilian rule. However, the
reemergence of mass-based social movements offering a direct political
challenge to the regime in 1983, and the subsequent radicalization of the
forms of struggle and leadership of these movements, eventually forced the
Reagan White House to move slowly, but surely, toward advocacy of a
regime change based on a negotiated transition that would divide the opposition and preserve the state. The goal was to facilitate the ascendancy

---

* On occasion, however, values may play a role in defining the kind of actions taken as a
result of the perceived need to defend the hegemonic state's permanent interests.

of the center-right "anti-regime" civilian forces over and against the ascendancy of the "anti-system" movements, while minimizing the changes in the existing socioeconomic model and the state institutions.

The United States conditioned its financial and political support for the conservative-moderate anti-Pinochet groups on their willingness to break ties with the left and participate in an electoral calendar outlined by the dictatorship. Following the July 2–3, 1986 general strike, Deputy Assistant Secretary of State for Inter-American Affairs Robert Gelbard flew to Chile and bluntly told the renovated Socialists and Christian Democrats that the Reagan administration opposed the tactics of "social mobilization" and alliances with the left. Immediately thereafter, the mass-based opposition movement broke apart, the center-right forces rejecting the strategy of mobilization politics.[1] In turn, Washington agreed to pressure Pinochet to comply with his electoral timetable and accept the outcome. The result was the best possible outcome from the point of view of U.S. permanent interests in Chile: a regime change that disarticulated the social movements challenging strategic state allies, and the legitimation, and (temporary) stabilization, of the Pinochet state and socioeconomic model by the new electoral regime.

Whereas the movements forced the issue of regime change, it was Washington that "brokered" the negotiation process that produced the hybrid political system – a popularly elected regime inserted in military-constructed state institutions. The Reagan-Bush White House sacrificed the Pinochet regime to save the neo-liberal state, and in the process took credit for promoting democracy. But it was a "redemocratization" process organized on the terrain of the authoritarian right. The presidential victory of the conservative Christian Democrat Patricio Aylwin was situated within the authoritarian parameters and rules of the game established by the Pinochet military dictatorship.

On the basis of these observations, a number of central propositions can be generated to account for U.S. policy toward political transitions in the Third World:

1. There is an underlying consensus among U.S. policymakers and the corporate elite to defend client-state structures in all circumstances.
2. When state structures are threatened by broad-based social and political movements, Washington will seek to divide these movements, hiving off sectors compatible with the state and U.S. permanent interests and promoting a political settlement in which electoral processes are incorporated within existing state structures.

1   See James Petras and Fernando Ignacio Leiva, "Chile: The Authoritarian Transition to Electoral Politics," *Latin American Perspectives*, Vol. 15, No. 3, Summer 1988, pp. 99–100.

3. The policy of dividing the opposition movement involves two approaches: pressure on the incumbent regime to modify its policies and coopt pliable sectors of the opposition; pressure to replace the regime with sectors of the opposition compatible with Washington's permanent interests – in recent times substituting military with electoral/civilian governments in cohabitation with the existing state.
4. The new regime will be embedded within the "old" state structures and join with the United States in demobilizing or repressing those sectors of the opposition movement oriented toward changing the state. Furthermore, the constraints imposed by U.S. policymakers on political and social changes in the post-transition period are defended by evoking a "concern with legitimate issues of national security." Under that rubric, the White House gains license to intervene and manipulate Third World internal political processes and institutions to accommodate U.S. hegemonic and corporate needs.

Hegemonic states face a particularly difficult task in effecting a political transition in circumstances where the incumbent client regime is tightly connected with the state, all the more so where the client dictator has built up strong political loyalties in the armed forces that resist pressure from the outside. The hegemonic power cannot isolate the regime from the state to sacrifice the former to save the latter. In this instance, the historic ties pass from the hegemonic power to the incumbent dictator, and from the dictator to the military hierarchy of the client state. This underscores the supreme importance of prior horizontal links at the sub-regime level, particularly with the commanding officers of the military, if the hegemonic power is intent on promoting a change of regime in the Third World.

As all of this suggests, Washington policymakers do not always achieve their sought-after objectives. Sometimes a regime change takes place that is deemed unacceptable. A second set of propositions lend themselves to examining under what circumstances this happens and also how the United States responds when the new regime pursues policies contrary to the former's definition of its permanent interests:

1. Regime changes may occur because of imperfect timing. Where the revolutionary process has advanced too far, and the radical forces have already assumed undisputed hegemony, no credible split-off from the opposition movement may be available.
2. Regime changes may occur as a result of non-synchronous perceptions between client regime and patron. Where the client-regime perceives its relations with the hegemonic patron as strategic, it will come into conflict

with the changing tactical policies of the patron who views the client as expendable. The conflict between the strategic perception of the client and the tactical needs of the patron can lead the former to adopt an intransigent position, refusing to leave office, thus delaying regime change and endangering the state. By tying the stability of the regime to the continuance of the state, the incumbent client may be attempting to reverse the pressure back onto the hegemonic power to force it to shift support back to the client.

3. Where regime changes take place that begin to challenge the permanent interests of the hegemonic power, the latter will exercise its historic ties with collaborator forces in the state and class structure to force the regime to reorient its policies to accommodate the state, or destabilize and overthrow the regime and replace it with one congruent with the state and its hegemonic patron.

4. Where the regime and the state have been transformed in a fashion to challenge the permanent interest of the hegemonic power, the latter will move to reverse the changes through a combination of policies, including the recomposition of the dismantled components of the old state apparatus as a counterrevolutionary army, an economic destabilization program, and the promotion of internal civilian restorationist forces. By attacking the state, economy, and regime simultaneously, the hegemonic power hopes to reconstitute an externally oriented state power linked to a pliable civilian-military regime.

5. Where revolutionary changes in state power preempt and short-circuit the process of reshuffling the regime, the hegemonic power embarks on a program of ideological warfare that focuses on two sets of issues: First, state transformation and the creation of a new revolutionary state structure is described as concentrating power and undermining pluralism. In this context, pluralism is identified with the presence of client groups in positions of influence in the state and hence the continuance of outside hegemonic leverage. Second, the presence of popular militias and mass organizations as centers of political and social power are described as precursors of authoritarianism or totalitarianism – even if elected processes and elected institutions operate. In operational terms, the code words "authoritarianism" or "totalitarianism" refer to popular control over the state within which the electoral regime functions.

Client dictators and elected presidents: U.S. policy and the Latin American state

U.S. policy toward political transitions in postwar Latin America has centered around the goal of securing regime changes that ensure the continuity of the state. Every president, from Eisenhower to Reagan, has accorded priority to the task of preserving the state while issues of democracy and dictatorship have remained secondary. The following examples (excluding Nicaragua) illustrate and illuminate this argument. Each case involves either a regime crisis in which Washington's traditional allies were challenged by democratic social movements and where U.S. policymakers sought to dump dictatorial regimes to save the state, or a situation in which the White House intervened on the side of the state against a regime that prefigured a threat to the state, and enforced a political transition to recreate a congruence between regime and state – and thereby eliminate a threat to U.S. permanent interests.

Cuba

Between 1952 and early 1958, the Eisenhower administration's policy of accommodation with the Batista military dictatorship was shaped by two general considerations: the Cuban regime's capitalist development strategy that provided favorable conditions for U.S. investment and trade expansion; and Batista's anti-communism and active support of U.S. regional and global objectives. The initiation of a guerrilla struggle in December 1956 and the increasingly repressive and corrupt policies of the dictatorship provoked a limited debate among mid-level American officials about the possibility of a more formal and correct bilateral relationship. But neither the White House nor the upper reaches of the State Department expressed much interest in Cuban developments, viewing the island basically as a "safe precinct."

In mid-1957, however, extensive interviewing of trade union leaders in Havana, Santiago de Cuba, and Pinar del Río led the *New York Times* correspondent on the island to conclude that "a majority of the rank and file [workers] are anti-Batista."[2] The Santiago proletariat was described as being in "open revolt" against the regime.[3] Meanwhile, influential segments of the Havana bourgeoisie had begun to defect from the strategy of "civic dialogue" and "compromise" politics. Industrialists whose declining economic position derived from "the intrusion of Batista and his cronies into the private business sector,"[4] and civic, religious, and professional groups

---

2 Herbert L. Matthews, "Situation in Cuba Found Worsening; Batista Foes Gain," *New York Times*, June 16, 1957, p. 26.
3 Herbert L. Matthews, "Populace in Revolt in Santiago de Cuba," *New York Times*, June 10, 1957, p. 1.
4 Alfred Padula, Jr., *The Fall of the Bourgeoisie: Cuba, 1959–1961* (Ph.D Dissertation, University of New Mexico, 1974), p. 101.

opposed to the manifest brutality and parasitism of the military-controlled state were instrumental in providing a structured urban opposition to Batista and providing material supports for the rurally based social revolutionaries.[5]

By early 1958, the regime's manifest political isolation, growing social polarization, and the appearance of a nationwide opposition movement led by insurrectionary forces had forced Washington to question its viability and its capacity to preserve the state and safeguard basic American interests over the long term. This sense of concern, even panic, was heightened with the collapse of Batista's major military offensive against the guerrillas in June and July of 1958. Eisenhower policymakers began to visualize the possibility of the disintegration of the Cuban armed forces. Officials expressed concern "that the breakdown of the military as an institution would present a threat to commercial interests" and also mean the loss of "a resource for the maintenance of order during a transition period."[6]

Defining this mass social movement as a primary threat, Washington hastily set about devising new strategies under the pressure of limited time constraints that would divide the opposition to the regime and preserve the state. The paramount concern was to deny political (and state) power to the Castro forces. "Nobody in the State Department," said one official, "wanted Castro to get in."[7] The preferred alternative was a pro-capitalist regime not identified with the excesses of the dictatorship but committed to the survival of a refurbished and reconsolidated Batista military state structure.

The problem of sifting the various strategy options, and settling on an appropriate response, was made more difficult by Batista's intransigent refusal to accommodate repeated U.S. requests for his voluntary resignation in favor of a transitional, anti-Batista, anti-Castro regime. Nevertheless, the State Department pushed ahead in an attempt to forestall a guerrilla victory, oust Batista from power, and impose an interim regime composed of selected anti-Castro civilian and military individuals. In a top secret memorandum to President Eisenhower in October 1958, acting Secretary of State Christian Herter outlined the immediate strategic priorities: "The Department has concluded that any solution in Cuba requires that Batista must relinquish power.... The Department clearly does not want to see Castro succeed to the leadership of the Government.... Therefore, we have been and are attempting in every appropriate way, through all means available, *without openly violating our non-intervention commitments*, to help create a situation in which a third force could move into the vacuum between Batista

5   Matthews, "Situation in Cuba Found Worsening; Batista Foes Gain," p. 26.
6   Quoted in Morris H. Morley, *Imperial State and Revolution: The United States and Cuba, 1952–1986* (New York: Cambridge University Press, 1987), p. 62.
7   Quoted in ibid., p. 63.

and Castro."[8] These efforts ranged from continued pressures on Batista to resign, to efforts to enlist regional support for its anti-Castro policy, to investigating the military coup option, to an active CIA presence in Cuba seeking to implement the "third force" solution. Ultimately, however, the belated nature of these endeavors, Batista's obduracy, and the strength of the revolutionary forces proved decisive. Not only had Washington failed to engineer a regime change in Cuba that denied political power to the social revolutionaries; with the collapse of the Batista armed forces, the Castro guerrillas automatically became the new military apparatus of the Cuban state.

The pro-capitalist orientation of senior economic officials in the first Castro cabinet and the decision to confine the first nationalizations to the local propertied class led some U.S. officials, especially in the State Department, to think that it might be possible to encourage the growth of a "manageable" Cuban political leadership. Initially, Washington pursued a dual approach: maintenance of diplomatic relations to facilitate communication with those forces inside the Cuban regime and society opposed to social revolution; and hostility to any program of large-scale social and economic change. But despite the allocation of key cabinet posts to conservative ministers, Castro did not transfer to this body the substance of political power.

In his role as commander-in-chief of the rebel army, Castro set about organizing a new state independent of the cabinet and anchored in the urban and rural working class. New military and security forces were created based on armed popular militias; the bureaucracy was remade from top to bottom to enable it to respond to class-anchored demands. As the process of state transformation gathered momentum, U.S. influence further dissolved. The closure of traditional U.S. points of access into the Cuban society eliminated the power of historic collaborator groups such as the church, sectors of the labor movement, and the network of professional and employer organizations of the bourgeoisie – sugar mill owners, sugar cane growers, cattlemen, industrialists, lawyers. A politically immobilized pro-U.S. bourgeoisie was no longer capable of responding organizationally or militarily to revolutionary initiatives backed up by an organized social force and an independent military apparatus. In December 1960, a number of changes ensured that almost all of the cabinet ministries were now headed by former guerrillas or Castro's close civilian supporters. The fit between revolutionary regime and revolutionary state was complete.[9] The post-revolutionary conflict be-

8 Memorandum from Acting Secretary of State (Herter) to President Eisenhower, Department of State 737.00/12-2358, December 23, 1958, Declassified Freedom of Information Act (hereafter DFOIA).
9 For an extended discussion, see Morley, *Imperial State and Revolution*, pp. 72–130.

tween the liberal regime and the revolutionary state was resolved in favor of the latter.

Operating within the state/regime framework, the Eisenhower administration unsuccessfully sought to dump the Batista dictatorship to save the state, in order to prevent the revolutionary forces from replacing it. Washington's belated recognition of the growing strength of the Castroist movement, policymakers' disagreements over the Batista regime, and the Cuban dictator's control over subordinate military officers undermined the hegemonic power's capacity to dictate the process of political transition. In the conflict between the U.S.-backed regime and the revolutionary state after 1959, the latter imposed its will, forcing Washington to subsequently attempt to restore the old order through a concerted military, economic, and political offensive that largely failed.

Dominican Republic

By early 1960, a combination of the Trujillo regime's repressive political rule and the need to avoid "another Cuba" forced the Eisenhower administration to seriously contemplate ways of accelerating a change of government in the Dominican Republic. Contingency planning "to quietly encourage a moderate pro-United States leadership among the civilian and military dissident elements to take over [in the event of Trujillo's demise]" was discussed at a mid-January National Security Council (NSC) meeting.[10] In April, the President approved a contingency plan to act swiftly if the situation deteriorated to a point where U.S. permanent interests were threatened: " ... the United States would immediately take political action to remove Trujillo from the Dominican Republic as soon as a suitable successor regime can be induced to take over with the assurance of U.S. political, economic, and – if necessary – military support."[11]

Throughout the latter part of 1960, Washington applied diplomatic and economic pressures on Trujillo in an unsuccessful effort to get him to voluntarily relinquish power. This preoccupation carried over into the Kennedy administration. An NSC meeting of May 5, 1961 "agreed that the Task Force on Cuba would prepare promptly both emergency and long-

10 Memorandum from Secretary of State (Herter) to President Eisenhower, Secret, April 14, 1960, Subject: "Possible Action to Prevent Castroist Takeover of Dominican Republic," DFOIA.
11 Memorandum from Secretary of State (Herter) to President Eisenhower, reprinted in U.S. Congress, Senate, Select Committee to Study Governmental Operations, *Alleged Assassination Plots Involving Foreign Leaders*, 94th Congress, 1st Session, Report No. 94–465, November 20, 1975 (Washington, D.C.: U.S. Government Printing Office, 1975), p. 192.

range plans for anti-communist intervention in the event of crises in Haiti or the Dominican Republic. [It] noted the President's view that the United States should not initiate the overthrow of Trujillo before we knew what government would succeed him.... "[12] Three weeks later, a group of Dominican dissidents with ties to Eisenhower and Kennedy officials assassinated the country's dictator.

Taking advantage of Trujillo's murder, the White House moved quickly in two directions: to ensure the end of the Trujillo political dynasty (regime) but the survival of the Trujillo military establishment (state). Initially, Washington sought to promote a political coalition of army officials, ex-Trujillistas, Ramfis Trujillo, and moderates to contest a future election.[13] The failure of this strategy, and the likelihood that the social reformist Juan Bosch would triumph in an open and honest election, led the Kennedy White House to refocus its efforts on reconsolidating the power of the Trujillista state. During 1962, the Pentagon provided intensive training for three companies of counterinsurgency troops, and the U.S. military mission pressured the National Police to increase its ranks from 3,000 to 10,000 members.[14] In December, Bosch won a sweeping electoral victory campaigning on a platform of moderate social and agrarian reforms and the expansion of civil liberties.

Seven months after his inauguration as President in February 1963, Bosch was ousted from office by the Trujillista army and police forces under the leadership of General Wessin y Wessin in alliance with the economic oligarchy that opposed the reformist programs. The coercive apparatus of the "old" state – refurbished and expanded at the behest of Washington – overthrew the elected regime. In its place, the military installed a three-member civilian triumvirate representing a cluster of right-wing parties and headed by Donald Reid Cabral, an oligarch with close links to the U.S. business community. Reid Cabral proceeded to terminate the Bosch economic and social legislation and the reformist constitution, savagely cut public works spending, and opened up the economy to U.S. investors. The result was a massive decline in living standards and a resurgence of support for the Bosch era among the urban and rural masses. Despite the triumvirate's lack of popular support, the Johnson administration continued to give its unquestioned backing to the Reid Cabral leadership.

Growing popular opposition to the military-dominated regime eventually fused with an internal upheaval in the armed forces in April 1965 to produce a social revolutionary challenge to the Dominican regime and state. A revolt

12 Quoted in ibid., p. 209.
13 Piero Gleijeses, *The Dominican Crisis: The 1965 Constitutionalist Revolt and American Intervention* (Baltimore: The Johns Hopkins University Press, 1978), pp. 41–43.
14 Ibid., p. 76.

by a group of officers against military corruption detonated an armed mass insurrection in Santo Domingo in support of Juan Bosch's return from exile, the 1963 constitution, and new elections. Constitutionalist military forces led by Colonel Francisco Caamaño and thousands of armed civilians raised the specter of a mass insurrection spreading throughout the country. The day the revolution began (April 25), a senior Embassy official telegrammed the State Department: "All members of the Country Team feel Bosch's return and resumption of control of the government is against U.S. interests in view of extremists in the coup and communist advocacy of Bosch's return."[15]

What triggered decisive action by Washington was the Constitutionalist military success over the "Loyalist" forces of Wessin y Wessin that was tantamount to the collapse of the Trujillista state. Determined to smash the mass social revolutionary movement, the Johnson White House unilaterally sent 23,000 U.S. marines into the Dominican Republic to "restore stability and order" and the authority of the rightist military faction. Having crushed the popular insurrection and restored the power of the Trujillista military state, Washington then proceeded to lay the foundations for a return to electoral politics. During the U.S.-imposed provisional government of Héctor García Godoy (April 1965-June 1966), the popular forces were demobilized, the Constitutionalist military demoralized, hundreds of leaders of the mass insurrection were assassinated, and the U.S. marines and other foreign military forces remained on Dominican territory. Meanwhile, to provide the illusion of a legitimate political contest, Washington convinced Juan Bosch to participate in new presidential elections even though it was actively supporting the candidacy of former Trujillista politician Joaquin Balaguer.

The election produced an overwhelming victory for the conservative Balaguer – an outcome determined largely by military power and intimidation. The country's predominantly rural population was under virtual military occupation for the duration of the political campaign. Only Balaguer was effectively permitted access to the voters. Bosch had limited organization and funds, minimal access to the media, and hardly left his home to campaign because of fear of assassination. The more important result of Washington's intervention was to restore to power the state apparatus that was perceived as critical to the long-term survival of U.S. permanent interests in the Dominican Republic.

The Balaguer regime opened up the economy to foreign capital, froze wages, eliminated price restraints, and confirmed in power all the Trujillista military officials the United States had rearmed and reorganized. The police

15   Quoted in ibid., p. 218.

state legislation, anti-working class measures, and newly established totalitarian state agencies were approved and to a large degree drawn up by U.S. advisors who were located in every major government ministry and state institution. In Washington, the Johnson administration moved swiftly to consolidate the client regime and the externally oriented state through new economic and military assistance programs.[16]

The Dominican Republic illustrates the centrality of the state-regime distinction in shaping U.S. policy responses to political change. In the face of a growing social movement and following the distinction between regime and state transformation, Washington supported the ouster of Trujillo to save the state. In the subsequent conflict between the democratic Bosch regime and the client Trujillista state, Washington sided with the latter. During the popular insurrection the White House intervened militarily to protect the authoritarian state, and then supported the election of a former Trujillista civilian. In this complex pattern, several threads appear: The U.S. government defended by all means possible, including a marine invasion, the restoration of the client state, thus demonstrating inflexible support for defenders of its permanent interests. At the same time, Washington demonstrated considerable flexibility toward regime changes by alternating support for the Trujillo military dictatorship for three decades, the elected nationalist Bosch regime for several months, and the post-intervention Balaguer regime, all of which adapted to hegemonic definitions of reality.

Brazil

Between late 1961 and early 1964, Brazil was governed by a popular-nationalist president, João Goulart, who espoused policies and instituted programs biased toward the country's poor. His actions polarized the society, generating widespread opposition among the bourgeoisie and petty bourgeoisie. The latter felt particularly threatened by the rising political and economic power of the working class and, over time, became increasingly attracted "to the authoritarian solutions presented by some sectors of the dominant class" as the only alternative to thwarted ambitions.[17]

In Washington, Goulart's election to the presidency was greeted less than enthusiastically by the Kennedy administration. A State Department memorandum to the White House summarized the basic posture: "We are pre-

---

16 See Fred Goff and Michael Locker, "The Violence of Domination: U.S. Power and the Dominican Republic," in Irving Louis Horowitz et al., *Latin American Radicalism* (New York: Vintage Books, 1969), pp. 287–288.
17 Octavio Ianni, *Crisis in Brazil* (New York: Columbia University Press, 1971), p. 129.

pared to give him the reasonable benefit of the doubt. . . . "[18] If this political transition created initial unease among U.S. officials, by the end of Goulart's first year in office it seemed more than justified. They singled out the Brazilian president's refusal to prevent state governments from nationalizing American-owned properties, "defects" in the government's profit remittance law, the absence of an International Monetary Fund (IMF) stabilization program to deal with balance of payments and debt crises, the worsening overall environment for foreign investors, and Brazil's refusal to break diplomatic relations with Cuba. At a December 1962 meeting with Goulart, Attorney General Robert Kennedy expressed considerable concern over Brazil's foreign policy and the extent of communist and radical nationalist influence within the government, trade union movement, and even the armed forces. He conditioned future large-scale American aid on Goulart's willingness to place pro-U.S. officials in key decision-making posts and take "effective measures to control the runaway inflation."[19]

Meanwhile, Washington had already begun to set in motion a strategy designed to exert maximum pressure on Goulart that involved consolidating ties with key Brazilian groups and individuals "who advocate domestic and foreign policies which we can support."[20] In October 1962, the Kennedy White House channeled approximately $20 million (through the CIA) into the campaigns of several hundred anti-Goulart candidates running for gubernatorial, congressional, state, and municipal office.[21] By early 1963, U.S. policymakers had abandoned efforts to force Goulart to the political center, having decided to systematically pursue the so-called islands of sanity tactic with a view to bolstering the anti-regime forces, exacerbating Goulart's economic problems and, ultimately, precipitating a change of government. The aim was to provide large-scale financial resources to selected state governments, autonomous public agencies, and private organizations hostile to the central administration.

In a situation where the Brazilian state had ceased to be a coherent body in which agencies and groups complemented one another, U.S. policy concentrated on disaggregating the state (those antagonistic national units such

18 Quoted in Phyllis R. Parker, *Brazil and the Quiet Intervention 1964* (Austin: University of Texas Press, 1979), p. 7.
19 Quoted in Ruth Leacock, *Requiem for Revolution: The United States and Brazil, 1961–1969*, (Kent: Kent State University Press, 1990), p. 137.
20 Memorandum for the National Security Executive Committee, Meeting of December 11, 1962, Subject: "U.S. Short Term Policy Toward Brazil", National Security Files, Vice-Presidential Security File, Box 4, Folder: National Security Council (1), Johnson Presidential Library, Austin, Texas. For an extended discussion of this strategy, see Jan Knippers Black, *United States Penetration of Brazil* (Philadelphia: University of Pennsylvania Press, 1977), passim.
21 Laurence Stern, "Ex-Spy to Give Detailed Account of Covert CIA Operations," *Washington Post*, July 11, 1974, p. 3.

as the armed forces and upper- and middle-class-dominated institutions) from the new national project, reorienting their allegiances externally, and then moving in concert with these affected groups to topple the regime, assert control over the state, and redirect both to serve the interests of the United States and its internal allies.

In the economic sphere, the United States not only halted virtually all bilateral assistance to Goulart's beleaguered regime but also influenced the multilateral development banks to do likewise. Though more than $600 million in Agency for International Development (AID) loans were approved for Brazil between 1960 and 1964, over three-quarters were not disbursed until after the civilian government was overthrown by the armed forces. The World Bank extended no credits to the Goulart regime; the Inter-American Development Bank provided a mere $66 million in urgently needed funds. Economic pressures were intensified by Washington's refusal to consider any renegotiation of Brazil's foreign debt to U.S. public institutions until Goulart had come to terms with his European creditors.[22]

However, efforts by Goulart to accommodate American concerns by settling the dispute over International Telephone & Telegraph's nationalized subsidiary, getting Congress to pass a tax reform bill, and taking new measures to force down inflation failed to impress a White House and State Department increasingly preoccupied with alleged communist influence in Brazil and Cuba's ties with Goulart and the country's political left. Washington demanded further concessions to foreign capital, an IMF "seal of approval" for the government's economic stabilization program, and the completion of debt negotiations with European creditors before any new large-scale aid was forthcoming.

In May 1964, Assistant Secretary of State for Inter-American Affairs Thomas Mann told a U.S. Congressional committee that sometime in 1963 the administration "devised" a policy "to help certain state governments" while simultaneously terminating all forms of economic aid "which benefit[ed] directly the central government of Brazil."[23] AID loan projects authorized and disbursed in the last year of the Goulart government were done so on the basis of overriding foreign policy considerations, leading the U.S. General Accounting Office to issue a report highly critical of AID's failure "to make dependable technical and economic analyses before making

---

22 Peter D. Bell, "Brazilian-American Relations," in Riorden Roett, ed., *Brazil in the Sixties* (Nashville: Vanderbilt University Press, 1972), p. 95; U.S. Agency for International Development, *U.S. Overseas Loans and Grants and Assistance from International Organizations, July 1, 1945–June 30, 1973*, p. 182; Thomas E. Skidmore, *Politics in Brazil 1930–1964* (Oxford: Oxford University Press, 1967), pp. 270–271.

23 Quoted in Carlos F. Díaz-Alejandro, "Some Aspects of the Brazilian Experience with Foreign Aid," in Jagdish N. Bhagwati et al, eds., *Trade, Balance of Payments and Growth* (New York: American Elsevier, 1971), p. 452.

[these] loans."[24] Between January and April 1964, the Johnson White House sought to tighten the financial and credit blockade against the Goulart regime in the knowledge that civilian and military *golpista* elements were steadily expanding their activities and influence within the state and society.

Economic assistance to the civilian antagonists of the Goulart government went hand in hand with funding of the Brazilian armed forces, which U.S. Ambassador Lincoln Gordon described as part of the strategy "for restraining the [regime's] left-wing excesses...."[25] Throughout 1963, CIA operatives and Defense Department attachés closely monitored the Brazilian military's plotting against Goulart, but some concern was expressed over the disorganized nature of these activities and the need to avoid "a premature coup effort" that would almost certainly lead to "the cashiering of those officers who are most friendly to the United States."[26]

While the CIA conducted a large propaganda and political-action campaign against Goulart and, together with Pentagon officials, retained extraordinary access to anti-regime military developments, the American labor movement (AFL-CIO) also played a role, albeit less direct, in support of the opposition forces. It sponsored the American Institute of Free Labor Development (AIFLD), which trained a number of anti-Goulart trade union leaders who, in the words of senior AIFLD official William Doherty, were "intimately involved in some of the clandestine operations of the revolution before it took place on April 1."[27]

Following the American Ambassador's public attack on communist influence within the central government, senior Embassy and Consulate officials in Rio de Janiero and São Paulo became increasingly accessible to the military and civilian coup plotters. The U.S. Defense Attaché Colonel Vernon Walters was "in daily contact" with coup leader General Humberto Castello Branco and the rest of the anti-Goulart high command.[28] Counsel General Niles Bond recalled that during the coup itself "our information about what was going on was very good.[29]

U.S. encouragement to the Brazilian military to move against Goulart came indirectly in the form of a special closed meeting of all regional am-

---

24   U.S. General Accounting Office, Report to the Congress, *Review of Administration of United States Assistance for Capital Development Projects in Brazil*, B. 133283, May 16, 1968, pp. 2, 5, 70.

25   Memorandum from Ambassador Gordon to Secretary of State Rusk, quoted in Parker, *Brazil and the Quiet Revolution 1964*, p. 102.

26   CIA memorandum, quoted in ibid., p. 40.

27   Quoted in Robert H. Dockery, "Labour Policies and Programs," in U.S. Congress, Senate, Committee on Foreign Relations, Subcommittee on American Republics Affairs, *Survey of the Alliance for Progress*, 91st Congress, 1st Session, Document No. 91–17, April 29, 1969, (Washington, D.C.: U.S. Government Printing Office, 1969), p. 586.

28   Parker, *Brazil and the Quiet Revolution 1964*, p. 103.

29   Quoted in Bell, "Brazilian-American Relations," p. 90.

bassadors, chargé d'affaires, and chiefs of AID missions called by President Johnson in mid-March 1964, less than two weeks before the coup. Assistant Secretary of State Mann informed the assembled officials of a shift in U.S. policy toward non-elected Latin governments: Henceforth, diplomatic recognition and future relations would no longer be based on "good or bad guys" criteria.[30]

Once the coup started, the White House approved a series of military contingency plans, including orders for a U.S. naval task force to sail into Brazilian waters and be ready "to carry out tasks as may be assigned."[31] But any need for direct American intervention to bolster a faltering operation proved unnecessary. The parliamentary regime was overthrown, and the victorious generals ushered in a period of repressive political rule and an economic development model that accorded foreign capital, freed from most restrictions, a central role. With Goulart's fall, and the changed environment for private investment, the foreign aid spigots were turned on full force: Before the end of 1964, aid commitments from the U.S. government, the IMF, the World Bank, and a number of private multinational banks totaled around $1 billion.[32]

Confronted by a nationalist regime increasingly defined as inimical to basic U.S. interests in Brazil, Washington disaggregated the state, withdrew economic assistance from the regime, provided financial support and training to key opposition institutions and individuals, and encouraged the armed forces to destroy the regime in the hope that it would recreate the state and the regime in the image of U.S. interests – which it did.

Chile

On September 15, 1970, Richard Nixon denounced the newly elected socialist government in Chile at a meeting with CIA Director Richard Helms and NSC Advisor Henry Kissinger. Terming it "unacceptable to the United States," the President instructed the covert agency "to prevent Allende from coming to power or to unseat him" by whatever means possible. Some of Helms notes taken during the meeting convey the extent of White House hostility to the election outcome: "Not one chance in ten perhaps, but save Chile!... not concerned risks involved... $10,000,000 available, more if

---

30 Tad Szulc, "U.S. May Abandon Efforts to Deter Latin Dictators," *New York Times*, March 19, 1964, pp. 1, 2.
31 Quoted in Parker, *Brazil and the Quiet Revolution 1964*, pp. 75–76.
32 See Juan de Onis, "U.S. Gives a Billion in Aid," *New York Times*, December 15, 1964, p. 11.

necessary, full time job, best men we have . . . make economy scream. . . ."[33]
A two-track strategy was implemented to prevent Allende's inauguration as
president, involving not only the CIA but other executive branch agencies
as well. Track 1 consisted of a political action, economic, and propaganda
program to induce Chilean opposition forces to politically or militarily block
the formal transfer of power. Track 2 concentrated specifically on efforts
to foment a coup by the armed forces.[34]

Washington's failure to achieve its desired outcome – a congressional
vote rejecting his confirmation as President on October 24 or a military
coup prior to his inauguration on November 3 – did not dissuade Nixon
and Kissinger from redoubling their efforts to ensure that a government
they viewed as a profound threat to U.S. permanent interests in Chile did
not last out its term of office. The policy was aptly summarized in a mid-
October cable from CIA headquarters to its Santiago Station following a
White House meeting on Chile: "It is the firm and continuing policy that
Allende be overthrown by a coup . . . We are to continue to generate maximum pressure toward this end utilizing every appropriate resource."[35]

U.S. policy was not determined by any particular economic decision in
Chile but derived from a commitment to oppose structural ideological developments: the transformation of the country into a democratic socialist
society. The changes envisioned by the Allende government not only restricted the capacity of U.S. capital to expand in Chile but threatened to
disarticulate the economic and trade patterns in the region. Changes in
Chile potentially laid the basis for modifying and redefining Latin America's
external economic relations. Under Allende, Chile was still in transition,
both in and out of Washington's orbit, and this accounted for its vulnerability
to U.S. pressures.

Nixon-Kissinger policy was dictated by the permeable nature of the Chilean state, the possibilities for reversing institutional changes, and the timing
of the socioeconomic transformation (its "gradualist" nature). In a context
where the new government only achieved control over the executive branch,
where sectors of the state apparatus remained linked to the old class structure, and where political channels remained open (thus giving external forces
unfettered access to opposition political parties, employer and professional
organizations, mass media outlets, and the like), the U.S. decision to maintain formal ties was an opportunity to reverse what was becoming an increasingly socialized economy. By taking advantage of the multiple points
of opposition permitted by the Allende government, Washington channeled

33 Quoted in U.S. Congress, Senate, *Alleged Assassination Plots Involving Foreign Leaders*,
   pp. 228, 27.
34 See ibid., pp. 229–254.
35 Quoted in Ibid., p. 243.

funds selectively to specific institutions (for example, armed forces), political parties (for example, Christian Democratic, National), media outlets (for example, *El Mercurio*) and class organizations of the bourgeoisie and petty bourgeoisie that would serve as spearheads or points of support for the counterrevolution.

Washington's policy of economic confrontation on a bilateral and global basis successfully hobbled Chile's access to funds from the multilateral development banks, U.S. private multinational banks, and the foreign investment community, as well as to Western export markets and U.S.-origin spare parts. The latter was particularly devastating for a country whose agro-industrial infrastructure was overwhelmingly dependent on purchases of these materials from American firms.[36]

Chilean efforts to cope with the economic problems resulting from U.S. pressures took the form of a non-confrontation strategy based on finding alternative sources of financing and new trading partners. Despite some success, these endeavors were ultimately not adequate to the situation: The government could not at one and the same time meet both past external obligations and current economic pressures and develop the economy.

The abortive efforts to promote a military coup in October 1970 led to the virtual collapse of the CIA's network of "assets" in the Chilean armed forces. The reconstruction of a new network of "assets" by late 1971 co-incided with a White House decision to massively expand its covert and propaganda war against the Allende regime.[37]

Between October 1971 and September 1973, the CIA subsidized a series of devastating political strikes against the government involving truckowners and other propertied petty bourgeoisie, copper workers, and professional groups (doctors, lawyers, and so on) that served as the basis for tens of millions of dollars in production and foreign exchange losses. It also played a key role in the organization of the first major strike of the capitalist class as a whole: the October 1972 lockout of workers from the industrial sector. During the twelve months prior to the coup, the CIA funded various private sector organizations that channeled monies to those domestic groups helping to coordinate and implement the anti-government strikes. *El Mercurio*, the leading opposition newspaper, received covert "subsidies" amounting to $1.5 million, which allowed it to play a key role in identifying the gradual economic deterioration with the policies of the regime, thus creating the

---

36 For a detailed analysis of the U.S. economic blockade, see James Petras and Morris Morley, *The United States and Chile: Imperialism and the Overthrow of the Allende Government* (New York: Monthly Review Press, 1975).

37 U.S. Congress, Senate, Select Committee on Intelligence, *Covert Action in Chile 1963–1973*, 94th Congress, 1st Session, December 18, 1975 (Washington, D.C.: U.S. Government Printing Office, 1975), pp. 36–37.

economic basis for polarizing Chilean society in a manner favorable to the large property-holding class and its allies. Finally, the major opposition political parties continued to benefit from U.S. financial largesse for the duration of the Allende presidency: "... CIA funds enabled the PDC [Christian Democratic Party] and PN [National Party] to purchase their own radio stations and newspapers.... Money provided to political parties not only supported opposition candidates in various elections, but enabled the parties to maintain an anti-government campaign throughout the Allende years...."[38]

Economic destabilization and covert subversion, paralleled by deepening ties (aid, training, dialogue) between the United States and the Chilean armed forces, had the effect of separating critical state and societal institutions from the national government and its development project – and mobilizing them in support of Washington's policy goals. As the level of class conflict rose, and preparations for the coup quickened, the CIA, already involved in mobilizing and channeling the political energies of the anti-regime social forces, now moved to give it support and direction. The Santiago Station began collecting "operational intelligence" vital to any successful *golpe* such as "arrest lists, key government installations that needed to be taken over and government contingency plans...."[39]

In September 1973, the armed forces terminated Chile's much vaunted democratic polity. The new military regime's economic development strategy, heavily influenced by proposals from the CIA-funded Institute for General Studies, envisaged a major "rollback" of the Allende reforms and an opening up of the economy to foreign investment. Almost overnight, the international financial community redefined Chile's economy as "creditworthy." With unseemly haste, the U.S. government, the multilateral development banks, and the private multinational banks offered the totalitarian generals large-scale funding: In its first two years, the dictatorship received approximately $2 billion in new loans and credits, of which $1.6 billion came from Washington and the "international banks."[40]

The United States intervened in Chile against a nationalist regime it defined as posing an even greater threat to its permanent interests than Goulart in Brazil. Employing a similar "state against regime" strategy, centered around strengthening bonds with the Chilean armed forces, Washington successfully laid the basis for a coup against the "intolerable" regime. Having enforced a regime change, the new ruling generals proceeded to

---

38 Ibid, pp. 28–30.
39 Ibid., p. 38.
40 See "Loans From Abroad Flow to Chile's Rightist Junta," *New York Times*, February 20, 1976, pp. 1, 47.

recreate the state and regime in the image of American political and economic interests.

El Salvador

Carter administration policy toward El Salvador during 1979 and 1980 was directed toward a single overriding goal: preserving a client state. Through the crisis and demise of the Romero dictatorship, the political transition and the subsequent regime reshuffles, Washington's direct involvement in shaping the trajectory of Salvadoran politics was inseparable from its preoccupation with strengthening, and ensuring the survival of, the state. The hegemonic power kept recomposing the new regime to find the right "mix" compatible with the state.

Between 1977 and 1979, the White House exerted diplomatic and economic pressures on the regime of General Carlos Romero to force a diminution in widespread human rights abuses by the armed forces in collaboration with the death squads – but to no avail.[41] The overthrow of the Somoza regime and state in July 1979 by a mass democratic social movement led by radical nationalist guerrillas accelerated State Department efforts to convince Romero and the military high command to institute limited political-economic reforms and advance scheduled 1982 elections to a much earlier date or risk a possible replication of the Nicaraguan upheaval. In return, Washington offered to provide increased economic and military assistance.[42] That October, however, a group of junior army officers who attributed the collapse of the Somoza National Guard to "repression without reforms" spearheaded a successful coup against Romero. The United States responded positively to the coup because the regime change had eliminated the chief symbol of the terror, but the government and state still remained under military control and the left was kept isolated from the centers of power.

Taking advantage of the opportunity created by the October coup, the Carter administration sought to forge a civilian-military coalition, composed of reformist and rightists, in the hope of producing a political as well as a military solution to the Salvadoran conflict. The governing junta consisted of Colonel Adolfo Majano (reformist military), Colonel Jaime Gutiérrez (right-

---

41   See Robert Pastor, "Continuity and Change in U.S. Foreign Policy: Carter and Reagan on El Salvador," *Journal of Policy Analysis and Management*, Vol. 3, No. 2, Winter 1984, pp. 175–190.
42   See ibid., p. 128; Karen DeYoung, "U.S. Attempting to Calm Strife in El Salvador," *Washington Post*, September 14, 1979, pp. A1, A24; John M. Goshko, "Salvadorans May Get Aid in Combating Extremists," *Washington Post*, October 31, 1979, p. A17.

ist military), Román Mayorga (civilian liberal), and Guillermo Ungo (civilian social democrat). Washington's aims were fourfold: to preserve the state and the power of the military; to divide the civilian opposition and limit the power of the reformist army officers; to enable the state and regime to control and demobilize the popular movement; and to maintain the capitalist economy. As a result, U.S. officials refused to pressure for any major changes in the state (military and police), opposed representation of the mass movement and popular organizations in the regime, and sided with the dominant rightist military forces who rejected any accord with the guerrillas. This strategy provided the basis for a dramatic increase in terrorist activities by the security forces and the death squads. In late December, the moderates and social democrats in the regime threatened to leave en masse unless their decision-making authority was enhanced. At a showdown meeting on the 27th, the senior military commanders rejected a cluster of civilian demands, leading junta members Ungo and Mayorga, approximately forty senior government officials, and ten of the eleven cabinet ministers (the exception was Defense Minister Colonel Guillermo García) to resign their posts – acknowledging their ineffectiveness and inability to generate support for social and economic reforms in a situation where they could not control the state.[43]

The United States did little to contribute to the junta's survival or encourage reforms. Ambassador Frank Devine maintained closer ties with the military rather than the civilian members of the junta, and during November – December 1979 Washington sent riot control equipment and technical advisors to help the security forces subdue the left and reprogrammed $300,000 for military training purposes.[44]

The Carter response to the collapse of the regime in January 1980 was revealing of the administration's priorities. Instead of siding with the civilian proponents of change, Washington set about brokering an agreement between a conservative group of Christian Democrats and the rightist military to form a second junta and maintain the illusion of civilian authority. Such was the hegemonic state's determination to establish a civilian regime congruent with, but prepared to subordinate itself to, the terrorist state – the vehicle for defending U.S. permanent interests in El Salvador.

Having revamped the regime, Washington announced increases in military and economic assistance, initiated discussions with Christian Democratic junta members about creating the conditions for pursuing a "clean

---

43 See Raymond Bonner, *Weakness and Deceit: U.S. Policy and El Salvador* (New York: Times Books, 1984), p. 163.
44 Cynthia Arnson, *El Salvador: Revolution Confronts The United States* (Washington, D.C.: Institute for Policy Studies, 1982), p. 45; John Eisendrath and Jim Morrell, *Arming El Salvador* (Washington, D.C.: Center for International Policy, August 1982), pp. 2–3.

counter-insurgency war,"[45] sought to promote an agrarian reform to create a social base of support for the regime, and encouraged the armed forces to institute reforms to make it a more professional and effective fighting force. At the same time, the White House refused to tolerate rightist military-oligarchy coup plotting on the grounds that any such move would almost certainly halt the flow of Congressional funds for both the regime and the state.

Meanwhile, the security forces and death squads accelerated their terrorist activities in the countryside, especially in those areas targeted by the regime for agrarian reform. The continuing savagery of the counterinsurgency war provoked the resignation of three civilian cabinet ministers at the end of March, a split among the Christian Democrats, and mass resignations by senior party officials and rank-and-file members over the decision of a small clique headed by José Napoleón Duarte to participate in the formation of a third junta in alliance with the military and paramilitary architects of the terrorist state. But the White House order of priorities remained intact: That April, it convinced a pliant Congress to reprogram $5.7 million in military aid to the new junta.

In May, Washington once again responded to reports of rightist military coup planning with the statements that it simply did not accord with U.S. strategic objectives in El Salvador. The newly arrived American Ambassador Robert White bluntly told the army high command that a coup would result in the complete termination of the Carter administration's aid program.[46] Because the strategic interest of the White House and the State Department was in protecting the Salvadoran state and securing legislative and public support for the U.S. aid program to promote class warfare against the mass-based social movement, they opposed rightist military coups that wanted to change the regime as endangering these efforts. Whereas a military regime was viewed as a liability, a civilian-led regime (irrespective of its figurehead status) constituted an asset in the administration's effort to maintain funding programs and domestic support for the terrorist Salvadoran state.

On December 5, the administration suspended new military and economic assistance to the junta pending clarification of the role of the Salvadoran security forces in the murders of four American churchpeople. Five weeks later, the suspension was lifted despite Ambassador White's categorical assertion that the regime had refused to conduct a "serious investigation" into the assassinations.[47] The decision to resume military aid was

45 Tommie Sue Montgomery, *Revolution in El Salvador* (Boulder: Westview Press, 1982), pp. 164–165.
46 Bonner, *Weakness and Deceit*, p. 186.
47 Karen DeYoung, "Carter Decides to Resume Military Aid to El Salvador," *Washington Post*, January 14, 1981, p. A18.

based on the "survival of the military" imperative. Even the "dissident" American envoy accepted this as justification: "The first priority of our policy is to support a reform-minded government... and to preserve the Salvadoran military as an institution. The military is the final barrier against a Marxist-Leninist threat."[48] On January 17, 1981, Carter authorized an emergency $5.6 million package of lethal military assistance to the junta, invoking special executive powers in order to circumvent the need for Congressional consent. His term of office ended before a final decision could be made on a State Department proposal to send $50 million in economic aid, up to $7 million in military sales and credits, and thirty-eight U.S. army advisors to El Salvador.[49]

El Salvador is an excellent illustration of the distinction that Washington makes between regime and state changes. Faced with a growing revolutionary social movement, Washington supported the overthrow of the Romero military regime in October 1979 and its replacement by a civilian-military coalition. The conflict between the reformers in this coalition regime and the U.S.-backed state led to the defeat of the former and its subsequent replacement by a second coalition regime more compatible with the state and U.S. permanent interests: The Carter White House was able to control the process of political change because of its ties with sub-regime-level military officers who were able to oust the military incumbent. The imperial state's willingness to support regimes operating within the parameters of the existing state structures revealed its tactical flexibility in pursuit of the strategic goal – a rigid commitment to defending the continuity of the state. In this case the appearance of civilian authority, despite its illusory or figurehead status, was a crucial ingredient in securing legislative approval for large-scale, sustained funding to support the state as the ultimate guarantor of U.S. permanent interests.

Guatemala

The Guatemalan military regimes of Ríos Montt (1982–83) and Humberto Mejía (1983–85) were among the most violent in recent Latin American history. The armed forces collaborated with rightist death squads to physically destroy political opposition in the cities and wage an escalating counterinsurgency war in the countryside. Workers' organizations were decimated and thousands of civilian non-combatants were killed. The Rea-

---

48 "Interview with Ambassador Robert White: El Salvador's Future – And How U.S. Can Influence It," *U.S. News & World Report*, January 26, 1981, p. 37.
49 Karen DeYoung, "El Salvador: Where Reagan Draws the Line," *Washington Post*, March 9, 1981, p. A18.

gan administration response was to describe these terrorist regimes as valued allies; human rights abuses were of minimal concern when set against the military's free market economic policies, its virulent anti-communism, its support of U.S. regional goals, and the fact that it was combating a guerrilla movement with a growing popular constituency.

The major problem for the military regimes, however, was that the successes against the guerrillas were not matched by similar gains in the economic sphere. Between 1980 and 1985, there was massive capital flight combined with sustained declines in levels of foreign investment, overseas economic aid, export earnings and tourist dollars. Nor was the resulting economic crisis helped by continued high military budgets or the absence of any pressure for concessions from the oligarchy.

Against the background of a deteriorating economy and an abysmal reputation abroad, the military, encouraged by the White House, agreed to return the country to civilian rule. Both the hegemonic state and its Guatemalan allies viewed elections as serving a threefold purpose: First, they would offset those factors (human rights abuses, military rule, political instability) perceived as inhibiting economic recovery; second, they would encourage increased levels of foreign aid, deemed critical to effectively prosecuting the anti-guerrilla war; and, third, they offered a means for producing a regime change that would achieve economic objectives without eroding the power of the military state or weakening the existing class linkages to the U.S. In return for allowing a political transition, the generals insisted on retaining a political and administrative structure that effectively ensured the armed forces a veto power over the new civilian government. And during the election campaign, General Mejía warned that it would be a mistake if the new president decided to investigate past human rights abuses by the military.

From Washington's vantage point, the November – December 1985 elections produced the best possible results. On the one hand, the victorious Christian Democratic Party had little or no history of involvement with the depredations of military rule, and the new president Vinicio Cerezo espoused the rhetoric of human rights. On the other, the civilian regime was prepared to accommodate, and collaborate with, the terrorist state structure, the oligarchy, and foreign multinationals. In the process, the regime facilitated efforts by Washington to bolster the authority and power of the armed forces while deflecting criticism of the coercive state by the U.S. Congress and West European governments.

The essential feature of the political transition is that it took place on terms established by the armed forces: no letup in the counterinsurgency program; army control over foreign policy, rural development policy, and all security matters; no prosecution of military officials for human rights abuses; and no socioeconomic reforms that threaten the position of the oligarchy. During his first year in office, Cerezo hewed to the course laid down by the generals. He selected a new Defense Minister from among the ranks of senior army officers. He refused to dissolve the military's civil defense patrol system that had forced almost one million rural villagers to join paramilitary units. He buckled to army pressure in abandoning a public offer to begin a dialogue with the guerrillas and in scrapping plans to name a civilian to head the National Police. And no attempt was made to overturn the Mejía regime's amnesty decree preventing indictments against army officials accused of terrorist activities.[50] "Cerezo recognizes the breaking points," a Western diplomat pointedly observed in March 1987. "He can't appoint generals, he can't set budgets, he can't do anything with the Army."[51]

But Washington did not promote the transition to civilian rule to weaken the power of the military state. On the contrary, it manipulated the Cerezo regime to preserve and enhance the power of the state in defense of U.S. permanent interests in Guatemala. To this end, the White House gained Congressional approval for a $5 million military aid package for Guatemala in 1986 even though Cerezo had only requested $1 million, thus reinforcing the parameters within which the regime could operate.[52]

The White House and the generals deemed the shift to an electoral-civilian regime a great success insofar as it achieved three priority objectives. First, it demonstrably improved Guatemala's image throughout the Western world. Cerezo retained his status as a reformist leader and an advocate of human rights despite the persistence of army-death squad political killings and disappearances of trade unionists, peasants, teachers, and students. Although the new president failed to prosecute the architects of the terror, he continually denounced such actions and took no responsibility for the violence attached to the regime. Second, the civilian government did not seek to enact major reforms in agriculture, banking, or commerce. Instead of confronting the oligarchy and foreign investors, Cerezo adopted an economic approach that disproportionately benefited the existing centers of wealth. Third, and perhaps the most important achievement of the transi-

50 See Stephen Kinzer, "Guatemalan Stays in Step With Army," *New York Times*, May 11, 1986, p. 4; Edward Cody, "Guatemala's Unspoken Bargain," *Washington Post*, July 3, 1986, p. A26; Terri Shaw, "Guatemala Said to Force Security Role on Civilians," *Washington Post*, August 14, 1986, p. A20; James Painter, *Guatemala: False Hopes, False Freedom* (London: Latin American Bureau, 1987), pp. 85–95; "Human Rights Abuses Continue Under Cerezo," *Central America Bulletin*, Vol. 6, No. 4, March 1987, pp. 4–5.

51 Quoted in Peter Ford, "The Army's Power Overshadows Guatemala's President Cerezo," *Christian Science Monitor* (International Edition), March 30–April 5, 1987, p. 9.

52 Painter, *Guatemala: False Hope, False Freedom*, p. 108; Stephen Kinzer, "Guatemalan Army Yields Little Power to Leader," *New York Times*, May 13, 1987, p. 10.

tion, was the ability of Cerezo to secure new commitments of large-scale economic assistance from Western governments and international banks, and to negotiate a debt restructuring with the country's foreign creditors. The level of foreign currency reserves increased from less than $8 million in 1985 to $484 million in September 1986.[53]

Guatemala is another illustration of U.S. support for regime change and continuity in the state apparatus. The catalyst was not an imminent political challenge but the profound economic crisis and the generals' desperate need for outside economic assistance. Although overwhelming military force had temporarily contained the revolutionary challenge, it isolated the regime in the world community. The shift to civilian government was perceived in Washington as an excellent mode of securing international economic assistance and strengthening the state. The Reagan administration and its military allies were able to control the process of regime change because the timing was propitious: Elections were held after the defeat of the guerrillas and the demobilization and decimation of the radical social movements, similar to the Dominican Republic experience of 1965–66. The process was aided by the synchronous perceptions between U.S. policymakers and the Mejía government: There was sufficient flexibility among the generals to accommodate a shift in regime as long as they retained control over the state apparatus. In the post-transition period, the elected regime revealed itself fully willing to cohabit with the military state. Meanwhile, Washington chose to turn a blind eye to the armed forces' continuing, large-scale human rights abuses, and its support of Cerezo never waivered.

Throughout both Republican and Democratic administrations, under conservative and liberal presidents, the state/regime distinction has been basic in explaining U.S. foreign policy toward political change and socioeconomic reform. As these case studies demonstrate, Washington's policy toward the state in Latin America has remained constant; toward the regime, variable. Whether we are discussing Eisenhower and Cuba, the Kennedy-Johnson approach toward the Dominican Republic and Brazil, Nixon's hostility toward Chile, Carter's policy toward El Salvador, or Reagan's approach toward the crisis of the dictatorship in Guatemala, the thread that links them is a singular determination to preserve the state, together with a flexible approach regarding support for elected regimes or dictatorial rulers.

Precisely because the state shapes the long-term policies of a political system, Washington is willing to accept changes in a regime in order to preserve the continuity of the state, including accommodations between

---

53 See "Economic Recovery: Who Pays?," *Central America Bulletin* Vol. 6, No. 3, February 1987, p. 2.

elected civilian regimes and terrorist military states. At the same time, it consistently opposes, by military, economic, and/or diplomatic means, political transitions that dismantle the existing state, particularly when the new state is organized to sustain a nationalist or anti-capitalist development project. U.S. governments are willing to sacrifice longstanding Third World clients and accommodate a transition from dictatorship to civilian rule as long as the state structure (or, at a minimum, its coercive arm) survives the transition process intact. Successive administrations have attempted, with mixed success, to take preemptive action when mass democratic revolutionary movements have threatened client states. Preemptive policies seek to create opportunities for sectors of these opposition movements (which share the U.S. view of the state) to form new regimes and thus ensure that the new government will collaborate with the existing state.

The cases of Cuba and (as we shall see) Nicaragua illustrate that the United States is not always able to reshuffle regimes, either due to conflicts with regime clients or because of inadequate policy calculations. Washington's unremitting hostility toward the Cuban and Nicaraguan revolutions – in contrast to its willingness to accommodate political shifts to civilian regimes elsewhere – is largely explained by the type of change that is proposed or takes place. The key issue in determining U.S. policy is not principled support for civilian-electoral systems or authoritarian-military regimes, but policy estimates in specific historical contexts as to the appropriate type of regime to defend existing state institutions that support U.S. permanent interests.

Approaching Nicaragua: The relevance of the framework

The state-regime distinction provides an indispensable key to understanding the shifts and changes, or lack thereof, in U.S. policy toward Nicaragua from the late 1960s to the early 1980s. In the absence of any fundamental challenge to the Somoza dictatorship, neither Nixon nor Ford expressed interest in withdrawing U.S. support and promoting a democratic transition. The impetus for a regime change occurred under Carter in a context of Somoza's growing political isolation, a rising level of social-class conflict, and an emerging perception among U.S. officials that the scope and composition of anti-regime movement offered, potentially, a threat to the state as well as the ruling dynasty. As a result, there was a policy shift that took the form of more active support for those sectors of the opposition willing to cohabit with the regime and work with the existing state, and it pressured the regime to negotiate and make concessions to these civilian elements. The failure of this strategy led Washington to promote a regime change by pressuring the client to leave office and "acceptable" civilian opponents to definitively split from the mass movement to form a new regime that would collaborate with the "old" state. In other words, confronted by a regime crisis in which a traditional ally was challenged by a mass-based democratic social movement, the White House sought to dump the regime in order to save the state. But success remained elusive, compounded by an inability to isolate the dictatorship from its coercive apparatus. The result was a virtual rerun of the Cuban scenario two decades earlier: The mass movement led by nationalist guerrillas overthrew a client regime and transformed the state. The Carter administration again revealed its flexibility by outlining a new strategy based on attempting to nurture divisions within the new regime in the ultimate hope of promoting a new collaborator regime as a manifestation of democracy accompanied by a reconstituted state that would be responsive to U.S. permanent interests.

Chapter 2 of this study presents an overview of the decades-long relationship between Washington and the Somozas. Without a historical setting it is not possible to understand why the family dictatorship survived so long, nor to fully comprehend the shaping of American policy during the latter half of the 1970s. In *Condemned to Repetition*, Robert Pastor has argued that "most administrations were uncomfortable" with the Somozas; that the policy pursued was largely one of benign neglect or indifference; that rather than being a close ally of the dynasty, Washington was more a reluctant collaborator attracted by its anti-communism and willingness to support U.S. interests in the region. He dismisses the notion that the Somozas were American "puppets" given that they always pursued their own interests, which on occasion conflicted with those of the imperial state.[54] Irrespective of the nature of the Somozas' clientelism, however, such an interpretation cannot obscure Washington's pivotal role in contributing to the longevity of the dynasty. As the events of 1978 and 1979 so graphically illustrate, its survival ultimately depended on the hegemonic power's continued support.

Chapter 3 tracks U.S. policy toward Nicaragua during the Nixon and Ford presidencies, highlighting the bureaucratic debate, confined primarily to State Department officials, over how closely Washington should tie itself to Somoza. Chapters 4–6 analyze Carter policy toward Somoza and the increasingly formidable polyclass, urban-rural opposition movement, at all times distinguishing between the basic consensus over policy objectives and the bureaucratic conflicts about how these goals could best be achieved. Chapter 7 focuses on the critical first eighteen months in the relationship between Washington and the Sandinista-dominated regime and state, dur-

---

54   Robert A. Pastor, *Condemned to Repetition: The United States and Nicaragua* (Princeton: Princeton University Press, 1987), pp. 271–272.

ing which time the White House embarked on a multitrack effort to limit the process of transformation consonant with U.S. permanent interests.

Throughout, this study makes extensive use of personal interviews and recently declassified U.S. government documents. Together, they cast fresh light on various aspects of American policy in a period of transition from dictatorial to revolutionary rule – ranging from Pentagon views of Somoza's demise to pressures on the Sandinistas to renegotiate Nicaragua's foreign debt as a precondition for access to large-scale sources of overseas reconstruction aid.

2

Washington and the Somoza dynasty: From consolidation to crisis of a client dictatorship

The historical setting of U.S.-Nicaraguan relations

Historically, Central America has been within the sphere of U.S. domination: frequent military invasions and occupations, economic and political interventions, and the routine manipulation of elected officials and army generals to suit overseas investor and strategic interests have been recurring themes in the twentieth-century relationship.

Starting in the late 1920s, Washington began the process of creating "national" armies in Central America and the Caribbean as the most cost-effective, long-term alternative to repeatedly "sending in the marines" to put down nationalist challenges to client rulers and protect U.S. economic and financial interests. Since World War II, tens of thousands of army, naval, and air force officers from the sub-region have honed their fighting skills at American military training centers in the Panama Canal Zone or on the mainland. They have also received political indoctrination in the values (for example, anti-communism, anti-nationalism, open capitalist economies), ideals and belief systems of the dominant power. The Defense Department's role as the most important weapons supplier for the Central American military, the stationing of U.S. army, naval, and air force missions in these countries, bilateral military pacts, and periodic joint maneuvers further consolidated professional and personal relationships. The two most consequential outcomes have been sub-regional armed forces prepared to support the political and economic status quo (and, by extension, U.S. permanent interests), and Washington's determination to safeguard the power and prerogatives of these coercive institutions in periods of societal upheaval and political transition.

Prior to World War II, U.S. economic interests focused on the agro-export sectors while its geopolitical interests centered on the control and operation of the Panama Canal. After 1945, however, the rapid and massive expansion of American multinational capital around the world relegated

Central America to a secondary position in Washington's global and regional concerns – except on those occasions when area regimes, notably Arbenz in Guatemala between 1950 and 1954, sought to challenge the role of foreign investors within the national economy. While the rest of the Third World was experiencing political and social upheavals, U.S. policymakers continued to support the entrenched landed oligarchies and military regimes in Central America. Supporters of capitalist development and expanding markets for U.S. products and services, they were dubbed "modernizing oligarchies" and "technocratic military." Washington encouraged the conversion of the oligarchs and generals to "entrepreneurial behavior" as part of its larger goal of promoting large-scale commercial agriculture and manufacturing based on cheap labor and major infusions of overseas capital.

Beginning in the mid-1950s, U.S. policymakers became increasingly linked to those sectors of the Central American ruling class involved in financial and industrial institutions and less tied to the direct ownership of land. The establishment of the Central American Common Market provided the catalyst for a shift in the pattern of multinational investments during the 1960s and 1970s, with industry absorbing an increased proportion of new capital commitments and agro-mining sectors a declining share. In 1960, only $12 million out of a total of $342 million in U.S. direct investment in Central America was located in manufacturing; by 1980, $417 million out of $1,033 million (approximately 40 percent of the total) was found in textiles, chemicals, food products, pharmaceuticals and other industrial activities.[1]

More diversified investments, however, did not lead to any change in Washington's policy toward those forces seeking to change the political and economic status quo. The convergence of the interests of the imperial state[2] and American investment capital with those of the local dominant groups produced a historic compromise in which successive U.S. administrations sacrificed democratic rights in exchange for capitalist economic opportunities and strategic objectives. The latter's support for Central American dictatorships was manifested through a vast program of bilateral and multilateral economic aid and various forms of military assistance. Between 1953 and 1979, Washington provided the rulers of El Salvador, Honduras, Guatemala, and Nicaragua with over $1.5 billion in economic and military assistance, a sum exceeded by the U.S.-influenced international banks who

---

1   U.S. Department of Commerce, *Selected Data on U.S. Investment Abroad, 1950–76* (February 1982), pp. 1–27; *Survey of Current Business* Vol. 61, No. 8, August 1981, pp. 31–32; *Survey of Current Business*, Vol. 63, No. 8, August 1983, pp. 23–24.
2   The notion of the U.S. as an imperial state is discussed in James F. Petras and Morris H. Morley, "The U.S. Imperial State," *Review* (Fernand Braudel Center for the Study of Economies, Historical Systems, and Civilizations), Vol. IV, No. 2, Fall 1980, pp. 171–222.

channeled more than $2.2 billion into their coffers.[3] At the same time, U.S. military assistance, arms sales, and training programs enabled these autocratic regimes to counter domestic challenges to their authority and White House interests. In return, Central America collaborated with Washington's geopolitical designs, acting as a staging ground for direct U.S. military intervention in the region, a training base for U.S. and Latin American military forces, and a testing area for counterinsurgency warfare methods.

United States and Nicaragua:
The political-strategic relationship

From the late 1940s to the mid-1970s, American presidents regarded the implacably anti-communist Somoza regime as a valued sub-regional ally and pursued policies that assured the consolidation and longevity of the Nicaraguan dynasty. The growing centralization of political and economic power in the hands of the Somoza family, senior National Guard officials, and assorted regime cronies was intertwined with continuing American political endorsements, military assistance, public economic aid, private bank loans, direct investments, trade relations, and support for Nicaraguan loan requests to the multilateral development banks. As a reward for Somoza's willingness to collaborate with Washington's strategic goals, promote an open economy, and support U.S. political positions in the Organization of American States and the United Nations, Democratic and Republican administrations alike accommodated the authoritarian rule, the rigged elections based on handpicked opponents and savage repression of independent challenges, and the corrupt, predatory state that operated largely as a vehicle for private capital accumulation by the Somoza family and its supporters.

Although the Somozas ruled on the basis of political manipulation, corruption, and repression, with minimal roots in any important social group or class in society, no White House prior to the Carter period deemed it necessary to actively encourage or pressure the regime to eliminate the worst excesses that accompanied its method of rule – precisely because such a concern was always subordinate to the fact of Somoza's willingness to accommodate fundamental American interests in Nicaragua and the Central American-Caribbean region. Washington's acquiescence was reinforced through the dynasty's longstanding ties with key legislative branch officials, and further cemented by a lavishly financed public relations/lobbying pro-

---

3   U.S. Agency for International Development, *U.S. Overseas Loans and Grants and Assistance from International Organizations, July 1, 1945–September 30, 1976*, pp. 47–48, 51, 54, 184–185; *U.S. Overseas Loans and Grants and Assistance from International Organizations, July 1, 1945–September 30, 1980*, pp. 47–48, 51, 54, 202–204.

gram that spanned almost two decades.[4] Successive U.S. Ambassadors behaved more as personal advisors to, and propagandists for, the Somozas than as diplomatic representatives of a foreign power. One of them, Thomas Whelan, who ran the Managua Embassy from 1951 to 1961, lauded Nicaragua as "our staunchest friend in Latin America" and the Somozas for "having done a good job of keeping it economically sound and politically stable."[5] A prominent Nicaraguan government official called Whelan "*our* Ambassador."[6] The Nixon White House appointee, Turner Shelton (1970–1975), "was so subservient to Somoza," a high-level State Department Central Americanist recalled, "that he was practically his ambassador rather than ours."[7]

The Somoza family's entrenched political and economic power was immensely facilitated by the links forged between the country's armed forces and the coercive agencies of the imperial state. Nicaragua's National Guard was a "creature" of U.S. policy from its inception in the late 1920s, when Washington decided to organize, finance, and train a "national" military force, to its demise at the hands of the Sandinistas in mid-1979.[8]

The Somozas built up and sustained a politically loyal officer corp by preventing non-family members from heading the organization, providing myriad opportunities for officers and enlisted men to accumulate wealth legally and illegally (in prostitution, gambling, bribery, and other rackets), and making devotion to the dictatorship the prime prerequisite for appointment to troop commands:

> Subject by Somoza to tight internal control through dispensation of favors, frequent rotation of postings, and occasional expulsion of ambitious officers, [the National Guard] was large enough to seem ubiquitous in a small country and yet too small to develop an institutional ethic beyond loyalty to its commander.[9]

---

4 Nicaraguan government spending on public relations activities in the United States between mid-1975 and mid-1979 averaged approximately $285,000 annually. For a discussion, see Lars Schoultz, *Human Rights and United States Policy Toward Latin America* (Princeton: Princeton University Press, 1981), pp. 58–65.

5 Letter from Ambassador Thomas E. Whelan to Assistant Secretary of State for Inter-American Affairs Roy R. Rubottom, September 9, 1957, in Department of State, *Foreign Relations of the United States, 1955–1957, Volume VII: American Republics Central and South America* (Washington, D.C.: U.S. Government Printing Office, 1987), p. 238.

6 Quoted in Thomas W. Walker, *Nicaragua: The Land of Sandino* (Boulder: Westview Press, 1986), p. 129 (author's emphasis).

7 Telephone interview with Lawrence Pezzullo, Maryland, September 27, 1989. The respondent was Deputy Director, Office of Central American Affairs, Department of State, 1972 to 1974.

8 For a detailed historical treatment, see Richard Millett, *Guardians of the Dynasty* (New York: Orbis Books, 1977).

9 James Dunkerly, *Power in the Isthmus* (London: Verso Books, 1988), p. 232.

However, the other side of the Guard's total identification with the Somoza family – its personal, private army – was its isolation from the rest of the population among whom it had developed the reputation as a brutal and corrupt occupation force, not a professional institution charged with protecting the country from external attack. Rooted in concrete historical experiences, this perception was to have profound consequences for Washington's efforts to promote a desired outcome to the anti-regime political upheaval in the late 1970s.

Even by Central American standards, Nicaragua under the Somozas was a most-favored recipient of U.S. military assistance and training, particularly after the establishment of Pentagon army and air force missions in the country in the early 1950s. A mid-1957 internal State Department memorandum referred to the United States as "the chief supplier of arms to Nicaragua."[10] During the 1960s, the Kennedy-Johnson preoccupation with avoiding a "second Cuba" and imposing regional "stability" triggered a substantial increase in military aid that, among other things, enabled Somoza to acquire "the largest force of jet aircraft in Central America."[11] Between 1963 and 1967, such assistance totalled $7.5 million, almost double the amount released over the previous thirteen years.[12] Training programs for National Guard officers and troops in the Panama Canal Zone or at military bases in the United States complemented these weapons sales to produce a formidable fighting force capable of easily overwhelming internal threats to the regime, including that posed by the Sandinista National Liberation Front (FSLN).

In the decade prior to Somoza's overthrow, Pentagon largesse reached new heights. Although figures vary from a low of approximately $20 million to a high of more than $32 million, what is indisputable is that between 1968 and 1978 Nicaragua was the largest per capita recipient of U.S. military assistance in Latin America.[13] Moreover, the number of National Guardsmen trained at U.S. military centers abroad in the two and a half decades after 1950 (well over 4,000) topped the list of Latin American armed forces.[14] The upshot of these historical processes, in the words of a

10 Memorandum from Office of Middle American Affairs (Moon) to the Director of the Office (Wieland), July 9, 1957, Subject: "Recent Arms Purchases by Nicaragua," in Department of State, *Foreign Relations of the United States, 1955–1957, Volume VII: American Republics Central and South America*, p. 235.
11 Millett, *Guardians of the Dynasty*, p. 226.
12 Walter LaFeber, *Inevitable Revolutions: The United States in Central America* (New York: W.W. Norton, 1983), p. 151.
13 *NACLA Report on the Americas*, Vol. XII, No. 6, November/December 1978, p. 32; Bernard Diederich, *Somoza and the Legacy of U.S. Involvement in Central America* (New York: E.P. Dutton, 1981), p. 133.
14 See Millett, *Guardians of the Dynasty*, p. 252; Don L. Etchison, *The United States and Militarism in Central America* (New York: Praeger Publishers, 1975), p. 105.

Pentagon official involved with Nicaragua during the 1970s, was the emergence of a multi-tiered relationship between the Department of Defense and the National Guard that "resembled social bonding." Formal military ties were complemented by what "turned out to be over the longer term much more important personal relations" developed through continuous interaction between Nicaraguan and American officers via training schools, military assistance advisory groups, and the like: "The result was pretty open dialogue not only on an official level but also through personal friendships."[15] Somoza himself went out of his way to maintain personal contacts with his fellow West Point Class of 1946 graduates. This included flying them to Managua to attend his presidential inauguration in May 1967 and celebrate the group's twenty-fifth anniversary in 1971.[16] Such long-term, large-scale U.S. military involvement in Nicaragua was to a considerable degree responsible for sustaining in power an autocratic political dynasty that refused to seriously tackle the country's underlying social and economic problems.

In exchange for consistent military support, Somoza became perhaps Washington's most important sub-regional ally. In 1954, Guatemalan army exiles, organized, financed, and trained by the CIA at the direction of the White House, mounted a successful invasion against the nationalist government of Jacobo Arbenz from staging bases in Nicaragua. Seven years later, in 1961, the Kennedy administration attempted to replicate the "Guatemalan tactic," again using Nicaraguan territory, in an unsuccessful effort to terminate the Cuban Revolution. In 1963, with Pentagon encouragement and support, Somoza played a leading role in the formation of the Central American Defense Council (CONDECA), a counterinsurgency regional military alliance, and became the dominant figure in the organization's "pacification" activities during the late 1960s and early 1970s. Hewson Ryan, the U.S. Ambassador to Honduras from 1969 to 1973, recalled that Somoza viewed CONDECA "as his tool...."[17] The Nicaraguan ruler reaffirmed his traditional commitment to furthering Washington's anti-nationalist and counterrevolutionary objectives following the 1965 U.S. military invasion in the Dominican Republic. He publicly supported the White House action and contributed troops to the regional "peacekeeping" force organized by Washington to help maintain "order" in the aftermath of the invasion.

15 Confidential telephone interview, Department of Defense official, Maine, September 26, 1989. The respondent was a senior Caribbean and Central American Affairs official, Office of the Assistant Secretary (International Security Affairs), 1979 to 1981.

16 See K. Bruce Galloway and Robert Bowie, Jr., *West Point: America's Power Fraternity* (New York: Simon & Schuster, 1973), p. 22.

17 Ambassador Hewson Ryan, *oral history interview*, April 27 and May 4, 1978, Association for Diplomatic Studies, Foreign Affairs Oral History Program, Lauinger Library, Georgetown University, Washington, D.C., p. 49.

Somoza's willingness to serve as a U.S. regional policeman and "enforcer" of political stability in Central America and the Caribbean went beyond CONDECA mobilizations against guerrilla movements to direct involvement in efforts to fend off domestic challenges and in other ways support allied military regimes. Two instances will suffice: In Guatemala, the Nicaraguan ruler actively supported the armed forces' candidates in the 1970 and 1974 presidential elections; in El Salvador, National Guard troops participated in quashing a junior officers' coup attempt against the military high command in the aftermath of the latter's rigging of the 1972 presidential election results to deny the clear-cut victory achieved by reformist political forces.

The dictatorship also vigorously supported Washington's global policies. Its actions ranged from consistently voting in favor of U.S. positions in the United Nations to offers to send troops to bolster American interventionist policies in the Third World (Korea in 1950, Vietnam in 1967). In an October 1975 dispatch to the State Department, U.S. Ambassador to Nicaragua James Theberge based his opposition to a proposed aid cutoff on Somoza's unquestioning support for American positions in international forums "especially when such support has been of crucial importance...." This included cosponsoring resolutions of "great importance to us" and "lobby[ing] intensively" on issues of high priority to the White House but "of little direct interest to Nicaragua." The Ambassador concluded by describing the Somoza regime as "one of the few remaining, reliable friends in Latin America that we can call on for assistance...."[18]

By no means, however, was the relationship totally devoid of conflict or disagreement. The Truman administration, for instance, opposed Somoza's presidential reelection bid in May 1947, which contributed to the latter's decision to withdraw from the race in favor of the Liberal Party's Leonardo Argüello. When the Somoza-led National Guard ousted Argüello from office soon after his election, the White House refused to recognize the new regime, imposed military aid sanctions, and over the next ten months applied "moral persuasion and diplomatic pressure"[19] in a failed effort to restore constitutional government to Nicaragua. Diplomatic ties were ultimately resumed – a testament both to the Guard's loyalty to Somoza and the latter's solid identification with the anti-communist ideology that more and more defined postwar American foreign policy.

18 Department of State Telegram, Confidential Managua 4144, American Embassy (Theberge) to Secretary of State, October 27, 1975, Subject: "OMB Proposed Aid Budget Cut for FY 1977," DFOIA.
19 Thomas M. Leonard, *The United States and Central America 1944–1949* (Tuscaloosa: University of Alabama Press, 1984), p. 148. Also see Millett, *Guardians of the Dynasty*, pp. 203–213.

Events in Costa Rica also precipitated some temporary rifts between Washington and Managua. Following the outbreak of civil war in 1948, Somoza's offer of military assistance to the embattled Picardo government was roundly condemned by American officials; seven years later, President Eisenhower authorized military aid to the regime headed by José Figueres, then under attack by an army of Costa Rican exiles organized by the Nicaraguan dictator. The White House rejected Somoza's request for a similar aid package, moving the client to wonder aloud: "What advantage do we get for being friendly."[20]

In late 1958, the possibility of a visit to the United States by [President Luis] Somoza led the State Department to advise against extending a formal invitation for a meeting with President Eisenhower to avoid giving "credence to any accusations that the United States favors the 'Somoza dynasty'..." At the same time, State had "no objections to informal arrangements being made [for such a meeting] should [Somoza] come to the United States for a medical checkup."[21] Public and private criticisms of this kind notwithstanding, Washington policymakers still refused to contemplate any measure that raised the specter of a major shift in policy toward Nicaragua.

The economic basis of U.S.-Nicaraguan relations: Contradictions of capitalist development

Capitalist development in post-1950s Nicaragua occurred within a socioeconomic and political framework that included (1) the continuity of the traditional ruling class increasingly diversifying its holdings but retaining its family-based sources of political and economic power; (2) rulership through a military-police state regime with ties to the military and intelligence agencies of the U.S. imperial state: and (3) multinationals, primarily American, with links to the Somoza family as well as to the economic and political agencies of the U.S. imperial state. This triumvirate of traditional family-based capitalism, foreign multinationals, and military-dominated political

---

20 Quoted in Thomas M. Leonard, *Central America and the United States: The Search for Stability*. (Athens: University of Georgia Press, 1991,) p. 144. Also see Stephen G. Rabe, *Eisenhower and Latin America: The Foreign Policy of Anticommunism* (Chapel Hill: University of North Carolina Press, 1988), p. 86.

21 Memorandum from the Director of the Office of Central American and Panamanian Affairs (Stewart) to the Assistant Secretary of State for Inter-American Affairs (Rubottom), Confidential, November 26, 1958, Subject: "Our Attitude Toward a Possible U.S. Visit by President Somoza", in Department of State, *Foreign Relations of the United States, 1958–1960, Volume 1: American Republics*, Microfiche Supplement (Washington, D.C.: U.S. Government Printing Office, 1991).

regimes provided the framework for a sustained period of economic development and growth preceding the Sandinista revolution of July 1979.[22]

Economic expansion in Nicaragua during the 1960s and 1970s featured two contradictory processes: a growing concentration of capital and declining wage and salary levels. While the Somoza family wealth, based on the ownership of agricultural estates, industrial enterprises, communications and banking operations, food processing companies, and joint ventures with foreign investors, increased from approximately $60 million in the mid-1950s to an estimated $400 million to $500 million in the mid-1970s,[23] real wage levels of Nicaraguan workers declined by 25 percent between 1967 and 1975.[24] These twin developments induced the growth of a mass-based opposition that linked demands for immediate improvements with a transformation of the social structure. The processes of capitalist development homogenized the conditions of heterogeneous social classes (salaried and wage workers, unemployed, landless rural wage workers, smallholding peasants, urban poor, and so on), creating the basis for a broad unified social revolutionary movement that ultimately terminated dictatorial rule in Nicaragua.

Origins of the political crisis (1): The economic development model

The political upheaval in Nicaragua in the late 1970s was rooted partly in the country's prior economic development experience. Autocratic government created optimal conditions for capitalist expansion: Between 1961 and 1977, the Gross Domestic Product (GDP) grew at an average annual rate of 6.5 percent. During this period, the yearly increase in industry and agriculture exceeded 9 percent and 6 percent respectively.[25] Although shifts in commodity export prices produced cyclical fluctuations, the overall picture was that of an economy enjoying a relatively dynamic industrial and agro-export based growth. In the early 1970s, however, portents of a serious, long-term economic decline began to emerge. Recessionary periods took an

22 For a discussion of family-based corporate capitalism in Latin America, see Maurice Zeitlin and R.E. Ratcliff, "Research Methods for the Analysis of the Internal Structure of Dominant Classes: The Case of Landlords and Capitalists in Chile," *Latin American Research Review*, Vol. X, No. 3, Winter 1965, pp. 5–61.

23 *NACLA's Latin America & Empire Report*, Vol. X, No. 2, February 1979, pp. 10–12; "Nicaragua: How the Local Boys Made Good," *Latin America Economic Report*, January 27, 1978, p. 27; Diederich, *Somoza and the Legacy of U.S. Involvement in Central America*, p. 132.

24 "Deepening Crisis Alarms Nicaraguan Private Sector," *Latin America Economic Report*, May 4, 1979, p. 133.

25 World Bank, *World Development Report 1980* (New York: Oxford University Press, August 1980), p. 112.

increasingly harsher toll on living standards, prefiguring major changes in the economy and the class structure that eventually spilled over into the political arena.

Agricultural expansion after midcentury, based principally on booms in cotton and beef production, was fueled by growing overseas (largely U.S.) demand and made possible by the introduction of new fertilizers, insecticides, herbicides, and other features of mechanization into the rural sector. Between 1950 and 1965, cotton jumped from 5 percent to 44 percent of total exports.[26] In the following decade the process of mechanization quickened, providing the basis for a new era of agro-export expansion. The fourfold increase in the number of tractors in operation and the amount of land under irrigation between 1965 and 1976 was accompanied by a 40 percent increase in beef exports and a 30 percent rise in cotton exports (from 1973 to 1978).[27] Despite a slowdown in the average annual growth rate of exports from 9.7 percent in the 1960s to (albeit a still healthy) 5.6 percent between 1970 and 1978, the average yearly increase for the entire period topped imports by a narrow margin. One index of the direct relationship between exports and economic prosperity was the marked increase in export earnings' share of GDP from 24 percent in 1969 to 33.7 percent in 1975.[28]

The major beneficiaries of this export growth were a small number of urban-based capitalists, wealthy rural families, the Somozas who owned vast amounts of ranchland, and foreign, mostly U.S., multinational corporations. The agro-export boom provided rich rewards for those American commercial traders and multinationals who sold most of the new pesticides, fertilizers, machine parts, raw materials, and transport equipment to the rural sector. The Monsanto Chemical Company, for instance, became a major supplier of insecticides to the expanding cotton industry. "Our business was very profitable," recalled a company executive. "We increased our market share in Nicaragua during the 1970s due to the growth of the cotton crop."[29] Agricultural sales composed a substantial part of U.S. exports to Nicaragua in the 1960s and 1970s. Although U.S. exports as a percentage of total

26 Dunkerly, *Power in the Isthmus*, p. 191.
27 James W. Wilkie, ed., *Statistical Abstract of Latin America, Volume 20* (University of California at Los Angeles: Latin American Center, 1980), p. 39; Robert G. Williams, *Export Agriculture and the Crisis in Central America* (Chapel Hill: University of North Carolina Press, 1986), p. 167. The cotton and cattle boom is discussed in Ibid. and Jaime Biderman, "The Development of Capitalism in Nicaragua: A Political Economic History," *Latin American Perspectives*, Vol. X, No. 1, Winter 1983, pp. 13–19.
28 World Bank, *World Bank Development Report 1980*, p. 124; John Weeks, *The Economies of Central America* (New York: Holmes & Meier, 1985), pp. 52, 67.
29 Telephone interview with Chad Engler, Missouri, September 13, 1988. The respondent is Monsanto's manager of credit and financing for Latin America. He was closely involved with the company's Nicaraguan operations during the 1970s.

Nicaraguan purchases abroad experienced a modest decline during the
1970s (from 38 percent in 1969 to an annual average of approximately 32
percent between 1971 and 1978), there was no lessening in the agro-export
sector's dependence on access to American-origin goods.[30]

Throughout the 1960s and 1970s, the United States remained an important, although declining, market for Nicaragua's exports. During the
early 1960s, American purchasers absorbed over 40 percent of the total;
between 1969 and 1973, this figure hovered at 33–35 percent annually.
Following a sharp drop to 19 percent in 1974, it regained lost ground in
1975 (28 percent) and 1976 (31 percent) before regressing again to 24
percent in 1977 and 23 percent in 1978. But despite Nicaragua's increased
access to European Economic Community, Japanese and Latin American
markets, over one quarter of all its exports continued to find their way to
U.S. ports between 1975 and 1978.[31]

Although primary products still accounted for 82 percent of total exports
in 1977, there was a steady, if incremental, expansion in non-traditional
exports after 1960 (from 2-18 percent) stimulated by rising foreign investments in the industrial/manufacturing sector of the economy.[32] The Kennedy administration's Alliance for Progress and the establishment of a
Central American Common Market (CACM) in the early 1960s initiated a
period of highly capital intensive industrialization in Nicaragua dominated
by American multinationals who actively exploited the advantages offered
not only by a protected regionwide market but also by government tax and
other fiscal inducements, a "docile" labor force, and low wage levels. According to an American businessman who worked in the construction industry, Nicaragua "was an easy place to do business in but you had to know
the type of business conducive to low labor costs. Much of the U.S. investment was to take advantage of the agrarian situation – fertile land and
low labor costs – or to take advantage of tariff barriers of the CACM."[33]

---

30 U.S. Department of Commerce, *United States Foreign Trade Annual 1969–1975* (Overseas
    Business Reports 76–24), May 1976, p. 30; *United States Foreign Trade Annual 1971–1977*
    (Overseas Business Reports 78–21), June 1978, p. 30; *United States Foreign Trade Annual
    1974–1980* (Overseas Business Reports 81–34), November 1981, p. 30. During the
    1960s, in particular, the quasi-U.S. government Export-Import Bank played an active
    role in underwriting American exporters selling in the Nicaraguan market.
31 U.S. Department of Commerce, *United States Foreign Trade Annual 1969–1975*, p. 30;
    United States Foreign Trade Annual 1971–1977, p. 30; *United States Foreign Trade Annual
    1974–1980*, p. 30; Robert Henriques Girling, "Nicaragua's Commercial Policy: Building
    a Socially Responsive Foreign Trade," *Latin American Perspectives*, Vol. X, No. 1, Winter
    1983, p. 35.
32 World Bank, *World Development Report 1980*, p. 126.
33 Telephone interview with Bruce Cuthbertson, Florida, October 17, 1988. The respondent
    was an American businessman resident in Nicaragua from 1965 to 1980 with economic
    interests in the construction industry. He was a founder member and director of the

The growth of a more diversified economy triggered largely by investment decisions made in the United States could not, however, mask a pattern of development based on a great deal of non-productive investments in the form of entrepreneurial and speculative activities (for example, large-scale investments in urban real estate) by the Somoza family, senior military officials, and representatives of the dominant local banking groups. The investment proclivities of the dictatorship and its supporters ensured that there would be no lessening in the importance of the service sector relative to industry and agriculture. In 1961, the service sector contributed 55 percent of the country's GDP, more than double that of both industry and agriculture; over a decade and a half later, this situation remained virtually unchanged.[34]

Probably the most distinctive feature of the Nicaraguan development model was its excessive dependence on access to multiple sources of foreign financing: private investment capital; government economic assistance; multilateral development bank loans; and private multinational bank funds. In each of these areas, the pivotal roles were played by United States actors and institutions.

Annual studies of the Nicaraguan economy prepared by the American Embassy in Managua during the 1960s and 1970s extolled the virtues of the country as a profitable locale for U.S. investors. They highlighted the lack of equity requirements, the absence of limitations on profit or royalty remittances, ease of access to local capital, no exchange controls, numerous tax concessions, duty-free entry of capital equipment and raw materials, a political environment that secured investors against expropriation or nationalization, the availability of all U.S. government Overseas Private Investment Corporation (OPIC) investment guarantee programs, and a foreign investment policy that accorded national and foreign firms identical treatment.[35]

Throughout the 1960s, U.S. direct investments flowed into agriculture, industry (mostly in joint ventures with Nicaraguan firms), natural resources, banking, and commerce-retail enterprises. Enticed by generous financial incentives, tariff protection, minimal constraints, and the expectation of large profits, American multinational giants such as Esso, Texaco, United Fruit,

American-Nicaraguan Chamber of Commerce from 1972 to 1978. He was also President of the organization during 1978 and 1979.

34 World Bank, *World Development Report 1980*, p. 114; Inter-American Development Bank, *Economic and Social Progress in Latin America: 1979 Report* (Washington, D.C., 1979), pp. 15, 21.

35 See, for example, U.S. Department of Commerce, *Foreign Economic Trends and their Implications for the United States*, prepared by the American Embassy, Managua, ET-68-75, December 1968, p. 10, ET-70-18, December 1969, pp. 10–11, ET-74-007, December 1973, p. 3, ET-75-013, February 1975, p. 7, FET-76-006, January 1976, pp. 3, 8, FET-77-037, March 1977, p. 8.

U.S. Steel, Bank of America, Citibank, and Sears invested at a faster rate in Nicaragua than in any other Central American country. Total U.S. investments increased from $18 million in 1960 to close to $80 million in 1970, the latter figure more than ten times the amount of the next biggest group of foreign investors (West Germany). Between 1970 and 1978, U.S. investments exhibited a "sawtooth" pattern of growth, with estimates of the overall increase varying from $45 million (Department of Commerce) to double that amount (NACLA Report on the Americas).[36] But whatever the precise rise, of greater significance was its strategic location. The sixty-three American-owned multinationals (out of a total of eighty-two foreign multinationals) operating in Nicaragua between 1976 and 1978 were entrenched in most key economic sectors: agribusiness and food processing, chemicals, forest products, banking, mining, petroleum, tourism, and transport.[37]

Discussing the treatment of overseas investment in a March 1966 cable, the Managua Embassy painted a glowing picture: "The treatment of foreign capital is very good and is expected to remain good for the foreseeable future." Most heads of American firms in Nicaragua concurred in this assessment. They characterized bureaucratic "red tape" and the "general lack of technical competence in the government agencies" as normal by Third World standards and "relatively minor" problems in any event. Moreover, easy access to cabinet ministers and other senior regime officials usually ensured that such problems were swiftly resolved. Some American companies employed local lawyers "to handle their business with the Government and get things done expeditiously." Although one U.S. firm complained that whenever a workers' grievance against management ended up in the Labor Court the decision was in favor of the employees, the Embassy downplayed the issue. The Court had only declared two strikes legal, both involving U.S. companies (Singer Sewing Machine Company and Tropical Radio Company), but "with the exception of these strikes American firms appear to have had generally amicable labor relations."[38]

36 U.S. Department of Commerce, *Selected Data on U.S. Investment Abroad, 1950–76*, p. 201, Table 9; Department of State Telegram, Managua 1852, American Embassy to Secretary of State, August 13, 1971, Subject: "Foreign Investment Survey," DFOIA; John F.H. Purcell, "The Perceptions and Interests of U.S. Business in Relation to the Political Crisis in Central America," in Richard Feinberg, ed., *Central America: International Dimensions of the Crisis* (New York: Holmes & Meier, 1982), p. 114; *NACLA Report on the Americas*, Vol. XII, No. 6, November/December 1978, p. 30.

37 Donald Castillo Rivas, *Acumulación de Capital y Empresas Transnacionales en Centroamérica* (Mexico: Siglo Vientiuno editores, 1980), p. 178. For a breakdown on sectorial investments, see *NACLA Report on the Americas*, Vol. XII, No. 6, November/December 1978, pp. 38–39, Appendix B.

38 Department of State Airgram, Managua Confidential No. A-247, American Embassy to Department of State, March 12, 1966, Subject: "Treatment of Foreign Investment in Nicaragua," DFOIA.

The U.S. capitalist class doing business in Nicaragua during the 1960s and well into the 1970s basically concurred with the Embassy's picture. For most, "Nicaragua was a very stable country, the cordoba was fairly convertible, it was an open economy, Americans were welcome, a laissez faire economy."[39] They lauded the Somoza regime for being "very pro-U.S. and open to business."[40] The "threat" to profitmaking posed by the organized working class was invariably minimized. Bruce Cuthbertson, an American citizen with economic interests in the construction industry, noted that "there were not really any labour problems. We were a unionized industry but had no more labor problems than in a unionized company in the United States."[41]

Like the Embassy, American businessmen took a rather low key, even sanguine, approach to the obstacles they did encounter. In the construction sector, explained Cuthbertson, "we had the problems of any developing country – inefficiencies, telephone didn't work, electricity problems, basic infrastructure problems."[42] A Westinghouse Electric Company executive singled out "language comprehension difficulties."[43] But the ability to gain rapid and direct entree to government agencies and officials, and the latter's always helpful and cooperative response, meant delays were kept to a minimum: "You had access up to the ministerial level with relative ease."[44] For Westinghouse, which supplied millions of dollars worth of equipment annually to the government's power utility agency, it was simply a question of directly informing the head of the agency, who happened to be the dictator's uncle: "We could call Dr. Debayle on the phone and he would discuss the problem and respond or set a date for us to meet him."[45]

Apart from the bureaucratic delays and the Somoza family's extensive economic holdings, which limited investment access to some areas (and ensured a small internal market), the most consistent problem American corporations and banks had to deal with was the regime's oft-demanded quid pro quo for profitable business opportunities: cash payments, minority equity participation, arranging loans or contracts for Somoza-owned companies, or some other kind of "fee" or "payoff." The examples are numerous: Loans to the dictator's cement works greatly facilitated First National City Bank's (Citibank) initial entry in the 1960s; according to the

39 Telephone interview with Bruce Cuthbertson.
40 Telephone interview with Chad Engler.
41 Telephone interview with Bruce Cuthbertson.
42 Ibid.
43 Telephone interview with Peter Strolis, Pennsylvania, October 17, 1988. The respondent is the director of International Operations for Westinghouse Electric Company. He was closely involved with the company's Nicaraguan operations during the 1970s.
44 Ibid.
45 Telephone interview with Bruce Cuthbertson.

then head of International Business Machines (IBM) World Trade Corporation Arthur K. Watson, Somoza "blatantly demanded a payoff" for allowing IBM to expand its Managua operations in the late 1950s or early 1960s; American mining and lumber companies paid an annual "fee" to avoid operating problems and taxes; joint ventures with Somoza-owned firms involving such prominent multinationals as U.S. Steel and Intercontinental Hotels became commonplace.[46] In 1973, an American businessman told the *Wall Street Journal:* "I don't care who you're dealing with – whether it's an assistant minister or the chief himself – you have to cut him [Somoza] in if you're going to close a deal."[47] Five years later, another U.S. executive knowledgeable about the Nicaraguan scene said virtually the same thing in an interview with *Business Week:* "You just don't do business here without offering the General a share in it from the beginning."[48]

Nonetheless, despite such "entry" requirements, the advantages of investing in Nicaragua outweighed any particular obstacle. Also, Somoza was willing to fend off hemispheric threats to American investor profits so long as they did not impinge on his family capital accumulation activities. In the early 1970s, for instance, he "protected U.S. economic interests at his own country's expense by helping to sabotage Latin American schemes to create coffee and banana cartels for the enforcement of higher commodity prices."[49]

In August 1975, the American Ambassador Turner Shelton cabled the State Department about the Somoza regime's attitude toward overseas investors: "The climate for U.S. investment is excellent. [There is] a proinvestment consensus among political leaders and Nicaraguan businessmen ... today, more than ever, the government encourages foreign investment and local entrepreneurs to actively seek joint venture arrangements."[50] Later that year, the regime announced a new range of incentives (sale of publicly owned land, ten-year tax exemptions, no import fees until operation estab-

---

46 See *NACLA's Latin American & Empire Report*, Vol. X, No. 2, February 1976, p. 20; Arthur K. Watson quoted in Jack Anderson and Les Whitten, "IBM Aide Told of Nicaragua Bribe Bid," *Washington Post*, March 19, 1976, p. B20. Another American enterprise, the International Systems and Controls Corporation, reportedly paid almost $300,000 to companies controlled by the Somoza family in an effort to win a $5.2 million contract in 1971 to build and supply a grain storage facility in Nicaragua. See "US Firm Accused of Overseas Payoffs Totalling $23 Million," *Journal of Commerce*, July 11, 1979, p. 33.
47 Quoted in Eric Morgenthaler, "Somoza Combines Politics, Business, Military to Rule Nicaragua as Undisputed Strong Man," *Wall Street Journal*, October 22, 1973, p. 22.
48 Quoted in "Nicaragua: Where U.S. Interests are Caught in a Crossfire," *Business Week*, February 27, 1978, p. 44.
49 Walker, *Nicaragua: The Land of Sandino*, p. 127.
50 Department of State Telegram, Managua 3002, American Embassy (Shelton) to Secretary of State, August 2, 1975, Subject: "Foreign Investment Climate and Statistics," DFOIA. Also see, for example, "Oilmen Rushing for Concessions in Nicaragua," *Miami Herald*, October 11, 1974, p. 2E.

lished as a going concern) in an effort to entice $1 million plus investment projects into the tourist industry.[51] On January 30, 1977, ten days after the inauguration of a new American president, the Nicaraguan dictatorship purchased a full page advertisement in the *New York Times* to promote foreign investment. The policy line was summed up in one pithy sentence: "Practically no restrictions limit the fields of endeavor which foreigners may enter."[52] The subsequent decision to establish a free-trade zone was made specifically with American investors in mind, and included incentives such as unlimited credit, no restrictions on capital outflows, and freedom from currency controls. "There are no strings attached," Somoza declared. "If [a businessman] wants to take a local partner he can. If he doesn't want a partner he can do it."[53]

Even more than overseas investment capital, the Somoza dictatorship was a leading beneficiary of the U.S. foreign aid program and the loan policies of the U.S.-dominated multilateral development banks. Between 1962 and 1978, Washington provided the Somoza clan with over $280 million in economic assistance, while the World Bank group and the Inter-American Development Bank (IADB) together channeled almost $394 million to the regime.[54] Officials of the IADB emphasized the institution's "normal relations with the Somoza government" during this period.[55] Arturo Cruz, a staff member through most of the 1970s, not only described the relationship as "very stable" but also commented on the bank's "lack of animosity towards Somoza."[56] U.S. aid policy toward Nicaragua remained quite consistent from the Kennedy administration onward, and when a change began to emerge (during the Carter presidency) it tended to be more symbolic or procedural than substantive.

The Nicaraguan economy first attracted the attention of American private banks during the 1950s. While Citibank and Bank of America were content to establish branch offices around the country, others entered into much more direct ties with the local capitalist class. Wells Fargo Bank and the

51 "Nicaragua Moves to Attract Tourist Dollars," *Wall Street Journal*, December 1, 1975, p. 6.
52 Government of Managua, "How to Invest in Nicaragua," *New York Times*, Section 12, Part II, January 30, 1977, p. 40.
53 Quoted in Patricia Alisau, "Riots in Nicaragua Close US Companies," *Journal of Commerce*, January 31, 1978, p. 2.
54 U.S. Agency for International Development, *U.S. Overseas Loans and Grants and Assistance from International Organizations, July 1, 1945–September 30, 1982*, p. 54, 205.
55 Interview with Tom Carson, Washington, D.C., October 5, 1990. The respondent was senior loan officer for Nicaragua, Inter-American Development Bank, 1969 to 1973.
56 Interview with Arturo Cruz, Washington, D.C., October 5, 1990. The respondent was on the staff of the Inter-American Development Bank, 1969 to 1979. In July 1979, he was appointed president of the Nicaraguan Central Bank by the Sandinista government. In April 1980, he became a member of the country's governing junta.

First National Bank of Boston joined forces with Banco de América (BAN-AMERICA) and Chase Manhattan Bank teamed up with Banco de Nicaragua (BANIC) – the two most powerful non-Somoza financial institutions that were formed by, and represented, the interests of the agro-export, industrial-manufacturing, and commercial elites not part of the ruling family's economic empire.[57]

It was not until the early 1970s, however, that U.S. private multinational banks in particular (and overseas capital in general) began to assume a commanding presence in the Nicaraguan economy. The impetus to this sudden increase in foreign bank exposure was twofold: the quadrupling of oil prices and the decision of the world's major petroleum exporting countries to channel their newly acquired windfall profits into Western commercial banks, and the impact of this dramatic rise in oil import costs on Nicaragua's terms of trade. Flush with petrodollars, the banks moved rapidly to recycle these monies at high interest rates, in most cases requiring only that the interest payments be made on time. To Somoza, this seemed the optimal solution to Nicaragua's growing, and potentially chronic, balance of payments deficit. And U.S. banks, in particular, were only too willing to oblige. According to a senior Managua Embassy official, they were not only "knocking on the door offering one more attractive loan package after another" but also "giving kickbacks and bribes in trying to get a part of the action."[58]

Almost every major American commercial institution lent to the Somoza dictatorship. In February 1973, bank syndicates headed by Wells Fargo and Manufacturers Hanover Trust negotiated $60 million in refinancing and $40 million in new loans with Nicaraguan government officials; in late 1974, a consortium of international banks led by First Chicago arranged a $30 million five year loan; in 1977, Citibank and the Banco Exterior de España jointly approved a $68 million credit line for the purchase of road-building equipment and machinery.[59] By early 1978, the total loan exposure of U.S. private banks had reached an estimated $350 million.[60] In January of that

57 See Norma Stoltz Chincilla and Nora Hamilton, "Prelude to Revolution: U.S. Investment in Central America," in Roger Burbach and Patricia Flynn, eds., The Politics of Intervention: The United States in Central America (New York: Monthly Review Press, 1984), pp. 234–236.

58 Interview with Thomas O'Donnell, Maryland, September 27, 1989. The respondent was a senior economic, and then political, official in the American Embassy, Nicaragua, 1972 to 1974. In mid-1979 he returned as Deputy Chief of Mission.

59 Department of State Telegram, Managua 2557, American Embassy to Secretary of State, May 25, 1973, Subject: "Status of Office Loans from Commercial Banks," DFOIA; Economist Intelligence Unit, Quarterly Economic Review of Nicaragua, No. 1, February 1975, p. 6; Quarterly Economic Review of Nicaragua, No. 3, August 1977, p. 14.

60 See John Huey, "Business Elite Joins Struggle to Displace Nicaraguan Dictator," Wall Street Journal, February 23, 1978, p. 22.

year, Somoza announced a new law allowing foreign banks to operate free from all regulation and taxes. Discussing the profitmaking climate in Nicaragua during the 1970s, one of Citibank's Managua branch managers noted Somoza's refusal to even "allow his own bank, Banco de CentroAmericano, to get special favors. Foreign banks had no problem with the Somoza government."[61]

Despite these infusions of finance capital, the external sector crisis continued to worsen, forcing the government to resort more to short-term commercial borrowings at higher rates of interest. Between 1976 and 1978, the short-term portion of the Nicaraguan bank system's overseas debt rose from 43 percent to an astronomical 80 percent of the total.[62] The country's fiscal problems were compounded by the fact that a substantial part of these funds (guaranteed by state agencies) were being lent to private companies "owned by the Somoza family, or its associates, and often already mortgaged to the hilt," or simply deposited into the dictator's personal bank account. The corruption was so blatant that even the lender banks, normally reluctant to comment on borrower countries use of loan funds, could not remain silent.[63] The American Ambassador, Mauricio Solaun, told Somoza in April 1978 that "he had received word from foreign banks that they were concerned about GON [Government of Nicaragua] practices such as the number of GON [Government of Nicaragua] officials skimming off large portions of new loans."[64] Nonetheless, these sentiments only translated into limited cutbacks in loan exposure by two or three banks. Surveying the relationship between the foreign banks and Nicaragua during the 1970s, a World Bank official accused them, in a masterpiece of understatement, of "injudicious" lending.[65]

Nicaragua's external public debt also skyrocketed in the years prior to Somoza's overthrow, thereby further exacerbating the state's fiscal crisis. Borrowings from Western governments (including the United States) rose from $332 million in 1972 to over $1.2 billion in 1978.[66] The severity of

61   Telephone interview with Onofre Torres, Florida, October 4, 1989. The respondent was the manager of Citibank's Managua branch, 1977 to 1980.
62   Michael E. Conroy, "Economic Aggression as an Instrument of Low-Intensity Warfare," in Thomas W. Walker, ed., *Reagan Versus the Sandinistas* (Boulder: Westview Press, 1987), p. 71.
63   "Nicaragua: Picking up Tacho's Banking Bill," *Latin America Economic Report*, October 26, 1979, p. 331.
64   Department of State Telegram, Confidential Managua 1945, American Embassy (Solaun) to Secretary of State, April 26, 1978, Subject: "Meeting with President Somoza, April 22," DFOIA.
65   Chandra Hardy, "Rescheduling Developing Country Debts," *The Banker*, July 1981, p. 37.
66   Inter-American Development Bank, *Economic and Social Progress in Latin America: 1983 Report* (Washington, D.C., 1983), p. 381, Table 56. On the growth of the foreign debt,

the debt crisis was not least revealed by the history of the debt-export ratio. In 1970, 10.6 percent of the country's export earnings was needed to pay interest on the total (public and private) foreign debt; in 1978, the figure stood at 17.3 percent.[67]

Although the type, scope, and direction of U.S. capital flows into Somoza's Nicaragua varied – beginning with direct investment in agro-mining, manufacturing, and other economic sectors, followed by state assistance and multilateral and private bank loans – there was no significant division among U.S. capitalist sectors regarding Washington's policy toward, or relations with, the dictatorial regime. Essentially, the process of incorporating new capital to old was an additive-accommodative one. The absence of any rupture between different forms of capital reflected the complementary role they performed, the interlocking interests they shared, and their narrow sociopolitical base of support in a country whose regime ruled partly on the basis of its dependence on the U.S. imperial state.

In the two decades prior to Somoza's downfall, Nicaragua pursued an economic development model based on the commercialization of agriculture, industrial expansion, urbanization, a large service sector, and access to large-scale borrowings of foreign capital. In the absence of a political regime supporting programs of social and economic redistribution, however, these parallel processes produced other, unanticipated, consequences: In a fundamental sense, they helped to create the social movements and social and class conflicts that more and more dominated Nicaragua's political horizon.

Origins of the political crisis (2): Capitalist transformation and the class structure

The processes of economic development in Nicaragua during the 1960s had a profound impact on the nation's class structure. In the countryside, the new emphasis on cotton production for export marginalized traditional crops for local consumption and led to a precipitous decline in the economic position of small landholders. Dispossessed of their land, small peasant producers of corn, sorghum, rice, and other subsistence crops became wage laborers forced to seek employment on large plantations where jobs were seasonal and insecure. Approximately one-third of the economically active

also see Victor Bulmer-Thomas, *The Political Economy of Central America Since 1920* (New York: Cambridge University Press, 1987), pp. 216–217.
67 Inter-American Development Bank, *Economic and Social Progress in Latin America: 1979 Report*, p. 448, Table 63.

rural population worked only during the three-month harvest period. The growth of huge beef cattle ranches (which doubled in acreage between 1960 and 1979) also quickened the proletarianization process: Peasants were ejected from lands they occupied without title and stripped of their livestock holdings. By 1970, Nicaragua had a higher percentage (nearly 34 percent) of landless rural families than any other Central American country.[68]

The expansion of large-scale agro-export farming exacerbated an already skewed pattern of land ownership. In the mid-1970s, 0.6 percent of the rural population owned 30.5 percent of the arable land, whereas 50.8 percent of farmers owned a mere 3.4 percent.[69] Meanwhile, rural unemployment climbed to 16 percent in 1977, doubling to 32 percent at the time of Somoza's ouster in July 1979.[70] In sum, the commercialization and mechanization of agriculture uprooted the peasant population, increased the number and importance of landless wage workers, depressed the conditions of petty commodity producers, worsened employment possibilities, and pushed a large segment of rural Nicaraguans to the margins of economic life.

In urban Nicaragua, the growth of commerce and industrial production and imperially capitalized enterprises had a dual impact on the class structure: First, it increased the number of industrial workers who benefited from relatively high wages and job security; second, it was linked to, and accompanied by, a substantial rise in the numbers of both property-owning and salaried petty bourgeoisie. The managers and clerical and technical workers who staffed the expanding state sector further increased the numerical power of the wage-earning middle sectors.

The transformation of rural land tenure relations also had important consequences for the urban class structure. Migration to the cities during the 1960s and 1970s increased the percentage of the population living in urban areas from 41 percent to 53 percent.[71] Attracted partly by the "pull" of industrialization, these new additions to the urban labor force soon discovered that the industrial expansion was capital, rather than labor, intensive. The resulting disjuncture between urban growth and capital intensive industry forced most of these new migrants to become part of an amorphous strata of "floating" poor looking for employment outside of the factory system. To the extent that they could find work it was usually in low paying and

68 Weeks, *The Economies of Central America*, p. 112. Also see Dunkerly, *Power in the Isthmus*, pp. 195–196.
69 Diederich, *Somoza and the Legacy of U.S. Involvement in Central America*, p. 118.
70 John A. Booth, *The End and the Beginning: The Nicaraguan Revolution* (Boulder: Westview Press, 1985), p. 84.
71 World Bank, *World Development Report 1980*, p. 148. The agricultural work force as a percentage of the total work force declined from 62 per cent in 1960 to 44 per cent in 1978. Ibid., p. 146.

unstable jobs in the service sector (personal services, and so on). In the process, the service sector ballooned while the industrial work force experienced relative stagnation in the decade prior to Somoza's overthrow. Between 1960 and 1978, the service sector as a percentage of the total work force almost doubled from 22 percent to 41 percent while the industrial work force declined marginally to 16 percent.[72]

Although a small proportion of rural migrants were integrated into the factory system, providing them with a class-anchored frame of reference through which to act politically, the mass of migrants were excluded from stable wage employment – either unemployed or underemployed in low paying, unproductive jobs – and were systematically concentrated in urban slums as a result of the organic ties between the state and real estate investors.

Changes in the Nicaraguan class structure were paralleled by economic setbacks for salaried and property owning groups in both the city and countryside. The periodic recessions and uncontrolled inflation during the 1970s compressed the real wages of urban (industrial and non-industrial) and rural workers and the incomes of small peasant producers. Combined with rising un- and underemployment, especially among the urban poor, and declining levels of social services, this created a situation in which a substantial part of the population lacked any real stake in the existing economic arrangements and thus were potentially open to appeals based on radical socioeconomic changes. Moreover, the petty bourgeois and bourgeois property-owning groups also began to express increasing dissatisfaction with Somoza economic policies. In Managua, the middle-sector commercial and industrial entrepreneurs who were affected by the December 1972 earthquake failed to recover economically during the rest of the decade. Bankruptcies became the order of the day as new recessionary cycles and massive capital flight forced a contraction in state credits upon which many of these businesses, however profitable, depended for their continued operations. On the other hand, those wealthy capitalists who had prospered from the 1960s industrial growth now had to contend with Somoza family intrusions into economic sectors (for example, banking, construction) they had traditionally dominated.

Ultimately, the general and chronic deterioration in economic conditions presided over by an autocratic and predatory state served to unite adversely affected groups – workers, peasants, urban poor, the business community, the church, students, and guerrilla forces – leading to united action across

---

72 Ibid., p. 146. For an interesting discussion of changes in the class structure, see David Close, *Nicaragua: Politics, Economics and Society* (London: Pinter Publishers, 1988), pp. 37–42.

class and occupational lines. Increasingly, these diverse classes and socio-economic groups linked the resolution of their specific problems to a change in political regime – and some to changes in the structure of society as a whole.

The shifting class structure and declining living standards forced Nicaraguan workers to resort to organization and struggle in an effort to recover past losses and promote new demands. Violent and indiscriminate resistance by the Somoza state, however, eventually blurred the distinction between the satisfaction of economic demands and a confrontation over political power.

Although large numbers of peasants had responded to the rise of plantation agriculture and the hegemony of the agro-exporters by migrating to the cities, and fewer relocated to the agricultural frontier areas, even as early as the late 1960s the countryside was the scene of numerous land invasions, calls for agrarian reform, and labor demands for wage increases and improved social services. To put an end to this rural militancy, the large landowners turned to Somoza and the National Guard. By the end of the decade the main centers of rural economic struggle had become the prime targets of the U.S.-trained and equipped Guard counterinsurgency forces.[73] A new cycle of strikes and land takeovers erupted in 1973 and 1974, provoking another bout of state repression. During 1975 and 1976, as part of its effort to isolate and physically destroy the Sandinista National Liberation Front (FSLN), the National Guard embarked on a program of wholesale terror against peasants and peasant communities "suspected" of collaborating with the guerrilla movement. An Amnesty International report on the Guard's activities paints a stark and gruesome picture:

> The wholesale killing of peasant farmers (campesinos) and their "disappearances" after detention is probably the most serious aspect of human rights violations in Nicaragua. The populations of entire peasant villages have been reported exterminated or taken away as prisoners by National Guard troops. The few who are released allege severe torture. The "disappeared" who aren't even acknowledged to be in custody and who never reappear must, in many cases be presumed to have died in custody.[74]

The report noted that the overwhelming majority of killings and disappearances occurred in the country's northeast, the area of most active FSLN operations. Despite this National Guard war against its rural population, land takeovers and strikes continued. The increased level of organization

73 See Williams, *Export Agriculture and the Crisis in Central America*, pp. 129, 151.
74 Amnesty International, *The Republic of Nicaragua* (includes the findings of a mission to Nicaragua 10–15 May 1976), p. 24. Also see Penny Lernoux, *Cry of the People* (New York: Penguin Books, 1986), pp. 82–84.

was reflected in the formation of the Association of Rural Workers (ATC) in 1977. By this time, economic and political demands were largely indistinguishable: Only a change of regime could lead to the satisfaction of economic grievances.

In the cities, confrontations with the regime developed at a slower rate, and only took on significant proportions after the cataclysmic earthquake that leveled Managua in December 1972, eliminating thousands of jobs and substantially increasing the size of the urban poor. Christian social activists inserted themselves into this milieu and began to organize these strata to make demands on the regime for financial assistance, improved social services, and other basic needs. These newly organized forces were among the more vociferous critics of Somoza's misappropriation of international reconstruction aid. The dictator's response mirrored that taken to deal with rural economic unrest: swift and savage National Guard repression. But once again this heavy-handed approach proved counterproductive. Instead of cowering the urban poor into submission, it radicalized and politicized many of them.

Other sectors of the urban population also began to challenge the regime's economic policies. During 1973 and 1974, factory workers in textile, construction, metal and other industries, hospital workers, and university employees participated in wage strikes.[75] Predictably, Somoza's response was hostile and, where necessary, force was used to end these mobilizations. The dictatorship's intransigence and willingness to resort to violence further alienated a business community unhappy over state corruption, economic competition from the Somoza family, and new taxes. Between mid-1978 and mid-1979, these various economic grievances helped detonate a major political offensive against the family dynasty, composed of multiple-class participants ranging from unemployed slum dwellers to the most privileged bourgeoisie.

Political crisis and revolutionary confrontation: The demise of Somoza family rule

Every crisis discards the conventionalities, tears away the outer wrappings, sweeps away the obsolete and reveals the underlying springs and forces.

V.I. Lenin

Like the Cuban revolution of January 1959, the Nicaraguan insurrection of July 1979 was the culmination of a prolonged domestic conflict featuring

---

75 See Diederich, *Somoza and the Legacy of U.S. Involvement in Central America*, p. 102.

many of the same kinds of political and socioeconomic factors that characterized the earlier upheaval: a corrupt and autocratic dictatorship with longstanding political, economic, and military ties to the United States; a capitalist development model that disproportionately benefited the ruling clique and a small coterie of local and foreign (mainly American) investors; the absence of reformist political channels through which regime opponents could express their discontent; and a method of rulership based on the repeated and indiscriminate use of force against the antagonists of government policy. The regime's political isolation and eroding legitimacy ultimately led to the growth of a formidable broad-based opposition movement hegemonized by radical nationalist guerrillas.

Revolutionary movements typically originate as processes of disengagement from established patterns of domination. The trigger may be a crisis situation or traumatic event that challenges traditional relationships or assumptions about the way in which society should be ordered and the role of individuals and institutions within that larger framework. In the case of Nicaragua, two moments of this kind were pivotal in accelerating the downfall of the Somoza dictatorship: the Managua earthquake of December 1972 and the Chamorro assassination of January 1978.

The capital city of Managua was virtually laid waste by the severity of the natural disaster that hit it at the end of 1972. Tens of thousands were killed or injured, hundreds of thousands left homeless, and over 80 percent of commercial enterprises destroyed. Maurice Williams, the Nixon administration's Special Coordinator for Emergency Relief, provides a detailed and graphic account of the earthquake's impact:

> Not only was the basic infrastructure of a modern city – electricity, communications, water supply and transport – immediately knocked out, but 50,000 homes were totally destroyed and thousands more made uninhabitable, forcing the survivors into the streets to fend for themselves. The gigantic dimensions of what was lost soon began to emerge. Gone was all of the physical plant of the national government; half the public schools in the city; all of its hospitals and practically all of the commercial services, markets and commodity stocks upon which an urban society depends. A preliminary estimate places the immediate losses at over $600 million. Additionally, almost half of the nation's GNP has been disrupted, more than half of the government's sources of revenue have been lost, and 25 percent of the population is now without the means to sustain even the minimum necessities of life.[76]

76 Department of State, Agency of International Development, Office of the Administrator, Memorandum for the President from Maurice J. Williams, President's Special Coordinator for Emergency Relief to Nicaragua, Subject: "Special Report on Emergency Relief for the Managua Disaster," January 8, 1973. White House Central Files, Collection: DI

What precipitated a crisis of political legitimacy, however, was not the earthquake itself but the bankruptcy and callousness of the regime's response – its decision to subordinate the basic needs of a devastated population to a headlong drive for private enrichment.

Somoza and senior National Guard officials personally commandeered tens of millions of dollars in reconstruction assistance provided by the international community that was subsequently invested in highly profitable real estate and commercial activities.[77] In the following years, the regime immersed itself in bribery, graft, and multifarious forms of public and private corruption that concentrated more and more capital in the hands of the few, while its continued failure to rebuild downtown Managua remained a visible symbol of the Somoza family's unpardonable behavior in a moment of acute socioeconomic crisis.

The earthquake and its aftermath ripped asunder traditional societal commitments, opening up thousands of individual minds to the possibility, indeed necessity, of mass political action against the dictatorship as the only means for gaining a redress of grievances. Over the next four years, the regime confronted a burgeoning urban-rural opposition movement as well as the still numerically small Sandinista guerrilla forces. Notwithstanding the imposition of a state of siege from December 1974 until September 1977, during which the National Guard waged a brutal counterinsurgency campaign against the rural population in and around the guerrilla strongholds, the genie of revolution could not be forced back into its bottle.

The second traumatic event that served to weaken the bonds of allegiance between the Nicaraguan people and the Somoza regime was the January 1978 assassination of Pedro Joaquín Chamorro, publisher of the newspaper *La Prensa*, a leading centrist political figure, and a member of one of the country's oldest and wealthiest families. The National Guard's involvement in the murder sent a message to the bourgeoisie that no one, however eminent and well-known, was safe from the depredations of the regime. The Guard's action had undermined part of the traditional consensus between Somoza and the capitalist class – that based on a mutual understanding about the rules of the political game. This latest outrage, on top of increasing hostility toward the government's economic policies, led influential sectors of the business community to move into opposition and become actively involved in efforts to force Somoza from office. In late January, for

(Disasters), Box 4, Folder: EX-DI 2/C) 101–150 [1973–74], Nixon Presidential Materials Project, National Archives, Alexandria, Virginia.

77 See Diederich, *Somoza and the Legacy of U.S. Involvement in Central America*, pp. 96–100; Millett, *Guardians of the Dynasty*, pp. 238–239; Alan Riding, "Nicaraguans Accused of Profiteering on Help the U.S. Sent After Quake," *New York Times*, March 23, 1977, p. 10.

the first time in its history, the local capitalist class stopped "obeying the law" and decided to participate in mass mobilization politics and a general strike to topple the regime from power.

By mid-1978, the dictatorship lacked solid roots in any significant class or social grouping in Nicaraguan society. Its support was primarily confined to Somoza's Nationalist Liberal Party (PLN), the Guard, and a small group of crony capitalists. For the moment, however, the existence of a hostile, unstable civil society was more than offset by the continued presence of an internally cohesive and disciplined armed forces loyal to the country's authoritarian leader. Somoza still presided over a strong state capable of "mediating" or controlling national-class conflict. But the regime's survival was becoming increasingly linked to its willingness to engage in high-level repression – a viable strategy only so long as there was no countervailing military power to complement those civilian forces demanding a political transition. This state of affairs did not last for long.

Throughout the 1960s, the FSLN struggled unsuccessfully to establish itself as a viable military alternative to the National Guard. A rurally based guerrilla movement lacking an organized social constituency (peasants), the Sandinistas could not withstand the superior numbers and firepower displayed by Somoza's praetorian army. During the first half of the 1970s, however, the FSLN began to develop effective rural and urban support systems. In the countryside, peasant mobilization was facilitated by the Guard's increasingly brutal and indiscriminate counterinsurgency warfare that produced more casualties among civilian noncombatants than guerrillas; in the cities, the FSLN built on prior ties "thrown down" among the student population and established new links with the numerically dominant urban poor through their post-earthquake community organizations. Paralleling this emerging nationwide political infrastructure was a series of successful, if small-scale, guerrilla military actions against National Guard rural posts. A key turning point in the fortunes of the FSLN was an adventurous December 1974 raid on the home of a former Agriculture Minister hosting a farewell party in honor of the departing American Ambassador Turner Shelton that brought the guerrillas "publicity, recruits and credibility."[78]

The setbacks of the 1960s had generated a volatile strategy debate among the three FSLN factions (Prolonged Popular War, Proletarian, and Insurrectional/Tercerista) over how best to confront the regime. Failure to agree on a common approach produced an organizational split in the wake of major guerrilla losses suffered during the 1975 National Guard campaign in northern Nicaragua. For the next three years, each faction pursued its preferred method of struggle, all the while expanding memberships, engaging in military actions and improving combatant skills, and gaining increased

---

78 Diederich, *Somoza and the Legacy of U.S. Involvement in Central America*, p. 106.

access to weapons through sympathetic regional governments – which gradually began to shift the balance of military power in favor of the guerrillas. The strategic differences were ultimately reconciled in early 1979 on the basis of according primacy to the insurrectionalist's approach: incorporating all opponents of the regime, including the petty bourgeois and bourgeois elements, into the broadest possible mass movement but in a way that did not allow any challenge to the FSLN's hegemonic status. The insurrectionalist's political flexibility and preparedness to embrace short-term alliances with diverse social and political groups represented an effort to adjust to immediate contingencies in order to maximize support for the guerrilla leadership within a disparate movement united only by its anti-dictatorial and democratic-nationalist aims.

The violent nature of Somoza rule between 1975 and 1979, legitimated by an almost permanent state of siege, directly or indirectly affected every major class and occupational and social group in society. The failure of the January and August 1978 bourgeois-led general strikes to topple the dictatorship undermined the viability of the centrist option in the minds of many, accelerating support for the guerrillas as the only alternative to a continuation of the Somoza family dynasty. The following months witnessed mass mobilizations in urban neighborhoods and the growth of a formidable FSLN political organization in the cities, increased Sandinista military confrontations with the National Guard in the countryside, and widespread human rights abuses by the Somoza state against the civilian population that, at one and the same time, totally isolated the regime and transformed the FSLN into a mass movement capable of challenging for governmental and state power on a national level. In the final offensive of May – July 1979, the locus of the struggle shifted to the nation's major provincial cities such as León, Estelí, Chinandega, and Matagalpa where the urban poor, unemployed youths, wage workers, students, skilled tradespeople and, to a lesser extent, small property owners, professionals, technicians, and teachers offered critical support to the FSLN including direct involvement in military battles against the Guard.[79] This urban resistance movement established the basis for the FSLN's crushing military victory over the Guard in Managua in July 1979.

Conclusion

Political revolution in Nicaragua was not the product of economic stagnation, underdevelopment, economic dependence, or the absence of capitalist

79   See Carlos M. Vilas, *The Sandinista Revolution: National Liberation and Social Transformation in Central America* (New York: Monthly Review Press, 1986), pp. 108–126; Booth, *The End and the Beginning*, p. 125.

production. On the contrary, it grew out of the very experience and processes of capitalist development and the political-social conditions under which it occurred.

During the 1960s and early 1970s, the Nicaraguan economy experienced a period of dynamic economic growth based on exports, external financing, and incentives to foreign capital. When the global economy began to contract beginning around 1973, however, the contradictions of the Somoza model were exposed: The economy was incapable of cushioning the impact of falling exports and commodity prices, declining markets, more stringent conditions attached to foreign loans, rising public and private debts, and interest payments to overseas banks and governments that absorbed an increasing percentage of export earnings. The result was chronic balance of payments problems, a slowdown in growth rates, and plummeting living standards. Neither worker nor peasant, slum dweller nor property owner were unaffected. More than ever, this new sense of deprivation required a repressive and autocratic state to sustain optimal conditions for capital accumulation and expansion. The collapse of the economic model accompanied by rising state corruption, widespread human rights abuses by the National Guard, and an expanding Somoza business empire began to erode regime legitimacy among all sectors of the community. This was the forerunner of the appearance of a mass-based, polyclass movement united in its determination to end dictatorial rule in Nicaragua.

One of the fundamental causes of the regime's growing isolation was the behavior of the National Guard: its assumption of functions beyond its original raison d'être, which in turn redefined its position in society. Initially, the Guard was established by the United States as a bulwark against the forces of political and economic nationalism, and associated challenges to foreign investment. Following its assumption of unlimited power over civil society at the time of the December 1972 earthquake, the Guard and its commander-in-chief revealed a propensity to wage indiscriminate warfare against its opponents (civilian or military) and to indulge in an array of nonmilitary objectives in the form of multiple corrupt enterprises, exchanges, and transactions that catered to the ruling elite's private accumulation drives.

The United States played a central role in implanting, consolidating, and sustaining the postwar political-economic environment in Nicaragua – and thus the long-term survival of the Somoza dictatorship. But this commitment was always a means to an end, based on a continuing determination by Washington that the regime was "doing the job." American presidents, Democratic and Republican alike, viewed Somoza as a key sub-regional political and strategic ally, a willing and effective supporter of U.S. permanent interests; American public agencies, private banks, and foreign investors, and American-dominated international financial institutions legitimated the Somoza development model through decisions that channeled hundreds of millions of dollars to the regime. Together, U.S. public and private institutions and individuals played a pivotal role in helping to create the conditions that produced economic expansion, political repression, popular mobilization, and revolutionary confrontation in Nicaragua within the space of two decades.

3

Supporting Somoza: Substance and symbol in American policy during the Nixon-Ford era

Introduction

Throughout the presidencies of Richard Nixon and Gerald Ford, American policymakers perceived Somoza as a viable dictator firmly in control of the Nicaraguan state and society, and promoting U.S. permanent interests. This despite increasing business sector hostility toward the regime's economic policies, the growth of a politically heterogeneous opposition movement, Somoza's willingness to use excessive force against peasant noncombatants in areas of guerrilla concentrations, and the appearance of institutional conflicts within the National Guard.

Toward the end of the 1960s, National Guard officers became embroiled in a divisive controversy over the twin issues of promotions and corruption. Many junior officers directed their criticism at Somoza himself over alleged favoritism toward family members, close cronies, and less-qualified individuals at the expense of younger, more professionally oriented officers and military academy graduates. But these conflicts had little or no impact on the overall cohesiveness of the Guard as a military organization capable of waging war against domestic opponents in the most efficient and ruthless fashion. In July 1969, amid disagreements among the officer corp, it "crushed" the Managua base of the Sandinista National Liberation Front (FSLN), the last in a series of major military defeats suffered by the guerrillas at the hands of Somoza's praetorian army since the early years of the decade.[1]

Confronting the formidable task of rebuilding its military capacities and establishing an organized mass political following, the FSLN moved its center of operations to the countryside in 1970 – to the large provincial towns (Masaya, Grenada, Carazo, Rivas) where it could operate out of the shadow of the regime's military-police force (Managua). In 1974, Somoza

---

1   See Millett, *Guardians of the Dynasty*, pp. 233–234.

initiated a merciless counterinsurgency campaign to eliminate the main centers of guerrilla activity in northern Nicaragua. The Guard revealed its continuing military superiority over the FSLN, inflicting substantial losses on the guerrilla forces. In the process it also perpetrated widespread human rights abuses against the surrounding peasant population. Some U.S. Embassy officials even began expressing concern "when credible reports started coming in of Guard officials forcing peasants from their land and taking it for themselves. This was particularly disturbing because the rural population was the most politically apathetic and at the same time generally supported Somoza. Beginning in 1974, we started hearing of more and more peasants supporting the Sandinistas with food and shelter. This was very worrisome."[2] Still, from Washington's vantage point, the counterinsurgency successes merely reinforced the perception of a regional ally well able to contain local challenges to its power and authority.

While Somoza was easily fending off the guerrilla challenge, however, economic downturns were beginning to create new centers of civilian opposition in the nation's most populous cities and towns. Government policy decisions and changes in the global economy combined to produce skyrocketing inflation, rising industrial production costs, declining exports, growing indebtedness, and a plethora of new direct and indirect taxes. The result was an erosion in living standards not only of wage workers, peasants, and the urban poor, but also of the property-owning class, especially the owners of small and medium-sized enterprises. In 1974, leading Conservative and Liberal politicians and moderate labor unions and political parties (for example, the Nicaraguan Socialist Party) joined forces with small shopkeepers, factory owners, cotton producers, construction firms, and other propertied petty bourgeoisie to form the Democratic Liberation Union (UDEL). The new political organization sought two interrelated objectives: political and economic reforms, and Somoza's ouster from office.

The behavior of the dictator and his cronies in the post-earthquake period also affected the country's two other powerful economic groups, BANIC and BANAMERICA. Flush with international reconstruction aid, Somoza decided to end the longstanding informal consensus on economic 'spheres of influence' and intervene in sectors (for example, construction and banking) traditionally the preserve of these competitor groups. This move to exploit his control over the state and public finances and form alliances with foreign multinationals and individual American entrepreneurs such as Howard Hughes, provoked some degree of bitterness and discontent within BANIC

2 Telephone interview with Leland Warner, Jr., Texas, September 21, 1989. The respondent was Deputy Chief of Mission, American Embassy, Nicaragua, 1972 to 1975.

and BANAMERICA. "After 1972," writes George Black, "the phrase on every businessman's lips was *competencia desleal,* unfair competition."[3] At the same time, neither was disposed to identify with the political opposition (UDEL) and support efforts to change the regime for two reasons. Both groups still benefited disproportionately from the development 'model.' Perhaps more important, they perceived no change in the correlation of military power (between the regime and the FSLN) on the horizon and thus no immediate threat to the survival of the dictatorship.

Washington's confidence in the National Guard was a decisive factor militating against any basic shift in U.S. policy toward the Somoza dictatorship during the Nixon and Ford presidencies. Spreading opposition to the regime's corruption and coercion was outweighed for American officialdom by the existence of a highly trained, battle-experienced armed forces loyal to a devoted regional ally – compounded by the manifest inability of the forces arraigned against Somoza to mount any coordinated and serious challenge for political power.

Nixon's Somoza: A favored client

Every American administration since Franklin Roosevelt contributed to the military, political, and economic consolidation of Somoza family rule in Nicaragua. The Somocista economic 'model' and willingness to support U.S. strategic interests in Central America and the Caribbean took precedence over the clan's autocratic political rule. No White House better exemplified its commitment to this order of priorities than Richard Nixon's.

The ascendancy of conservative civilian regimes and the growing militarization of Latin American civil society during the late Kennedy and Johnson presidencies was welcomed by Richard Nixon when he entered the White House in January 1969. Against this background of a quiescent hemisphere and a determination to prevent any erosion of U.S. hegemony, the new president proposed to take a "low profile" approach in relations with his southern neighbors. Henceforth, Washington would deal "realistically" with all governments (except Cuba) irrespective of their origins (elected or military coup) or methods of rule (democratic or dictatorial), so long as they accommodated U.S. permanent interests. To this end, National Security Council Advisor Henry Kissinger announced, questions of morality would not be allowed to "distract" foreign policymakers "from pursuit of their more traditional national security interests."[4] This "low profile" strategy

---

3 George Black, *The Good Neighbor: How the United States Wrote the History of Central America and the Caribbean* (New York: Pantheon Books, 1988), p. 130.
4 Schoultz, *Human Rights and United States Policy Toward Latin America* p. 112.

prefigured a shift away from the direct military intervention of the Johnson period to an emphasis on more indirect forms of involvement in the hemisphere's social and political struggles. Allies threatened by domestic political (electoral defeat) or military (revolution) challenges would receive sufficient covert funding, public economic aid, and military assistance and training to rebuff such threats to their own survival and, by extension, to American "national security" as well.

In Central America, Washington employed this new approach to forge ever closer ties with repressive military or military controlled "collaborator" regimes throughout the area. With compliant authoritarian rulers in the ascendency, there was little enthusiasm at the highest U.S. policymaking levels for proposals seeking to change the status quo. The American Ambassador to Honduras from 1969 to 1973, Hewson Ryan, remembered "a great deal of difficulty in getting any attention to Central America in the Washington bureaucracy."[5] The State Department official in charge of Central American affairs during the Nixon and Ford presidencies described the sub-region as "a low priority area."[6]

In Guatemala, the regime of Colonel Carlos Arana (1970–1974) was showered with U.S. economic and military assistance while it engaged in a ferocious terror campaign, in alliance with rightist death squads, to eliminate all vestiges of opposition – civilian and guerrilla – to military rule. Regarding El Salvador, White House policy was most notable for its silence over the massive electoral fraud perpetrated by the armed forces during the 1972 presidential elections that assured Colonel Arturo Molina victory over a popular-based center-left coalition led by Christian Democrat José Napoleón Duarte.

The stridently anti-communist Somoza regime in Nicaragua was a particularly willing client, prepared to do Washington's bidding on most regional and global matters: from votes in the United Nations and Organization of American States to allowing the use of its territory to train contra movements. In return, the Nixon White House offered unswerving political, economic, and military support. Some U.S. Embassy officials attributed the closeness of bilateral ties to strategic factors, including "the importance of the Panama Canal." Others focused on Nicaragua's "very prosperous and booming economy," its role in the Central American Common Market, and the large number of "U.S.-financed macro-infrastructure projects" underway.[7] To Leland Warner, the Embassy's Deputy Chief of

5 Interview with David Lazar, Washington, D.C., October 6, 1988. The respondent was Officer in Charge of Central American Affairs, Department of State, 1972 to 1975.
6 Ambassador Hewson Ryan, *oral history interview*, p. 53.
7 Interview with James Cheek, Washington, D.C., September 18, 1989. The respondent was Political counsellor, American Embassy, Nicaragua, 1971 to 1974.

Mission (DCM) from 1972 to 1975, administration policy seemed a mixture of "two attitudes that were sometimes blurred. One was that we considered Nicaragua pretty reliable as far as helping us in a regional context. The other attitude was a general 'Nicaragua is down there, a nice country, staying that way, and it doesn't bother us.'" Discussing Pentagon-National Guard relations, though, he characterized them "as about as good as you can have with a Latin American military."[8]

In June 1971, Somoza was "a special honored guest" at an informal White House dinner hosted by President Nixon for Washington, D.C. area graduates of the 1946 West Point Class on its twenty-fifth anniversary.[9] A high-ranking Central Americanist in the State Department attributed the "close, real affinity" between Nixon and Somoza not merely to the Nicaraguan leader's consistent support for U.S. foreign policy objectives ("he acted as a friend and ally of the United States at all times"), but in no small measure to his consummate understanding of how that country's political system worked. The official, Lawrence Pezzullo, remarked on Somoza's ability to manipulate the system to his own ends, especially his skill at cultivating the most influential decisionmakers within both the governmental and corporate spheres: "Somoza was a cunning fellow. Not only was he friends with [Nixon's crony] Bebe Robozo . . . he cultivated lots of people in the U.S. government and in the Congress over the years. And because of that, he was a difficult man to go up against and change policy on. Somoza knew people in government, banking, investments, and different political parties."[10]

In 1970, Turner Shelton arrived in Nicaragua as the new American Ambassador – reportedly a "payoff" for financial contributions to the Nixon presidential campaign – convinced that Washington and Managua had shared, identical interests. Thomas O'Donnell, a senior Embassy officer during the first half of the 1970s, elaborated:

> Shelton felt that Somoza was Washington's best friend in Central America and his job was to do everything he could to strengthen and reinforce not just relations between the U.S. and Nicaragua but to strengthen Somoza's position in his government and in Latin America. Shelton believed that anything that strengthened Somoza was good for

8 Telephone interview with Leland Warner, Jr.
9 Telephone interview with Lawrence Pezzullo, Maryland, September 27, 1989.
10 White House Central Files, Memorandum, Kissinger to Nixon, May 18, 1971, Subject: "Dinner for President Somoza of Nicaragua," Collection: CO (Countries), Box 55, Folder: [EX] CO III Nicaragua 1/1/71-, Richard M. Nixon Presidential Materials Project. This dinner party was of historical significance for another reason: While Nixon was entertaining Somoza, NSC Advisor Henry Kissinger received word that China had agreed to direct talks between the American president and Chairman Mao Tse Tung in Peking later that year. See Henry Kissinger, *The White House Years* (London: Weidenfeld and Nicolson and Michael Joseph, 1979), p. 727.

the United States. He saw no divergence over any issue between U.S. interests and Somoza interests.[11]

Shelton's first DCM, Robert White, described the envoy's relationship with Somoza as equivalent to that of a courtier to a regent, a "cheerleader" approach that meshed perfectly with the requirements of both the White House and the Nicaraguan leader: "When the White House thought about Nicaragua... their thoughts were directed toward supporting Somoza. Turner Shelton knew that he would never get anything but 'well dones' from the Nixon White House if he made Somoza feel good and he set out to do that to the exclusion of everything else."[12]

In the State Department, the Bureau of Inter-American Affairs (IAA) was rife with anti-Shelton sentiment. According to one official, Shelton was held in such low regard that scheming to force his premature recall began almost from the time he arrived in Managua:

> Two days before I went down to Nicaragua in 1972 [to take up an Embassy post], I went to see Bob Hurwitch, acting Deputy Assistant Secretary at the time. Hurwitch said 'we don't like our Ambassador, his closeness to Somoza. We are making a case against Somoza and the Ambassador, and would you participate in this effort. If you agree, and write to us like Bob White and continue to help us we will help you.' I had had similar hints from Larry Pezzullo, the Deputy Director of the Office of Central American Affairs. Bill Bowdler, Ambassador to Guatemala, questioned me about Somoza in 1972 during a stop-off in Guatemala. I think Bowdler was also part of this anti-Shelton group.[13]

Leland Warner, who succeeded White as Embassy DCM, targeted IAA as the locus of opposition to Shelton's "warm and close embrace" of Somoza; the predominant sentiment there favored a "much more formal relationship," one that piaced some "distance" between the U.S. and the dictatorial regime.[14] But the fundamental obstacle to any significant policy shift was the continuing Nixon-Kissinger support for Somoza. Hence the reluctance of IAA to press the issue vigorously. In his position as Secretary of State, Kissinger's "basic view was that Nicaragua was a backwater and

11   Interview with Thomas O'Donnell, Maryland, September 27, 1989.
12   See Diederich, *Somoza and the Legacy of U.S. Involvement in Central America*, p. 91; interview with Robert White, Washington, D.C., September 23, 1988. The respondent was Deputy Chief of Mission, American Embassy, Nicaragua, 1970 to 1972.
13   Confidential telephone interview, Department of State official, Texas, September 21, 1989. The respondent was a senior official in the American Embassy, Nicaragua, during the Nixon-Ford period.
14   Telephone interview with Leland Warner, Jr.

Shelton couldn't do much damage."[5] Warner recalled "seeing two letters in which the White House urged Shelton to stay close to Somoza and assure him of U.S. support."[6]

On at least two occasions, with tacit White House support and no apparent State Department opposition, Shelton intervened directly into the Nicaraguan political arena to defuse or remove potentially serious domestic challenges to the Somoza family dynasty. The first contributed to prolonging Somoza's control of the presidency, the second to reestablishing the authority of the National Guard in a moment of acute national crisis.

In 1967, Somoza won the presidency of Nicaragua running as the 'civilian' candidate of the Nationalist Liberal Party (PLN) with the help of the National Guard, which brutally clamped down on the electoral activities of opposition groups. As his term entered its final year, Somoza gave notice of his intention to seek reelection despite a constitutional prohibition against an incumbent succeeding himself. This decision triggered widespread opposition, particularly among political, labor, student, and church groups. By early 1971, Somoza also found himself beset by an additional problem: institutional conflicts within the National Guard. To reinforce Somoza's authority at home, Shelton organized a trip to the United States and a private meeting with President Nixon; to facilitate Somoza's political ambitions, he arranged discussions between his "regent" and the Conservative Party leader Fernando Agüero over the succession issue. The Nixon talks served the purpose of defusing the civilian opposition while the meeting with Agüero produced a formula allowing Somoza to contest the next presidential election. According to one Central American foreign minister, Somoza contributed $1 million to Nixon's 1972 presidential reelection campaign.[17]

Under the agreement worked out with Agüero, an interim junta composed of the Conservative Party leader and two Somoza appointees would govern the country from May 1972 to December 1974, at which time new elections would take place. For all practical purposes, though, Somoza remained the de facto ruler of Nicaragua. "While the triumvirate exercised nominal power," writes Richard Millet, "all real decisions were made by Somoza."[18] In September 1974, Somoza won another six year presidential term in another suspect election. Only one-third of eligible voters went to the polls amid a boycott call by sectors of the civic opposition on the grounds that the process was rigged to guarantee a Somoza victory.

The other major domestic crisis, which exposed the Somoza dynasty as

15   Confidential telephone interview, Department of State official, Maryland, September 30, 1989. The respondent was Nicaraguan Desk Officer, 1973 to 1974.
16   Telephone interview with Leland Warner, Jr.
17   Diederich, *Somoza and the Legacy of U.S. Involvement in Central America*, p. 89.
18   Millett, *Guardians of the Dynasty*, p. 236.

more vulnerable than at any other time in its history and prompted decisive intervention by Ambassador Shelton, occurred in the aftermath of the December 1972 Managua earthquake when the National Guard momentarily disintegrated as an organized institution. Officers and enlisted men deserted their posts, most in search of their families, some to engage in "massive looting. . . ." Alarmed by this turn of events, Shelton pressed Somoza "to seize total power" from the governing triumvirate in order to gain time to reconstitute the Guard as a unified, mobilized fighting force.[19] Somoza heeded the advice, invoking constitutional authority to allow rule by decree – graphically exposing the facade of junta government. "Some administration officials argued that we should not by-pass the triumvirate," Lawrence Pezzullo recalled, "but Nixon would have none of that."[20] Indeed the White House put through a "direct call to Somoza assuring him of U.S. support and help" within 24 hours of the earthquake.[21]

Meanwhile, the American Ambassador "was doing everything he could to support and reinforce Somoza's position. He just asked Somoza what he needed." Shelton speedily arranged for a contingent of U.S. Southern Command troops stationed in Panama to be dispatched to Managua to provide 'emergency' disaster assistance. When they arrived "they chose to set up their mobile military field hospital in Somoza's front yard. The Nicaraguans picked up on this right away."[22] Writing to President Nixon to express his appreciation for U.S. assistance, Somoza "highlight[ed], in particular, the rapid reaction of U.S. forces stationed in the Panama Canal Zone."[23]

The White House showered Nicaragua with emergency economic aid, which a number of Embassy and State Department officials believed was motivated by a need to divert public attention from the pre-Christmas American bombing of Cambodia. Thomas O'Donnell was one of these:

> The context within which U.S. earthquake assistance was provided had little to do with Nicaragua. The day before Christmas, the U.S. had resumed bombing in Cambodia producing an upsurge of domestic criticism of U.S. policy in South-East Asia. The Nicaraguan earthquake presented an opportunity to demonstrate the humanitarian side of the administration. The earthquake gained wide media coverage and in this

19   Ibid., p. 237.
20   Telephone interview with Lawrence Pezzullo.
21   Telephone interview with Leland Warner, Jr.
22   Ibid.
23   White House Central Files, Department of State Memorandum, Theodore L. Eliot, Jr., Executive Secretary, to Henry A. Kissinger, White House, May 4, 1973, Collection DI (Disasters), Box 4, Folder: EX DI 2/CO 101–150 [1973–74], Richard M. Nixon Presidential Materials Project.

context Nixon decided to act for political as much as humanitarian reasons.[24]

In the following months, largely on the basis of Shelton's reports, the United States channeled massive amounts of economic reconstruction aid to Nicaragua. Agency for International Development (AID) post-earthquake assistance (loans and grants) totaled $120 million, with an additional $48 million coming from the multilateral development banks (World Bank, Inter-American Development Bank).[25] Instead of reaching its designated target(s), however, much of these relief funds were siphoned off by the Somoza family and a small coterie of military and civilian cronies for their own private enrichment. A 1976 AID-funded inquiry into charges that Somoza-owned companies were the sole suppliers of materials used to build hospitals, schools, roads, and drainage canals (projects receiving AID monies) noted that the regime had purchased land for five district centers at above-market prices and for amounts much greater than paid by the sellers.[26] Although a subsequent AID investigation was unable to find evidence of diversion of funds and equipment to Somoza family-owned companies, an internal memorandum conceded that some of these enterprises "unavoidably benefited from the large-scale procurement which AID helped finance as part of the reconstruction of Managua."[27]

Although pronouncements from the Nixon White House and the Seventh Floor of the State Department raised little prospect of any change in U.S. policy toward Nicaragua, the post-earthquake political repercussions served to exacerbate divisions within the Embassy throughout 1973 and 1974 "over how to relate to the Somoza regime." DCM Leland Warner identified two groups of protagonists: "On the one side was the Ambassador, myself, and the military attaches. On the other was the political-economic-counsellor section, the James Cheek group."[28] The most significant individual confrontation erupted between the Ambassador and his political counsellor James Cheek who complained about reports critical of the Somoza regime being edited before transmission to the State Department or not sent at all: "I was saying that Somoza had lots of trouble, that new forces were emerging but Shelton was censoring the reports from the Embassy to Washington or

24 Interview with Thomas O'Donnell.
25 U.S. General Accounting Office, Report, *Nicaragua – An Assessment of Earthquake Relief and Reconstruction Assistance*, ID-77-25, March 17, 1977, p. 3.
26 Alan Riding, "Nicaraguans Accused of Profiteering on Help the U.S. Sent After Quake," *New York Times*, March 23, 1977, p. 10.
27 Quoted in Charles Stafford, "Somoza Holds a Firm Grip on Nicaragua," *St. Petersburg Times*, October 31, 1977, pp. 1A, 7A.
28 Telephone interview with Leland Warner, Jr.

was refusing to send the cables. This led to a constant conflict between Shelton and myself and to the use of the dissent channel."[29]

The broad thrust of Cheek's dissent cables was that "the earthquake had changed the economic and social landscape of the country and inevitably a political earthquake had to come and that that was going to be the rub and challenge for Somoza and, therefore, Somoza was going to have to change or there would be no long-term stability."[30] Included among these cables was one referring to a hospital strike and censorship of *La Prensa* that particularly angered the Ambassador. He refused to transmit it through normal channels because he objected to a comment that the strike "showed that people were organized and getting unhappy with Somoza."[31] Cheek's reports finally led Deputy Secretary Hewson Ryan to visit the country himself to make an on-the-spot assessment of the Nicaraguan political scene. What he saw seemed to confirm Cheek's views. Soon after Ryan's return to Washington, the administration decided to make substantial cuts in a $100 million to $125 million reconstruction aid package "it was on the verge of committing" to the Somoza regime.[32]

In recognition of his dissent channel cables, Cheek received the State Department's prestigious William R. Rivkin Award for being "the first to recognize, seek out, and report on the new sociopolitical forces in Nicaragua. …"[33] But the Nicaraguan Desk officer at the time stressed that Cheek's report did not "suggest a major change in policy" or differ markedly from "most of the cables coming out of the Embassy during that period. It was just a little stronger criticism of Somoza. There were lots of cables with the Ambassador's signature that talked about corruption in government, suffering, political maneuvering, unhappy middle classes, and so on." The political counselor was honored "simply because he managed to argue with the Ambassador and get the cables out, not because of the dissent itself."[34] Indeed, at the awards dinner, Secretary of State Kissinger was heard "to comment that he didn't think that Cheek's award was deserved."[35]

Efforts by IAA officials to promote a limited policy change on Nicaragua continued to founder on the shoals of Nixon and Kissinger's refusal to consider any revision of the status quo. To the Secretary, Nicaragua was a "backburner issue" and little was to be gained from raising it with a White House that still viewed Somoza as a valued and supportive regional ally.

29 Interview with James Cheek.
30 Ibid.
31 Confidential telephone interview, Department of State official, September 30, 1989.
32 Interview with James Cheek.
33 Quoted in Jeremiah O'Leary, "Diplomatic Problem," *Washington Star*, November 28, 1974, p. A6.
34 Confidential telephone interview, Department of State official, September 30, 1989.
35 Telephone interview with Leland Warner, Jr.

Notwithstanding, the Latin Americanists, discomforted over Somoza's "maneuverings to keep himself in office" and concerned over "what comes after him," kept the issue alive. As one of their number explained: "The State Department was looking for alternatives, whereas the White House was content with the situation staying as it was and was not really interested in interfering. Its attitude was 'let Somoza work out his own thing.' The White House looked to Somoza to make changes but were not about to push him, whereas the State Department was saying change is coming and we have to push him."[36] But such differing perceptions and attitudes should not be exaggerated. To the extent that a conflict existed it was tactical rather than strategic. State officials, for instance, repeatedly urged Ambassador Shelton to be "less effusive" in his praise of and support for Somoza, and to "keep a little distance. 'You don't have to go out to the airport and meet him every time he comes back from a trip.' "[37] Yet even those who "were beginning to have doubts about Somoza's survivability did not suggest that Somoza was evil and had to go. Nobody in Washington did."[38]

One aspect of Shelton's behavior that enormously irritated those State officials responsible for implementing Nicaragua policy was the Ambassador's repeated insistence that in his dealings with Somoza he was only answerable to the White House: "Turner Shelton would go to Somoza and say 'don't take any notice of what the State Department said. I take orders from the White House and they say to support you 100 percent.' "[39] Lawrence Pezzullo, one of those most convinced that Shelton was "taking orders from the White House," recalled how he "would just ignore statements from the State Department."[40] None of this was lost on Somoza, who started giving short shrift to Embassy officials attempting to convince him that one or other of his actions was undermining his standing within the Department. "On a couple of occasions," Leland Warner recalled, "when I was in charge and had talks with Somoza and tried to tell him that he was damaging himself with Washington by doing things such as censorship of *La Prensa*, it had no effect."[41]

What posture to adopt toward the civilian opposition also served to bedevil Ambassador Shelton's relations with his Embassy colleagues. According to DCM Malcolm Barnaby (1967–1970), neither Shelton's predecessor nor the State Department attempted to limit Embassy efforts to establish ties

---

36 Confidential telephone interview, Department of State official, September 30, 1989.
37 Telephone interview with Lawrence Pezzullo; interview with Robert White; interview with David Lazar.
38 Interview with James Cheek.
39 Confidential telephone interview, Department of State official, September 30, 1989.
40 Telephone interview with Lawrence Pezzullo.
41 Telephone interview with Leland Warner, Jr.

with leading representatives of the anti-regime forces in Managua: "We had open and full communication with the Conservative party and with a whole range of parties from left to right, excluding the extreme left, during 1969 and 1970. We dealt with the Social Christians, conservatives, dissident liberals, Somoza's own party, but not with the FSLN."[42] After Shelton arrived, some Washington officials perceived little or no change in this area. Until the December 1972 earthquake, the new Ambassador allowed the existing practice to continue even though he "was not very keen on his subordinates dealing with these groups. Basically, Shelton maintained that they were not really important. His attitude was 'I'll talk to Somoza if I want something done. It's a waste of time to talk to the others.' " Occasionally, he conversed with "the house opposition" or with "top echelon" Somoza protagonists such as the Chamorros but refused "to talk to any of the others."[43] Robert White, who succeeded Barnaby as DCM in 1970, perceived the situation differently from his colleagues, insisting that Shelton actively "discouraged" contacts with the moderate and conservative opposition groups well before the natural disaster that befell Managua. According to White, this issue soured relations between the two diplomats because of what the Ambassador's deputy said was his insistence that such contacts "were one of the few ways we had of trying to impress upon Somoza that he didn't have us locked up."[44]

The events surrounding the earthquake and its aftermath precipitated increasingly sharp disagreements between Shelton and those Embassy officials who desired an end to the longstanding U.S. policy of complete, uncritical support for the Somoza dictatorship.[45] Tensions were further heightened by Shelton's "harder-line" stance on consorting with the regime's critics: "He didn't like the idea of Embassy officials getting too cozy with opposition politicians." Henceforth, the Ambassador studiously avoided such individuals "on the grounds that working with Somoza was in the best interests of the United States." But IAA officials "believed that it was now more important than ever to talk with all areas of opinion across the political spectrum."[46] Taking their cue from their colleagues in Wash-

---

42 Interview with Malcolm Barnaby, Washington, D.C., October 4, 1988. The respondent was Deputy Chief of Mission, American Embassy, Nicaragua, 1967 to 1970. He was also involved with Nicaragua policy during the Carter presidency. Between 1977 and 1980, he was the Director of the Andean Office, Department of State, and Director of the NSC Departmental Groups.

43 Confidential telephone interview, Department of State official, September 30, 1989; interview with James Cheek; interview with Thomas O'Donnell.

44 Interview with Robert White.

45 See Alan Riding, "Hopes of Nicaraguan Opposition Rise With Shift of the US Envoy," *New York Times*, August 11, 1975, p. 3.

46 Confidential telephone interview, Department of State official, September 30, 1989.

ington, Embassy officers increasingly and openly defied Shelton on this point. Leland Warner described the widening chasm between the Ambassador and his subordinates:

> The State Department wanted the Embassy to expand its links with the opposition and this was one of the bones of contention between the State Department and the Ambassador. One big mistake the Ambassador made was to try to stop visiting U.S. government officials, members of Congress, etc. from seeing some of the opposition. The Embassy fought him as a unified group on that. We refused to support that and would take these people to see Somoza *and* the opposition leaders.[47]

What the dominant Embassy sentiment favored was not a fundamental policy shift but a less cozy and more dignified bilateral relationship with the regime, accompanied by greater efforts to get Somoza to implement limited changes in his method of political rule.

Undeterred, Ambassador Shelton continued to act "as though he didn't need the State Department to tell him what to do."[48] Toward the midpoint of the second Nixon administration, however, developments in Nicaragua and the United States began to noticeably weaken and erode Shelton's Washington support network. While a more assertive State Department started treating his reports on the Nicaraguan political scene with growing skepticism, and to distance itself more and more from his actions in support of Somoza, the Ambassador's most prominent executive branch ally – Richard Nixon – was much too preoccupied with the Watergate scandal and the very real possibility of impeachment during 1974 to devote even limited attention to Nicaragua policy.

The Ford administration and Somoza:
New rhetoric and old policy

In August 1974, the long-running presidential crisis reached its denouement when Richard Nixon resigned from the country's highest political office in disgrace and was replaced by his Vice-President Gerald Ford. Over in the State Department, William D. Rogers, a proponent of a new approach toward dealing with Nicaragua, was appointed Assistant Secretary for Inter-American Affairs. Although Rogers immediately discovered that "Nicaragua was very low on the [Ford White House] priority list," he nonetheless set about lobbying within the foreign policy bureaucracy for authority to place

47   Telephone interview with Leland Warner, Jr. (Warner's emphasis).
48   Interview with David Lazar.

relations between Washington and Managua on a more professional and diplomatically correct foundation. This necessitated, first and foremost, a change of Ambassador:

> The day I went into office, the first task was to get rid of Turner Shelton. It was not an easy task on which Larry Eagleburger [Executive Assistant to Secretary of State Kissinger] and I conspired almost daily because he had a lot of friends and he was persistent in involving them. Somoza was very active in pulling in all his chips on behalf of Turner Shelton in the Congress and the White House had a lot of fish to fry and didn't want another in terms of getting rid of Shelton. So it took a little while to do it.[49]

Almost twelve months passed before Shelton was removed from his post. Meanwhile, relations between the Ambassador and his Embassy colleagues worsened apace: "The staff was going in one direction, the Ambassador was going in another. The staff was trying to do a professional job while the Ambassador was trying to do everything he could to support Somoza and to be sure the United States supported Somoza."[50] When the Office of Management and Budget proposed that the U.S. eliminate new aid programs to all countries (including Nicaragua) with per capita incomes in excess of $300 per annum, Shelton immediately cabled his opposition on the grounds that "an abrupt ending of the AID program would lead over time to a reduction of our influence with President Somoza and the GON [Government of Nicaragua]."[51]

Assistant Secretary Rogers' hard-won effort to get Shelton out of the Managua Embassy was only a partial victory because of his failure to gain a free hand in the choice of a successor. Under pressure from Vice-President Nelson Rockefeller and the Secretary of State's wife Nancy Kissinger, Rogers was forced to accept the appointment of James Theberge, a traditional "cold war" academic attached to the conservative Georgetown Center for Strategic and International Studies where he specialized in studies on the "communist threat" to the hemisphere and how best to counter it. Some years earlier, Theberge had worked as a "staff person" on a Latin American project supervised by Kissinger under the Vice-President's overall authority.[52]

49 Interview with William D. Rogers, Washington, D.C., September 7, 1988. The respondent was Assistant Secretary for Inter-American Affairs, Department of State, 1974 to 1976, and Under-Secretary of State for Economic Affairs, Department of State, 1976 to 1977.
50 Interview with David Lazar.
51 Department of State Telegram, Managua 3002, Ambassador Shelton to Secretary of State, August 1975, Subject: "Foreign Investment Climate and Statistics," DFOIA.
52 Telephone interview with Hewson Ryan, Massachusetts, September 16, 1988. The re-

This decision to replace Nixon's "courtier" to Somoza with someone "to the right of the Bureau of Inter-American Affairs and Assistant Secretary Rogers" was a disappointment to the Latin Americanists in State.[53] Still, Rogers was determined to move Nicaragua policy "off dead center," and the first step in this process was to leave Somoza in no doubt that the ambassadorial reshuffle was "a signal of our displeasure" with his performance and a move toward "distancing" the United States from the regime.[54] Because Theberge was to play an important role in carrying out this policy shift, the Assistant Secretary intended to keep the new Ambassador "on a very short leash. He had conservative instincts that could have led him off the reservation."[55]

The first order of business was to give State's imprimatur to Embassy contacts with a civilian opposition that "had become more potent, larger, more important,"[56] especially as a result of the growing capitalist class disillusionment with the regime's economic policies. Henceforth, Washington intended to pursue an evenhanded approach in its dealings with the Nicaraguan government and the non-radical opposition, including regular Embassy staff communications with leading political and business critics of the regime. Assistant Secretary Rogers elaborated:

> We sent Theberge down with very clear instructions to make clear to Somoza that the United States was now neutral with respect to the political struggle and that he was to establish relations with the opposition. I accompanied Theberge either the first time he met with Somoza or shortly thereafter to underline the point that we were sending a new Ambassador down to open a new era of American-Nicaraguan relations and that Theberge was instructed to avoid any action that would give the impression that we favored any particular regime and to open channels of communication with the political opposition.[57]

As Ambassador, Theberge, like his predecessor, preferred to limit personal contacts with the opposition to "top echelon" figures, and was particularly "enchanted" by the Chamorros.[58] This attitude probably

spondent was Deputy Assistant Secretary for Inter-American Affairs (Political), Department of State, 1974 to 1976.

53 Ibid.
54 Confidential telephone interview, Department of State official, Washington, D.C., October 4, 1989. The respondent was a senior official in the Office of Central American Affairs, 1974 to 1976.
55 Interview with William D. Rogers.
56 Confidential telephone interview, Department of State official, Washington, D.C., September 14, 1989. The respondent was a senior official in the Bureau of Inter-American Affairs, 1976.
57 Interview with William D. Rogers.
58 Telephone interview with Leland Warner, Jr.

contributed to the strained relations that developed between the new head of mission and his Embassy colleagues. Theberge, his longest serving DCM observed, "felt uncomfortable with the Embassy staff in many ways."[59] Nonetheless, he carried out his responsibilities to the satisfaction of his superiors in Washington: "He was very obedient. He did what we told him to do."[60] The only exception was a minor one: He failed, said a member of the State Department's briefing team, "to move out of the U.S. residence on the hill that was next to the Somoza residence" after being told to do so.[61]

At the time of Theberge's appointment, the White House assured Somoza that the change of envoys was "not to be taken as representing any change in United States policy" toward Nicaragua.[62] Even senior State officials who were most active in "searching for ways of distancing ourselves from Somoza and trying to persuade him to modify his behavior" were at pains to stress that they wanted to achieve these goals "without jeopardizing the overall relationship between the United States and Nicaragua."[63] Nothing the administration did was "carried to extremes."[64] No thought was given to rupturing ties or dumping the client, not least because such an approach was anathema to the Secretary of State. As one of Kissinger's senior hemispheric advisors put it: "No serious contemplation was given to drastic measures against Somoza because this was entirely against Henry's general approach to things."[65]

The fundamental realization that took hold within State during the Ford presidency was that "some kind of public distancing was required *to preserve our long term interests.*" Simultaneously, the Department embarked on an effort "to encourage Somoza to open up the political system." Between mid-1975 and mid-1976, Embassy reporting "tracked [developments in this area] very carefully" and despite frustration over the lack of movement "we continued to press for it."[66] Washington also targeted the issue of government corruption. During a visit to Nicaragua in October 1976, for

59 Confidential interview, Department of State official, Washington, D.C., October 3, 1990. The respondent was Deputy Chief of Mission, American Embassy, Nicaragua, 1976 to 1978. He was in charge of Embassy affairs during the 4–5 months interval between the recall of Ambassador James Theberge and the arrival of Ambassador Mauricio Solaun.
60 Interview with William D. Rogers.
61 Confidential telephone interview, Department of State official, New York, October 5, 1989. The respondent was a senior official in the Bureau of Inter-American Affairs, 1975 to 1977.
62 Quoted in "U.S. Reassures Nicaragua," *New York Times*, August 11, 1975, p. 3.
63 Confidential telephone interview, Department of State official, October 4, 1989.
64 Telephone interview with Hewson Ryan.
65 Confidential telephone interview, Department of State official, September 14, 1989.
66 Confidential telephone interview, Department of State official, October 4, 1989 (my emphasis).

example, a senior U.S. diplomat conferred with Somoza and "pressed him hard on corruption."[67] In other words, whereas Ford policy was based on "distancing ourselves so as not to be seen by other political elements in Nicaragua as favoring Somoza's stay in power,"[68] accompanied by discreet criticisms of particular aspects of regime policy, the actual measures taken were restricted to what Deputy Secretary of State Hewson Ryan termed "low-level diplomatic pressures" and "subtle signals" of displeasure.[69] At the end of 1976, the administration was, as one high-ranking Embassy official put it, doing no more than "trying to nudge Somoza to open up the political process."[70]

Throughout this period, the State Department was particularly concerned to deny the Nicaraguan leader any opportunity to exploit the bilateral relationship for his own domestic or regional purposes. In April 1976, the dictator arrived in Washington to confer with Vice President Nelson Rockefeller. A State Department memorandum to Rockefeller in preparation for the meeting noted that "there are no bilateral issues of significance" between the two countries. "Somoza has based his foreign policy consistently on close identification with the United States and on a rigid anti-communism...." It counseled the Vice-President to assuage Somoza's concern that the ambassadorial change signaled "a basic decision to cool relations with him" by emphasizing that the U.S. "ha[s] neither any reason nor the intention to make any fundamental change in our relations with Nicaragua. They have traditionally been close and mutually helpful." However, regarding Somoza's interest in inviting a senior administration official to Managua "to permit a public expression of gratitude" for U.S. post-earthquake assistance, the memorandum offered Rockefeller the following advice in the event an offer was made to him: "Such a visit would have the primary purpose of bolstering his personal political position domestically and reinforcing his self-assumed image as 'our man' in Central America vis-à-vis the other heads of state. A polite brush-off would be the best response."[71]

President Ford refused to meet with Somoza during another of his U.S. trips later that year for basically the same reasons. Meanwhile, officials continued to emphasize that such "brush-offs" did not signify any erosion

67 Confidential telephone interview, Department of State official, September 14, 1989.
68 Confidential telephone interview, Department of State official, October 4, 1989.
69 Telephone interview with Hewson Ryan.
70 Confidential telephone interview, Department of State official, October 3, 1990.
71 Department of State, Memorandum for the Vice President (Rockefeller), April 19, 1976, Subject: "Your Meeting with Nicaraguan President Somoza," Gerald R. Ford Presidential Library, Ann Arbor, Michigan. Also see The White House, Memorandum for the Vice President (Rockefeller), Subject: "Call on Nicaraguan President Anastasio Somoza, April 20, 1976," Ibid.

of "the continuity of our relationship with Nicaragua."[72] Only changes in economic or military ties would indicate movement in this direction, and there was no evidence to even suggest that the administration was interested in pursuing a shift of that kind. On the contrary, in November 1976, as Ford was about to leave the White House, the United States Southern Command sent observers (and had Senate permission to send troops, which the Pentagon declined to do) to Central American Defense Council (CONDECA) tactical military maneuvers, code-named "Eagle Six," held in Nicaragua.[73]

The Ford-Kissinger refusal to contemplate any major shift in relations with the Somoza regime, and the basic White House perception of Nicaragua as a minor or backburner issue, was partly explained by the lack of a serious *radical* challenge to the family dynasty and the state. Even those State Department officials most critical of Somoza's behavior readily agreed that the FSLN was still "a very minimal blip on the horizon," which was "the real key" to understanding the administration's relative indifference to reports of institutional conflicts within the National Guard.[74] Insofar as State had decided to actively cultivate sectors of the civilian opposition movement, it was doing so in the belief that Somoza's political base was beginning to crumble, which necessitated some kind of contingency planning. This included aiding the non-Sandinista forces within what Assistant Secretary Rogers called "the growing tide of popular opposition." The Department was encouraged by the fact that "the anti-Somoza civilian opposition was stronger than the guerrillas at this time. There was no sense that if we did get Somoza out and the moderates in, the radicals would take over."[75] And America's long-term interests in Nicaragua could only be enhanced by taking whatever initiatives were possible to consolidate the leadership of the conservative and moderate opposition sectors within the anti-regime movement.

American policy also was influenced by Nicaragua's declining strategic importance. Responding to a letter from the leader of the anti-Somoza group in the House of Representatives Edward Koch in late January 1976, the Assistant Secretary of State for Congressional Relations wrote that "we do not consider that the United States has any major strategic interests in Nicaragua."[76] William Rogers concurred in this estimate: "There was no

72 Department of State, Memorandum for the Vice President (Rockefeller), April 19, 1976.
73 See Diederich, *Somoza and the Legacy of U.S. Involvement in Central America*, p. 120, Foreign Broadcast Information Service, *Daily Report: Latin America*, December 14, 1976, p. 2.
74 Confidential telephone interview, Department of State official, September 14, 1989.
75 Interview with William D. Rogers.
76 Quoted in "The Koch-State Department Correspondence on U.S. Relations with Nicaragua," *Inter-American Economic Affairs*, Vol. XXIX, No. 4, Spring 1976, p. 88.

strategic concern. At that time the United States was engaged in secret negotiations with Castro and Nicaragua was not even considered a serious problem to be dealt with during those negotiations."[77]

The Ford administration's refusal "to place much pressure on him"[78] encouraged Somoza to deflect or ignore calls for political reform in the knowledge that such requests were not backed by significant penalties. His confidence, already bolstered by the attitude of the White House and Secretary Kissinger, was reinforced by the existence of influential supporters within the foreign policy bureaucracy. Perhaps no executive branch agency lobbied more strongly on Somoza's behalf than the Department of Defense, which looked upon Nicaragua "as a far more reliable partner for Central American activities compared to El Salvador, Honduras, and Guatemala."[79] A graduate of the U.S. West Point Military Academy in the late 1940s, Somoza went out of his way to maintain personal as well as professional contacts with his classmates over the following quarter century. This was an integral aspect of his continuing effort to "identify himself with the United States and to portray himself as representing the United States in Central America." Embassy DCM Robert White described Managua as "crawling with [U.S.] generals" during the twenty-fifth anniversary reunion of Somoza's graduating class in 1971.[80] Throughout the Ford years, the dictator also kept "inviting [American] major generals, lieutenant generals, and generals to come down and go hunting with him."[81]

Somoza had equally powerful allies on Capitol Hill. In the House, John Murphy of New York and Charles Wilson of Texas were among the more influential members willing to lobby on his behalf; in the Senate, no one was more supportive of the Nicaraguan dictator than Senator Jacob Javits, the liberal New York Republican and a prominent member of the Foreign Relations Committee. "Nobody in the administration wanted to start a fight over Somoza with Senator Javits," Deputy Secretary of State Hewson Ryan recalled. "Javits had long been a strong supporter of Somoza because of the Israeli connection and as a key liberal leader of the Republican Party no one wanted to initiate a confrontation with him over this issue."[82]

During the final year of the Ford presidency, Nicaragua became one target of a growing U.S. Congressional focus on human rights abuses in the Third World, particularly by governments receiving American economic and military aid. The White House refusal to comply with non-binding

77 Interview with William D. Rogers.
78 Telephone interview with Hewson Ryan.
79 Confidential telephone interview, Department of State official, October 4, 1989.
80 Interview with Robert White.
81 Telephone interview with Hewson Ryan.
82 Ibid.

legislation calling for the termination of military assistance programs to repressive allies failed to slow down the groundswell of legislative support for sanctions against offending regimes. Subsequently, Congress passed the Harkin amendment, legally mandating the executive branch to halt all economic aid to governments deemed guilty of a gross and consistent pattern of human rights violations. In May 1976, the amendment was extended to U.S. policy in the Inter-American Development Bank and the African Development Bank. U.S. representatives in these regional economic institutions were now required to vote against loan requests from designated human rights abusers except where the monies were intended to "directly benefit the poor." Congress also directed the Secretary of State to submit an annual report on the status of human rights in all countries receiving U.S. aid. Finally, legislative pressure was instrumental in the administration's decision to establish a human rights office in the State Department.

Irrespective of these Congressional demands for greater attention to human rights questions in the conduct of foreign policy, the overall Ford White House posture remained a mixture of reluctant accommodation, subtle resistance, and outright rejection. The major stumbling block was Secretary of State Henry Kissinger, who exhibited a palpable lack of enthusiasm over the idea that morality had any, let alone a prominent, role to play in the making of foreign policy – and a President willing to defer to his Secretary's judgment on this issue. A senior Inter-American Affairs official summarized the basic approach:

> Ford policy remained essentially the Kissinger policy which basically placed considerably less emphasis on human rights issues and more on government stability and friendly relations. Governments supportive of the United States were basically viewed as good governments. The policy of the Kissinger period was to do what was necessary to satisfy Congress on human rights but not to take any measures to distance the U.S. from governments helpful to us.[83]

Neither the Harkin amendment nor the newly formed State Department's Office of Human Rights substantially interfered with this general policy line. In the multilateral development banks, the administration applied pressure to force postponements of final decisions on loan submissions from repressive Third World allies. "Our general tactic," an involved official observed, "was to get loan requests put off so we didn't have to vote either way."[84] Meanwhile, Kissinger ensured that the Office of Human Rights was kept outside of the policymaking "loop." According to the Office's first coordinator James Morrison Wilson, he routinely ignored Office memoran-

83 Confidential telephone interview, Department of State official, October 5, 1989.
84 Confidential telephone interview, Department of State official, September 14, 1989.

dums recommending greater attention to human rights factors in America's relations with autocratic governments.[85] As a result, it wielded virtually no influence over Third World aid decisions.

Not surprisingly, the Secretary was harshly critical of any subordinates who publicly diverged from his approach. In June 1976, for instance, Kissinger "laid out the administration's line" on human rights in an opening address to the Organization of American States which was meeting to consider the issue. In the debate that followed, comments by U.S. Ambassador to El Salvador Robert White "went a considerable way to specifically condemn Somoza and the Chilean dictator Pinochet." Kissinger was "outraged" and accused White of having "overstepped his instructions."[86]

The deterioration of the human rights situation in Nicaragua began soon after the transition from Nixon to Ford. On December 1, 1974, Somoza engineered his reelection to a new six-and-a-half year term as President over a "handpicked puppet opponent...."[87] That same month, Sandinista guerrillas successfully executed a military action that severely embarrassed the regime, capturing the home of former Nicaraguan Agriculture Minister José Maria Castillo during a party being held in honor of the departing U.S. Ambassador Turner Shelton. Several high-ranking politicians were taken hostage and only released after Somoza agreed to pay a $5 million ransom, free a number of FSLN prisoners, and guarantee safe passage for the guerrilla force and their "liberated" comrades out of the country.

In line with the "distancing" strategy, Washington was reluctant to assist its Nicaraguan client extricate himself from each and every domestic crisis. "Somoza tried very hard to get the U.S. directly involved in dealing with the hostages," a State Department official with major responsibilities for Central America explained. "At a minimum, he wanted us to advise him, to send down to Nicaragua a former FBI officer. We declined and told him to deal directly with the guerrillas. We refused to become directly involved in the negotiations, even after his personal request for support."[88]

Furious over this turn of events, Somoza declared an immediate state of siege, which was the prelude to a large-scale National Guard military offensive against the FSLN in the guerrillas' northern strongholds. Supported by CONDECA troops, the Guard waged a prolonged and brutal counterinsurgency war employing such methods as "free-fire zones," which not only resulted in heavy Sandinista casualties but also indiscriminate abuses

85   See Jeffrey D. Merritt, "Unilateral Human Rights Intercession: American Practice Under Nixon, Ford, and Carter," in David Newsom, ed., *The Diplomacy of Human Rights* (Lanham: University Press of America, 1986), pp. 45, 48.
86   Confidential telephone interview, Department of State official, October 5, 1989.
87   Millett, *Guardians of the Dynasty*, p. 242.
88   Confidential telephone interview, Department of State official, October 4, 1989.

(summary executions, torture, disappearances, incarcerations) against the local civilian population.[89]

Denunciations of National Guard terrorism against the peasant population by Amnesty International, the Nicaraguan church, and leaders of the moderate political opposition focused the U.S. Congressional spotlight on Nicaragua. In July 1976, a House International Relations subcommittee held hearings on the status of human rights in Nicaragua, Guatemala, and El Salvador. In testimony before the subcommittee, executive branch officials basically conceded the accuracy of some of these reports of Guard human rights abuses but questioned whether they were so extensive and systematic as to justify the termination of U.S. economic aid or some equivalent dramatic response by Washington. Deputy Assistant Secretary of State for Inter-American Affairs Hewson Ryan stated that the administration could find no evidence of "a consistent pattern of gross violation of human rights" but acknowledged that U.S. Embassy officials had been instructed to voice "our concern" to the Somoza regime on a number of occasions. Nevertheless, Ryan's answers to subcommittee questioning led the chairman, Representative Donald Fraser, to conclude that the Embassy was guilty of a marked disinclination to investigate reports of Guard human rights abuses.

Also revealing of Washington's reluctance to consider any kind of major policy shift was Ryan's effort to partially justify the Guard's counterinsurgency operations insofar as their primary target was "a movement [the FSLN] which has a very strong base of support in Cuba.... " This attempt to redefine an organization with deep roots in Nicaraguan politics and society as externally supported and manipulated elicited skeptical subcommittee responses. Edward Koch expressed amazement and incredulity at the evidence presented to support the Cuba connection – the fact that the FSLN prisoners freed in December 1974 received sanctuary in Cuba and that two of their number returned to Nicaragua two months later to renew anti-Somoza activities. Seeking clarification of the State Department position, Koch asked Ryan the following question: "Is it your position that external aggression exists when an insurgent in one country is able to receive sanctuary or guns in another country? Would you define that as the kind of external aggression that allows us to assist the government in putting down the insurgency in its own country?" The Deputy Assistant Secretary answered in the affirmative and then presumed to bolster his argument by concluding that the Sandinistas received "psychological support" as well as weapons and refuge from Cuba.[90]

89 See Amnesty International, *The Republic of Nicaragua*, p. 39; Alan Riding, "Rights Organization Accuses Nicaraguan Regime of Widespread Abuses," *New York Times*, August 16, 1977, p. 6.
90 U.S. Congress, House, Committee on International Relations, Subcommittee on Inter-

The Ford administration differed from its predecessor in its willingness to at least privately raise the issue of human rights violations with the Somoza regime. Assistant Secretary of State William Rogers maintained that part of his original instructions to Theberge was "to communicate our view about human rights violations" to the Nicaraguan leader.[91] And, if the former Ambassador is to be believed, "our concern was made clear to the Nicaraguan Government on various occasions" after his posting to Managua.[92] Hewson Ryan told a House subcommittee considering the foreign aid program to Nicaragua that State officials had regularly discussed National Guard human rights abuses with Somoza and other regime influentials during 1976.[93] But as Department officials were quick to point out, there was no attempt "to single out or target" the dictatorship. "The effort to get Somoza to behave better, to reduce the number of human rights violations, was simply part of a general effort in Latin America."[94]

Just as significantly, diplomatic representations were unaccompanied by sustained and consequential pressures (for example, aid sanctions) to force a change in Guard behavior. U.S. economic assistance to Nicaragua in 1976, through bilateral and multilateral agencies, totaled more than $100 million.[95] Officials in both Washington and Managua rationalized this "soft" approach partly on the grounds that the documented cases of abuse were not as excessive and widespread as critics of the dictatorship contended. "Ambassador Theberge," one of his Embassy subordinates remarked, "didn't think it was very important and thought the Somoza regime was not guilty of any serious human rights violations and certainly didn't think it was a consistent government policy."[96] Consequently, he was "somewhat reluctant to push as hard on the human rights issue as on corruption," an approach that received a sympathetic hearing among some senior Latin Americanists in State. Said one: "I was sympathetic to some extent to his approach because it wasn't clear that the U.S. government per se was going to do much good in terms of overall results by being too public and too strong [about human rights]."[97]

national Organizations, *Human Rights in Nicaragua, Guatemala, and El Salvador: Implications for U.S. Policy,* 94th Congress, 2nd Session, June 8 and 9, 1976 (Washington, D.C.: U.S. Government Printing Office, 1976), pp. 112, 115, 121.

91 Interview with William D. Rogers.
92 Statement made in March 1977 and quoted in *Keesing's Contemporary Archives,* October 21, 1977, p. 28625.
93 U.S. Congress, House, Committee on Appropriations, Subcommittee on Foreign Operations and Related Agencies, *Foreign Assistance and Related Agencies Appropriations For 1978, Part 3,* 95th Congress, 1st Session, April 5, 1977 (Washington, D.C.: U.S. Government Printing Office, 1977), p. 3.
94 Confidential telephone interview, Department of State official, September 14, 1989.
95 See Karen DeYoung, "Somoza's Nicaragua," *Washington Post,* October 16, 1977, p. A30.
96 Telephone interview with Leland Warner, Jr.
97 Confidential telephone interview, Department of State official, September 14, 1989.

Efforts by the Ford White House to get Somoza to govern in a less repressive fashion, without provoking a rupture in bilateral relations, seemed constrained by much the same sentiments that shaped U.S. policy during the Nixon era. Rising, but uncoordinated, political opposition was incapable of challenging the military power of the Somoza state and in the absence of an acceptable alternative it was important to avoid taking measures that might undermine a reliable hemispheric supporter. "The general feeling around was don't bother us on the Seventh Floor [Secretary Kissinger's office] with Nicaragua," a prominent State Department official with hemispheric responsibilities explained. "We have other more important things to deal with. Don't rock the boat."[98]

Conclusion

I have argued in this chapter that the Nixon-Ford White House viewed Somoza as a consolidated strategic ally willing to support and safeguard basic U.S. interests in Nicaragua and Central America; that in the absence of any serious challenge to his survival, senior policymakers were uninterested in contemplating a fundamental change in the existing relationship despite their client's increasingly corrupt and repressive rule. The emergence of a growing cross-class opposition movement after the December 1972 earthquake did little to weaken the perception of a regime well able to dispose of any internal challenge given its near monopoly over coercive power. At the same time, I have also identified and emphasized the importance of growing divisions within sectors of the foreign policy bureaucracy over the extent of Washington's support for Somoza: Officials in the State Department and the Managua Embassy advocated more "distancing" from a regime that was mired in corruption, a ruler who was "a pain in the ass [and] just not a situation that we enjoyed at all,"[99] and increased ties with a civilian opposition perceived as politically viable and likely to be just as accommodative of U.S. permanent interests as the dictatorship.

Although the Ford administration adopted a relatively more neutral posture toward the regime and its critics, and was forced by Congress to address Nicaragua's human rights record, there was "no radical change in the direction of policy."[100] Apart from the perceived absence of any serious threat to American interests, Secretary of State Kissinger believed that moral considerations (human rights) had little or no place in the making of U.S.

98 Telephone interview with Hewson Ryan.
99 Confidential interview, Department of State official, September 14, 1989.
100 Confidential interview, Department of State official, Washington, D.C., October 3, 1990. The respondent was involved with Nicaragua policy in the Bureau of Inter-American Affairs, 1974 to 1976.

foreign policy, and therefore opposed rupturing ties with Third World allies simply on the basis of methods of political rule. Furthermore, Somoza had influential supporters within the Defense Department and the Congress whose activities were aided and abetted by a highly effective Nicaraguan government-funded public relations campaign in the national capital.

Nor were the "dissident" foreign service officers advocating a major policy change. Their behavior was motivated by a concern over the long-term future of U.S. permanent interests in Nicaragua; it was also revealing of the way in which the ideology of particular administrations and a policy based on enduring interests are interrelated. Many of these same individuals' formative diplomatic experiences with Latin America occurred during the Kennedy administration and the Alliance for Progress. The Alliance was fundamentally an effort to promote "reform to avoid revolution"– Washington's response to the demise of the client Batista dictatorship in Cuba, the capture of political and state power by radical nationalist guerrillas, and the rapid elimination of American influence on the island. One of its central features was hostility to dictators and support for elected regimes willing to implement socioeconomic reforms and maintain the continuity of existing state institutions. And since the early 1960s, "avoiding a second Cuba" had become one of the central preoccupations of career diplomats involved with the making and implementation of U.S. hemispheric policy.

The State Department "dissidents" did not believe there was any impending threat of revolution in Nicaragua at that time. But, in light of recent developments – especially the regime's response to the December 1972 earthquake and growing local capitalist class hostility toward Somoza's policies – they at least wanted discussion of a possible future regime crisis placed on the bureaucratic agenda. In advocating expanded ties with the civilian opposition, they were motivated by a concern to position the United States so it would have a viable and acceptable alternative to the dictatorship it could support in the event of a political transition. They were looking both to the past and the future rather than reacting to the present, anticipating that the Somoza's behavior might well create problems for the state in the near term. If this circumstance arose, as professional diplomats they wanted room to maneuver. Therefore, it was in Washington's basic interests to move away from too close an identification with the longstanding client and establish links with all those opposition forces that did not pose a threat to state. The emphasis was on political flexibility: Opposing Somoza within the framework of existing institutional and economic structures, these officials perceived U.S. support for a bourgeois opposition willing to cohabit with the National Guard as the best means of defending U.S. permanent interests in a post-Somoza Nicaragua.

Finally, they were also influenced – and appalled – by the manifestly undiplomatic behavior of an Ambassador (Turner Shelton) who "used to spend at least ten hours a week alone with the General, counseling and guiding him..."[101] Said one: "He simply didn't conduct himself in a professional manner."[102] Exclaimed another: "He was not performing the job of Ambassador."[103] This criticism extended to Somoza's ability to exploit Shelton's obsequious and fawning support for his own ends. "Somoza," in the words of the Nicaragua Desk officer in State during 1973 and 1974, "played him like a violin."[104]

The debate among Nixon and Ford diplomats over how closely Washington should tie itself to Somoza foreshadowed the Carter administration's policy of "distancing" and the inter- and intra-agency conflicts that re-emerged in the late 1970s.

101   "Nicaragua: Shaky Satrap," *Latin America*, September 19, 1975, p. 294.
102   Interview with Robert White.
103   Telephone interview with Thomas Mehen, Washington, D.C., September 14, 1988.
       The respondent was the Country Director/Nicaragua in the Bureau of Inter-American
       Affairs, Department of State, 1974 to 1975.
104   Confidential interview, Department of State official, September 30, 1989.

4

The Carter administration and Nicaragua: Human rights and the politics of accommodation

Introduction

Shifts and changes in U.S. policy toward Third World allies are dictated by variations in the level of political and class struggles: In periods of low or declining levels of conflict where there is no need or imperative to contemplate a change of regime, Washington continues to support the incumbent, no matter how repressive or corrupt the method of political rule. In periods of medium- or high-level confrontation, Washington tends to throw its support behind the more conservative and moderate sectors of the opposition and encourage the client regime to begin a dialogue with these elements and make concessions in order to isolate the more radical opposition forces, the greatest potential threat to U.S. permanent interests.

During the first nine months of the Carter presidency, the Somoza dictatorship easily brushed aside isolated, individual protests against its policies and continuation in office. The dominant perception among American officials was of a consolidated regime that had time and again proved its military superiority over the Sandinista guerrillas. Given the absence of any consequential domestic challenge to Somoza rule, the incoming U.S. administration felt no pressing reason to undertake a major reassessment of bilateral ties. Diplomatic initiatives to encourage reforms were largely confined to the discrete issue of human rights abuses.

In mid-October 1977, however, the Tercerista faction of the FSLN launched a nationwide military offensive against the coercive Somoza state, attacking National Guard posts near the Costa Rican and Honduran borders and in numerous provincial cities.[1] "What was very significant," wrote Ber-

---

1 See Department of State Telegram, San Jose 4745, American Embassy to Secretary of State, October 14, 1977, Subject: "FSLN Attack on Nicaraguan Border Town," DFOIA; Department of State Telegram, State 247051, Secretary of State (Vance) to American Embassy, Port au Prince, October 15, 1977, Subject: "FSLN Attacks in Nicaragua," DFOIA; Department of State Briefing Memorandum, Confidential, William P. Stedman

nard Diederich, "was that the Sandinistas had for the first time shown themselves capable of launching coordinated attacks in diverse parts of the country and of achieving brief occupations of small towns from north to south."[2] In a number of these towns, FSLN actions triggered spontaneous mass uprisings, with guerrillas and civilians fighting side-by-side against the Guard.

Opposition to the Somoza regime was not confined to the guerrillas. The local capitalist class had become increasingly disillusioned over the dictator's economic policies and dynastic ambitions in the period since the December 1972 earthquake. The return of Somoza's Harvard-educated son ("Tachito III") to manage the family enterprises was interpreted by many in the business community as meaning "that Somoza was not planning for any interim figure between himself and Tachito Tres."[3] A State Department official monitoring these developments observed: "The Nicaraguan business community could live with Somoza himself but did not want to see the reigns of power passed on to Somoza's son."[4] The notion of "a dynasty 'Somoza forever' " was anathema to many entrepreneurs, who equated new possibilities for capital accumulation with access to political power. "The business community had a big piece of the economic pie and seemed very prosperous, but it knew it could do even better," said a knowledgeable U.S. Embassy officer. "It wanted a piece of the political action and Somoza wouldn't go for it."[5] After dining with a group of Nicaraguan business leaders at the Embassy residence in October 1976, a leading State Department Latin Americanist concluded "that Somoza had clearly lost the support of the business community."[6]

In the years following the earthquake, capitalist class discontent was also fueled by the ruling family's abuse of power for personal financial gain (for example, misappropriation of international reconstruction aid, nonpayment of import taxes), the rising public debt, electricity shortages, new taxes, increased prices for petroleum imports, industrial stagnation, and declining prices for coffee and cotton exports. The business community accused the regime of responsibility for stifling foreign investment by demanding family involvement in the most promising ventures. Nor was the situation helped by the lack of planning and coordination within public agencies, the inability

(ARA) to Deputy Secretary, October 14, 1977, Subject: "FSLN Attacks on Nicaragua, October 14," DFOIA.

2 Diederich, *Somoza and the Legacy of U.S. Involvement in Central America*, p. 146.
3 Interview with Thomas O'Donnell, Maryland, September 27, 1989.
4 Confidential telephone interview, Department of State official, Maryland, September 30, 1989.
5 Interview with James Cheek, Washington, D.C., September 18, 1989.
6 Confidential telephone interview, Department of State official, Washington, D.C., September 14, 1989.

of non-Somoza enterprises to compete with the dictator and his military-civilian cronies for state contracts, and the regime's monopoly over economic decisionmaking.[7] The resulting crisis in confidence translated into declining private investment, rising liquidity and savings, spiraling inflation, and capital flight, which reached $90 million during the last six months of 1977.[8]

Less than three months after the National Guard violently suppressed the October 1977 Sandinista military challenge to the dictatorship, Somoza confronted a new crisis that writ large the increasingly heterogeneous nature of the opposition movement. In early January 1978, members of the ruling clique apparently participated in the decision to assassinate the prominent anti-Somoza newspaper publisher and politician Pedro Joaquín Chamorro. The murder not only produced widespread popular outrage accompanied by riots and attacks against Somoza-owned enterprises, but also galvanized large sectors of the business community and a number of reformist political and labor organizations into direct confrontation with the dictatorship. These non-Sandinista forces coalesced to organize a general strike whose major strategic goal was to force Somoza from office.

Initially, the strike attained a high degree of effectiveness. In early February, however, the bourgeois leadership decided to push for an end to its political challenge on the grounds that: (1) the strike had failed to weaken Somoza's hold on political power, and (2) the situation was beginning to move beyond the control of the moderates and increasingly take on the appearance of a mass movement of workers against the regime – that is, a class struggle. Meanwhile, spontaneous insurrections, spearheaded by the urban poor with only minimal FSLN participation, erupted in a number of provincial cities, inducing more unease among Somoza's non-radical adversaries. The National Guard ruthlessly crushed these popular uprisings with little concern for the high number of non-combatant civilian casualties – further contributing to the regime's political isolation.

The failure of the general strike to topple Somoza began to shift public opinion toward the belief that only armed struggle could eventually achieve the opposition objective. In the following months, the Sandinistas sought to capitalize on this trend, stepping up their organizational activities in the cities and military operations in the countryside. At the same time, urban Nicaragua well and truly established itself as the locus of anti-government resistance. Mass demonstrations by the poor and unemployed, workers' strikes, and student unrest were common occurrences.[9] The American Embassy reported that June had seen "a plethora of labor activity" over wages

7 "Nicaraguan Businessmen Come Out Against Somoza," *Latin America Economic Report*, December 2, 1977, p. 231.
8 "Deepening Crisis Alarms Nicaraguan Private Sector," p. 133.
9 See Dennis Gilbert, *Sandinistas* (New York: Basil Blackwell, 1988). p. 9; Walker, *Nicaragua: The Land of Sandino*, p. 35.

and working conditions, continuing land takeovers which had now spread from the provinces to Managua, and confrontations between students and the National Guard "in most major cities...."[10] In July, seeking to consolidate mass support for its claim to the leadership of the anti-Somoza struggle, the FSLN established the United People's Movement (MPU) composed of newly formed mass organizations, labor unions, and left-wing political parties.

The conservative and moderate opposition, with Washington's encouragement, also moved to develop a structured, viable organizational presence that could compete for hegemony within the anti-dictatorial movement. In March 1978, Alfonso Robelo, a wealthy businessman with close ties to the BANIC economic group and U.S. multinationals, founded the Nicaraguan Democratic Movement (MDN), whose membership consisted primarily of small capitalists and members of the most highly-paid professions. But the MDN was saddled with a serious dilemma from the outset. On the one hand, it could not ignore the mass demand for Somoza's ouster; on the other, its capacity to achieve such a goal through its own actions was severely limited by the regime's economic and military power. In other words, the bourgeois opposition seemed incapable of changing the regime in the absence of pressure from either Washington or the Sandinistas.

Reluctant to intervene directly, the Carter White House encouraged its Nicaraguan allies to reach out to the center-left opposition in order to construct the broadest-based alternative to both Somoza and the most radical factions of the FSLN. In May, the MDN, the Democratic Liberation Union (UDEL), the liberal "Group of Twelve," and selected labor federations and opposition political parties amalgamated into the Broad Opposition Front (FAO). The most significant bourgeois absentees were BANIC and BANAMERICA. Both had consistently refused to participate in efforts to challenge Somoza on the grounds that the National Guard could rebuff any threat to the survival of the regime. Having been on the receiving end of Somoza's economic ambitions, neither was resolutely opposed to his ouster. But they preferred to plot with dissident high-ranking National Guard and government officials to achieve the common goal. Still, the FAO offered the Carter administration and the civilian opposition at least some hope of a non-revolutionary outcome to Nicaragua's crisis. On July 19, in a show of strength, the FAO organized a successful one day general strike that closed down 70 percent of businesses nationwide and 90 percent in Managua.[11]

The evolution of a national, mass-based polyclass movement, incorpo-

---

10 Department of State Telegram, Confidential Managua 3019, American Embassy (Solaun) to Secretary of State, July 3, 1978, Subject: "Continued Turmoil in Nicaragua," DFOIA.
11 "Nicaragua Strike," *Central America Report*, July 24, 1978, p. 231.

rating divergent political and ideological views, but lacking a high degree of coordination, did not produce a major reevaluation of U.S. policy prior to September 1978. Somoza's repeated and successful military crackdowns on the civilian and guerrilla opposition sustained the appearance, in the minds of American officials, of a regime well able to impose controls over an increasingly volatile population. Despite the rising level of political and military struggle after October 1977, the power of the National Guard and concern over a viable, acceptable alternative tempered U.S. initiatives that might have presumed a fundamental restructuring of Washington's historic relationship with the Somoza dynasty.

Human rights and Nicaragua: Pushing reforms "through" Somoza

When Carter entered the White House declaring his intention to elevate human rights to the center stage of U.S. foreign policy, he signaled that the executive branch would assume the leadership from Congress in this area. Human rights would "be actively pursued as a matter of legitimate U.S. policy interests."[12] The legislative framework for a more aggressive approach was already in place. The Harkin amendment terminated bilateral economic aid to highly repressive governments and instructed U.S. representatives to vote against loans from the regional development banks; in October 1977 this was extended to all multilateral development banks.[13]

Initial measures taken by the incoming administration to fulfil its promise included an upgrading of the State Department's Coordinator of the Office of Human Rights to Assistant Secretary (or full bureau) status and the establishment of an Interagency Group on Human Rights and Foreign Assistance (the "Christopher Committee") to examine U.S. bilateral and multilateral economic assistance programs in the context of human rights situations in the recipient countries. Yet, from the beginning, the symbolic gesture coexisted with the substantive act. "Quiet" or private diplomacy still remained the preferred means for confronting regimes deemed to be widespread human rights abusers. At the same time, the Carter White House, unlike Ford's, was more than willing to voice public criticism and apply aid sanctions if traditional diplomacy failed to produce the desired results. Dep-

---

12 Confidential interview, Department of State official, Virginia, September 20, 1989. The respondent was a senior official in the Bureau of Inter-American Affairs, 1978 to 1980.

13 For an excellent discussion of Congressional human rights legislation between 1975 and 1978, see W. Frick Curry and Joanne Royce, *Enforcing Human Rights: Congress and the Multilateral Banks* (Washington, D.C.: Center for International Policy, February 1985), pp. 1–11.

uty Assistant Secretary of State for Human Rights Mark Schneider described the approach as a "sequential and calibrated diplomatic strategy."[14] But it was one applied with considerable selectivity: Excluded from sanctions were such key Third World allies and "regional influentials" as Iran, Indonesia, Brazil, and the Philippines. Moreover it did not seek to challenge the origins or legitimacy of offending regimes, or the institutions upon which their power typically rested that were largely responsible for the violence. The fundamental aim of the diplomatic and economic pressures was to get these governments to assert greater control over their armed forces and police, and to eliminate the excessive use of force against the domestic opposition.[15]

The Carter approach toward Nicaragua and the other Central American dictatorships was symptomatic of a reluctance to translate human rights criticisms into measures prefiguring a fundamental change in bilateral ties. At the peak of their influence during 1977 and 1978, the human rights advocates within the executive branch did not preside over any decisive shift in economic relations between Washington and its subregional allies. Nicaragua was a perfect example of the anomalies that were a feature of the way in which the policy was applied in practice. Between November 1977 and May 1978, for instance, administration criticism of National Guard behavior was interspersed with votes in favor of three Nicaraguan loan requests to the World Bank and the Inter-American Development Bank totaling more than $62 million. That May, the "Christopher Committee" also recommended that the Agency for International Development (AID) proceed with five grants to the regime totaling $589,000.[16] Regarding military aid cutbacks to the dictatorships in Nicaragua, El Salvador and Guatemala, the trigger was always specific, discrete conflicts; such decisions never reflected any thought-out, consistent, or committed opposition to rule by the generals. Nor did the Carter White House take action to prevent Israel, its strategic Middle East ally, from substituting itself for the United States as the major foreign weapons supplier to these Central American regimes.

Despite this rather narrowly conceived approach to human rights, it still constituted a shift of sufficient proportion to engender resistance within key sectors of the foreign policy bureaucracy, principally the Departments of the Treasury and Defense, and among career officials in the Department

---

14 Quoted in Merritt, "Unilateral Human Rights Intercession: American Practice Under Nixon, Ford, and Carter," p. 46.
15 See James Petras, "President Carter and the 'New Morality,' " *Monthly Review*, Vol. 29, No. 2, June 1977, pp. 42–50.
16 Department of State Telegram, State 117777, Secretary of State to American Embassy, May 9, 1978, Subject: "Recommendations – Interagency Group on Human Rights and Foreign Assistance," DFOIA.

of State's geographic bureaus. Treasury officials were concerned that using human rights criteria to determine U.S. policy on loan requests to the multilateral development banks might be interpreted by member governments as an attempt "to politicize these institutions," thereby complicating efforts to achieve broader American foreign policy goals in these lending agencies.[17] As a result, although Treasury-appointed Executive Directors adhered to the letter of the law and voted against loans to human rights abusers, the agency "would not put pressure on these banks or their members to defeat or delay loans opposed by the United States."[18] The Pentagon considered the human rights policy an unwelcome intrusion on regional military assistance programs that could only weaken its influence or leverage over the armed forces of Third World allies. The head of the Department's Inter-American Region insisted that the Pentagon "always supported human rights but it didn't support the manner in which human rights were being implemented in Latin America. The Carter administration picked and chose who they were going to apply human rights to."[19] Another U.S. military official was less circumspect, saying Defense "was concerned about the application of the policy, why it was so arbitrarily applied to basically friendly nations."[20]

In the State Department, the political appointees in charge of the Bureau of Human Rights and Humanitarian Affairs (HA) conducted running battles with the five regional offices during 1977 and 1978 over foreign aid to repressive regimes – an internecine warfare characterized by turf battles, personality conflicts, and differing interpretations of the agency's diplomatic responsibilities and how best to manage and pursue bilateral relations. The career foreign service officers believed an excessive emphasis on human rights would only lead to the downgrading of "more objective national interests."[21] HA's Assistant Secretary Patricia Derian and her most senior advisors, however, repeatedly accused the regional bureaus of "overstat[ing] the extent of U.S. interests at stake in particular cases and the damage that could possibly result from failure to approve proposed security assistance."[22]

17 Quoted in Caleb Rossiter, *Human Rights: The Carter Record, The Reagan Reaction* (Washington, D.C.: Center for International Policy, September 1984), p. 18.

18 Interview with Richard Feinberg, Washington, D.C., October 17, 1988. The respondent was a member of the Policy Planning Staff, Department of State, 1977 to 1979. He also held previous positions in the Treasury Department.

19 Interview with Admiral Gordon Schuller, Virginia, September 20, 1988. The respondent was the Director of the Inter-American Region, Department of Defense, 1977 to 1980.

20 Confidential telephone interview, Department of Defense official, Maine, September 26, 1989.

21 Wade H.B. Matthews, *Human Rights and the National Interest: Our Policy in Central America and the Philippines.* Executive Seminar in National and International Affairs, Twenty-Second Session, Department of State, June 1980, p. 16.

22 Stephen B. Cohen, "Conditioning U.S. Security Assistance on Human Rights Practices,"

They coupled this criticism with an attack on State's annual country reports on human rights prepared by the geographic bureau officers, accusing the authors of "consistently underreport[ing]" abuses perpetrated by pro-U.S. governments in the Third World.[23]

Of all the regional bureaus, Inter-American Affairs and its then Assistant Secretary Terence Todman waged the most aggressively obstructionist campaign against the human rights policy during the early period of the Carter presidency. Todman adhered to "a traditional conception of realpolitik, that the U.S. needed to maintain alliances in Central America and that no single country was that important but the region as a whole was because of the proximity of Central America to the United States. Therefore, he was an advocate of maintaining alliances and of quiet diplomacy."[24] His principal deputy assistant William Stedman attacked the need to put "every single foreign policy operation through one single lens, which was human rights," terming "the exclusivity of this one approach...overbearing."[25] Todman opposed HA sanction proposals at every opportunity and was unwilling to brook any disagreement from his subordinates. Deputy Assistant Secretary Sally Shelton recalled one such experience involving a projected Nicaragua aid package under consideration by the "Christopher Committee":

> I was yanked off the Committee by Todman as a result of a virulent argument over economic assistance to Somoza. When he learned that I had encouraged either an abstention or a no vote or a suspension of some development project, he yelled at me that we should not use economic assistance to the poor to express our unhappiness with the political complexion of another government.[26]

Such reluctance to publicly pressure allies over their human rights records and Todman's repeated attempts to block aid cutbacks to autocratic governments in Latin America finally gave way to a full-blown attack on the human rights policy in a February 1978 speech to the Center for Inter-American Relations in New York City. The State Department leadership,

American Journal of International Law, Vol. 76, No. 2, April 1982, p. 260. Cohen was Deputy Assistant Secretary of State for Human Rights and Security Assistance, 1978 to 1980.

23 Ibid., p. 259.
24 Telephone interview with Mauricio Solaun, Illinois, September 15, 1989. The respondent was American Ambassador to Nicaragua, 1977 to 1979.
25 Ambassador William P. Stedman Jr., *oral history interview*, February 23, 1989, Association for Diplomatic Studies, Foreign Affairs Oral History Program, Lauinger Library, Georgetown University, Washington D.C., p. 54. The respondent was principal Deputy Assistant Secretary of State for Inter-American Affairs, 1977 to 1978.
26 Interview with Sally Shelton-Colby, Washington, D.C., October 12, 1988. The respondent was Deputy Assistant Secretary for Inter-American Affairs, Department of State, 1977 to 1978.

severely embarrassed by the outburst, decided it had no alternative but to move him to another position within the foreign policy bureaucracy. He was replaced by Viron Vaky and subsequently reassigned as U.S. Ambassador to Spain.[27]

The Carter administration's late January 1977 global agenda did not assign a high priority to Central America. Although "a broad review of our overall policy toward Latin America and the Caribbean" identified the sub-region as one of the "special country problems,"[28] more pressing concerns in other parts of the world ensured that hemispheric issues received limited attention from senior officials during 1977 and much of 1978. In the State Department bureaucracy, however, the new human rights emphasis guaranteed the region would loom larger in discussion. Advocates of "quiet diplomacy," for instance, accused Secretary of State Cyrus Vance's deputy Warren Christopher, Assistant Secretary for Human Rights Patricia Derian and others of targeting Central America as "a relatively cost-free area" in which to pursue an activist human rights policy:

> Some State Department officials in preparing a transition paper for the Carter administration, as well as some transition team officials, said that in Central America we had no vital interests and therefore Central America can be a great testing ground for the new administration's human rights policy (excluding Panama). Therefore, we can try and adopt a human rights policy almost to the exclusion of everything else in dealing with Central America.[29]

During the first twelve months of Carter's tenure, Nicaragua policy was almost exclusively filtered through the human rights prism. "Outside of this framework," writes Robert Pastor, the National Security Council's (NSC) Latin American staff specialist, "U.S. relations with Nicaragua received low priority."[30] Officials attributed the White House decision to pressure Somoza to curb human rights abuses rather than implement political and economic changes to the country's limited strategic importance and Carter's desire to avoid the interventionist policies associated with his predecessors.

---

27 For excerpts from Todman's speech, see Schoultz, *Human Rights and United States Foreign Policy Toward Latin America*, p. 118.
28 Presidential Review Memorandum/NSC-17, Secret, Zbigniew Brzezinski, National Security Council, to the Vice-President, Secretary of State, Secretary of Defense, et al., January 26, 1977, Subject: "Review of U.S. Policy Toward Latin America," National Archives, Washington, D.C.
29 Matthews, *Human Rights and the National Interest: Our Policy in Central America and the Philippines*, pp. 13–14; Interview with Wade Matthews, Washington, D.C., October 6, 1988. The respondent was the Director of Central American Affairs, Bureau of Inter-American Affairs, Department of State, 1977 to 1978.
30 Pastor, *Condemned to Repetition*, p. 52.

Discussing the former, American Ambassador to Panama Ambler Moss (1978–82) observed that Central America "had become a political backwater that didn't pose any threat to U.S. interests." This lack of concern produced a feeling within the administration that Somoza might well be "susceptible to reform if pushed hard enough by the human rights policy."[31] Another senior State Department official spoke of "a very strong reluctance" on the President's part to his government's being tagged with the interventionist label: "Having viewed the past U.S. exercise of power in Latin America as inappropriate, particularly Chile, intervening to alter a political system was a no no, even if it was a horrible political system. Intervening to protect human rights was acceptable...."[32]

As a designated human rights target, Nicaragua soon became a battleground between the State Department's warring parties. Assistant Secretary for Inter-American Affairs Terence Todman and the Director of the Office of Central American Affairs Wade Matthews charged that U.S. permanent interests were too "complex and subtle" to be allowed to fall under the influence of "a simplistic ideology, a good and evil moralistic sort of thing" like human rights. Washington "had neither the will nor the resources to decisively determine events in these countries." In such circumstances, they argued, it seemed "more efficacious to obtain the support of those in power to affect changes that would be beneficial to both sides." Applied to Nicaragua, this meant "that we should work with Somoza, encourage him, and give aid to encourage reform. Somoza could be encouraged to change if we adopted the right set of policies." To Patricia Derian and other Department advocates of a more aggressive approach, "working through Somoza" had already been "found wanting." Reforms were a forlorn hope unless the United States "moved away from the regime, sent signals to the opposition, and continued to get tough with Somoza."[33] This bureaucratic tug-of-war – within and between foreign policy agencies – did not produce a decisive and consistent approach in dealing with the Somoza dictatorship's human rights record. Instead, ambiguity, inconsistency, and contradiction became the order of the day.

Appearing before a Congressional committee in early April 1977, Deputy Assistant Secretary of State Charles Bray testified that "the Nicaraguan National Guard has used brutal and, at times, harshly repressive tactics in maintaining internal order." Since the beginning of 1976, the Ford and Carter administrations had made almost monthly diplomatic representations

31 Interview with Ambler Moss, Washington, D.C., September 21, 1988. The respondent was American Ambassador to Panama, 1978 to 1982.
32 Confidential interview, Department of State official, Washington, D.C., September 8, 1988. The respondent was a high-ranking Department official, 1977 to 1979.
33 Interview with Wade Matthews; interview with Sally Shelton-Colby.

"at the highest levels" to complain about human rights abuses. Bray then qualified his initial comments by describing the human rights picture in Nicaragua as "mixed" as well as "in some respects a stark one." The continuation of a state of siege (imposed in December 1974) and strict press censorship had to be weighed against the availability of legal remedies to redress grievances, a government decision to allow political exiles to return home, minimal constraints on freedom of association, and the apparent decline "in the number of abuses attributed to the National Guard and to other instrumentalities of the Nicaraguan Government over the past year."[34]

Taking into account this "mixed" picture, the administration requested Congressional passage of its fiscal year 1978 foreign aid authorization bill, which included $15.1 million in economic assistance (loans and grants) and $3.1 million in military aid ($2.5 million Foreign Military Sales credits and $600,000 training funds) for the Somoza regime. The State Department argued that the Nicaragua submission satisfied legislative requirements because it "focused on selected development bottlenecks and is designed to benefit the poor." Deputy Assistant Secretary Bray warned against any resort to aid sanctions because the only result would be to eliminate U.S. "leverage" on Somoza to push for reforms.[35]

The need for maximum flexibility was also trotted out by State officials to justify the administration's military assistance program. Any perceived strategic interest was given short shrift by Under Secretary of State for Security Assistance Lucy Benson during an appearance before a House Appropriations subcommittee. "What," asked Representative Clarence Long, "would be lost to the United States and would there be a violation of our security interests?" Benson's reply was succinct and revealing: "I cannot think of a single thing."[36]

Congressional debate on the foreign aid bill began in the House Appropriations subcommittee on Foreign Operations where Edward Koch, a liberal Democrat and leading Capitol Hill opponent of the Somoza regime, sponsored an amendment to ban all military assistance to Nicaragua. The amendment carried by a narrow majority. Prior to full House consideration of the entire bill, State Department officials verbally informed members of Koch's staff on three separate occasions that the administration would not

34 U.S. Congress, House, *Foreign Assistance and Related Agencies Appropriations for 1978, Part 3*, pp. 1–5.
35 Ibid.
36 U.S. Congress, House, Committee on Appropriations, Subcommittee on Foreign Operations and Related Agencies, *Foreign Assistance and Related Agencies Appropriations for 1978, Part 1*, 95th Congress, 1st Session, March 24, 1977 (Washington, D.C.: U.S. Government Printing Office, 1977), pp. 724, 748–749.

"actively lobby" to overturn his amendment.[37] Thus, Koch was surprised and angered to discover that on June 21, the day before the start of debate, Assistant Secretary Todman wrote to Clarence Long urging that the military package for Nicaragua be restored to the bill for national security reasons and because "there has been a marked decline in reports of human rights abuses attributed to the National Guard" over the past four months.[38] Koch denounced Todman's intervention in a letter to President Carter and reminded the White House of Benson's testimony before the same subcommittee that a military aid cutoff would not affect any American security interest in Nicaragua.[39] Unbeknownst to Koch, however, administration officials had approached a leader of the Congressional "Somoza lobby," conservative Texas Democrat Charles Wilson, prior to the Appropriations subcommittee vote, for help in retaining the military assistance program – for use as a lever to pressure Somoza to improve Nicaragua's human rights image.[40] If Wilson, together with long-time Somoza friend and ally John Murphy, the powerful chairman of the House Merchant Marine and Fisheries Committee, constantly opposed U.S. efforts to pressure Somoza to institute reforms, they were more than willing to lobby on the floor of the House of Representatives on behalf of Nicaragua's foreign aid program.

Wilson offered an amendment to the Foreign Assistance Appropriations Act to restore the administration's military aid request, which passed by a vote of 225 to 180 following a highly acrimonious debate. In the Senate, Edward Kennedy withdrew his amendment to terminate military aid to Nicaragua after being assured by the State Department that no monies or weapons would be released pending major human rights improvements and the full chamber followed the House example. Even though anti-Somoza legislators believed that financial sanctions would send an "unequivocal signal"[41] to the dictator that Washington was no longer prepared to maintain

37 Letter from Edward I. Koch, House of Representatives, U.S. Congress, to President Jimmy Carter, The White House, July 1, 1977.
38 *Security Assistance for Nicaragua.* Attachment with Letter from Terence A. Todman, Assistant Secretary for Inter-American Affairs, Department of State, to Clarence D. Long, Chairman, Subcommittee on Foreign Operations, Committee on Appropriations, House of Representatives, U.S. Congress, June 21, 1977.
39 Letter from Edward I. Koch to President Jimmy Carter, July 1, 1977. The State Department's Assistant Secretary for Congressional Affairs Robert McClosky made this same point in January 1976, more than a year prior to Benson's testimony, in response to a letter from Representative Koch: "We do not consider that the United States has any major strategic interests in Nicaragua.... The Department does, however, consider that our military assistance program assists us in sustaining a cooperative relationship with the Nicaraguan Government which has been mutually beneficial." Quoted in "The Koch-State Department Correspondence on U.S. Relations with Nicaragua," p. 88.
40 See Anthony Lake, *Somoza Falling* (Boston: Houghton Mifflin, 1989), p. 205.
41 Senator Edward Kennedy, quoted in *Congressional Record-Senate*, Vol. 123, Part 11, 95th Congress, 1st Session, August 5, 1977, p. S13915. For the entire debate on the 1978

traditional relations with repressive Third World allies, the combined forces
of the "Somoza lobby" and the State Department with its strictures on the
need for flexibility carried the day. Secretary of State Vance sought to mollify
the critics of military aid by insisting that no funds would be disbursed until
there was an "improvement in the human rights situation in Nicaragua."[42]

Paradoxically, while Secretary Vance, Under Secretary Benson, and other
State officials were preaching the advantages of "flexibility" in dealing with
the Nicaragua aid question, Bureau of Inter-American Affairs officers were
criticizing the policy on the grounds that it lacked flexibility and was even
"counterproductive." Wade Matthews leveled precisely this kind of attack
against the Bureau of Human Rights and Humanitarian Affairs (HA) over
its refusal to approve an export license for a U.S. company to replace non-
lethal rusted sling swivels on several thousand rifles sold to the National
Guard during the Ford presidency. Matthews contended that the timing of
the HA action, coming amid reports of Somoza successes in curbing National Guard abuses, justifiably raised the dictator's ire about Washington's
support for reforms. It had the result of making the Nicaraguan leader very
pessimistic about the likelihood of any "positive" Carter policy response no
matter how effective the crackdown on Guard violence against the civilian
population.[43]

In August 1977, the newly confirmed American Ambassador Mauricio
Solaun arrived in Managua with instructions "to implement our human
rights policy" and "avoid any commitment to either side." Instead of the
close embrace of the Nixon period, the Carter White House was intent on
"maintain[ing] a distance from the government, and establish[ing] broad,
active contacts with the unarmed opposition."[44] However, putting some
distance between Washington and Somoza, allowing the Embassy to cultivate a wide spectrum of anti-regime political and business figures, and even
making occasional public criticism of Somoza or the National Guard did

foreign assistance bill, see ibid., pp. S13907–13916. On the House debate, see *Congressional Record-House*, Vol. 123, Part 17, 95th Congress, 1st Session, June 23, 1977,
pp. 20574–20595, especially the comments by Edward Koch. The debate on the amendment to eliminate military assistance to Nicaragua for fiscal year 1978 is in *Congressional
Record-Senate*, Vol. 124, Part 22, 95th Congress, 1st Session, August 5, 1977, pp. 27440–
27449.

42 Department of State Telegram, State 148790, Secretary of State (Vance) to American
Embassy, June 25, 1977, Subject: "Press Release on U.S. Military Assistance to Nicaragua," DFOIA.

43 Matthews, *Human Rights and the National Interest: Our Policy in Central America and the
Philippines*, p. 17.

44 Quoted in Diederich, *Somoza and the Legacy of U.S. Involvement in Central America*, p. 144;
Mauricio Solaun, "Comment," in Alan Adelman and Reid Reading, eds., *Confrontation
in the Caribbean Basin* (University of Pittsburgh: Center for Latin American Studies, 1984),
p. 78.

not mean that the United States was contemplating more drastic measures or involvement in any opposition attempts to topple the dictator. Although Solaun was told "don't get too close" to the Nicaraguan leader,[45] the administration was reluctant to force the pace of regime change.

In early September, Vice President Walter Mondale told the President of the Nicaraguan Congress Cornelio Hüeck that the United States "[was] encouraged by the marked decrease in reported violations by the Nicaraguan National Guard."[46] Less than two weeks before the administration deadline for signing the aid agreement (September 30), Somoza lifted the state of siege that had been in force for almost three years. The State Department response was twofold: On the one hand, it applauded the move as a step in the right direction and certain to be viewed favorably when it came time to make a final decision on the economic and military aid package passed by Congress in August; on the other, officials wanted to signal the regime that it still had some way to go to satisfy Washington's human rights concerns.

On September 27, the "Christopher Committee" reconvened to discuss the fate of almost $14 million out of the $15.1 million AID economic program for Nicaragua (including rural education and nutritional assistance loans totalling $10.5 million) and also how the U.S. should vote on a $455,000 Inter-American Development Bank (BID) technical cooperation grant. State Department members Sally Shelton and Mark Schneider joined forces with the NSC's Robert Pastor to recommend deferring final action on the aid package until the next fiscal year to allow sufficient time to assess the genuineness of Somoza's new found commitment to eliminating National Guard abuses. According to Nicaragua Desk officer Daniel Welter, State in particular "did not want to seem to be overreacting to the lifting of the state of siege."[47] Warren Christopher, who "exercise[d] the ultimate authority" over the fate of each individual project,[48] concurred despite the

45 Anastasio Somoza, *Nicaragua Betrayed* (Boston and Los Angeles: Western Islands, 1980), p. 60.
46 White House Central Files, Department of State Memorandum, Peter Tarnoff, Executive Secretary, to Zbigniew Brzezinski, White House, Subject: "Vice-President's Meeting with Cornelio Hüeck, President of the Nicaraguan Congress [September 6, 1977]," Briefing Memorandum, Box 46, Folder: CO 108 1/20/77–1/20/81, Jimmy Carter Presidential Library, Atlanta, Georgia.
47 Quoted in Paul E. Sigmund and Mary Speck, "Virtue's Reward: The United States and Somoza, 1933–1978," Senior Conference, Hispanic Studies, June 8, 1978, reprinted in U.S. Congress, Senate, Committee on Foreign Relations, Subcommittee on Western Hemisphere Affairs, *Latin America*, 95th Congress, 2nd Session, October 4, 5 and 6, 1978 (Washington, D.C.: U.S. Government Printing Office, 1979), p. 211. Also see Department of State Telegram, Confidential Managua 5563, American Embassy (Solaun) to Secretary of State, December 9, 1977, Subject: "Interagency Group Decisions re Pending IFI Loans for Nicaragua," DFOIA.
48 This was the conclusion reached by a congressional study following interviews with committee members from State, Treasury, Defense, the Agency for International Develop-

objection of NSC official Jessica Tuchman that postponing "basic human needs" funds was tantamount to using aid as a political weapon. Justifying his decision to withhold the bulk of the package (except for some small grants to nongovernmental organizations), Christopher termed it part of Washington's goal to convince Somoza of the administration's commitment to human rights. He described the action as "a big enough signal for the time being." But, as *Washington Post* journalists John Goshko and Karen DeYoung observed, given the confusion generated by the decision in official U.S. circles it was unlikely that Somoza would divine the intended message.[49]

The Committee action provoked an immediate and angry response from Terence Todman. In a strongly worded memorandum to the Secretary's office, he expressed dismay over the failure to sign the agreement to release already appropriated funds, especially after Somoza had lifted martial law and loosened constraints on the mass media.[50]

In December 1977, the "Christopher Committee's" Working Group met to consider additional AID loan requests for Nicaragua. The Group concluded that proposed $296 million Small Farmers Enterprise and $60,000 Rural Women Leadership loans could be justified with reference to "basic human needs" criteria, and that a convincing case could be made for passage of three more loans totaling $300,000. Its final report, though, recommended that these and earlier AID proposals should all be considered "in context with" current Nicaraguan loan submissions to the Inter-American Development Bank.[51]

The administration debate over human rights and Nicaraguan aid programs also flared over what to do about the $3.1 million military assistance

ment, and the National Security Council. U.S. Congress, Senate, Committee on Foreign Relations, *Human Rights and U.S. Foreign Assistance,* Report prepared by the Congressional Research Service, Library of Congress, 96th Congress, 1st Session, November 1979 (Washington, D.C.: U.S. Government Printing Office, 1979), p. 41.

49 Quoted in John M. Goshko and Karen DeYoung, "U.S. Aid to Nicaragua: "Garbled" Rights Message," *Washington Post,* October 24, 1977, p. A8. Also see Karen DeYoung, "Nicaragua Denied Economic Aid, Gets Military," *Washington Post,* October 5, 1977, p. A10.

50 Department of State Action Memorandum No. 7725101, Terence A. Todman (ARA) to Acting Secretary of State, September 30, 1977, Subject: "Nicaragua AID Loans and Grants," DFOIA. In congressional testimony in March 1978, Todman contended that the Somoza regime had made "notable progress" in human rights during 1977. U.S. Congress, House, Committee on International Relations, Subcommittee on International Development, *Rethinking United States Foreign Policy Toward the Developing World: Nicaragua, Part II,* 95th Congress, 2nd Session, March 9, 1978 (Washington, D.C.: United States Government Printing Office, 1978), p. 8.

51 Department of State Memorandum on Nicaragua for January 20, 1978 meeting of the Christopher Group, Christopher Files, 81D 113, Box 8588, "Nicaragua II," Department of State, DFOIA.

authorization passed by Congress in June. In this case, postponement was not a solution. Agreements not signed in the current fiscal year were automatically canceled. This precipitated another bitter dispute between the State Department Bureaus of Human Rights, Inter-American Affairs and Politico-Military Affairs over the issue of aid to repressive Third World allies in general, and Nicaragua in particular. Human Rights officials opposed arms sales to regimes such as Somoza's in the belief they only served to enhance the ability of these autocratic rulers to entrench themselves in power and ignore calls for redemocratization. They argued that disbursement of the Nicaraguan military package would send the wrong signal to both the opposition and the regime: Undermining the former's morale and easing pressure on the latter to participate in negotiations to resolve the conflict. Inter-American Affairs and Politico-Military Affairs countered that each case should be assessed on its individual merits and not automatically rejected as lacking in merit.[52]

In the absence of a formal interagency mechanism for considering military aid issues, the State Department made sure it solicited the views of the Pentagon and other interested executive branch agencies before making a final determination. Tactical considerations ultimately carried the day. "We had to decide," Under Secretary Benson declared, "whether we were going to throw this weapon away or try to preserve it as a weapon of future leverage."[53] On September 29, 1977, the Department informed Somoza that it would sign the military agreement "in view of the diminution of charges of serious human rights abuses by the Nicaraguan National Guard over the past months and particularly in view of termination in Nicaragua of the state of siege."[54] But Deputy Secretary Christopher stipulated that all arms shipments would be withheld pending hard evidence of a continuing improvement in the human rights situation.

Daniel Welter attributed the administration's reluctance to simply terminate the military aid program to a continuing perception of Somoza as a reliable ally with whom the U.S. could still do business. Why? Because of his "close ties to the United States. He is West Point-educated and his son is a Harvard graduate. He's a leader we can bargain with and influence. To cut off all FMS [Foreign Military Sales] would have deprived us of some

---

52 See Schoultz, *Human Rights and United States Foreign Policy Toward Latin America*, pp. 330–331.
53 Quoted in Goshko and DeYoung, "U.S. Aid to Nicaragua: "Garbled" Rights Message," p. A8.
54 Department of State Noon Briefing, "Department Approval for Assistance to Nicaragua," cleared by Assistant Secretary Derian and Deputy Secretary Christopher (ARA), September 29, 1977, Christopher Files, 81D 113, Box 8588, "Nicaragua 1," Department of State, DFOIA.

valuable leverage."[55] Human Rights official Michelle Bova said the decision to sign but not disburse reflected a concern to avoid any precipitous action "that would reduce our flexibility in dealing with Somoza," and stressed the symbolic relevance of the measures taken: "The important thing is that Somoza has gotten the message and he's not at all happy about the situation."[56]

The civilian opposition was both encouraged and energized by the implications of Washington's action: Somoza could no longer automatically expect U.S. support to consolidate his political rule. Yet, it was still not possible to speak of a consistent American policy. Accompanying this decision to withhold military aid was a State Department agreement to release an assignment of 5,000 M16 rifles valued at almost $800,000, negotiated with the Ford administration and in the pipeline during the presidential transition.

Amid Washington's limited efforts to pressure Somoza to liberalize his regime, a Sandinista-led nationwide uprising in October 1977 revealed growing political disaffection with the Somoza dictatorship and revived the prospects of the guerrilla movement emerging as a viable alternative to the government – a pole around which a still disparate, unstructured, and uncoordinated movement could cohere. To avoid such an outcome, American Ambassador Mauricio Solaun began advocating a more activist U.S. collaboration with the conservative anti-regime forces in the hope of exerting sufficient pressure on Somoza to accept a timetable for redemocratization and possibly relinquish power before (but no later than) May 1981. His superiors were not convinced, more or less pouring cold water on the whole idea. During State Department meetings in late 1977, Solaun's proposal that the United States work more closely with Somoza's Nationalist Liberal Party (PLN) and the centrist opposition to open up the political system and accelerate the process of regime change met a wall of opposition. Some termed it unrealistic; others, like Terence Todman, were still convinced that Somoza was strong enough to overcome any internal challenge, and believed the administration should not participate in any joint action with his civilian protagonists. The only support for the Ambassador's idea came from some junior career officers in Inter-American Affairs who thought that Somoza's power rested on a more fragile base than was generally appreciated, that his regime could not survive indefinitely, and that the United States should act to speed up the process of political transition.[57]

55 Quoted in Sigmund and Speck, "Virtue's Reward: The United States and Somoza, 1933–1978," p. 213.
56 Quoted in Ibid., pp. 211, 214.
57 See Shirley Christian, *Nicaragua: Revolution in the Family*, (New York: Vintage Books, 1986) pp. 52–53; Pastor, *Condemned to Repetition*, p. 59.

The Carter refusal to go substantially beyond human rights criticisms during 1977 and the first half of 1978 reflected a belief that it was still possible to pursue reforms "through" the client regime. The prevailing (official) wisdom also extended to Somoza's continuing firm hold on political power, based on one of the most formidable coercive structures in the hemisphere. In any event, as the dictator told a group of church and private sector leaders in late 1977, he had no intention of voluntarily relinquishing office before his term expired in May 1981.

The inconsistencies and contradictions that were so much a part of the application of the human rights policy to Nicaragua must also be seen in the context of a White House and State Department reluctant to become involved in a visible, public effort to change the government, especially in the perceived absence of a satisfactory political alternative. The known client was preferable to the possible negative consequences of an immediate regime change. The activities of the Congressional "Somoza lobby" and a high-powered team of public relations consultants based in Washington further constrained the administration from contemplating any measures that might prematurely destabilize a longstanding ally and threaten U.S. permanent interests in Nicaragua and Central America.

When the "Christopher Committee" reconvened on January 20, 1978 to discuss the Nicaraguan situation it noted some improvement in National Guard behavior but refused to identify "a positive human rights trend" or change the existing designation of the regime as "a repressive one" on the grounds of continuing reports of military abuses against the civilian population.[58] Within State, however, the gap between the human rights advocates and the Latin Americanists over aid policy remained as wide as ever. A draft paper prepared by Inter-American Affairs for the January 20 meeting highlighted the benefits the U.S. derived from its relationship with the Somoza dictatorship; human rights was almost an afterthought. The document summarized the key objectives of American policy as follows: maintenance of a favorable trade and investment climate; ensuring the continuation of Somoza's "consistently strong support for [the] U.S. position in international forums" and the regime's role in preserving subregional stability "and [the] protection of U.S. flanks"; avoiding any interruption to the "mutually beneficial and cooperative relations" between the two countries; and promoting improvements in the human rights situation.[59]

58 Department of State Memorandum on Nicaragua for January 20, 1978 meeting of the Christopher Group.
59 Department of State, Meeting on Nicaragua, January 20, 1978, Christopher Files, 81D 113, Box 8588, "Nicaragua II." Attachment: Country Paper, "Nicaragua," drafted by ARA, January 12, 1978, Department of State, DFOIA.

The Chamorro assassination and the rise of mass mobilization politics: Washington's ambivalent response

The regime's involvement in the January 1978 assassination of newspaper publisher and prominent opposition leader Pedro Joaquín Chamorro became the trigger for major political realignments inside Nicaragua, accelerating movement toward the creation of a pre-insurrectionary situation. Still wedded to the human rights "through Somoza" policy, this event, observed Assistant Secretary of State Viron Vaky in a masterpiece of understatement, "was not fully appreciated by the administration."[60]

In Managua, Chamorro's murder sparked mass demonstrations and riots, including attacks on Somoza-owned enterprises and some U.S. firms. A senior American executive in Citibank's local branch recalled the occasion: "Our offices at the time were directly across the street from *La Prensa* and in the fighting that followed part of our branch was burned, but not intentionally. They were going after a Somoza-owned bank. In the turmoil they torched the [Somoza] bank and our building also burnt down. It was clear [to the U.S. business community] that the Chamorro assassination had changed things dramatically and permanently for the worse."[61] Determined to bring an end to the dictatorship, a coalition of business, political, and labor leaders issued an immediate call for a general strike. An official of the centrist Democratic Liberation Union (UDEL), originally founded by Chamorro, emphasized that the coalition's goal was to change the regime, not the state: "We have made it clear we are not opposed to the National Guard."[62] Although one private sector "influential" told the U.S. Embassy he doubted the strike could sustain itself for any length of time in the absence of a single dynamic figure around which conservatives and moderates could rally, within 48 hours (January 23 to 24) approximately 80 percent of Managua's commercial and industrial establishments closed their doors – forcing the heart of the nation's economy to a virtual standstill. The summons to strike achieved equally successful results in the large provincial cities of León, Granada, Chinandega, and Matagalpa.[63] Reporting on the

---

60 Interview with Viron Vaky, Washington, D.C., September 15, 1988. The respondent was Assistant Secretary for Inter-American Affairs, Department of State, 1978 to 1979.
61 Telephone interview with William Dewey, Florida, October 17, 1988. The respondent was second-in-command of Citibank's Nicaragua branch, 1977 to 1979.
62 Quoted in Diederich, *Somoza and the Legacy of U.S. Involvement in Central America*, p. 159.
63 See Department of State Telegram, Confidential Managua 0340, American Embassy (Solaun) to Secretary of State, January 24, 1978, Subject: "Closure of Businesses Continues," DFOIA; Department of State Telegram, Confidential Managua 0371, American Embassy (Solaun) to Secretary of State, January 25, 1978, Subject: "General Strike Called," DFOIA; Foreign Broadcast Information Service, *Daily Report: Latin America*, January 25, 1978, p. 6.

status of this national mass mobilization against the regime at the end of its first week, an Embassy official cabled the State Department that it continued "effective" in Managua, León, Granada and Chinandega.[64]

The Chamorro assassination significantly widened the cracks that had already developed between the Nicaraguan bourgeoisie and the regime. On January 24, the Nicaraguan Development Institute (INDE), the Nicaraguan Chamber of Industries, the Nicaraguan Chamber of Construction, the Managua Chamber of Commerce, and four other prominent business organizations issued a joint communique in support of the strike. Even the two most powerful non-Somoza economic groups, Banco de América (BANAMERICA) and Banco de Nicaragua (BANIC), which had taken no part in opposition political activities, were apparently only restrained from joining the strike movement because "the[ir] Association as a whole [would] not take a stand owing to the objection of foreign [primarily U.S.] and Somoza-owned or controlled banks."[65] The scope and depth of the opposition moved Ambassador Solaun to comment in a message to the State Department that, irrespective of the final outcome, the strike "has already demonstrated that Somoza is no longer in as complete control of events in Nicaragua as he was six or seven months ago, say."[66]

On February 1, sixteen private sector organizations issued a statement denouncing the lack of progress in the Chamorro murder investigation and the failure to halt National Guard abuses, and called for a return to democracy. At the same time, however, the business community was starting to become uneasy over the direction in which the strike was moving. Of particular concern was the growth in worker militancy which, if allowed to proceed unchecked, might conceivably transform this effort to overthrow the dictatorship into an anti-capitalist movement as well. A growing resolve to end the strike, the American Ambassador reported, "was apparently stiffened by the walkout of many National Bank and Ministry of Agriculture employees. The increasingly militant behavior of workers, both in government and private firms, indicates work stoppage is evolving from being mostly a lockout into becoming a genuine strike."[67] Public sector workers staged mass walkouts and many employees of large private industrial and commercial firms rebuffed management entreaties to resume operations, contending that "their strike is not against management but against the

64 Department of State Telegram, Confidential Managua 0425, American Embassy (Freres) to Secretary of State, January 27, 1978, Subject: "Report on Status of General Strike," DFOIA.
65 Department of State Telegram, Confidential Managua 0397, American Embassy (Solaun) to Secretary of State, January 26, 1978, Subject: "Strike Enters Fourth Day," DFOIA.
66 Department of State Telegram, Confidential Managua 0371.
67 Department of State Telegram, Confidential Managua 0525, American Embassy (Solaun) to Secretary, February 2, 1978, Subject: "National Strike Developments, DFOIA.

Somoza regime."[68] Taken aback by this unanticipated development, the owners of capital began to reconsider their position: "[The Embassy] impression is that many firms who originally backed the strike are having second thoughts about what forces they may have unleashed, i.e., Nicaragua workers who heretofore have been poorly organized may now realize their potential strength and apply it against management on future occasions."[69] On February 4, Ambassador Solaun cabled Washington that the private sector had decided to abandon the strike, fearful "that their workers may be getting out of hand."[70]

Despite its failure to achieve Somoza's ouster, the general strike exposed a regime that lacked legitimacy among a large, heterogeneous segment of the Nicaraguan population. The U.S. Embassy questioned whether a government as politically isolated as Somoza's could serve out its term of office, notwithstanding its impressive military capabilities: "The GON [Government of Nicaragua] can no longer credibly claim its only opposition is from revolutionaries and small groups of political oppositionists. To the extent that the anti-GON [Government of Nicaragua] protest constitutes a plebiscite, the results appear to have been a large majority of the urban population of all cities expressing support for the challenge to the GON [Government of Nicaragua]." While this time around a loyal and disciplined National Guard had enabled Somoza to overcome his most serious political challenge to date, the Ambassador was not sanguine about the regime's long-term prospects. "Although the appearance of normality has returned," he cautioned the State Department in a February 10 cable, "the situation has not returned to the status quo ante and likely will not."[71] He expected the political and social polarization to worsen, triggering new challenges to the autocratic dynasty: "Whether [Somoza] can continue to maintain firm control over the GON [Government of Nicaragua] and the GN [National Guard] to 1981 is problematic."[72]

Of particular concern to Solaun was the looming presence of the Sandinista National Liberation Front (FSLN) in the context of the failure of the general strike to topple Somoza. He singled out two "apparently well

68 Department of State Telegram, Confidential Managua 0529, American Embassy (Solaun) to Secretary of State, February 2, 1978, Subject: "Nationwide Strike Enters Tenth Day," DFOIA.

69 Department of State Telegram, Confidential Managua 0558, American Embassy (Solaun) to Secretary of State, February 3, 1978, Subject: "Strike Situation at Crucial Point?," DFOIA.

70 Department of State Telegram, Confidential Managua 0562, American Embassy (Solaun) to Secretary of State, February 4, 1978, Subject: "Uncertainty and Frustration Mount," DFOIA.

71 Department of State Telegram, Confidential Managua 0707, American Embassy (Solaun) to Secretary of State, February 10, 1978, Subject: "Watchful Waiting," DFOIA.

72 Department of State Telegram, Confidential Managua 0562.

executed" hit and run attacks against the National Guard that "coincided with the faltering in the peaceful protest movement. Thereby they identify themselves with the movement to overthrow Somoza but only after non-violent protest has fallen short of its goal." Such military actions have gained the FSLN "increased sympathy" and simultaneously put the regime on notice that it "is still a serious challenge and the pressures that can be brought to bear on the GON [Government of Nicaragua] come from a wide spectrum."[73]

In the post-strike period, Somoza moved swiftly to shore up the Guard's authority and battle-readiness and avoid the possibility of defections through promotions, pay increases, and a decision to expand the number of troops eligible to attend the elite Basic Infantry Training School.[74] Efforts to solve his two other most pressing problems – the economy and the Sandinistas – proved more difficult. A return to economic normalcy had to contend with the ongoing political crisis, the business community's anxiety over possible reprisals for participating in the general strike and the growing influence of the FSLN, and the worsening debt-trade-fiscal situation.[75] What to do about the Sandinistas was not just the subject of concern and debate in Managua.

The scope and depth of the January upheaval visibly surprised U.S. pol-icymakers, renewing the interagency debate over whether a more activist U.S. involvement would produce a quicker solution to the conflict than the current "distancing and reforms" approach. However, many Inter-American Affairs officials were still basically unwilling to concede any significant ero-sion of Somoza's hold on power, and remained optimistic about his com-mitment to political change, much to the surprise of a visiting Embassy official: "I came up and talked to people in the State Department and said I felt there was a 50/50 chance that Somoza would not last out 1978, and that the odds were against him lasting out 1979. But the Bureau people said 'oh no, he was going to have elections in 1980.' The Bureau was optimistic that we would get elections and something would happen."[76] Even though Assistant Secretary Todman and his deputy Wade Matthews "were taken aback by the assassination and the national revulsion that followed," Todman was reluctant to abandon a planned visit "in the midst of wide-

73 Ibid.
74 See Richard Millett, "From Somoza to the Sandinistas: The Roots of Revolution in Nicaragua," in Wolf Grabendorff. et al. eds., *Political Change in Central America: Internal and External Dimensions* (Boulder: Westview Press, 1984), p. 44.
75 "The predominant psychological attitude among private sector elements, insofar as we can gauge it, remains one of tension and fear...." Department of State Telegram, Con-fidential Managua 0619, American Embassy (Solaun) to Secretary of State, February 9, 1978, Subject: "Strike Seems Nearly Over," DFOIA.
76 Confidential interview, Department of State official, Washington, D.C., October 3, 1990 (American Embassy, Nicaragua, 1976 to 1978).

spread rioting that followed Chamorro's assassination," and only did so under pressure from his superiors.[77]

Nonetheless, Chamorro's assassination and its aftermath, as one Department official put it, "opened up a wider administration debate over what to do about Nicaragua," including a reassessment of "the possibilities for a change of government."[78] Nicaragua policy was the only agenda item at a mid-February 1978 meeting in the State Department attended by the NSC's Robert Pastor and senior State officials from Inter-American Affairs, Humanitarian Affairs, and Policy Planning. There was no clearcut consensus over the best way to proceed. Some argued that the situation would almost inevitably deteriorate unless the United States pressured Somoza to negotiate with the leaders of the civilian opposition. Those skeptical of this approach worried out loud about the possible negative consequences for American policy if an initiative of this kind failed to achieve its objective. Among State officials there was also support for getting Somoza to leave office before his term expired on the grounds that otherwise the current moderate leadership of the anti-dictatorial movement "would become more radicalized and increasingly threatening to American interests." For the time being, Warren Christopher decided against any shift in the existing policy.[79] Secretary Vance cabled Ambassador Solaun to "avoid being seen to be propping up Somoza government or supporting efforts by the opposition to unseat Somoza."[80]

Once it became apparent that the general strike was not going to force Somoza from office, members of the local business community turned to the American Embassy for help in their efforts to change the regime. The Ambassador, although a confirmed advocate of "the U.S. playing a mediating role in the conflict," was under strict instructions from State "that the Embassy could not mediate or even serve as a messenger" between the protagonists. Thus, he was forced to parry opposition appeals for support under the cover of "neutrality" – a stance that confused and frustrated Washington's bourgeois allies. To them it indicated a lack of understanding of the dynamics of the unfolding political struggle. Solaun elaborated:

> In the light of my instructions, I did not promise that we would get Somoza out or discourage them from the path they were taking. I told them we were not going to intervene. The business community was very upset. They did not understand why we could not intervene but

77 Interview with Sally Shelton-Colby.
78 Confidential interview, Department of State official, September 8, 1988.
79 See Lake, *Somoza Falling*, pp. 26, 39–42.
80 Department of State Telegram, Secret State 41757, Secretary of State (Vance) to American Embassy, February 16, 1978, Subject: "Role of U.S. Embassy in Nicaragua," DFOIA.

could interfere through preaching reforms. They felt Somoza would not give up power without American pressure. They couldn't understand U.S. policy and why the U.S. government wouldn't deliver in view of the fact that Venezuela, Costa Rica, etc. were helping. They could not believe U.S. policy.[81]

The White House refused to become directly involved in attempts to terminate the dictatorship and remained opposed to even brokering (as distinct from encouraging) a dialogue between Somoza and the moderate-conservative opposition. "We've quite clearly put some distance between ourselves and Somoza," a State Department official observed, "but we don't want to shift from a policy of actively backing Somoza to a stance of actively seeking this overthrow."[82] Another, on the "Seventh Floor," put it even more succinctly: "Our focus was on Somoza and attempts to find some way to achieve a better government rather than to oust him."[83]

One of the concerns uppermost in the minds of senior U.S. policymakers was the importance of avoiding a premature transition. Like President Kennedy's sentiments about the Dominican Republic at the time of the Trujillo assassination in 1961, a return to political democracy was the preferred alternative, but the continuation of Somoza rule had to be supported if it meant blocking the likelihood of an FSLN victory. In early February, as the guerrillas were beginning to substitute themselves for the general strike, one American official commented: "There is no telling what would fall out if Somoza was toppled."[84]

By acquiescing to Somoza's determination to serve out his current term, while reserving the right to discreetly criticize the more repressive and brutal aspects of National Guard behavior, the U.S. hoped to establish the necessary groundwork for an eventual peaceful political transition dominated by "responsible" anti-regime forces. Instead of public pressure, therefore, the White House settled for a more low key triple-track approach: private diplomacy, selective public pronouncements on human rights abuses, and the "carrot and stick" of economic assistance. It supported Venezuelan efforts to get Somoza to endorse a visit by the Inter-American Human Rights Commission (IAHRC) of the Organization of American States but distanced itself from a proposal by Venezuelan President Carlos Andrés Pérez that the regional organization be asked publicly to investigate the

81 Telephone interview with Mauricio Solaun.
82 Quoted in Graham Hovey, "Venezuela to Urge Investigations by O.A.S. of the Somoza Regime," *New York Times*, February 8, 1978, p. 3.
83 Confidential telephone interview, Department of State official, California, September 18, 1989. The respondent was a senior Department policymaker, 1977 to 1981.
84 Quoted in "U.S. Risks Toppling an Ally in Nicaragua 'Test Case,'" *Miami Herald*, February 8, 1978, p. 7B.

human rights situation in Nicaragua. "Quiet diplomacy" was still the preferred option.[85]

The Nicaraguan human rights-aid question resurfaced in February 1978 when the State Department presented its annual country report to Congress, noting a decline in the number of reported National Guard abuses over the preceding twelve months. In follow-up testimony, Deputy Assistant Secretary Sally Shelton told a House International Relations Subcommittee that "marked progress," including the lifting of martial law, influenced the administration to sign the Foreign Military Sales (FMS) agreement "so as to allow us to retain the option of providing these military credits, if circumstances warranted."[86] For fiscal year 1979, though, the White House would only request $150,000 in military training grants and $3,000 for "supply operations" for Nicaragua. Some career Latin Americanists in State criticized this minuscule funding package as harsh punishment of a traditional and friendly ally, especially in light of the Department's stated belief that political repression had "markedly diminished" over the past year.[87] Remarked one of these dissenting officials: "The issue is not human rights. The objective is the ouster of Somoza."[88]

In terms of the overall policy approach, the proposed reduction in the military aid program was less significant than the failure to terminate the program completely. Even a small amount of aid was fraught with symbolic overtones: Washington was telegraphing not only its continuing reluctance to break relations with the regime but also with the most important of all the state institutions. During her Congressional testimony, Shelton stressed the importance of the bilateral military relationship to Central American stability and U.S. regional collective security (Rio Treaty) commitments, and spoke of the need "to maintain our cooperative political relationship" with a government that had consistently supported U.S. positions in the United Nations, the Organization of American States, and other key forums.[89]

In Nicaragua, the moderate opposition was becoming increasingly vocal in attacking what it viewed as the disproportionate emphasis in American policy on the human rights issue to the seeming exclusion of far more serious

85   See Hovey, "Venezuela to Urge Investigations by O.A.S. of the Somoza Regime," p. 3.
86   U.S. Congress, House, Committee on International Relations, Subcommittee on International Organizations, *Foreign Assistance Legislation for Fiscal Year 1979, Part 4*, 95th Congress, 2nd Session, February 15, 16, 28; March 7 and 8, 1978 (Washington, D.C.: U.S. Government Printing Office, 1978), p. 127.
87   Quoted in "Arms Cutoff Sparks Policy Fight," *Miami Herald*, February 24, 1978, p. 22A. Also see John M. Goshko, "Nicaraguan Human Rights Situation Caught in a Crossfire," *Washington Post*, February 17, 1978, p. A22.
88   Quoted in "Arms Cutoff Sparks Policy Fight," p. 22A.
89   U.S. Congress, House, *Foreign Assistance Legislation for Fiscal Year 1979, Part 4*, p. 128.

problems: political polarization and spreading radicalization among wage workers, the poor and unemployed, students, and other segments of the urban population, and "periodic" land invasions, some involving more than a thousand campesinos.[90] With the most politically and ideologically diverse forces demanding Somoza's ouster, the hegemonic power's apparent belief that elections in 1981 would provide the solution to the crisis also came in for severe criticism. "Washington seems to have lost touch with events here," lamented a businessman who identified with the moderate opposition. "It's talking about human rights when people here are calling for arms to overthrow the dictatorship. This situation can't last until 1981."[91]

American policy was caught in a dilemma. Its closest allies were seemingly incapable of politically or militarily affecting a regime change while support for the anti-system FSLN was growing apace. Efforts during April to promote a coup by dissident Guard officers came to nothing.[92] Hoping to isolate the Sandinistas and improve the standing of its allies, Washington shifted policy gears slightly, repeating its call for negotiations between the moderate and conservative opposition and Somoza but also prodding the latter to consider some form of power-sharing arrangement. The U.S. Embassy encouraged the formation of the Broad Opposition Front (FAO) in May 1978, impressing upon wealthy business and conservative political leaders such as Alfonso Robelo and Adolfo Calero that without a structured organization and a coherent, thought-out strategy, their constituencies were unlikely to survive as influential actors in opposition or government.[93]

Having overcome the latest challenge to his authority through the application of overwhelming force, Somoza exuded confidence in his ability to serve out his term of office. At a meeting with Ambassador Solaun in early May, he dismissed calls for his resignation as U.S. "inspired," and contended that his bargaining position had been considerably strengthened by recent developments: Post-strike measures had reinforced the Guard's loyalty, the family business enterprises were flourishing, and there was a marked improvement in the government's economic and financial position. Acknowledging Somoza's "political strength," Solaun broached the possibility of rescheduling the next presidential elections for 1980 "as a compromise with demands for his early resignation." Somoza said that he might be

---

90 See Alan Riding, "Nicaraguan Dissidents Say U.S. Does Not Appreciate Gravity of Crisis," *New York Times*, March 5, 1978, p. 14; Department of State Telegram, Managua 2277, American Embassy (Solaun) to Secretary of State, May 17, 1978, Subject: "Nicaragua – Tense and Uncertain," DFOIA.

91 Quoted in Riding, "Nicaraguan Dissidents Say U.S. Does Not Appreciate Gravity of Crisis," p. 14.

92 See Stephen M. Gorman, "Nicaragua," in Melvin Gurtov and Ray Maghroori, *Roots of Failure: United States Policy in the Third World* (Westport: Greenwood Press, 1984), p. 134.

93 See Christian, *Nicaragua: Revolution in the Family*, p. 69.

willing to advance the election date but repeated his oft-stated position that under no circumstances would he leave office before May 1981.[94]

In May 1978, the administration once more revealed the confused and contradictory nature of its human rights policy toward Nicaragua when it released the $10.5 million AID loans for education and health projects held over from the previous year. The decision was occasioned not by any dramatic decline in National Guard abuses but over fear that the Congressional "Somoza lobby" would sabotage the foreign aid program and passage of the Panama Canal Treaty legislation. Led by influential conservative Democrats Charles Wilson and John Murphy, the dictator's supporters on Capitol Hill had worked tirelessly "to force the administration to lay off Somoza," achieving some victories along the way.[95] In his capacity as a member of the House Appropriations Committee, Wilson had previously shown that he was not given to idle threats when he persuaded the Committee to block a White House request for increased U.S. contributions to the multilateral development banks. Therefore, on informing the White House official in charge of foreign economic policy, Henry Owen, that no part of the 1979 foreign aid bill could be considered safe from attack if the AID loans for Nicaragua were not disbursed, Owen needed no convincing that this was "a credible threat" – an assessment he quickly conveyed to Deputy Secretary of State Warren Christopher.[96]

The Panama Canal Treaty legislation, which had to pass through the House Merchant Marine and Fisheries Committee chaired by longtime Somoza crony John Murphy, was a considerably higher White House priority than Nicaragua. Given the importance President Carter attached to passage of this legislation, he was prepared "to make concessions to the pro-Somoza lobby which overruled some actions taken by the Christopher Committee." According to Deputy Assistant Secretary of State for Inter-American Affairs John Bushnell, "one set of issues that President Carter overrode the Christopher Committee on dealt with the two AID loans. The President agreed that those loans that fell within the realm of basic human needs would go ahead." In Bushnell's opinion, however, "a credible case could be made that one of these loans was not a basic human needs loan." Nonetheless, "the President had already decided to release the two loans before they were debated in the Committee."[97] Carter officials insisted that

94 Department of State Telegram, Confidential Managua 2163, American Embassy (Solaun) to Secretary of State, May 10, 1978, Subject: "Amb[assador] Conversation with Somoza – May 8," DFOIA.
95 Interview with John Bushnell, Washington, D.C., September 8, 1988. The respondent was Deputy Assistant Secretary for Inter-American Affairs, Department of State, 1978 to 1981. Also see Lake, *Somoza Falling*, pp. 205–206.
96 Quoted in Pastor, *Condemned to Repetition*, pp. 65–66. Also see John M. Goshko, "U.S. Frees Aid to Nicaragua in a Policy Reversal," *Washington Post*, May 16, 1978, p. A18.
97 Interview with John Bushnell.

this decision did not constitute "an expression of political support for Somoza."[98]

In mid-May, the State Department also reversed itself on a blocked $160,000 loan to Nicaragua for the purchase of military hospital equipment. On this occasion, Congressman Wilson waged another successful campaign, again exploiting the foreign aid bill "pressure point" in meetings with Christopher and other Department officials. His message was blunt and threatening: "that we release the funds for Nicaragua, if we know what's good for us...."[99]

More disturbing to opponents of the dictatorship was President Carter's idea in June to send a personal letter of encouragement following Somoza's announcement that he proposed to invite an IAHRC mission to visit Nicaragua, would consider ratifying the Inter-American Convention of Human Rights, expressed a willingness to negotiate with the opposition over amnesty for political prisoners, and declared that the "Group of Twelve" were free to return from exile. In a memorandum to Robert Pastor, NSC Advisor Zbigniew Brzezinski wrote that the President wanted "a message...prepared for him to send Somoza encouraging these moves."[100]

The State Department response – in the Secretary's office and the relevant Bureaus – was exceedingly cool and unenthusiastic on the grounds that such an initiative ran counter to the basic thrust of American policy over the preceding 18 months. Under Secretary for Political Affairs David Newsom appended a number of critical comments to the first draft of the letter prepared by the NSC's Pastor. The Department expressed additional reservations about a second draft authored by the President himself but was instructed to transmit this version to Ambassador Solaun for presentation to Somoza. Neither Secretary Vance nor Assistant Secretary Vaky wanted the letter (dated June 30) forwarded to Managua. But none of Carter's senior foreign policy officials (including Brzezinski) was willing to personally argue the case with a President whose mind seemed made up. The most State could do was delay sending the letter for almost a month on the outside chance that the White House would have a change of heart.[101]

Finally, resigned to the inevitable, the Seventh Floor instructed Ambassador Solaun to deliver the communication to the Nicaraguan dictator. It

98 Quoted in Alan Riding, "Somoza and His Foes Both Looking to U.S. for Aid," *New York Times*, July 26, 1978, p. 3.
99 Quoted in Karen DeYoung, "Somoza's Friends in Congress Seen Threatening Aid Bill," *Washington Post*, July 26, 1978, p. A19. Also see Goshko, "U.S. Frees Aid to Nicaragua in a Policy Reversal," p. A18.
100 White House Central Files, Memorandum, Zbigniew Brzezinski to Robert Pastor, June 21, 1978, Subject: "Human Rights in Nicaragua," Box 46, Folder: CO III 1/1/78–12/31/78, Jimmy Carter Presidential Library.
101 See Pastor, *Condemned to Repetition*, pp. 67–68; John M. Goshko, "Carter Letter to Somoza Stirs Human-Rights Row," *Washington Post*, August 1, 1978, pp. A1, A9.

lauded Somoza for the human rights initiatives he was "considering" (for example, an amnesty for political prisoners, electoral reforms) but had not actually put into practice. This, at a time when the State Department was receiving new reports of an increase in National Guard violations and abuses.[102] One telegram from Ambassador Solaun, dated July 7, noted that although the regime "appears to be actively moving to improve its image," prior to upcoming visits by Amnesty International and the United Nations Human Rights Commission, "the usual pattern of protest demonstrations, arrests and allegations of disappearances continued into June [accompanied by] a tendency of the GN [National Guard] to over-react."[103]

Ever the opportunist, Somoza used the letter to deflect hemispheric pressures on him to institute changes or resign from office. The most prominent "casualty" was Venezuelan President Carlos Andrés Pérez. At a secret meeting between the two heads of state in August 1978, Pérez said "that he and Jimmy Carter had decided that Somoza must shape up or get out. But with that," Pérez told a senior Inter-American Affairs official, "Somoza pulled this letter from Carter out of his pocket. Carlos Andrés Pérez thought he had been sandbagged, double-dealt by Carter. To Pérez, the letter was a signal that Carter was not nearly as committed on the issue of Somoza's having to leave as Pérez thought had been the case in his earlier meeting with the President."[104]

Carter's letter clearly did not produce the effect the White House intended. The consequences were precisely the opposite of the overarching objective toward which the actions of U.S. policymakers had been directed: It reinforced Somoza's belief that he would be able to govern until his term expired; it demoralized the conservative and moderate opposition upon whom Washington's political hopes were based; it increased support for the advocates of a military confrontation (FSLN) as offering the only realistic means of getting rid of the autocratic dynasty.

Conclusion

Carter administration policy toward Nicaragua during 1977 and the first half of 1978 presumed that Somoza would serve out his term of office ending in May 1981. Washington's reluctance "to clearly distance ourselves

---

102 See ibid. The letter is reprinted in Christian, *Nicaragua: Revolution in the Family*, p. 67.
103 Department of State Telegram, Confidential Managua 3087, American Embassy (Solaun) to Secretary of State, July 7, 1978, Subject: "Human Rights Situation – June," DFOIA.
104 Confidential telephone interview, Department of State official, New York, October 5, 1989.

from Somoza"[105] or "do anything active to unseat him"[106] stemmed largely from a triptych of concerns: Somoza's military power; the perceived incapacity of the non-FSLN opposition forces to threaten the regime or gain hegemonic status within the anti-dictatorial movement; and the fate of key Congressional legislation that led the White House to avoid giving undue offence to Somoza's supporters on Capitol Hill, especially those who held "positions of power" on House committees responsible for scrutinizing the foreign aid bill and the Panama Canal treaty legislation.[107] Hence, the continued definition of Nicaragua as preeminently a human rights problem. "The focus," in Assistant Secretary Vaky's words "was on how to get the regime to reform itself."[108]

The emphasis on human rights did not reflect any sense of misplaced values, any downgrading of traditional priorities, but was at all times anchored within the broader objective of safeguarding U.S. permanent interests in Nicaragua. State and NSC officials were consistently seeking to estimate the possibility and type of changes likely to occur in Nicaragua as well as the individual and collective strength of the various forces ranged against Somoza in relation to continuing U.S. support for the dictatorship. Although interagency discussions revealed different perceptions of the relative strengths and weaknesses of the combatants, the regime's coercive capabilities and the absence of a viable political alternative dictated that American interests would still best be served by working "through" Somoza to institute desired reforms.

The erosion of Somoza's political support and regime legitimacy was not paralleled by any weakening of the institution that underpinned his power: the National Guard. Thus, although Carter policymakers "became more and more disillusioned with Nicaragua," said State's Nicaragua country officer Thomas Mehen, "they basically felt that it was very unlikely that Somoza would be overthrown. State Department and Embassy cables during 1977 and 1978 were saying it would be very difficult for any force to defeat the Guardia. The Guardia was so strong that the regime was not likely to be overthrown militarily."[109]

The Chamorro assassination in January 1978 was a watershed event for the Nicaraguan bourgeoisie, transforming simmering economic grievances into a full-blown political effort to topple Somoza in alliance with other

105 Interview with Sally Shelton-Colby.
106 Interview with Ambler Moss.
107 Confidential interview, Department of State official, September 8, 1988; interview with Sally Shelton-Colby.
108 Interview with Viron Vaky.
109 Telephone interview with Thomas Mehen, Washington, D.C., September 14, 1988. The respondent was the Country Officer for Nicaragua, Department of State, 1977 to 1978.

non-radical groups. Although the failure of the general strike to unseat the family dynasty (the strategic goal) could not obscure the fact that the regime was losing its control over civil society, senior U.S. officials expressed reluctance to entertain a major policy reassessment, in part because of continuing uncertainty over the ability of the "acceptable" anti-regime forces to assume power in the event of a political transition. As one senior U.S. diplomat involved in Central American affairs at the time put it: "There was a concern that the opposition was not viable or very visible."[110] Ambassador Solaun criticized the opposition for "its lack of a negotiable specific program to dismantle the Somoza regime, and of an effective structure with a universally recognized leadership."[111] Deputy Assistant Secretary of State John Bushnell offered a blunt summary of Washington's basic dilemma: "The question I asked in the [Department and interagency] debates was 'If somebody shot Somoza tomorrow, who would take over?' The National Guard was no improvement. If an election was held, the [pro-U.S.] political forces were terribly splintered. The alternatives were Somoza and the communists [Sandinistas]." The timing of any political transition was critical: "We needed a game plan so that the moderates and democrats could take over."[112]

To the extent that the Sandinistas were equated with "communists," this preoccupation with the timing of any regime change also reflected a concern to deny new "targets of opportunity" in the region to either Havana or Moscow. "This was an unpredictable situation," said Viron Vaky, "a vacuum into which Cuba and other countries could enter."[113] President Carter raised this issue during his June 1978 meeting with Panamanian leader General Omar Torrijos. One question they discussed was "how to constrain Cuba and other communist intrusion in the internal affairs of Caribbean and Latin American countries, and how to encourage freedom and democracy in Nicaragua...."[114]

In Nicaragua, both conservative and moderate opposition leaders voiced increasing dismay over Washington's preoccupation with human rights and what they viewed as its failure to understand the internal political dynamics of the situation that was polarizing and radicalizing the population with each passing day – carrying with it a potentially explosive challenge to U.S. permanent interests. The June 1978 Carter letter to Somoza congratulating

110 Interview with Ambler Moss.
111 Department of State Telegram, Confidential Managua 2068, American Embassy (Solaun) to Secretary of State, May 4, 1978, Subject: "Somoza's Initiatives – Report Card," DFOIA.
112 Interview with John Bushnell.
113 Interview with Viron Vaky.
114 Jimmy Carter, *Keeping Faith: Memoirs of a President* (London: William Collins Sons, 1982), p. 178.

him on proposed human rights initiatives (ironically at a time of increasing reports of National Guard abuses) merely confirmed the civilian opposition in its belief that Washington lacked an adequate understanding of the strengths and weaknesses of the contending forces. The letter not only demoralized the anti-regime moderates who interpreted it, accurately, as a signal to Somoza that the U.S. would not force him from office, but it also bolstered support for those anti-system elements who contended that a change of government could only be achieved by military means – a solution that posed the greatest threat to historic imperial interests in Nicaragua.

Washington policymakers during the first 18 months of the Carter presidency exhibited a strong grasp of U.S. interests in Nicaragua but a much more limited feel for the Central American country's internal political dynamics. Flawed judgments about the capacities of the major antagonists in an increasingly fluid and uncertain political situation translated into a profound underestimation of the dictator's present and future strength, and hence the regime's ability to meet fundamental U.S. needs. Consequently, the widespread administration perception that Somoza had restabilized his political authority in the months following the January – February 1978 upheaval, based on a relative decline in the level of political and military struggle, did not prepare Carter policymakers for what Ambassador to Panama Ambler Moss termed the "big surprise" of late August and September.[115]

115 Interview with Ambler Moss.

5

The Carter administration and Nicaragua: Mediation and the politics of frustration

Introduction

A proper conception of U.S. policy toward Somoza's Nicaragua must follow the multiple tracks that it pursues, as well as its capacity and willingness to shift track depending on the contextual situation, above all the scope and depth of the political-class struggle. Explanations for Washington's failure to distance itself from the regime during the 1960s and the first half of the 1970s must be sought in the continuing inability of the opposition to weaken Somoza's hold on political power and the regime's economic policies that favored foreign (primarily American) investment and banking interests. Through 1976 and 1977, a more complex U.S. policy approach emerged in response to the incremental growth of localized, relatively uncoordinated opposition to the dictatorship. Although supportive of the latter's crackdown on the FSLN and the political left, the State Department began to issue occasional public criticisms of National Guard "excesses" and Somoza's lack of tactical flexibility in refusing to talk with even his most conservative opponents. Simultaneously, the American Embassy in Managua expanded its links with the non-radical, anti-regime civilian leadership.

Despite two major opposition attempts to overthrow Somoza before the halfway point of the Carter administration, U.S. policy oscillated between limited pressures for reform and "business as usual." On the one hand, it suspended military aid and encouraged Somoza to negotiate with, and make concessions to, the "acceptable face" of the opposition movement. On the other, it continued to voice optimism that such reforms could be achieved without rupturing the historic collaborative relationship. For most Carter policymakers, there was a manifest reluctance to break with a government highly supportive of American political, economic, and strategic interests, and still perceived to be firmly in control of political and state power.

The overwhelmingly human rights and "reforms through Somoza" focus of U.S. policy was abruptly challenged in August and September 1978 by a combined political-military upheaval – the bourgeois-led general strike and the Sandinista-led national insurrection – that graphically exposed the dictator's political isolation, forcing a now perturbed White House to undertake a major reassessment of its relations with the Somoza regime.

For Washington, the growth of a mobilized democratic mass movement under increasingly radical (Sandinista) leadership and Somoza's loss of control over whole sectors of society raised the hitherto unforeseen possibility of a future regime change based on the worst case scenario. As the level of popular pressure for political change increased, and as the Sandinistas emerged as a potent and consequential force within the anti-regime movement, the United States began to pressure Somoza – albeit gingerly – to lay the groundwork for an eventual return to electoral/civilian rule. Initially Carter policymakers looked toward some form of power-sharing arrangement with the moderate-conservative opposition, and subsequently to Somoza's ouster either through voluntary resignation or electoral defeat. But the fundamental strategic objective remained unchanged: to marginalize or, preferably, exclude the FSLN as an influential actor in post-Somoza Nicaragua.

Washington's decision to support a mediation strategy in the aftermath of the August-September upheaval can only be understood in terms of the emergence of a heterogeneous anti-regime and anti-system movement that raised the possibility of a future serious threat to U.S. permanent interests in Nicaragua and Central America. "It was now increasingly evident," in the words of one involved State Department official, "that Somoza was not going to make it, that his government was simply imploding, collapsing from within. We were concerned about what that would mean for American interests and what we might try to do to maintain stability and safeguard U.S. interests on the assumption that Somoza was not able to hold out."[1] This situation created a new policy imperative: to promote the interests of those groups opposed to Somoza's emphasizing electoral/political changes rather than transformation of the state and polity – the structures and institutions that underpinned Somoza power. For the Carter administration, the basic issue was how to come to terms with the possible collapse of a longstanding client regime and influence the process of change in a way that conserved the institutional power of the National Guard and preserved other fundamental American interests during and after any political transition.

1   Confidential Interview, Department of State official, Virginia, September 20, 1989.

National insurrection and U.S. policy: Prelude to mediation

Developments in late 1978 revealed the extent to which opposition to the Somoza dictatorship had cut across political, class, and occupational lines. Multiple challenges from Sandinista guerrillas, owners of capital, salaried workers, urban unemployed, political parties, and labor unions revealed the broad-based nature of the forces ranged against it. The Nicaraguan business community, for instance, had accumulated a string of economic (and some political) grievances since the early 1970s. Not the least of these was Somoza economic competition and the fear of displacement from traditional areas of activity. Local capitalist class discontent intensified during the first year of the Carter presidency,[2] erupting into an organized political effort to oust Somoza after the January 1978 assassination of opposition leader Pedro Joaquín Chamorro. New government economic measures to reduce a budget deficit in excess of $40 billion – in particular, the reimposition of a profit tax on industry, the announcement of sales levies on 166 new products, an increase in existing levies on 249 items, and a rise in invoice taxes – provided the catalyst for a return to the political barricades in August.[3]

A new phase in the anti-Somoza struggle was inaugurated with the spectacular and audacious seizure of the National Palace by a Sandinista guerrilla force on August 21–22, 1978. An estimated 1,500 people, including most of the Nicaraguan Congress, were taken hostage and released only after Somoza agreed to a series of guerrilla demands, among them a ransom payment and the freedom and guarantee of safe passage out of the country for a substantial number of political prisoners. The attack was a major political embarrassment to Somoza but, more importantly, it served to undermine any aura of invincibility surrounding the regime. It showed that the dictatorship was safe nowhere in Nicaragua. Three days later, on August 25, the Broad Opposition Front (FAO), a coalition of business, political and labor organizations, launched a general strike aimed at toppling the regime. Informal U.S. Embassy surveys characterized the strike as 80–90 percent effective.[4] In the key northern provincial city of Matagalpa, the strike call detonated a spontaneous military uprising spearheaded by "los muchachos" (young unemployed workers). On September 1, Ambassador Solaun wrote that the strike continued to

2 See "Nicaraguan Businessmen Come Out Against Somoza," *Latin America Economic Report*, December 2, 1977, p. 231.

3 See "Somoza Defies New Pressure to Step Down," *This Week: Central America & Panama*, August 21, 1978, p. 166. Also see Alan Riding, "National Mutiny in Nicaragua," *New York Times Magazine*, July 30, 1978, p. 39; "Nicaragua: The Squeeze Is On," *Central America Report*, August 21, 1978, p. 262; Huey, "Business Elite Joins Struggle to Displace Nicaraguan Dictator," pp. 1, 22.

4 See "Nicaragua: Uneasy Stalemate," *Latin America Political Report*, September 8, 1978, p. 273.

gain momentum in Managua and gave no indication of leveling off in the provinces: "The country remains tense with discontent and anti-GON [Govern-
ment of Nicaragua] sentiment remaining high."[5]

Amid this groundswell of domestic opposition, Somoza's troubles were
compounded by the appearance of cracks in National Guard unity – which
went to the very foundation of the regime's power base. In early August,
rumblings of unrest within the officer corp over Somoza's policies precipitated a major shakeup in the Guard high command. Acting to reassert and
reinforce his personal authority, the commander-in-chief dismissed a number of senior officers, appointed his half brother General José Somoza to
commander of a Managua-based armored battalion, and promoted his son
Lieutenant Colonel Anastasio Somoza to head the elite Basic Infantry
Training School. These moves, however, failed to prevent an attempted
military coup at the end of the month that resulted in the arrest of more
than forty colonels, lieutenant colonels, majors, captains, and other disillusioned Guard members. Two explanations were offered to explain the
institutional upheaval: anger over Somoza's concessions to the guerrillas to
end the National Palace takeover, and the possible existence of elements
within the Guard "who may be more willing to open the political system to
change."[6]

The National Palace episode made Somoza more determined than ever
to break the FAO-led general strike and bring the business community to
heel – by whatever means necessary. Initially, he resorted to economic pressures, targeting those striking companies with outstanding loans from private
local banks. Among new regulations promulgated on August 28 was one
requiring domestic commercial banks to maintain a 25 percent reserve
against loans made over the next 12 months to any enterprise that participated in the general strike. But neither Somoza nor Central Bank president
Roberto Incer anticipated the private sector response: increased support for
the anti-regime political offensive. Angered by what they described as "a
threat of blackmail," the influential Nicaraguan Development Institute
(INDE) and the no-less prominent Nicaraguan Federation of Chambers of
Commerce both voted to join the strike.[7] Within days, the Chamber of

5 Department of State Telegram, Secret Managua 4135, American Embassy (Solaun) to
   Secretary of State, September 1, 1978, Subject: "Sitrep 6–1 September," DFOIA.
6 State Department official, quoted in John Huey, "Split in Nicaragua's Army Seen Ominous
   For Somoza Regime; Violence Continues," *Wall Street Journal*, August 30, 1978, p. 38.
   Also see Foreign Broadcast Information Service, *Daily Report: Latin America*, August 14,
   1978, p. 4, August 29, 1978, pp. 3–4, August 30, 1978, pp. 3–4.
7 Department of State Telegram, Managua 4081, American Embassy (Solaun) to Secretary
   of State, August 30, 1978, Subject: "GON [Government of Nicaragua] Begins to Take
   Economic Measures Against the Private Sector," DFOIA. Also see Joseph Mann, "Nicaraguan Bankers Under Loan Pressure," *Financial Times*, September 8, 1978, p. 4.

Industries followed suit. A "fear of three more years of Somoza in power" had begun to grip the non-Somoza capitalist forces who believed such a scenario would set the stage for an eventual victory of the "leftwing extremists."[8] For them, the key to resolving the country's problems was removing the dictator, not changing the structures and institutions of Somocismo. In the words of an INDE official at the time of the general strike: "The problem is the man. He's taking over our market. We have no quarrel with anyone else or the system. Just get rid of him."[9]

Whereas Somoza's resort to economic sanctions proved counterproductive, the shift to more overtly repressive measures achieved greater success. On September 4, American Ambassador Mauricio Solaun reported that "in an apparent effort to neutralize the opposition, the GON [Government of Nicaragua] has begun to arrest opposition leaders."[10] The incarceration of hundreds of business, political, and trade union officials effectively terminated the strike. In the process, however, the leadership of the anti-dictatorial struggle began to shift toward the one group in Nicaraguan society willing to militarily challenge the Somoza coercive apparatus – the Sandinista National Liberation Front (FSLN).

On September 9, the dominant Tercerista faction of the FSLN launched a series of coordinated military attacks in major urban centers throughout Nicaragua, hoping to ignite a mass popular insurrection that would overthrow Somoza political rule. In the Departmental capitals of Matagalpa, León, Estelí, Masaya, and Chinandega there occurred spontaneous mass uprisings of urban poor, unemployed youths, students, churchpeople, middle-class individuals, rural wage workers, and peasants.[11] Popular support for the guerrillas enabled them to temporarily take control of a number of provincial cities and shake the regime to its foundations. In cables to Washington, Ambassador Solaun remarked on the "increased level of [FSLN] military capability and organization than heretofore" and noted that "they have received significant support from certain sectors of the population" such as students.[12]

8 Department of State Telegram, Managua 4138, American Embassy (Solaun) to Secretary of State, September 1, 1978, Subject: "A View of the Private Business Sector Strikers in Nicaragua," DFOIA.
9 Quoted in George Black, *Triumph of the People: The Sandinista Revolution in Nicaragua*, (London: Zed Press, 1981), p. 64.
10 Department of State Telegram, Secret Managua 4140, American Embassy (Solaun) to Secretary of State, September 4, 1978, Subject: "Nicaragua Update," DFOIA.
11 See Ricardo E. Chavarria, "The Nicaraguan Revolution," in Thomas W. Walker, ed., *Nicaragua In Revolution* (New York: Praeger Publishers, 1982), p. 33; Black, *Triumph of the People*, p. 129; Diederich, *Somoza and the Legacy of U.S. Involvement in Central America*, pp. 189–197.
12 Department of State Telegram, Secret Managua 4246, American Embassy (Solaun) to Secretary of State, September 9, 1978, Subject: "FSLN Attacks," DFOIA; Department

Somoza's response to this challenge to his authority was swift and brutal. In a display of maximum force, he unleashed the National Guard who proceeded to drown the uprising in blood – several thousand civilians were killed by bombs, mortars, and heavy artillery. The Inter-American Commission on Human Rights called the National Guard counterattack "excessive and disproportionate." It accused the airforce of "indiscriminate" bombing of guerrilla-held towns "without prior evacuation of the civilian population," and the army of violating human rights "in a grave, persistent and widespread manner" during the so-called Operation Mop-Up and also following the cessation of hostilities:

> ...many persons were executed in a summary and collective fashion for the mere reason of living in neighborhoods or districts where there had been activity by the Frente Sandinista de Liberacíon Nacional (FSLN); and young people and defenceless children were killed.[13]

An angry Carter administration urged Somoza to "discipline and control" his troops.[14]

The general strike, the national insurrection, the anti-regime mass mobilizations, and the violent National Guard response created the objective conditions for revolution in Nicaragua. The Guard, however, still posed a formidable obstacle: Although it "encounter[ed] difficulty in re-establishing complete control in some cities" and suffered unprecedented casualties, it maintained an "internal cohesion"[15] and stayed loyal to Somoza. If necessary, the dictator could continue to rule on the basis of force alone. After two abortive efforts to change the regime, the civilian opposition decided to seek greater U.S. involvement in its struggle to bring down the ruling family.

In cables to the State Department during the last week of August, Ambassador Solaun had already concluded that the opposition was "too weak

of State Telegram, Confidential Managua 4248, American Embassy (Solaun) to Secretary of State, September 11, 1978, Subject: "Violence Continues," DFOIA.

13 Organization of American States, Inter-American Commission on Human Rights, *Report on the Situation of Human Rights in Nicaragua* (Finding of the "on-site" observers in the Republic of Nicaragua, October 3–12, 1978), OEA/Ser.L/V/II.45, November 17, 1978, p. 76.

14 Quoted in John Goshko, "U.S. Urges Somoza to Discipline Troops, Investigate Slaying," *Washington Post*, September 21, 1978, p. A21. In a letter to President Carter in mid-September, representatives of the Sacerdotal Council of the Managua Archdiocese and the National Council of Clerics denounced the Somoza regime for engaging in "institutionalized violence," including summary executions and the routine torture of prisoners, and requested a total U.S. aid cutoff. Quoted in Department of State Telegram, Managua 4391, American Embassy (Solaun) to Secretary of State, September 16, 1978, Subject: "Church Letter to President Carter," DFOIA.

15 Department of State Telegram, Confidential Managua 4268, American Embassy (Solaun) to Secretary of State, September 11, 1978, Subject: "Sitrep 12–11 September, Afternoon," DFOIA.

now to topple [the] GON [Government of Nicaragua]" or even wrest "significant concessions," and "Somoza knows this." Although Somoza remains more determined than ever to cling to power, encouraged by the "blandness" of current American policy, conversations with government and opposition leaders have convinced the Embassy that only "effective USG [United States Government] policy designed to pressure him to make reforms necessary to permit effective elections in 1981 or earlier" was likely to effect a political transition. Unless Washington shifted to "a new course of action," preferably "some form of mediation by a third party," it risked a growing "anti-American sentiment [and] the moderate opposition becoming more radicalized and eventually los[ing] influence."[16]

Among the Nicaraguan bourgeoisie, there was a growing consensus that although Somoza now lacked the political credibility to govern effectively, a more active Washington role was the key to forcing his resignation. In order to blunt the growing radicalism of the anti-Somoza movement, leading members of the business community told the American Embassy, it was imperative to end hostilities as quickly as possible. Otherwise control of the movement "would soon slip from the hands of the moderates." Also of concern was the likely devastating consequences of a prolonged conflict on the critical agricultural (coffee and cotton) export sectors.[17] But, wrote Solaun, they remained "puzzled by what they see as a lack of USG [United States Government] response to [the] situation."[18] On September 24, the Ambassador cabled State that almost all the "acceptable" opposition influentials perceived U.S. policy as "ambiguous and vacillating," and were convinced that only Washington could force Somoza to the bargaining table, thereby "strengthen[ing] their hand vis-à-vis the radicals."[19] And these Nicaraguans were not the only American allies calling for a more interventionist approach. There was also what a senior State Department official

16 Department of State Telegram, Managua 3998, American Embassy (Solaun) to Secretary of State, August 27, 1978, Subject: "Ambassador Talks with Somoza – August 26," DFOIA; Department of State Telegram, Secret Managua 4022, American Embassy (Solaun) to Secretary of State, August 28, 1978, Subject: "Ambassador's Conversations with Political Leaders," DFOIA; Department of State Telegram, Confidential Managua 4099, American Embassy (Solaun) to Secretary of State, August 31, 1978, Subject: "Ambassador Meets with Somoza – 30 August," DFOIA.
17 Department of State Telegram, Confidential Managua 4139, American Embassy (Solaun) to Secretary of State, September 3, 1978, Subject: "INDE Leaders Initiate Contacts for Possible Mediation of Nicaraguan Strike," DFOIA.
18 Department of State Telegram, Confidential Managua 4185, American Embassy (Solaun) to Secretary of State, September 6, 1978, Subject: "Sitrep 8–6 September," DFOIA.
19 Department of State Telegram, Secret Managua 4609, American Embassy (Solaun) to Secretary of State, September 24, 1978, Subject: "Perceived Needs of Nicaraguans for US Involvement," DFOIA.

described as "incessant pressure from friendly governments in the region to become more involved, to go beyond the human rights focus."[20]

What most surprised senior administration officials about the events of August-September was the "scope" of the anti-dictatorial movement that united groups espousing the most diverse outlooks, ranging from conservative businessmen to radical nationalist guerrillas.[21] As the Sandinista insurrection began to peter out, a high-ranking Inter-American Affairs official arrived in Managua "to get a reading on events" for the State Department. He discovered a "politically polarized" country governed by a regime that lacked any semblance of popular support:

> What surprised me most was to run across a situation in which all of the business forces had declared against him. They were absolutely obdurate that Somoza had to leave. There were advertisements in all of the papers from the bankers and coffee growers and other associations calling on Somoza to step down. I told Washington that the situation was militarily improving but politically and psychologically was not getting better. Washington was definitely surprised at the scope of the opposition, especially my telling them flatly that the business community had turned completely sour on Somoza. He was bereft of allies.[22]

Bemoaned one frustrated American official: "This crisis has been coming for months but no one in Washington seemed to recognize the seriousness of the trend. Now, suddenly, we have a crisis and we find it's almost too late for us to adopt a useful position."[23]

Ambassador to Panama Ambler Moss blamed the administration's misreading of Nicaraguan political developments on an inordinate preoccupation with shutting off the guerrillas access to military aid from sympathetic regional governments. U.S. intelligence operatives had "a tendency to explain it all in terms of gun running to the Sandinistas. They didn't realize

20 Telephone interview with Peter Tarnoff, New York, September 19, 1988. The respondent was Executive Secretary and Special Assistant to the Secretary of State for inter-American affairs, 1977 to 1981.
21 Interview with Sally Shelton-Colby, Washington, D.C., October 12, 1988; interview with Viron Vaky, Washington, D.C., September 15, 1988.
22 Interview with Malcolm Barnaby, Washington, D.C., October 4, 1988. According to Barnaby, the State Department had become "very uncomfortable with the performance of Ambassador Solaun." He described Solaun as "one of the worst people we could have sent to Nicaragua. He couldn't figure out what was going on." Citibank branch official William Dewey was similarly dismissive of Solaun's competence: "He was intimidated and scorned by Somoza who didn't even feel he had to deal with him." Telephone interview with William Dewey, Florida, October 17, 1988.
23 Quoted in Alan Riding, "Supplementary Material," New York Times, September 3, 1978, p. 38.

how quickly Somoza's authority was eroding or how quickly Sandinista power was increasing." Panama was a prime target of these pressures. "I was sent with instructions from the State Department at least 13 times during 1978 and 1979," said Moss, "to ask General Torrijos to refrain from sending arms to the Sandinistas because it was not conducive to working out a settlement." President Carter himself told the Panamanian leader during their June 1978 meeting that Somoza "can hold out for quite a while and if only people like you would stop running guns [to the guerrillas]."[24]

The need for a wide-ranging policy review seemed all the more pressing in the light of Somoza's continued refusal to entertain any compromise that might weaken his personal authority – evidenced by his heavy-handed crackdown on the leadership of the general strike. Deputy Secretary of State Warren Christopher criticized the arrests or detention of business leaders and directed Ambassador Solaun to convey "our strong concern at the effect this undoubtedly is having on preventing moderate opposition businessmen from expressing their concern over the growing strength of the radical left by supporting negotiations and moving along that route." The State Department feared that Somoza's intransigence and his repeated use of "armed force or intimidation" to quell domestic unrest would bury the anti-FSLN "centrist" option ("further polarize the situation and radicalize the opposition") and leave behind a militarily powerful regime but one whose eroding political legitimacy would probably redound to the ultimate benefit of the most radical opponents of the dictatorship.[25]

Pressured to do something to abort the drift toward large-scale confrontation, and even social revolution, in Nicaragua, the Carter administration moved to establish a centralized decisionmaking structure in an effort to get on top of the rapidly unfolding events and anticipate and shape their direction. Responsibility for formulating and executing policy was concentrated in two executive branch interagency bodies: the Special Coordination Committee (SCC), a crisis management group chaired by NSC Advisor Zbigniew Brzezinski, and the Policy Review Committee (PRC), chaired by Secretary of State Cyrus Vance. The chairmanships of both committees reflected the fact that although Defense, Treasury, Central Intelligence, and other agencies participated in the policy-strategy deliberations, it was State and the NSC that basically controlled the proceedings.

24 Interview with Ambler Moss, Washington, D.C., September 21, 1988.
25 Department of State Telegram, Confidential State 233537, Secretary of State (Christopher) to American Embassy, September 14, 1978, Subject: "Démarche to Somoza on Release of Arrested Politicians and Vacating Arrest Orders," DFOIA. Also see Department of State Telegram, Secret Managua 4369, American Embassy (Solaun) to Secretary of State, September 15, 1978, Subject: "Ambassador's Call on President Somoza – September 15," DFOIA.

At this juncture, Washington's objectives were essentially threefold: the short-term restoration of political stability, the eventual transition to a post-Somoza regime that excluded the Sandinistas from political power, and the survival of the National Guard as the coercive apparatus of the Nicaraguan state. Insofar as the subsequent policy debate generated any disagreements, it was over the means to arrive at a common goal: a negotiated settlement that protected U.S. permanent interests.

Within the State Department, there was a broad consensus that Somoza's resignation offered the "best hope" for an orderly and satisfactory political transition.[26] The newly appointed Assistant Secretary for Inter-American Affairs Viron Vaky believed Somoza's rapid ouster was imperative, and advocated forceful U.S. action ("go in as a catalyst") to get him to make concessions to the moderate opposition and accelerate his departure timetable. But such an activist approach did not find favor with Secretary Vance or President Carter, both of whom desired Washington's involvement as part of a multilateral mediation involving other regional governments, which was first proposed by Costa Rican President Rodrigo Carazo. "Let's not get in the middle of this," they said.[27] The White House was particularly keen to avoid identification with the interventionist behavior of past administrations and take no measure that might be construed as violating the OAS Charter on national sovereignty and non-intervention in the domestic affairs of member countries. Meanwhile, NSC Advisor Brzezinski, Deputy Secretary of State Christopher, and other foreign policy officials continued to emphasize the danger of a "premature" regime change leading to something that "could be worse than what we have now...."[28] In the Defense Department, the concerns were both local and subregional: Developments inside Nicaragua seemed to be creating "an ideal situation for the Communists to take advantage of."[29] If Somoza were overthrown, it might increase the vulnerability of allied military regimes in Guatemala and El Salvador also under pressure from mass revolutionary movements.

During the first week of September, Washington supported a Venezuelan request to the Organization of American States (OAS) to convoke an extraordinary meeting to discuss the Nicaraguan situation. In Managua, Ambassador Solaun presented Somoza with "four hypothetical [U.S. policy] options": bolster the regime, terminate economic and political support, intervene to assist in his overthrow, or mediation. The United States, he said,

26 John M. Goshko, "U.S. Is Nudging Somoza Toward OAS Mediation," *Washington Post*, September 16, 1978, p. A12.
27 Interview with Viron Vaky.
28 Quoted in "Nicaragua: Cuba All Over Again?" *U.S. News & World Report*, September 11, 1978, p. 37. Also see Lake, *Somoza Falling*, pp. 115–118.
29 Interview with Admiral Gordon Schuller, Virginia, September 20, 1988.

had reservations about all but the last one. The client, however, was decidedly unenthusiastic about any kind of third party mediation, which suggested that he intended to offer stubborn resistance to any attempt to chip away at his political authority. Or, in the Ambassador's own words, Somoza "remains unwilling to initiate dramatic reforms that might strengthen the center of the political spectrum."[30] In follow-up reports he described Somoza's determination to remain in office until his term expired as "non-negotiable." Somoza "was willing to talk, but was not willing to leave before 1981." The Nicaraguan leader was confident "that he can surmount the present crisis" – using force if required. In any event, he saw no reason to contemplate concessions to a weak and divided civilian opposition. The Ambassador should inform the State Department "that the situation was under control and going to calm down."[31]

In Washington, high-level discussions were also taking place between American and Nicaraguan officials. On September 8, Assistant Secretary Vaky told Somoza's Ambassador to the United States Guillermo Sevilla-Sacasa and Foreign Minister Julio Quintana that "there was a wide range of opposition to the regime from respectable and moderate elements," that the internal political situation was becoming more polarized with each passing day, and that repressive measures by the government against the moderates only served to "legitimize the violent extreme." Therefore, he concluded, "the important thing was to negotiate a new [domestic] consensus so that chaos would not develop."[32] The State Department believed that only by "establish[ing] the proper environment for such negotiations," which included releasing moderate politicians and businessmen arrested for merely supporting the general strike, would it be possible to undermine "the growing strength of the radical left. . . ."[33]

In closed testimony before the Senate Foreign Relations Committee on September 13, Vaky stressed the "very widespread opposition" to the Somoza dictatorship, extending "across the spectrum from conservative businessmen to leftist revolutionaries." And, he continued, the "polariz[ation]" was likely to worsen so long as Somoza refused to even consider relinquish-

---

30 Department of State Telegram, Confidential Managua 4176, American Embassy (Solaun) to Secretary of State, September 6, 1978, Subject: "Conversation with Somoza – 5th September," DFOIA.

31 Department of State Telegram, Confidential Managua 4197, American Embassy (Solaun) to Secretary of State, September 7, 1978, Subject: "Conversation with Somoza – 7th September," DFOIA; Department of State Telegram, Secret Managua 4245, American Embassy (Solaun) to Secretary of State, September 9, 1978, Subject: "Conversation with Somoza – 8th September," DFOIA.

32 Department of State Telegram, Secret State 228709, Secretary of State (Christopher) to American Embassy, September 9, 1978, Subject: "Conversation with Nicaraguan Foreign Minister Quintana [on 8th September]," DFOIA.

33 Department of State Telegram, Confidential State 233537.

ing power before 1981 and the moderate opposition was convinced he was someone who could not be trusted to bargain in good faith. Against this background, the Sandinista strategy of active confrontation with the regime "[is] gaining some legitimacy among the opposition." By posing the issue as a "choice ... between him and chaos, between him and Castroites," Vaky declared, Somoza was undermining the moderates and in danger of bringing about "a self-fulfilling prophecy." His actions were effectively "chew[ing] up [or] destroying [the] moderate, or let me call it the responsible, opposition...." Given the continuing National Guard loyalty to the dictator, "the real question is whether it is not possible to create some moderate third force choice between these two poles that are emerging...." Vaky expressed uncertainty as to "what that might be." He ended with the warning that a "reconciliation" (i.e., mediation) between the regime and the nonradical opposition was probably the only way to arrest the polarization and radicalization, and diminish the "risk ... of the leftist extremists coming into power." Among the moderate leaders who enjoyed the Department's "stamp of approval" were Alfonso Robelo and Arturo Cruz. Both were described "as responsible people who are capable of exercising power."[34]

Within days of the September 16 OAS vote to hold a special meeting on Nicaragua, the White House accepted an SCC recommendation to dispatch a Special Ambassador to Central America and the Caribbean to gather support for a multilateral mediation of the Nicaraguan conflict. The administration hoped the diplomat, just retired Ambassador to Panama William Jorden, could convince Somoza that a refusal to participate risked a major shakeup in bilateral ties and "prevail upon the governments that were helping the anti-Somoza forces with material and moral support to reduce their actions and give the mediation effort a chance to succeed."[35]

In outlining the case for mediation to the heads-of-government and foreign ministers, Jorden was instructed to emphasize three key points: First, "the political situation in Nicaragua was polarizing rapidly with growing popular support for the Sandinistas. So something had to be done quickly to get discussions going and make a solution possible." Second, "pressure on Somoza from his neighbors could be helpful in encouraging him to at least consider laying the groundwork for stepping down." Third, they should ignore Somoza's rhetoric that " 'the choice was either back him or the

---

34 Stenographic Transcript of Hearings before the Committee on Foreign Relations, United States Senate, Administration briefing on the current situation in Nicaragua, Washington, D.C., September 13, 1978, pp. 6–12, DFOIA.
35 William J. Jorden, *Panama Odyssey* (Austin: University of Texas Press, 1984), p. 669. Also see Department of State Telegram, Confidential State 236887, Secretary of State (Vance) to American Embassy, September 19, 1978, Subject: "Ambassador Jorden's Trip," DFOIA.

communists.' We felt that there were other possibilities and a lot of people in Nicaragua that were moderate and democratic and offered a good deal of hope for the future. But they needed encouragement and the faster the better."

During 10 days of intensive shuttle diplomacy between Costa Rica, El Salvador, Honduras, Guatemala, and Colombia, the Special Ambassador discovered "enthusiastic support for a mediation effort," and gained commitments from each government "to take part" in the process if requested. He also visited Panama and Venezuela for meetings with two of the more outspoken opponents of the Somoza regime, Presidents Omar Torrijos and Carlos Andrés Pérez. His brief was to dissuade both leaders from "any precipitous military action" against the Nicaraguan dictatorship:

> At the time, Torrijos and Pérez were beating the drums and advocating military action, and Venezuela had moved some planes into Panama and Costa Rica. The great fear was that Pérez would do something rash such as attack Managua and Somoza's headquarters. Pérez was suspicious of the Sandinistas and very afraid that if they were allowed to continue and then forced Somoza out militarily and took over, then this was going to open the door to Castro. One of the first things I had to do was talk to Torrijos and try to calm him down and get him to calm Pérez down. Indeed, I did succeed in that no military action was taken and Pérez did pull his planes out of Costa Rica (except for two transports) and held his fire.[36]

After meeting with Somoza to inform him about the purpose of Jorden's visit and restate Washington's "concern over the outstanding arrest orders for a number of moderate politicians and businessmen who had not been engaged in violent activities," Ambassador Solaun cabled State that the Nicaraguan dictator still "does not perceive the 'carrot and stick' combination that might induce him to accept mediation."[37] Twenty-four hours later, Somoza delivered a stinging attack on Carter's human rights policy and the "incompetence" of the domestic opposition, insisting they were the root causes of the current unrest. He termed U.S. support for an on-site inspection by the Inter-American Human Rights Commission simply a Carter effort to "further 'kick him.' " Despite this outburst, Solaun sensed a "slightly more flexible position" on the mediation question, a greater re-

36 Telephone interview with William Jorden, Washington, D.C., October 13, 1988. The respondent was American Ambassador to Panama, 1974 to 1978. During 1978, he was appointed Special Ambassador by the State Department, charged with mobilizing regional support for the mediation strategy.

37 Department of State Telegram, Secret Managua 4477, American Embassy (Solaun) to Secretary of State, September 20, 1978, Subject: "Conversation with Somoza, September 19," DFOIA.

ceptivity to Embassy "suggestions," and a willingness on Somoza's part to shift positions so long as he could avoid the appearance of taking actions "determined by the USG [United States Government]."[38] This was all to the good because the special envoy was under orders "to get Somoza to accept the mediation effort," promise U.S. participation if he requested it, and warn him that "there would be real trouble in the bilateral relationship if he didn't accept this."[39]

On September 23, the day of Jorden's first meeting with Somoza, the OAS Foreign Ministers gathered in special session to debate the Nicaraguan crisis and a U.S. proposal that the regional body send a human rights mission to investigate reports of National Guard abuses and take the lead in the search for a "democratic solution" to the unrest. The proposal was coldly received by a number of Latin American military dictatorships on the grounds that it violated the OAS prohibition on intervention in the internal affairs of sovereign states but who privately were more likely concerned over the precedent that might be established. The final result was passage of a compromise measure calling on the Nicaraguan government to accept the "friendly cooperation" of the hemisphere in negotiating a settlement to the political conflict. The watered down resolution satisfied Washington's basic objective – OAS support for proceeding with the mediation effort – and within days the State Department announced the successful conclusion of talks between Ambassador Jorden and Somoza to establish a "framework for mediation" based on the "friendly cooperation" of outside parties.[40]

As both sides moved to address the question of the composition of the mediation team, it became evident that Somoza's decision to go along with the mediation was partly a tactical ploy based on an apparent belief that he could sufficiently influence the selections to ensure a committee biased in his favor. When Jorden suggested representatives from the United States, the Honduran military government, and the conservative civilian regimes in the Dominican Republic and Colombia, Somoza counterproposed delegates chosen by the military dictatorships in Argentina, Brazil, El Salvador, and Guatemala. Deputy Secretary of State Warren Christopher accused Somoza of "stacking the deck," declaring that his panel would neither be acceptable to the civilian opposition nor produce "a stable and lasting solution." He cabled the Embassy to "make clear to Somoza that this effort must be even

38 Department of State Telegram, Confidential Managua 4537, American Embassy (Solaun) to Secretary of State (Vaky), September 21, 1978, Subject: "Conversation with Somoza – 21st September, 11.00am," DFOIA.
39 Telephone interview with William Jorden.
40 See John M. Goshko, "OAS Approves Compromise on Nicaragua Role," *Washington Post*, September 24, 1978, p. A15; John M. Goshko and Karen DeYoung, "Peace Efforts Advance in Nicaragua, U.S. Says," *Washington Post*, September 27, 1978, p. A1.

handed" and underlined how essential it was "not... to begin this process by allowing Somoza to control it since it will not get off the ground under those circumstances."[41] On September 26, Jorden met with Somoza for a third time and relayed the State Department's "unwillingness to get into [the mediation] game if [the] main participants were shuffling feet and trying [to] load [the] dice against us." Unless the panel was "more balanced," U.S. participation could not be guaranteed.[42] Part of the problem throughout the negotiations, Jorden remembered, was "the bad advice Somoza was getting from his friends in Congress who were telling him to just hold firm."[43]

Somoza finally relented and subsequent discussions produced agreement on the acceptability of negotiators from the United States, Colombia, Guatemala, El Salvador, and the Dominican Republic. Soon after, Colombia fell by the wayside when its President, Julio Turbay, wrote a letter to the head of the United Nations General Assembly denouncing the Nicaraguan regime for human rights abuses. Somoza was outraged and Washington was forced to "reluctantly conclude that Colombian participation under these circumstances cannot be sold."[44] In order to maintain a balance between elected and non-elected Latin governments, the Carter administration persuaded Somoza to accept a three-person mediation panel: William Bowdler, a former U.S. Ambassador to El Salvador and Guatemala, and currently the State Department's Director of Intelligence and Research; Ramon Emilio Jiménez, the Dominican Republic's Foreign Minister; and José Alfredo Obiols Gomez, a former Guatemalan Deputy Vice Foreign Minister.

At the time of the Jorden mission, the issue of U.S. economic and military assistance policy toward Nicaragua temporarily returned to center stage. The White House announced the suspension of all new military shipments and training programs on the same day (September 22) that the Senate approved the fiscal year 1979 foreign assistance appropriations bill after voting to delete $8 million in economic aid to the Somoza regime on an amendment offered by Foreign Relations Committee chairman Frank Church. Invoking arguments similar to those made by leading State Department "liberals," the Democratic senator from Idaho warned his col-

---

41   Department of State Telegram, Secret State 244326, Secretary of State (Christopher) to American Embassy, September 26, 1978, Subject: "Nicaraguan Mediation," DFOIA; Department of State Telegram, Secret State 244327, Secretary of State (Christopher) to American Embassy, September 26, 1978, Subject: "Nicaraguan Mediation," DFOIA.
42   Department of State Telegram, Secret Managua 4656, American Embassy (Solaun) to Secretary of State, September 26, 1978, Subject: "Jorden Mission – Talk with Somoza (3)," DFOIA.
43   Telephone interview with William Jorden.
44   Department of State Telegram, Secret State 247454, Secretary of State (Christopher) to American Embassy, September 28, 1978, Subject: "Structure of Nicaraguan Mediation Team," DFOIA.

leagues that Somoza was so politically isolated, his demise was all but certain, and it was incumbent upon Washington do all it could to avoid a protracted military struggle that could only play into the hands of "the extremists" [i.e., the Sandinistas] and lead to the emergence of "another Castro-type revolutionary government" hostile to U.S. permanent interests.[45] The amendment passed the Senate after it was modified to allow the President to use the funds if he could certify that such action would directly contribute to the redemocratization process. The amendment was subsequently dropped following a September 27 joint House-Senate conference committee meeting that could not resolve differences over the 1979 aid bill. But Deputy Secretary of State Christopher emphasized that the administration would still only release the $8 million "to promote the progress of democratization" and the funds would not be disbursed in the absence of presidential certification that such a development was occurring.[46]

Washington confronts an intransigent client: The mediation process

In the aftermath of the September 1978 insurrection, a "general conviction" took hold in Washington "that Somoza had to go" and that "a formula was needed to make changes."[47] The "distancing" and human rights policy was no longer adequate to deal with what one American official characterized as "a pressure-cooker situation building up down there...."[48] In settling on an alternative approach, however, the U.S. faced a dilemma. The options, explained the Under Secretary of State for Political Affairs David Newsom, "were limited and almost all unsatisfactory for one reason or another." Mediation was chosen as "the least unappealing" option.[49] Above all, it held out the best possibility of "involving the Latin Americans." The administration wanted "to build up regional pressure on Somoza to get out" and,

---

45 Quoted in the debate on foreign assistance appropriations for 1979, in *Congressional Record-Senate*, Vol. 124, No. 149, 95th Congress, 2nd Session, September 22, 1978, p. S15739. Also see "Senate Votes to Cut off Most Aid to Nicaragua," *Washington Post*, September 23, 1978, p. A9; "Nicaragua Funds Cut From Aid Bill," *Congressional Quarterly Weekly Report*, Vol. XXVi, No. 39, September 30, 1978, p. 2642.

46 Department of State Telegram, Confidential State 249653, Secretary of State (Christopher) to American Embassy (Solaun), September 30, 1978, Subject: "Proposed Statement on AID," DFOIA.

47 Interview with Viron Vaky.

48 State Department official, quoted in John Goshko, "Nicaragua: Case of Limits on U.S. Clout Abroad," *Washington Post*, September 30, 1978, p. A4.

49 Interview with David Newsom, Washington, D.C., October 6, 1988. The respondent was Under Secretary for Political Affairs, Department of State, 1978 to 1979.

in the words of Deputy Assistant Secretary John Bushnell, mediation "was the most we thought we could get the Latins to go along with."[50] The White House reluctance to contemplate a more aggressive approach to force Somoza to make concessions to the civilian opposition and accelerate his departure timetable was symptomatic of the incremental nature of the policy shift. "We weren't in the business of forcing reforms," Ambassador to Panama Ambler Moss remarked. "If you look back, the human rights record was largely hortatory."[51] Washington's "restraint," according to another State official, was powerfully influenced by "domestic political considerations and other important issues on the President's foreign policy political agenda, including relations with the Soviets."[52] Last, but not least, in the view of a number of policymakers, Somoza "seemed to still have a lot of cards."[53]

The Carter administration hoped the mediation strategy would achieve four interrelated objectives: contain what Secretary of State Vance described as the "increasing radicalization" of the Nicaraguan population[54]; "head off an explosion by pushing Somoza to ease up and get into a dialogue with his opposition"[55]; encourage the dictator's voluntary resignation and replace autocratic family rule with a moderate-conservative civilian government; and ensure the survival of a reformed National Guard, thus "avoiding a radical outcome inimical to our interests."[56]

From the outset, American officials envisaged grafting a new regime, albeit one that included "members of Somoza's political party [the PLN],"[57] onto the coercive apparatus of the old state. John Bushnell was quite specific on this point: "Our game plan in organizing the moderate middle (liberals, conservatives, social democrats) was that they would provide the civilian control of the National Guard and the Guard would provide the law and order, and fight against the guerrillas and the left."[58] A member of State's

---

50 Interview with John Bushnell, Washington, D.C., September 8, 1988.
51 Interview with Ambler Moss.
52 Telephone interview with Peter Tarnoff.
53 Confidential telephone interview, Department of State official, California, September 18, 1989.
54 Secretary of State Vance, press conference (Transcript), January 11, 1979, Bureau of Public Affairs, Department of State.
55 State Department official, quoted in Goshko, "Nicaragua: Case of Limits on U.S. Clout Abroad," p. A4.
56 Quoted from Letter, dated September 8, 1979, by Assistant Secretary of State for Inter-American Affairs Viron P. Vaky, reprinted in U.S. Congress, House, Committee on Foreign Affairs, Subcommittee on Inter-American Affairs, *United States Policy Toward Nicaragua*, 96th Congress, 1st Session, June 21 and 26, 1979 (Washington, D.C.: U.S. Government Printing Office, 1979), p. 72.
57 Interview with David Newsom.
58 Interview with John Bushnell.

Policy Planning Staff called the survival of the Guard an "absolute priority" if the U.S. wanted to avoid any future likelihood of "a Sandinista takeover lock, stock, and barrel."[59]

It was hoped that the FSLN could be excluded from a significant role in any new political order. A Sandinista-dominated regime was termed "highly undesirable" and "an alternative devoutly to be avoided."[60] On this point, recalled Secretary Vance's special assistant on regional matters," there was a firm consensus: "There were no voices reaching the top of the administration making the case that a Sandinista regime would be a good replacement *in relation to our interests.* Due to strong reservations about the Sandinistas and their intentions, it was important to have an armed counterweight to the Sandinista military force."[61] To the extent that Washington contemplated any guerrilla representation in a post-Somoza government, only "the Terceristas were looked upon in a reasonable light," particularly the faction's most conservative leader, Eden Pastora.[62]

The importance attached to preserving the National Guard explained the White House concern that Somoza not be ousted by force of arms. "If Somoza goes, we would prefer to see him go peacefully," commented a State Department official at the time. "We would not like to see him toppled in an armed revolt."[63] Such a preoccupation contributed to U.S. tolerance of Israel's emergence as the dictator's most important foreign arms supplier during 1978 and the first part of 1979. It also explained the State Department pressure on Somoza to investigate reports of National Guard human rights abuses during the September insurrection and take the necessary legal action where it was justified. Deputy Secretary Christopher argued that "plac[ing] the blame on individual guilty parties [would] keep the National Guard *as an institution* free from such allegations."[64]

In a confidential cable to all Latin American diplomatic posts on the eve of the mediation, Christopher summarized the U.S. objective as "the achievement of a national consensus on Nicaragua's future political evolution," leading to a democratic political transition.[65] Initial signals, however,

59 Interview with Richard Feinberg, Washington, D.C., October 17, 1988.
60 Interview with Wade Matthews, Washington, D.C., October 6, 1988; interview with Richard Feinberg; interview with Viron Vaky.
61 Telephone interview with Peter Tarnoff (my emphasis).
62 Interview with Wade Matthews.
63 Quoted in "U.S. Letting Israel Resupply Somoza," *Washington Star,* November 18, 1978, p. A6; "U.S. Won't Bar Israeli Arms to Somoza," *Los Angeles Times,* Part 1, November 18, 1978, p. 3.
64 Department of State Telegram, Confidential State 239655, Secretary of State (Christopher) to American Embassy, September 21, 1978, Subject: "Concern over Alleged Human Rights Violations," DFOIA (my emphasis).
65 Department of State Telegram, Confidential State 254339, Secretary of State (Christopher) to American Embassy, Bogotá, Caracas, Panama, Information All American Re-

were not promising. Although Washington had managed to coax Somoza to participate in the negotiations, the Nicaraguan leader soon dampened any suggestions that he might be willing to make substantive concessions to the opposition. When the three-person mediation team, led by the American diplomat William Bowdler, arrived in Managua on October 6, Somoza's welcome consisted of a public restatement of his intention to remain in office until May 1981. Adjourning to the dictator's "bunker," the mediators, accompanied by Ambassador Solaun, were regaled by a Somoza monologue critical of Washington and Caracas for encouraging the FSLN to believe it could oust him from office. He expressed pleasure that the negotiating group had arrived to "help them [the guerrillas] climb down from the coconut tree." On leaving the meeting, Solaun remarked to his colleagues that "our task will be to persuade Somoza that he is higher up the coconut tree" than the Sandinistas.[66]

Some days later, Somoza launched a blistering attack against all those demanding his early resignation, calling such statements the meanderings of "dreamers...full of illusions." In the same speech he announced that the defense budget and the size of the National Guard would be doubled, and that the state of siege (recently extended until April 30, 1979) would not be lifted.[67] Secretary of State Vance was in no doubt as to the meaning of the speech and the decree: It was a signal to all "that he has no intention of leaving and is going to hang tough."[68] The daunting prospect of having to bargain with an obstructionist head of state, and a National Guard and Nationalist Liberal Party (PLN) that both lacked "a strong institutional identity or capability of action independent from Somoza,"[69] was not the least of the mediators' tasks. They also had to negotiate with an ideologically and politically diverse opposition movement. Grouped under an umbrella organization, the Broad Opposition Front (FAO), it included conservative business interests, moderate political groups, social democratic trade unions, and the so-called Group of Twelve (Los Doce) – a mixture of liberal academics, professionals, businessmen, and churchpeople recently returned from exile, who reflected the views of the "insurrectional" or Tercerista faction of the FSLN.

public Diplomatic Posts, October 5, 1978, Subject: "Nicaraguan Mediation Effort," DFOIA.

66 Department of State Telegram, Managua 4935, American Embassy (Solaun) to Secretary of State, October 7, 1978, Subject: "Nicaraguan Mediation Team No. 7–Mediators' First Meeting with Somoza," DFOIA.
67 Alan Riding, "Supplementary Material," *New York Times*, October 15, 1978, pp. 08, 09.
68 Department of State Telegram, Confidential State 260247, Secretary of State to American Embassy, October 14, 1978, Subject: "Nicaraguan Situation Update," DFOIA.
69 Department of State Telegram, Secret Managua 4858, American Embassy (Solaun) to Secretary of State, October 5, 1978, Subject: "Mediation – A Difficult Road," DFOIA.

Within the FAO there were different, often contradictory, agendas, ranging from those conservative elements who identified with Washington's policy goals to the "Group of Twelve" who insisted "...there is no solution
to this crisis if the Somocist system isn't dismantled; if the FSLN does not
have participation in whatever future step of national life."[70] Ambassador
Solaun termed the FAO structure "inherently unstable – united principally
by anti-Somoza sentiment...."[71] These various political orientations were
reflected in the FAO's negotiating team: Alfonso Robelo, a pro-U.S. business
leader; Rafael Córdova Rivas, an influential figure within the Democratic
Liberation Union (UDEL); and Sergio Ramírez, a member of the "Group
of Twelve." Cognizant of the potential problems involved in backing such
a heterogeneous civilian opposition, the State Department instructed the
American Embassy "to continue to urge that FAO leaders remain united
as the mediation process gets underway, and that they and other opposition
figures such as the Archbishop [Miguel Obando Y Bravo]...strive to the
extent feasible to coordinate their views and the presentations they plan to
make to the mediators."[72]

In the course of initial discussions with the mediators, the FAO submitted
a proposal based on the premise that there could be no satisfactory political
solution to the conflict without "an immediate separation of the entire Somoza family from any position of power."[73] The proposal demanded a complete reorganization of all military, political, juridical, and other state and
governmental institutions tainted by Somoza influence as a prelude to the
formation of a transitional government of national unity. Such sweeping
changes were unacceptable to the United States, particularly those relating
to state institutions. As a result, it began to differentiate more sharply between the groups making up the coalition, and set about cultivating the
conservative FAO elements – those most willing to collaborate in the pursuit
of imperial objectives.

After both Washington and Somoza rejected the original FAO proposal
for uprooting and terminating the family dictatorship, representatives of the
more conservative forces offered the mediators a new proposal that immediately exposed the brittleness of the Front's unity. It allowed the governing PLN to retain its congressional power and a reorganized National

---

70 October 14 communique, quoted in Department of State Telegram, Managua 5088,
     American Embassy (Solaun) to Secretary of State, October 16, 1978, Subject: "The
     Group of 12 (G-12) on Mediation," DFOIA.
71 Department of State Telegram, Secret Managua 4858.
72 Department of State Telegram, Secret State 245639, Secretary of State (Christopher) to
     American Embassy, September 27, 1978, Subject: "Conversations with Oppositionists,"
     DFOIA.
73 Quoted in "Nicaragua: Commission for Peace," *Central America Report*, October 16, 1978,
     p. 327.

Guard to keep its monopoly over coercion under a new regime. On October 25, the "Group of Twelve" publicly withdrew from the mediation, charging that the Carter administration had exerted undue pressure to force the FAO to moderate its demands for Somoza's immediate ouster, the expropriation of the family economic empire, and the dismantling of the National Guard. Any attempt to include the PLN and the Guard in a transitional government was denounced as tantamount to supporting Somocismo without Somoza. Soon after, the Union of Nicaraguan Workers (CTN) resigned also citing U.S. pressures and FAO concessions to Somoza.[74] The Nicaraguan Socialist Party (PSN) did likewise. As the FAO began to unravel, with defecting liberal and progressive sectors shifting their allegiances to the FSLN, the dictatorship began to express increasing confidence in its ability to withstand the challenge to its power and survival.

In Washington, policymakers' frustration over FAO disunity and the absence of leadership was palpable. One senior State Department official wistfully recalled the successful resolution of a transition crisis in the Dominican Republic in 1965 when President Johnson dispatched 23,000 marines to crush a mass social revolutionary movement, restore the power of the "old" Trujillo military state, and establish the foundations for a return to electoral politics based on a handpicked candidate acceptable to the White House and its local military-oligarchy allies. The subsequent election produced an overwhelming victory for the conservative politician Joaquin Balaguer, confirmed the power of the rightist military establishment, and opened up the economy to foreign capital. In a conversation with former Costa Rican president José "Pepe" Figueres, the aforementioned American diplomat emphasized the need to "avoid another Cuba" in Nicaragua as well as "another mess like the invasion of the Dominican Republic. We've been looking everywhere for another Balaguer, but we can't seem to locate him."[75]

Within days of their arrival, the mediators concluded that Somoza was so politically isolated that no peaceful settlement of the conflict was possible as long as he remained in office. Special Ambassador Bowdler recommended that the administration "bite the bullet" and apply sufficient pressure to achieve the dictator's resignation as quickly as possible. The issue was heatedly debated at an October 31 Policy Review Committee (PRC) meeting on Nicaragua. Siding with Bowdler, Assistant Secretary of State Viron Vaky argued that if Somoza stayed there would quite likely be additional FAO

74 Foreign Broadcast Information Service, *Daily Report: Latin America*, November 3, 1978, p. 6.
75 Quoted in "Nicaragua: The Beginning of the End," *Latin America Political Report*, September 22, 1978, p. 289.

defections, thus further weakening those anti-regime forces Washington hoped would dominate a post-Somoza government. NSC Advisor Zbigniew Brzezinski shot back that if the FAO was such a fragile and vulnerable organization there must be serious doubts about its current ability to assume a hegemonic role within any new government. In Brzezinski's opinion, there was no justification in calling for sanctions to force Somoza from office if Washington's preferred alternative, as seemed to be the case, was incapable of seizing the opportunity. Instead, the United States should focus its efforts on developing a "post-Somoza leadership and on making contacts with the National Guard." The Brzezinski view prevailed. The Committee also agreed on the importance of selecting a new Guard commander as quickly as possible.[76]

At the beginning of November, the mediation tottered on the brink of collapse. Following a Somoza speech attacking the United States and the internal opposition, Ambassador Solaun cabled the Secretary of State that "if his words are to be believed, he is committed to resisting outside pressures and hanging on to power at all costs."[77] On November 6, the FAO, severely weakened by defections, announced that it would consider the talks at an end if Somoza did not resign, leave the country, and pave the way for new elections within 15 days. Somoza and the PLN responded that the government would run its full course. But just as Washington sought to avoid a "premature" collapse of the dictatorship, so too was the Nicaraguan dictator intent on stringing out the mediation process for his own purposes. To this end, he counterproposed a national plebiscite to determine the strength of the FAO's popular support. Based on the result, the FAO would be offered a role in a reorganized government, still under Somoza's leadership, to last until May 1981. Not surprisingly, the internal opposition denounced the scheme. Even Somoza's most conservative critics termed the plebiscite idea totally unacceptable.[78] The response in Washington, however, testified to Somoza's political acumen.

On November 13, the PRC reconvened to consider this latest proposal. Once more, Bowdler (recalled for consultations) and Vaky argued the case for economic and political sanctions to force Somoza to leave the country,

76 Pastor, *Condemned to Repetition*, pp. 103–104.
77 Department of State Telegram, Confidential Managua 5621, American Embassy (Solaun) to Secretary of State, November 6, 1978, Subject: "Nicaragua Mediation No. 103–Somoza's Speech and Opposition Developments," DFOIA.
78 See Alan Riding, "U.S. Strategy in Nicaragua Keeps the Time Bomb Ticking," *New York Times*, December 17, 1978, p. E3; Karen DeYoung, "U.S.-Led Mediation in Nicaragua Feared Near Collapse," *Washington Post*, November 14, 1978, p. A13; "Somoza Rejects Last-Minute U.S. Mediation Effort," *Washington Post*, November 22, 1978, pp. A1, A10.

describing the plebiscite as just another ploy. Once again, they failed to persuade the President's senior foreign policy officials – Secretary of State Vance, Deputy Secretary Christopher, and NSC Advisor Brzezinski – who took a more charitable view of the Somoza initiative and were able to convince the White House that instead of dismissing the plebiscite idea it should try to turn it into a referendum on the fate of the dictatorship. The meeting "also emphasized again that the unity of the Guard was an important objective of U.S. policy."[79]

In discussions with U.S. Embassy officials, however, the anti-regime civilian leadership expressed its opposition to this latest Somoza gambit in unequivocal terms. One told Ambassador Solaun that it "was a Somoza trick," and that even if it became a referendum on whether the dictator goes or stays there was every likelihood of the latter "manipulating" a victory, which "could lead to renewed violence." Others now advocated a "quick solution even if this entailed the use of U.S. military force." The only circumstances under which the opposition was prepared to consider participation in the plebiscite process would be if the National Guard were confined to barracks during the voting period. In its place, they suggested an "interamerican force" to guarantee security, observe the election procedures, and tabulate the results. If the plebiscite were held under these conditions "they were confident that Somoza would be overwhelmingly defeated."[80]

The shifts and changes in American policy at the operational level should not obscure the fact that it operated at all times within the broader state-regime framework. Saving the state was uppermost in the minds of William Jorden and Mauricio Solaun when they conferred with the Nicaraguan dictator, amid the debate over the latter's plebiscite proposal, in yet another effort to get him to consider resignation and exile. Jorden turned first to the problem of the regime's growing political isolation. "If it was only the Sandinistas, the situation would be manageable," he said. "But it has developed into something quite different."[81] Jorden later amplified on this statement: "What I meant was that if we were talking about a minority that was clearly extremist and violent and to a large extent pro-Communist, the solution for both the U.S. and other neighbors would be simpler and easier.

79 See Pastor, *Condemned to Repetition*, pp. 106–107.
80 Department of State Telegram, Secret Managua 5883, American Embassy (Solaun) to Secretary of State, November 15, 1978, Subject: "Wrapup of Ongoing Political Consultations," DFOIA.
81 Quoted in Somoza, *Nicaragua Betrayed*, p. 315, (my emphasis). This study contains verbatim transcripts of tapes of conversations between Somoza and high-ranking Carter administration officials. William Jorden confirmed the authenticity of this particular tape in Alfonso Chardy, "U.S. Broke Promises, Somoza Book Claim," *Miami Herald*, October 29, 1980, p. 13A.

But it had gone beyond that. There were lots of people non-violent, non-left wing, not communist increasingly opposed to the Somoza regime. *Therefore, it was getting to be a national struggle.*[82] Then he zeroed in on the institutional "foundations" of the regime: The society had become so polarized that it threatened the survival of those very institutions, such as the National Guard, which Washington deemed critical to the success of its transition strategy. "We are terribly concerned," the special envoy told Somoza, "that everything you have built up, and your brother before you, is in danger of being destroyed. *And that means the political structure, institutions.*"[83]

This determination to confine the process of change to the regime co-existed with a fear over the possible regional implications of a Sandinista victory. The American diplomats underlined Washington's belief that if the political situation were allowed to deteriorate further, it could ultimately destabilize the whole of Central America, which would "play into the hands of the Communists and Castro."[84] The discussion ended with Somoza's being asked to reconsider his options.

In a November 16 cable to all regional embassies, Secretary of State Vance wrote that the "central objective" of U.S. policy "[is] to try to prevent further polarization and radicalization of the situation which would facilitate a Sandinista takeover that could destabilize the Isthmian region."[85] Alan Riding, the *New York Times* correspondent in Central America, reported that U.S. officials had privately informed Nicaraguan opposition leaders that the White House was "determined to see General Somoza out of office as soon as possible."[86]

On November 21, the mediators presented both sides with Washington's compromise for breaking the stalemate: an internationally supervised national referendum within 60 days to decide whether Somoza retained power, or was replaced by a government of national unity and went into exile. In constructing this latest proposal, the State Department heeded Embassy advice that the dictatorship must be excluded from any involvement with the voting process. Ambassador Solaun explained why:

> The reason is that the GON [Government of Nicaragua] from Somoza down to the last Juez de Mesta (essentially a combination of sheriff and

82 Telephone interview with William Jorden (my emphasis).
83 Quoted in Somoza, *Nicaragua Betrayed*, p. 315.
84 Quoted in ibid.
85 Department of State Telegram, Secret State 2914/7, Secretary of State (Vance) to All American Republic Diplomatic Posts, November 16, 1978, Subject: "Nicaragua Mediation," DFOIA.
86 Alan Riding "U.S. Leads Efforts to Oust Somoza and Lead Nicaragua to Democracy," *New York Times*, November 16, 1978, p. 3.

Justice of Peace in each Canton) is controlled and staffed by the Liberal Party. Polling places are often as not in the homes of local Liberal Party leaders. Jueces de Mesta and National Guard Capitanes de Canada are the local officials who normally supervise the elections; they frequently observe and even ascertain how each person votes. Electoral tribunals at the National and Departmental levels are made up of members of both Liberal and Conservative Parties, with the Liberals enjoying a majority in every case; election disputes are almost invariably decided in favor of the Liberal Party.[87]

The PLN rejected the mediators' proposal outright, while the FAO leadership declared that it was impossible to contemplate "clean" democratic elections so long as Somoza and his relatives were allowed to retain control of the National Guard. According to a State official involved in formulating the referendum plan, Somoza's response was equally dismissive. " 'I can lose that kind of election,' " he told Special Ambassador William Bowdler.[88]

After six days of no progress, the mediators set a 72 hour deadline for an agreement to be reached. Otherwise, they threatened to leave the country. Before the deadline expired, each side modified its initial position. The FAO gave conditional support to the plebiscite proposal after receiving the mediators' opinion that the resignation of the head of state prior to the election was not, as the governing PLN maintained, unconstitutional. An influential conservative political leader offered another explanation for the FAO change of heart: "it ha[d] no other resources than to rely on the mediation."[89] Somoza shifted from his original position even more reluctantly. At first, he continued to reject any possibility of abandoning power voluntarily prior to 1981, irrespective of whether a plebiscite was held or not. Then, in an abrupt turnabout, he offered to participate in a plebiscite if the PLN were guaranteed a leading political and constitutional role in the establishment of a transitional regime should he lose the election – instead of the formation of an FAO government. Of course, Somoza also had other reasons for wanting to avoid a "premature" collapse of negotiations.[90]

87 Department of State Telegram, Secret Managua 5950, American Embassy (Solaun) to Secretary of State, November 19, 1978, Subject: "Nicaragua Mediation No. 141–Plebiscite Conditions," DFOIA.
88 Interview with Malcolm Barnaby.
89 Department of State Telegram, Confidential Managua 6242, American Embassy (Solaun) to Secretary of State, December 1, 1978, Subject: "Nicaragua Mediation No. 193–FAO Consideration of Plebiscite Proposal," DFOIA.
90 See Department of State Telegram, Managua 6225, American Embassy to Secretary of State, November 30, 1978, Subject: "Nicaragua Mediation No. 186–English Translation of FAO Reply to NG [Negotiating Group] Proposal," DFOIA; Department of State Telegram, Managua 6240, American Embassy (Solaun) to Secretary of State, December 1, 1978, Subject: "Nicaragua Mediation No. 189–English Translation of Somoza's Reply to NG's [Negotiating Group] Plebiscite Proposal," DFOIA.

In a revealing conversation with Ambassador Solaun at the time of this "change of heart," Somoza rejected any "up or down vote on his continuing in office" and strongly intimated that he would only support a plebiscite that tested "relative party strength." Solaun came away from the meeting with "the clear impression that he does not think the pressures bearing down on him are yet sufficient to compel him to throw in the sponge." This "refusal to accept our formula" strongly reinforced the impression that he was "string[ing] this process out in order to gain time." The moment had arrived when Washington should consider "specific measures" such as economic and military aid sanctions. Otherwise, the Ambassador believed, Somoza was unlikely to budge from his current stance and would continue to dismiss administration warnings as "not credible. . . ."[91]

Having momentarily saved the plebiscite proposal by threatening to discontinue the talks, the mediators recommended direct negotiations between the parties before the vote, but insisted that whatever the outcome of the election it must be accepted by the PLN and the FAO. If Somoza won, he would remain as head of state. If he lost, resignation would follow, and a joint session of Congress would elect a new president put forward by the FAO, but acceptable to the PLN, who would serve until May 1981; the new cabinet would be composed of one-third FAO representatives, one-third PLN members, and one-third independents approved by the FAO and the PLN; the judicial system would be reorganized; the National Guard would be restructured through the creation of three separate branches (army, navy, air force); a national police force would be created; and a new electoral law would be drafted to guarantee the long-term survival of a democratic, pluralist political system. The FAO responded that prior to any face-to-face discussions with the PLN, the regime must honor a series of minimum demands including an end to the state of siege, changes in the National Guard leadership, an amnesty for political prisoners, the lifting of press censorship, and a promise to confine the Guard to barracks during the pre-plebiscite period.[92]

After conferring with Solaun, the Nicaraguan dictator agreed to end the state of siege, introduce a general amnesty law, relax the radio-TV censorship code, and enter into direct negotiations with the FAO. The official

91 Department of State Telegram, Secret Managua 6205, American Embassy (Solaun) to Secretary of State, November 30, 1978, Subject: "Nicaragua Mediation No. 183, Private Conversation with Somoza," DFOIA.
92 See Department of State Telegram, Confidential Managua 6281, American Embassy (Solaun) to Secretary of State, December 2, 1978, Subject: "Nicaragua Mediation No. 195–Translation NG [Negotiating Group] Reply [to FAO and Somoza/PLN response on plebiscite]," DFOIA; Department of State Telegram, Managua 6367, American Embassy (Solaun) to Secretary of State, December 6, 1978, Subject: "Nicaragua Mediation No. 214–Translation of FAO Response to NG [Negotiating Group] Proposal," DFOIA.

PLN communication was delivered to the mediators on December 6. Under heavy pressure from Washington to participate in a solution to the conflict that "ignore[d] the guerrillas,"[93] the FAO decided that these concessions were sufficient for talks to begin. Throughout this maneuvering, the U.S. Embassy worked closely with the most right-wing FAO members such as Adolfo Calero, the Conservative Party leader and president of Coca Cola Nicaragua, whom Ambassador Solaun described as "one of the most level-headed and moderate leaders in the FAO."[94] To ensure the success of the talks, Solaun urged influential conservatives and business leaders, including Archbishop Obando Y Bravo and officials of the Superior Council of Private Enterprise (COSEP) to attend as observers.[95] Embassy activity was complemented by new State Department pressures on the Sandinistas closest regional allies – Venezuela, Panama, and Costa Rica – to withdraw their support for the guerrillas "unless they accept the plebiscite."[96]

Almost three months of mediation, however, had seen a conviction take hold among a large segment of the political opposition that the U.S. solution to the Nicaraguan crisis began and ended with Somoza's replacement by an equally conservative but less repressive successor. Certainly, the State Department linked the fortunes of the FSLN to Somoza's ultimate fate. Assistant Secretary Vaky called the dictator "the main argument for the Sandinista's existence."[97] Policy Planning's Richard Feinberg noted that "at the time of the mediation the general view [within the administration] was that the Sandinistas were still distinctly a minority and that once you get rid of Somoza they would become an even smaller minority."[98] A senior Central Americanist expanded on the thinking behind this "hitting at the top" strategy: "If you could get Somoza out and if you could get [Alfonso] Robelo or some other leading opposition figure as a successor, we thought that there was a very good chance of mobilizing the anti-Sandinista forces under one banner and thereby drain a very large measure of Sandinista support."[99]

93 Riding, "U.S. Strategy in Nicaragua Keeps the Time Bomb Ticking," p. E3; Department of State Telegram, Managua 6425, American Embassy (Solaun) to Secretary of State, December 7, 1978, Subject: "Nicaragua Mediation No. 219–Translation of PLN Communication," DFOIA.
94 Department of State Telegram, Confidential Managua 6105, American Embassy (Solaun) to Secretary of State, November 25, 1978, Subject: "Nicaragua Mediation No. 171–Opposition Leader to Visit Washington," DFOIA.
95 Department of State Telegram, Confidential Managua 6510, American Embassy (Solaun) to Secretary of State, December 12, 1978, Subject: "Nicaragua Mediation No. 236–Developments on the Amnesty Front: Church and Cosep Attitudes," DFOIA.
96 Alan Riding, "Amnesty in Nicaragua Expected to Speed Negotiations," *New York Times*, December 11, 1978, p. 3. Also see Karen DeYoung, "U.S. Mediation in Nicaragua Set Back," *Washington Post*, December 27, 1978, pp. A1, A8.
97 Interview with Viron Vaky.
98 Interview with Richard Feinberg.
99 Confidential interview, Department of State official, September 20, 1989.

Or, as William Jorden pithly observed, "the feeling was that with him gone the basic problem would be settled."[100]

For U.S. policymakers, Somoza's willingness to yield political power sooner rather than later also held out the possibility of containing popular demands for socioeconomic change within "acceptable" limits. In mid-December, the *New York Times* correspondent in Managua reported that "Washington is gambling that, once Somoza resigns, support for the guerrillas and pressures for reform will evaporate."[101] But these objectives began to founder on the shoals of an increasingly unrepresentative FAO, under more or less constant State Department pressure to moderate its demands in order to keep Somoza at the bargaining table and sustain the possibility of a non-military solution to the conflict.

A vulnerable pressure point: U.S. policy and the fiscal crisis of the Nicaraguan state

Prior to the Chamorro assassination in January 1978, foreign capital saw little reason to change its long-held view of Nicaragua as a safe and profitable haven for investment and accumulation. "For the most part," a knowledgeable American banker observed, Somoza "created a very positive environment for foreign business in general and U.S. companies in particular. It was stable politically and a profitable place to do business."[102] Following Chamorro's murder and Somoza's ruthless response to the partially business-led general strike, new American investments slowed down to what one Nicaraguan economist called "a glacial pace,"[103] and even some foreign banks began "to talk about reconsolidating their operations."[104] Responding to Somoza allegations of an "economic boycott" by finance capital, U.S. Ambassador Mauricio Solaun told the dictator that the banks had also become increasingly disturbed about the practice of government officials siphoning off portions of each new loan for their own private use.[105]

No foreign bank was more concerned over unfolding developments in Nicaragua than Citibank whose exposure, estimated at $128 million in mid-1977, exceeded that of any of its competitors. Of this amount, about $60 million had been lent directly to the regime, while millions more in loans

100 Telephone interview with William Jorden.
101 Riding, "U.S. Strategy in Nicaragua Keeps the Time Bomb Ticking," p. E3. Also see Riding, "Amnesty in Nicaragua Expected to Speed Negotiations," p. 3
102 Telephone interview with William Dewey.
103 Quoted in "Nicaragua: Investment Inhibited," *Financial Times*, August 17, 1978, p. 32.
104 Telephone interview with William Dewey.
105 Department of State Telegram, Confidential Managua 1945.

were made to government banks and other state-related institutions. According to Onofre Torres, who arrived in Managua in May 1977 to manage the Citibank branch, "prior to that time, headquarters had not shown much concern about loans made to government entities or whether money was being siphoned off by Somoza personally." Torres and his deputy William Dewey began "to take a hard look at Citibank's exposure to certain business groups and try to determine if these companies were economically viable or not. We began to get concerned about the financial situation of the companies we were lending to because of the general deterioration of the economy." The major targets of the investigation were companies owned by the Somoza family. The objective was "to reduce outstanding loans and to require the Somoza companies to repay, not roll over, loans. For the most part, the General was prepared to accede to our demands because this was not a problem he needed."[106]

Amid the generalized economic crisis, the Chamorro assassination sent "another important message" to Citibank officials in Managua: "Things are bad and getting worse."[107] But New York headquarters was reluctant to embrace such pessimistic reports, especially in the light of more positive assessments they were receiving from the Carter administration. "New York didn't see the situation was deteriorating as fast as it was from our perspective in 1978," said William Dewey. "They were getting briefs in Washington and reporting that Somoza was once again going to weather the storm, that the opposition was not large or powerful enough to mount a two-front war."[108] Still, around the middle of the year, a Citibank executive informed Ambassador Solaun that New York was contemplating "a gradual decrease in the bank's exposure in Nicaragua due to political trends in the country." Soon after, a decision was taken to reduce the total portfolio by around $10 million. Other U.S. banks also indicated their anxiety over Nicaragua's future by placing "country limits" on new loans that effectively meant a refusal to provide additional lines of credit unless a particular regime proposal seemed extraordinarily attractive (profitable).[109]

Not all the American or other foreign banks in Nicaragua followed Citibank's example. Indeed, at this stage the cautious approach adopted by

---

106   Telephone interview with Onofre Torres, Florida, October 4, 1989; telephone interview with William Dewey. Also See Department of State Telegram, Confidential Managua 3365, American Embassy (Solaun) to Secretary of State, July 25, 1978, Subject: "Decrease in Activities of U.S. Banks in Nicaragua," DFOIA.
107   Telephone interview with Onofre Torres.
108   Telephone interview with William Dewey.
109   Department of State Telegram, Confidential Managua 3365; Department of State Telegram, Managua 5149, American Embassy (Solaun) to Secretary of State, November 8, 1978, Subject: "Liquidity in Nicaraguan Banking System Evaporates – Some Economic Problems Lie Ahead," DFOIA.

Citibank seemed more the exception than the rule. A number of competitor banks still had unqualified confidence in Somoza's ability to prevent the internal conflict from getting "out of hand" and aggressively sought to increase their exposure: "None of the U.S. banks that didn't have a local presence, or even Bank of America which did, were intimidated by the Chamorro murder and burning down of Citibank's branch. We [Citibank] did everything after that to collect on everybody. We began pulling in and not extending new loans. The Bank of America used this as a competitive opportunity to lure clients away from us. There were varying perceptions among the banks and that continued for many months."[110] On the eve of the August-September upheaval, William Dewey recalled, "there was still lively competition. We were taken out in several cases by the Lloyds Bank affiliate, Bank of London. Other foreign banks did not show our concern about the country credit risk. They believed that Somoza could deal with the crisis and were not prepared to abandon him or other members of the private sector. There was still the perception that Somoza would weather the political crisis, that the National Guard was capable."[111] Among the major foreign banks still willing to underwrite the Somoza regime was Italy's Banco Ambrosiano, which established an office for offshore business in the government's newly created free zone "and did a lot of business directly with the government and the Somozas,"[112] and Swiss Bank Corporation, which had agreed to lend the dictatorship $15 million "without strings" just prior to the national insurrection.[113]

If Citibank's pessimistic assessment of the Nicaraguan situation were not shared by many of its own fraternity, foreign investors and the multilateral development banks (MDBs) were another matter entirely. Both contracted their lending to Nicaragua during 1978. Loans from the MDBs, which totaled $120 million in 1976–77, almost dried up completely. The Inter-American Development Bank refusal to approve loan requests was instrumental in forcing the regime to shelve its multi-million dollar Copolar hydroelectric project.[114] With the exception of two $20 million credits from the Central American Monetary Stabilization Fund, the Somoza dictatorship became increasingly reliant on foreign commercial banks. But even these institutions began to impose harsher lending conditions (shorter terms, higher interest rates) than previously.

110 Telephone interview with Onofre Torres.
111 Telephone interview with William Dewey.
112 Telephone interview with Onofre Torres.
113 Department of State Telegram, Confidential Managua 4202, American Embassy (Solaun) to Secretary of State, September 7, 1978, Subject: "Sitrep 8–7 September," DFOIA.
114 "Nicaragua: The Capitalists Battle for a Capital," *Latin America Economic Report*, October 20, 1978, p. 323.

The Nicaraguan economy was further undermined by the domestic unrest in the form of large-scale capital flight. It reached record levels in 1978 as between $230 and $255 million left the country, more than half at the instigation of the Somoza family and its closest supporters, for deposit boxes in foreign financial institutions or to purchase arms for the National Guard.[115] Nicaraguan exporters also began to channel more and more of their foreign exchange (hard currency) earnings into overseas banks.

Against this background of declining access to funds from abroad and massive outflows of capital, the revival of high-level social and military struggle in August-September 1978 had a particularly devastating impact on the Nicaraguan economy. The popular insurrection destroyed over 600 factories, and enterprise losses in the provincial cities of Masaya, León, Chinandega, and Estelí alone totaled more than $66 million. Capital flight quickened apace: An estimated $60 million decamped between August 25 and September 21. The inability to maintain normal levels of tax collection due to the hostilities so contracted public revenues that the regime was forced to borrow money from the Central Bank to cover shortfalls in its regular operating expenses. However, the problem of debt interest repayment obligations could not be resolved in this fashion, raising the distinct possibility of a default, thus alienating the country's foreign private bank creditors – the dictator's only remaining significant source of overseas credits. Compounding these economic woes, Nicaragua's foreign exchange reserves were almost exhausted and international insurers were refusing to make payments on $60 million in war-related damage claims.[116]

With the central government about to be overwhelmed by the cumulative impact of these economic and fiscal pressures, Somoza turned for a way out of his predicament to the International Monetary Fund (IMF) – one of the capitalist world's preeminent financial institutions, which had emerged in the 1970s as perhaps the most important social and economic agenda-setting agency in the Third World. His government formally applied for a Special Drawing Rights (SDR) $21.6 million loan from the Fund's Compensatory

115 James Nelson Goodsell, "Economic Pressures Could Prove Somoza's Undoing," *Christian Science Monitor*, February 15, 1979, p. 7; James Nelson Goodsell, "IMF Loans to Nicaragua Give Somoza Breathing Space," *Christian Science Monitor*, May 16, 1979, p. 7; "Big Devaluation Angers the Opposition in Managua," *Latin America Economic Report*, April 13, 1979, p. 113.

116 "Nicaragua; Trouble Economy," *Central America Report*, October 23, 1978, pp. 329–330; Frank Del Olmo, "Run on Banks Draining Capital From Nicaragua," *Los Angeles Times*, Part 1, September 3, 1978, p. 21; Don Bohning, "Big Money Is Fleeing Nicaragua," *Miami Herald*, September 22, 1978, pp. 1A, 23A; "Nicaragua: An Ostracized Regime Runs Out Of Money," *Business Week*, February 5, 1979, p. 38; "Tax War in Nicaragua," *Central America Report*, April 9, 1979, p. 113; Economist Intelligence Unit, *Quarterly Economic Review of Nicaragua*, No. 1, January 1979, pp. 13–14; *Quarterly Economic Review of Nicaragua*, No. 2, May 1979, p. 12.

Financing Facility (CFF), which had been established to help Third World countries experiencing balance of payments difficulties resulting from severe, but temporary, losses in export earnings due to circumstances beyond their control (for example, an abrupt fall in global commodity prices).

Following normal procedure, the Fund dispatched an inspection mission to Managua to make an on-the-spot assessment. Although unable to travel beyond the capital because the regime could not guarantee its safety, the team prepared an informal report to the IMF Executive Board that was sharply critical of the submission. It argued that primary responsibility for the country's economic plight did not rest with export price fluctuations but was linked to the economic activities of the Somoza family and its allies – specifically, the siphoning off of millions of dollars in foreign aid, year after year, for purposes of private enrichment or equipping the National Guard.[117]

On September 15, the Executive Board met to consider the Nicaraguan request, and decided to postpone a final judgment but to keep it under "active consideration." The U.S. Executive Director Sam Cross lobbied hard to have the request deferred rather than rejected outright on the grounds that recent political developments in Nicaragua may have further weakened the country's export prospects, thus invalidating the calculations upon which the CFF request was originally based. Deputy Assistant Treasury Secretary for Developing Nations Arnold Nachmanoff put it more succinctly: "The U.S. wasn't satisfied that Nicaragua had met the conditions for the CFF."[118] NSC Latin American staff specialist Robert Pastor maintained that State and Treasury "were united on an overall strategy" despite the latter's "stress on the importance of guaranteeing the integrity of the IMF. This was not difficult because Somoza had not fulfilled the requirements. [Assistant Secretary of State] Vaky used [Deputy Assistant Secretary] Bushnell to come up with a whole variety of specific technical criteria by which the IMF should not consider giving the loan. As long as the State Department came forward with technical criteria, Treasury did not question the IMF's right to deny the loan."[119]

Both Treasury and State Department officials agreed that more time was needed to clarify the economic situation inside Nicaragua. Treasury official Thomas Leddy recalled that the decision not to "knock it back completely

117 See Lewis James, "The Truth Behind the Nicaraguan Row with Carter and the IMF," *Euromoney*, January 1979, pp. 109, 111.
118 Telephone interview with Arnold Nachmanoff, Washington, D.C., October 2, 1989. The respondent was Deputy Assistant Secretary for Developing Nations, Department of the Treasury, 1977 to 1981. U.S. Executive Director to the IMF during 1978, Sam Cross, also described the CFF proposal as having "technical deficiencies in it." Telephone interview with Sam Cross, New York, October 5, 1989.
119 Telephone interview with Robert Pastor, Georgia, October 5, 1989. The respondent was the National Security Council Staff specialist on Latin America, 1977 to 1981.

involved a strong tactical consideration and an underlying feeling that it would not be proper to try and defeat something that might in substance have been right and would have been damaging to the U.S. position in the Fund."[120] State was also reluctant to see the request voted down to avoid unnecessarily alienating the "Somoza lobby" while Congress was debating important international financial institutions legislation.[121] After the IMF announced its decision to put off a final vote, negotiations between Nicaragua and eight foreign and American banks involving loans totalling $40 million (with the exception of $4 million already disbursed by the Bank of London) – conditioned on a successful Fund outcome – collapsed.[122]

Predictably, the Somoza government responded to the IMF action with a mixture of anger and bewilderment. A delegation of senior Nicaraguan officials led by Central Bank president Roberto Incer complained to U.S. Executive Director Cross and Assistant Treasury Secretary Nachmanoff that without a Fund "seal of approval" it would be impossible for the Central Bank "to maneuver financially, repay its debts, and maintain access to [the] private international [banking] sector." The Carter officials restated the Board's concern over "uncertainties" about the calculations in the CCF submission but attempted to reassure the delegation that the postponement should not be interpreted "as a negative judgment of the request." Washington "remains open-minded" and would base its final decision on an updated assessment of Nicaragua's economic situation.[123]

In mid-October, Central Bank president Incer told a high-ranking American Embassy official that Nicaragua's foreign reserves were fast disappearing (they plummeted from $87 million in 1977 to no more than $5 million by February 1979) and that the government intended to submit new requests to the IMF and the Central American Common Market for $30 million and $20 million loans respectively. But the severity of the fiscal crisis was such,

120 Telephone interview with Thomas Leddy, Washington, D.C., October 5, 1989. The respondent was special assistant to the Under Secretary for Monetary Affairs, Department of the Treasury, and alternate U.S. Executive Director to the IMF during 1978.
121 Department of the Treasury, Internal Memorandum, Confidential, Prepared by Brian Zipp (I/IDN), September 22, 1978, Subject: "Nicaraguan Request for Compensatory Financing Facility Credit," DFOIA.
122 Karen DeYoung, "Nicaragua Asks Loan From IMF to Prevent Collapse of Economy," *Washington Post*, November 3, 1978, p. A16; "Famine and Economic Collapse Threaten Strife-Torn Nicaragua," *Washington Post*, September 19, 1978, p. A18; Department of State Telegram, Managua 4202.
123 Department of State Telegram, Confidential State 260248, Secretary of State (Vance) to American Embassy, October 14, 1978, Subject: "Discussions with Nicaraguans during Fund/Bank Meetings," DFOIA. The Nicaraguan participants were Central Bank President Roberto Incer, Minister of Economy Blandon Valasquez, Vice President Finance Rueben García, and IMF alternative Nestor Caldera.

he believed, that it would also be necessary to convince the foreign commercial banks to provide an extra $30 million in new credits during 1979.[124]

While the Nicaraguan government was still reeling from its treatment at the hands of the IMF, State Department officials broached the possibility of exploiting the parlous state of the country's economy to pressure Somoza to take the mediation negotiations more seriously. In early October, Deputy Secretary of State Warren Christopher had sent a telegram to the Managua Embassy that read in part: "While our basic position is that existing loan and grant agreements constitute binding obligations on the USG [United States Government], timing of certain disbursements may be important and in some projects consideration might be given to delaying major new steps which would give rise to significant disbursements depending on the progress of mediation."[125] Ambassador Solaun was a strong advocate of using aid as a form of leverage to facilitate a successful political outcome. Recent discussions with Incer and a representative of the powerful non-Somoza Banco de América economic group, Ernesto Fernandez, reinforced this conviction. They told him that the government was "in dire financial straits [with] no relief in sight until early next year.... For the purpose of the mediation effort, the implication is clear: maximum financial pressure can be exerted on Somoza and GON [Government of Nicaragua] in the next two or three months." Nicaragua's economic crisis, the Ambassador cabled Washington on October 13, constitutes "a potential plus in bringing about a settlement."[126]

Despite Embassy urging, the administration moved with great circumspection, and ultimately resisted the imposition of significant economic sanctions, preferring to accommodate Somoza's idiosyncrasies and encourage him to take the desired measures voluntarily or risk some vague future retaliation. A few days after Solaun's conversation with Incer and Fernandez, the U.S. Export-Import Bank announced that henceforth the export credit programs to Nicaragua would be assessed on a case-by-case basis. But Warren Christopher was quick to assuage Managua's fears by saying that the Bank had not gone "off cover." It was merely taking a "very cautious

---

124 Department of State Telegram, Managua 5074, American Embassy (Solaun) to Secretary of State, October 14, 1978, Subject: "Conversation with Central Bank President," DFOIA; "Nicaraguan Debt Reschedule Likely Despite US Aid Ban," *Latin America Economic Report*, February 16, 1979, p. 50.

125 Department of State Telegram, Confidential State 255841, Secretary of State (Christopher) to American Embassy, October 7, 1978, Subject: "Aid Loan Disbursements," DFOIA.

126 Department of State Telegram, Confidential Managua 5025, American Embassy (Solaun) to Secretary of State, October 13, 1978, Subject: "Nicaragua Mediation No. 24– Scraping the Bottom of the Barrel," DFOIA.

approach" given the current depressed state of the Nicaraguan economy.[127] In early November, the opposition newspaper *La Prensa* reported subtle U.S. threats to revise Nicaragua's annual 900,000 pound meat export quota to the American market.[128] "Lots of things were being proposed," Assistant Secretary of State Vaky recalled, "up to and including the cutting of the meat quota. The question was how to convince Somoza that we were serious, whether about the sugar quota, the meat quota, or suspending aid. The White House would say 'rather than invoke those sanctions, let's say to Somoza that if you don't do these things bad things are going to happen.' We [Vaky, Special Ambassador Bowdler, etc.] were saying 'do them' and then say to Somoza what are you going to do."[129] The White House approach prevailed.

As Carter officials considered the economic sanctions option, the IMF Executive Board prepared to reconvene for another round of discussions on the Compensatory Financing Facility (CFF) loan request. After what the London-based *Financial Times* characterized as "much U.S. arm twisting," the Directors once more adjourned without taking a final vote.[130] Secretary of State Vance reported that "a clear majority" of the Board (United Kingdom, West Germany, France, the Scandinavians, Belgium, Italy) supported this second postponement "at our initiative."[131] An involved Treasury official attributed the White House stance to the September insurrection and its aftermath, which rendered a second IMF inspection team visit to Nicaragua to assess the quality of the technical data included in the loan request impossible because this time around the Somoza government could not even guarantee its safety in the capital city. Washington's support for another deferral was also linked to the State Department's continuing preoccupation with minimizing "Somoza lobby" attacks on key executive branch legislation before the House and Senate. Indeed, State went out of its way to assure one of Somoza's leading Congressional standard bearers, Texas Democrat Charles Wilson, that administration votes in the IMF were dictated exclusively by neutral economic factors and did not indicate a shift in policy or a disposition to use economic pressures to force the dictator to accept the

127   Department of State Telegram, State 261627, Secretary of State (Christopher) to American Embassy, October 16, 1978, Subject: "Export Import Bank Programs in Nicaragua," DFOIA.

128   See Foreign Broadcast Information Service, *Daily Report: Latin America*, November 8, 1978, p. 7.

129   Interview with Viron Vaky.

130   Hugh O'Shaughnessy, "Carter's Blow to Somoza's Financial Underbelly," *Financial Times*, November 8, 1978, p. 4.

131   Department of State Telegram, Confidential State 278417, Secretary of State (Vance) to American Embassy, November 3, 1978, Subject: "Nicaraguan Situation Update," DFOIA.

mediators' plebiscite proposal. "On the IMF," Secretary Vance wrote, "we explained to Wilson, at all levels including very senior levels in Treasury and State, that the action we took [deferral] was for technical reasons."[132]

Interpreting the IMF's decision to table the CCF loan request for a second time as tantamount to a rejection, the Nicaraguan government withdrew the submission. According to Viron Vaky, the Fund's action "really rocked" Somoza.[133] It certainly had a powerful negative impact on his relations with the foreign private banking community. Having conditioned the release of major new credits on IMF passage of the CCF request, American, British, Canadian, and other banks with long histories of exposure in Nicaragua began shelving some large pending loan applications on the grounds that the country had failed to regain international financial respectability. During November, the American Embassy in Managua witnessed an upsurge in visits by senior officials of U.S. commercial banks expressing concerns about the worsening economic and financial climate. This unease soon turned to alarm when the government resorted to new controls to tackle the problem of a severe shortage of foreign exchange. The Embassy reported that two American banks had already cut existing lines of credit to Nicaraguan banks (thereby decreasing the amount of capital available to the private sector) and that "others are looking hard at their posture vis-à-vis the GON [Government of Nicaragua]. They have long-range interests in Nicaragua and would like to take a long range point of view."[134] With a gross domestic product of less than $2 billion, a small, resource-weak Central American economy had managed to accumulate over $800 million in long-term debts, more than half of which was owed to these private financial institutions.[135] Against that background, the move by foreign banks to contract their private and public portfolios was quite understandable.

By mid-November, the Nicaraguan economy had reached breaking point, forcing the Central Bank President to officially notify the country's principal foreign creditors that it could not meet its current obligations – an estimated $150 million in interest payments due before the end of 1978 – and was applying for a refinancing or "rollover" of its overseas debt.[136] Instead of

---

132   Department of State Telegram, Secret State 287379, Secretary of State (Vance) to American Embassy, November 12, 1978, Subject: "AID and IMF Matters," DFOIA.

133   Interview with Viron Vaky.

134   Department of State Telegram, Managua 6087, American Embassy (Solaun) to Secretary of State, November 24, 1978, Subject: "Economic-Financial Situation in Nicaragua Continues," DFOIA. Also see Department of State Telegram, Confidential Managua 5926, American Embassy (Solaun) to Secretary of State, November 17, 1978, Subject: "US Commercial Banks and the Nicaraguan Financial Situation," DFOIA.

135   James, "The Truth Behind the Nicaraguan Row with Carter and the IMF," p. 111.

136   "Nicaraguan Debt Reschedule Likely Despite US Aid Ban," p. 50; Edward P. Foldessy, "Nicaragua's Central Bank Asks Creditors in U.S. and Elsewhere to Refinance Loans,"

panicking, though, most creditor banks still remained optimistic about a quick resolution to the problem. The manager of Citibank's Managua branch explained: "The banks said the reason why the government couldn't make the payments was political, a war was going on, it would be resolved soon, and the money would flow back in. That was the belief. Everybody blamed it on a temporary political situation that would be resolved when Somoza left."[137]

American diplomacy stalled: The collapse of the mediation track

With the passage of time, the Broad Opposition Front (FAO) began to increasingly reflect the views of a narrowly based agglomeration of right-wing organizations and individuals rather than those of a mass-based, polyclass antidictatorial movement. The mediation strategy had not only split the civilian opposition; it had failed to dislodge Somoza from power and increased support for the FSLN – to the point where most of the anti-Somoza forces inside (as well as outside) Nicaragua were willing to let the plebiscite collapse rather than endorse any outcome that excluded the Sandinistas from a role in the political transition commensurate with their contribution to the anti-regime struggle.

In the large urban centers, the insurgents' growing popularity also gave them a powerful weapon to render any plebiscite meaningless – either by directing its constituencies to abstain from voting or preempting the vote by launching a new military offensive. To undercut the latter option, Washington again resorted to diplomatic pressures, targeting the anti-Somoza regimes in Caracas, Panama City, and San José in an effort to curtail any planned FSLN attack. But what Ambassador Bowdler discovered upon his arrival in Costa Rica and Panama to press for a rupture in ties with the FSLN unless the Sandinista high command accepted the plebiscite proposal was that "the anti-Somoza struggle [was] so popular in these countries that such antirebel moves [were] politically impossible for their governments."[138]

On December 20, amid threats by Nationalist Liberal Party (PLN) negotiators to halt talks unless the FAO agreed to participate in a government of national unity if Somoza topped the plebiscite vote and to withdraw a demand that the dictator go into exile if he lost, the mediators presented an expanded and revised plebiscite draft to the warring parties. Although it still

Wall Street Journal, November 14, 1978, p. 36; David Lascelles, "Somoza Seeks Relief on Foreign Debts," *Financial Times*, February 1, 1979, p. 3.
137 Telephone interview with Onofre Torres.
138 Riding, "U.S. Strategy in Nicaragua Keeps the Time Bomb Ticking," p. E3.

retained such key features of the original document as an internationally supervised vote and reform of the National Guard, there were changes designed to make it more palatable to Somoza. For instance, the dictator no longer had to abide by an FAO demand to leave the country during the election campaign; he was only required to resign from his National Guard post. The plebiscite (to take place between January 5 and February 28, 1979) would determine Somoza's political fate and the results would only be accepted as meaningful if there was effective compliance with measures adopted for the full observance of constitutional guarantees, amnesty, pardons, and media reforms. Effective compliance included immediate overseas postings for two leading National Guard officials, the dictator's half brother General José Somoza, Director of the National Guard, and his eldest son, Major Anastasio Somoza, head of the military training school, until the process was completed, the Guard's confinement to barracks (except units engaged in routine police and border control duties) 72 hours before voting began, international supervision of the state-run media to ensure both sides equal access during the campaign period, and a prohibition on either the FAO or the PLN using government personnel or resources in support of their electoral goals.

A Somoza victory would empower him to form a new government and require the FAO to accept the role of a "constructive and peaceful opposition." A defeat would be followed by resignation and exile within three days although his obligatory sojourn abroad would only extend until May 1981.[139] In the event of an FAO triumph, the new president would name a cabinet composed jointly of FAO, PLN, and independent representatives along the lines set out in the earlier document. Significantly, the mediators demanded no changes in, or reorganization of, the pro-Somoza Congress. Thus, whatever the outcome, conservative political forces would still play a prominent role within a new government of national reconciliation.

The day of the mediators' latest proposal, Ambassador Solaun cabled the State Department to the effect that Somoza was intent on deliberately sabotaging the negotiations in the belief "that he has weathered the storm and can now dispense with the mediation," pinning responsibility for its failure on the FAO's refusal to participate in a Somoza-led government should he

---

139 Department of State Telegram, Confidential State 321699, Secretary of State (Christopher) to All American Republic Diplomatic Posts, December 22, 1978, Subject: "Nicaraguan Mediation Update," DFOIA. Also see Department of State Telegram, Confidential Managua 6687, American Embassy (Solaun) to Secretary of State, December 20, 1978, Subject: "Nicaragua Mediation No. 259: English Translation of Draft Agreement [presented by mediators to PLN and FAO]," DFOIA; Department of State Telegram, Confidential Managua 6710, American Embassy (Solaun) to Secretary of State, December 20, 1978, Subject: "Nicaragua Mediation No. 263–Revised Text of Draft Agreement," DFOIA.

win the plebiscite. A combination of factors explained the dictator's growing confidence: the defeat of Acción Democrática (AD) in the Venezuelan presidential elections (outgoing AD president Carlos Andrés Pérez was a leading hemispheric critic of the Somoza regime); new Costa Rican government curbs on Sandinista guerrilla activities in that country; indications that Panamanian president General Omar Torrijos was waning in his support for the FSLN; an easing of financial pressures on the regime; and the absence of a unified and effective civilian opposition.[140] Secretary Vance instructed the Embassy to tell Somoza that the FAO's refusal to join a regime led by him "is not a valid argument for refusing to negotiate a plebiscite package," and that in the absence of "a rapid and successful conclusion" to negotiations, bilateral ties "will be strongly affected."[141]

In another attempt to persuade Somoza "to modify [his] apparent stonewalling,"[142] State enlisted the help of the Defense Department, historically the dynasty's most consistent bureaucratic ally. Since Carter's election, the Pentagon had opposed any policy shift on strategic grounds or in the belief that Washington's options were limited in any case. "If the Department thought about Nicaragua at all," said Assistant Secretary for International Security Affairs David McGiffert, "it was 'well Somoza's there, an unsavory fellow, but there is not much we can do about it.' "[143]

However, the events of August–September jolted the Pentagon no less than the rest of the imperial state. Officials started pondering whether the upheaval signaled the beginnings of "a very unhealthy period of instability that might have strategic implications for the rest of Central America. They felt that some of Somoza's internal policies weren't necessarily conducive to long-term interests of the government or Nicaragua or the United States."[144] But, at least initially, there was considerable hesitation about going down the mediation road. The Department "was nervous about mediation," State's Wade Matthews remembered. "They didn't like it and thought it would come a cropper."[145] Many within the coercive agency still adhered to the notion that " 'the devil you know is better than the devil you

140   Department of State Telegram, Secret Managua 6686, American Embassy (Solaun) to Secretary of State, December 20, 1978, Subject: "Nicaraguan Mediation No. 260–GON [Government of Nicaragua] Intransigence in Mediation," DFOIA.
141   Department of State Telegram, Secret State 319955, Secretary of State (Vance) to American Embassy, December 20, 1978, Subject: "Nicaragua Mediation – New Démarche to Somoza," DFOIA.
142   Department of State Telegram, Confidential State 321699.
143   Interview with David McGiffert, Washington, D.C., October 7, 1988. The respondent was Assistant Secretary (International Security Affairs), Department of Defense, 1977 to 1980.
144   Confidential telephone interview, Department of Defense official, Maine, September 26, 1989.
145   Interview with Wade Matthews.

don't.' "[46] At the same time, senior officials began to accept the reality of the situation: A regime change was increasingly likely, probably sooner rather than later. In that circumstance, the Pentagon's Director of Inter-American Affairs Admiral Gordon Schuller explained, the overriding issue became that of preventing a "second Cuba":

> The Pentagon recognized a change had to take place and wanted change to take place but in an orderly fashion. The Pentagon didn't want the Marxists-Leftists Sandinistas to be in charge. All Defense wanted was stability. If a dictatorship that's fine. If a democracy that's fine. But a stable government. Didn't want another Cuban situation. That worried Defense. All Defense was after was stability. A good military dictatorship was fine, a good civilian government was better.[47]

A mid-November background paper prepared by the Western Hemisphere Division for Defense Secretary Harold Brown also dwelt on the likely negative strategic implications for U.S. interests throughout Central America if Somoza sought to hold onto political power.[48]

Hoping to persuade Somoza of the Pentagon's equally strong commitment to achieving a "peaceful resolution of the crisis,"[49] Secretary Vance authorized Lieutenant General Dennis McAuliffe, the head of Southern Command in Panama, to accompany William Bowdler to a December 21 meeting with the Nicaraguan leader. McAuliffe dispelled any illusions Somoza may still have harbored about the agency's stance: There was broad acceptance, including the Joint Chiefs of Staff, of the necessity for a regime change. The prospect of a more radical outcome increased the longer the conflict persisted, bringing with it the threat of shockwaves throughout the region. At the same time, McAuliffe gave the dictator assurances that the National Guard would "play an important role in any future government of the country," even though it might be necessary to change the institution's "makeup, complexion and image."[50] This was the subject of ongoing discussions between U.S. military officials and Guard officers.

Ambassador Bowdler confined his remarks largely to criticism of Somoza's obstructionist attitude toward the mediation proceedings, singling out his "insisten[ce] that the FAO agree to join the government if he won the plebiscite."[51] Both American officials cautioned that failure to achieve

146 Confidential telephone interview, Department of Defense official, September 26, 1989.
147 Interview with Admiral Gordon Schuller.
148 Department of Defense Working Paper, Secret, Background Paper prepared by Lt.Col. H.M. Cueller, USAF, Western Hemisphere Division for Policy Review Committee meeting re Nicaragua, November 13, 1978, Subject: "Nicaragua," DFOIA.
149 Karen DeYoung, "U.S. Mediation in Nicaragua Set Back," *Washington Post*, December 27, 1978, pp. A1, A8.
150 Quoted in Somoza, *Nicaragua Betrayed*, pp. 332–333.
151 Christian, *Nicaragua: Revolution in the Family*, p. 96.

a swift and successful outcome would "strongly affect" the overall relationship between Washington and Managua.[152]

But not even Pentagon entreaties could change Somoza's mind about the mediators' December 20 plebiscite proposal. He persisted in his objections to overseas assignments for National Guard family members, or to his own exile for any time period should he lose the election. The official PLN reply accused the document of violating the constitution, and refused to countenance the elimination of the voter inscription system and other specific changes. What angered the dictator most, though, was the proposed control and organization of the referendum – instead of mere oversight of the process – by an international authority. This latest example of Somoza intransigence produced new divisions and morale problems among an opposition that had already agreed to abide by the mediators' plan.[153] Political commission member Alfonso Robelo declared that the FAO/PLN negotiations were now on "the verge of a breakdown."[154] Meanwhile, those groups that had withdrawn from the FAO – the "Group of Twelve", the Union of Nicaraguan Workers, the Popular Social Christian Party, the United Peoples Movement, and the Independent Liberal Party – charged that by continuing to participate in the U.S.-orchestrated peace process the FAO "remnants" bore major responsibility for the disunity of the anti-Somoza forces.

Upon their return to Washington, Bowdler and McAuliffe proposed that Somoza be given an ultimatum: Adopt a more flexible negotiating posture or the Ambassador, Defense personnel, Agency for International Development officials, and Peace Corp workers will be recalled. At its December 22 meeting (the same day the PLN formally rejected the plebiscite proposal), the Special Coordination Committee (SCC) decided to send Bowdler to meet again with Somoza and issue a "stern démarche" calling for a definitive response to the plebiscite plan by December 28. The interagency committee also recommended simultaneous statements by prominent legislators and a private communication from President Carter to Somoza to the effect that a further rebuff to the mediators would lead to retaliatory measures along the lines proposed by the envoys.[155] Deputy Secretary of State Warren

152 Department of State Telegram, Secret State 319955.
153 Department of State Telegram, Managua 6745, American Embassy (Solaun) Secretary of State, December 22, 1978, Subject: "Nicaragua Mediation No. 268: FAO Reply to Plebiscite Proposal," DFOIA; Department of State Telegram, Managua 6747, American Embassy (Solaun) to Secretary of State, December 22, 1978, Subject: "Nicaragua Mediation No. 269–PLN Reply to NG's [Negotiating Group] Proposal," DFOIA.
154 Quoted in Foreign Broadcast Information Service, Daily Report: Latin America, December 20, 1978, p. 4.
155 Department of Defense Joint Talking Paper, Secret, Prepared for the Secretary of Defense and the Chairman of the Joint Chiefs of Staff for a meeting of the Policy Review Committee on December 26, 1978 (approved by Assistant Secretary of Defense, International Security Affairs), Subject: "Nicaragua," DFOIA.

Christopher, though, was pessimistic about the outcome. In an update to all regional embassies, he wrote that the negotiations were at "an impasse which could lead to [their] collapse." The PLN had "adopted a tough and uncompromising line" and there was a real possibility that Somoza "may now be prepared to torpedo the mediation and the plebiscite."[156]

The flurry of high-level activity was not confined to Washington. In Managua, Ambassador Solaun kept up a busy schedule of meetings with opposition leaders "to urge support for the mediation effort."[157] Instead of compliant allies, however, he ran into a barrage of criticism over Washington's perceived lack of "pressure" on Somoza to do likewise. And there was a second blunt message: Efforts to resolve the conflict were not helped by Carter administration hostility toward the FSLN. The White House must adopt a more flexible approach toward the Sandinistas, including "some public action to explain to the FSLN that the U.S. was not hostile to true change in Nicaragua and would stop undermining their international collections."[158] While the Ambassador baulked at raising this issue with his superiors, he dismissed any plebiscite counterproposal as an attempt by Somoza "to escape shouldering full responsibility for failure of the talks." But should the mediation fail, he warned the Department against a "return to business as usual with Somoza" on the grounds that it would destroy "our credibility with the moderate democratic forces in Nicaragua. . . ."[159]

By the fourth week of December, Embassy reports were suggesting that neither the FAO nor the government would be unduly disappointed if the mediation process did indeed collapse. Somoza had strengthened his military position and appeared supremely confident that he could "resist both internal attacks and international pressures." In any event, he was likely to seize on the opposition's refusal to serve under him should he win the election as the most convenient pretext for sabotaging the talks. The FAO, on the other hand, although still uncertain about its electoral prospects, was convinced that the outside world would blame the dictator for any breakdown of negotiations, which would inevitably produce increased American pressure on him to resign.[160]

156 Department of State Telegram, Confidential State 321699.
157 Department of State Telegram, Confidential Managua 6772, American Embassy (Tucker) to Secretary of State, December 23, 1978, Subject: "Conversations with Oppositionists," DFOIA.
158 Ibid.; Department of State Telegram, Confidential Managua 6746, American Embassy (Solaun) to Secretary of State, December 22, 1978, Subject: "Oppositionists Comments on the December 20 NG [Negotiating Group] Proposal," DFOIA.
159 Department of State Telegram, Secret Managua 6748, American Embassy (Solaun) to Secretary of State, December 22, 1978, Subject: "Nicaragua Mediation No. 270–PLN Response to NG Proposals," DFOIA.
160 Department of State Telegram, Confidential Managua 6768, American Embassy

On the day (December 27) the White House finally expressed a willingness to impose sanctions in an effort to force Somoza to participate in elections, the dictator unveiled his long-awaited counterproposal. The document turned out to be nothing more than a composite of earlier positions that had already been rejected by the mediators and the FAO. These included four key demands: The plebiscite must be organized and controled by a national authority; the vote must only determine whether Somoza finishes his constitutional term as president or convenes a constituent assembly to organize a provisional government; neither Somoza nor members of his family would be required to leave the country if the opposition won the plebiscite; and the ground rules operating in previous "elections" (for example, advance inscription of voters, a 5 percent deduction from government employees' salaries to the PLN campaign) would remain in force during the plebiscite.[161] Under Secretary of State David Newsom predicted that this scenario "will almost certainly be unacceptable to the FAO."[162]

The State Department immediately recalled Ambassadors Bowdler and Solaun and General McAuliffe for consultations. In Bowdler's view, the next move was obvious: Somoza was deliberately "nickel and diming" the mediation to death and, at the risk of a further deterioration in U.S.-FAO relations, the counterproposal must be rejected out of hand. He told Secretary Vance that a prolonged crisis could well destabilize other allied governments and American interests throughout the subregion.[163] Vaky and other senior Department officials agreed. The FAO poured scorn on the Somoza document, reaffirmed its support for the mediators' December 20 plan, and expressed the hope that Washington would at last stop mollycoddling the dictator. To keep the process alive, however, the opposition intimated that it might be willing to relent on its public demand that General José Somoza and Major Anastasio Somoza leave their National Guard posts and go into exile "prior to the plebiscite."[164]

Still reluctant to give up on a mediated solution, the President (supported by Vance and Brzezinski) insisted that Somoza receive another benefit of the doubt. It was little wonder that the dictator paid scant attention to what

(Tucker) to Secretary of State, December 23, 1978, Subject: "Prospects for Renewed Violence," DFOIA.

161   Department of State Telegram, Managua 6812, American Embassy (Solaun) to Secretary of State, December 27, 1978, Subject: "Nicaraguan Mediation No. 275–English Translation of PLN Counterproposal," DFOIA.

162   Department of State Telegram, Confidential State 326504, Secretary of State (Newsom) to All American Republic Diplomatic Posts, December 29, 1978, Subject: "Nicaragua Mediation Update," DFOIA.

163   See Christian, *Nicaragua: Revolution in the Family*, p. 97.

164   Department of State Telegram, Confidential Managua 6858, American Embassy (Solaun) to Secretary of State, December 30, 1978, Subject: "FAO Position," DFOIA.

must have sounded like hollow warnings from other officials that unless he adopted a more flexible posture "the whole gamut of [bilateral] relations" could be affected.[165] The mediators were instructed to revise the December 20 proposal on the basis of a formula allowing the election to be "formally administered by a national plebiscite authority" in accord with PLN-Somoza demands while simultaneously preserving "the control, integrity and acceptability provided by an internationally-conducted vote...."[166] Terming Somoza's scheme "a joke and a fraud," the American Embassy's Deputy Chief of Mission James Cheek "asked to be relieved of his post after it became clear that Carter would not get tough and insist that Somoza had to go."[167]

Ambassador Solaun continued to bear the brunt of opposition frustration over what it viewed as Washington's excessive forbearance in the face of Somoza's electoral machinations. On January 4, 1979, he was sharply rebuffed by an FAO-Conservative Party delegation when he "tried to test FAO willingness to accept any further changes in their position." Undeterred, the Ambassador probed for a new opening, "wonder[ing] about the FAO attitude [toward a nationally supervised plebiscite] if the GON [Government of Nicaragua] would make concessions and accept a plebiscite free from coercion and honestly administered." An FAO leader said that the Front would agree to "cosmetic changes" in the December 20 plan "if there were effective controls over the plebiscite and some public evidence that Somoza is willing to cede power."[168] Later that day, Solaun briefed officials of the Nicaraguan Development Institute (INDE) who expressed profound displeasure over the Carter administration's failure to denounce Somoza for the apparent breakdown of negotiations. Furthermore, they called on the White House to mobilize global financial sanctions against the dictatorship, maintaining "that Somoza only understands pressure and that violence is the only alternative to international pressure. If violence increases, they believe, it will be at the expense of the moderate, pro-U.S. groups."[169]

The American Ambassador termed this view that Somoza could be forced from office "provided there is strong U.S. pressure," unrealistic, even naive:

165 Quoted in Karen DeYoung, "U.S. Warns Somoza Mediation Rebuff May Affect Relations," *Washington Post*, December 28, 1978, p. A16.

166 Department of State Telegram, Confidential State 3773, Secretary of State (Vance) to All American Republic Diplomatic Posts, January 5, 1979, Subject: "Nicaraguan Update," DFOIA.

167 Interview with James Cheek, Washington, D.C., September 18, 1989.

168 Department of State Telegram, Secret Managua 0076, American Embassy (Solaun) to Secretary of State, January 5, 1979, Subject: "Conversation with FAO – January 4," DFOIA.

169 Department of State Telegram, Secret Managua 0086, American Embassy (Solaun) to Secretary of State, January 5, 1979, Subject: "Conversation with INDE Leaders – January 4," DFOIA.

"They apparently have not considered, or are unwilling to contemplate, the possibility that despite all possible external pressure Somoza may have sufficient holding power to continue in control for [a] prolonged period."[170]

The mediators' revisions of the December 20 plebiscite proposal were completed by the second week of January 1979. In a concession to Somoza, it provided for a referendum administered by a bipartisan national agency composed of members of the governing PLN, the FAO, and independents. But the mediators stood firm on the need to vest ultimate responsibility for the plebiscite in an international authority – either the Organization of American States or (Washington's preference) a "multi-national commission."[171] Predictably, Somoza and the PLN balked, insisting on a nationally supervised election as well as the prior inscription of voters and other traditional features of past "elections." In the absence of this kind of control over the process, the regime had apparently concluded it could not win a popular mandate. This response finally exhausted the limits of White House tolerance. A frustrated Ambassador Bowdler was reported favorably disposed to a National Guard coup if the outcome was a business-dominated government.[172]

The mediation collapse was a devastating political blow to the conservative and moderate anti-Somoza forces. Washington had extracted one concession after another from the FAO in the process of trying to "get Somoza out without leaving a power vacuum into which the Sandinistas could jump,"[173] eventually fracturing whatever consensus it may have initially enjoyed, paralyzing its ability to act, and destroying its credibility as a viable, structured alternative to the dictatorship. By January 1979, the FAO had lost one-third of its original membership (five out of fifteen), leaving the organization dominated by conservative-business-rightist groups and individuals with little or no popular base of support. As the mediation ground to a halt, one opposition leader remarked to State Department officials that those groups leaving the FAO "are being drawn to join forces with [the] more radical opposition."[174]

Washington's ability to promote an "acceptable" regime change in Nicaragua during the latter part of 1978 was enormously complicated, and eventually undermined, by Somoza's obdurate and stubborn behavior. Em-

170 Department of State Telegram, Secret Managua 0086.
171 Department of State Telegram, Confidential State 324154, Secretary of State (Vance) to All American Republic Diplomatic Posts, December 26, 1978, Subject: "Nicaragua Plebiscite," DFOIA.
172 See "Nicaragua: Tachito's Theme," *Latin America Political Report*, January 5, 1979, p. 7.
173 Karen DeYoung, "Somoza Jogs as U.S. Tries to Set Pace," *Washington Post*, January 14, 1979, p. A22.
174 Department of State Telegram, Confidential State 2596, Secretary of State (Vance) to American Embassy, January 5, 1979, Subject: "Views on Mediation," DFOIA.

boldened by a White House that "was not firmly resolved to force his departure,"[175] the client kept throwing up roadblocks to each of the mediators' proposals and declared time and again that he would not abandon power voluntarily before his term expired in May 1981. Throughout the negotiations, Somoza concentrated his energies on military matters: The strength of the National Guard almost doubled from 7,500 to over 14,000 troops, augmented by large-scale weapons purchases from Israel and smaller arms acquisitions from Argentina, El Salvador, Guatemala, Brazil, South Africa, and the Bahamas. Jerusalem had earlier provided the weapons and transport planes that enabled Somoza to crush the September FSLN insurrection, and its continued military support added to the dictator's confidence that he could surmount any forseeable domestic challenge.[176] American reluctance to challenge this Israeli-Nicaraguan alliance was not unrelated to the Camp David Mideast summit, which more or less coincided with the Sandinista uprising, and its aftermath. As one commentator observed: "The U.S. government didn't want to squander its capital on Nicaragua when it had something that appeared infinitely more important going."[177]

In the most candid official assessment of the mediation failure, Assistant Secretary of State Viron Vaky admitted that Washington had anticipated neither Somoza's "fundamental rigidity" and refusal to make any concessions indicating a willingness to eventually relinquish power nor his intention to string out the talks "to gain time in the belief that he could strengthen the National Guard and simply hold on."[178] Missing from this statement was any reference to the administration's apparently inept efforts to exploit moments of institutional discord within the National Guard officer corp over the dictator's behavior. According to Richard Millett, the one former

---

175 Richard E. Feinberg, "The Rapid Redefinitions of U.S. National Interests and Diplomacy in Central America," in Feinberg, ed., *Central America: International Dimensions of the Crisis*, p. 66.

176 On the National Guard figures, see Alan Riding, "Nicaraguans Brace for Fresh Violence," *New York Times*, January 17, 1979, p. 5; The American University, Foreign Area Studies, *Nicaragua: A Country Study* (Department of the Army, Washington, D.C.: U.S. Government Printing Office, September 1981), p. 51; Booth, *The End and the Beginning*, p. 169. On Israeli military assistance to the Somoza dictatorship during 1978 and 1979, see Bishara Bahbah, *Israel and Latin America: The Military Connection* (New York: St. Martins Press, 1986), p. 83–85, 149; Christian, *Nicaragua: Revolution in the Family*, p. 91; "Problems From the Barrels of Israeli Guns," *Latin America Weekly Report*, May 16, 1980, p. 9; "Israeli-Made Weapons Helped Save the Somoza Dynasty," *Miami Herald*, October 18, 1978, p. 20A.

177 Richard Millet, "Shooting Ourselves in the Foot," in Hans Binnendijk, ed., *Authoritarian Regimes in Transition* (U.S. Department of State: Foreign Service Institute, June 1987), p. 129.

178 Quoted from Letter, dated September 8, 1979, reprinted in U.S. Congress, House, *United States Policy Toward Nicaragua*, p. 74.

U.S. military attache "who really knew the National Guard received only one phone call from the State Department during the entire crisis. When some National Guard officers revolted in September 1978, the State Department called him at Fort Bragg and asked if he knew them. That was it."[179]

The mediation episode graphically exposed the gap between Washington's rhetoric and practice. Despite periodic threats of retaliation and warnings of a major policy reassessment, the White House appeared always willing to go the extra step to accommodate Somoza's maneuvers and delaying tactics. It repeatedly backed away from a more forceful approach, what Ambassador Solaun called a "credible ultimatum."[180] One State Department "Seventh Floor" policymaker laid the blame squarely at the door of a "vacillating" President who "was unsure of how to proceed and let policy drift." He elaborated:

> The plebiscite proposals gave the White House good warm feelings. There was strong resistance in the White House to anything anti-Somoza. Every time Somoza came up with the plebiscite, it carried weight with senior political levels in the White House. Basically the White House considered this an eggshells issue and was tip toeing around when it should have been far more forceful in pursuing policy.[181]

The uncertain fate of the administration's two key legislative programs – the foreign aid bill and Panama Canal treaties – also affected Carter's handling of the Nicaragua issue. Confronting a situation where Somoza's Congressional allies were capable of, and threatening to, sabotage these requests, Chief of Staff Hamilton Jordan repeatedly told the President that "you can endanger the greatest achievement of your administration, the Panama Canal legislation. And for what? Nicaragua!"[182]

The administration went to extraordinary lengths to avoid provoking the ire of the dictator's most prominent and influential cronies on Capital Hill. Ambassador Solaun gave one example:

> I remember one day, during the mediation, Somoza was told privately by the administration that foreign assistance would be curtailed. Congressmen John Murphy and Charles Wilson came to Managua to see what the mediation was doing to help Somoza. I received a cable from the State Department that when they came to see me I should not tell them we had curtailed the disbursement of loans. Immediately,

179 Richard Millet, "Shooting Ourselves in the Foot," p. 130.
180 Telephone interview with Mauricio Solaun, Illinois, September 15, 1989.
181 Confidential interview, Department of State official, Virginia, September 20, 1989.
182 Interview with James Cheek.

Wilson and Murphy went back to Somoza and said to him that he didn't have to worry about these loans.[183]

Viron Vaky thought that Murphy and Wilson "put such a lot of pressure on the administration that it became a little intimidated," while his State Department colleague David Newsom accused the two legislators of almost singlehandedly "sabotaging the mediation. Murphy was in constant contact with Somoza and encouraged him to resist the suggestions of the mediators and was citing his own clout on Capitol Hill. Somoza felt up to the end that he had political clout on Capitol Hill and didn't have to pay attention to what the Carter administration was trying to do."[184]

On January 26, 1979, the Policy Review Committee (PRC) convened to discuss Nicaragua. A State Department paper seriously questioned whether there was any point in further negotiations with Somoza given his apparent refusal to support a plebiscite process "that he could not manipulate." The FAO opposed additional concessions on the grounds that it would trigger more "defections from its ranks" and the mediators did not want to continue a dialogue "that would only serve to weaken the position of the moderate forces." But this deadlock posed "the danger that the moderate opposition ... will disintegrate ... lead[ing] to further polarization and radicalization of the body politic" with the attendant "negative impact on other Central American countries [i.e., El Salvador and Guatemala]." Therefore, the critical question for the PRC was "whether to distance ourselves from Somoza ... and thereby encourage the moderate opposition, or simply allow the mediation to lapse and maintain [pre-September 1978] relations with Somoza...." In reaching its decision, the PRC had to weigh a number of factors, not least Washington's responsibility for the fate of the "moderate forces" whom it "actively encouraged ... to negotiate with Somoza," and who "are now exposed and look to us for moral support."[185]

The meeting quickly agreed that sanctions against the Somoza regime could no longer be avoided, if only to reinforce U.S. support for the civilian opposition. But still not wishing to signal a major break with its client, it recommended "symbolic" retaliation only.[186] The White House concurred. In early February, the State Department announced the cancelation of the U.S. military aid program (suspended since September 1978), which meant the loss of $800,000 "in the pipeline," the withdrawal of American military personnel in Nicaragua, the permanent suspension of two development

183 Telephone interview with Mauricio Solaun.
184 Interview with Viron Vaky; interview with David Newsom. Also see statement by a U.S. official quoted in "Somoza Under Fire," *Newsweek*, June 18, 1979, p. 23.
185 Department of State Memorandum, Secret, To Zbigniew Brzezinski, The White House, January 22, 1979, Subject: "PRC Meeting on Nicaragua," DFOIA.
186 Pastor, *Condemned to Repetition*, p. 116.

loans totaling $10.5 million, a freeze on new economic assistance except for "basic human needs" programs nearing completion, and a reduction of the Managua Embassy staff by more than 50 percent.[187] To one career diplomat, however, this "punishment" was further confirmation of a President who "wouldn't bite the bullet either way. That is, he wouldn't say 'let's get out of this mess and let Somoza stew in his own juice' or 'no, let's get tough with Somoza.' "[188]

Legislative concerns, the illusory belief among some policymakers that "a settlement is still possible,"[189] a lull in the military struggle, the perception of a divided and paralyzed opposition incapable of seriously challenging the regime or the state, and CIA reports that Somoza's chances of remaining in office until May 1981 were "better than ever"[190] all contributed to the White House's rejection of more drastic sanctions (for example, recall the Ambassador, break diplomatic relations). Arguably, though, no one factor was more important in constraining a "harder-line" approach than the lack of certainty over what would follow in the event of Somoza's ouster. The Secretary of State's special assistant on regional affairs Peter Tarnoff emphasized the constant worry over a "premature" transition:

> There was considerable concern over the absence of a Third Force alternative. When it looked obvious that was not going to happen, the administration became concerned about a too rigid movement from one regime to another. The democratic opposition was not capable or viable and there seemed no way to guarantee the democratic opposition a prominent position in the post-Somoza period.[191]

Conclusion

U.S. efforts to mediate a solution to the Nicaraguan crisis during the latter months of 1978 illustrate the centrality of the state-regime distinction in the making of American foreign policy. The possibility of a challenge for political and state power by a democratic mass social movement forced Washington to begin the process of disengaging from a traditional Third World ally in order to promote a regime change that would ensure the continuity of the "old" state – thereby preventing any likelihood of a chal-

---

187 See John M. Goshko, "U.S. Retaliates Against Somoza, Cuts Back Aid," *Washington Post*, February 9, 1979, pp. A1, A10.
188 Confidential interview, Department of State official, September 20, 1989.
189 State Department spokesman Hodding Carter, quoted in Goshko, "U.S. Retaliates Against Somoza, Cuts Back Aid," p. A1.
190 Pastor, *Condemned to Repetition*, p. 116.
191 Telephone interview with Peter Tarnoff.

lenge to U.S. permanent interests. The White House push for a "negotiated transition" was an attempt to focus the debate on a narrow set of political/legal changes; the goal was to facilitate the ascendency of the center-right "anti-regime" opposition forces over and against the guerrilla-political left "anti-regime" movements, while minimizing changes in the socioeconomic model as well as the state institutions.

Between January 1977 and mid-1978, Carter administration policy was confined to human rights criticisms, military aid sanctions, and diplomatic pressures on Somoza to begin a dialogue with, and make concessions to, those civilian protagonists who were willing to cohabit with the regime and work with the existing state institutions. These efforts were frustrated by a recalcitrant client and Washington's preference for "working through" Somoza, which blinded it to the emergence of a broad-based opposition movement and the regime's eroding political support. The upheavals of August–September 1978 – a general strike and mass insurrection – dramatically revealed Somoza's vulnerability and forced U.S. policymakers to acknowledge that the dictatorship was less firmly in control of its population than they had previously believed. Forced to take account of these internal developments, but still reluctant to apply direct and forceful pressure on the client, the White House settled on a strategy of mediation as "the most elegant way of being activist at the time."[192]

The U.S. hoped this proposed political solution to the Nicaraguan crisis would halt the growing popular radicalization, get Somoza to voluntarily leave office, ensure that non-Sandinista forces would dominate the new regime, and preserve the traditional role of the National Guard as *the* coercive apparatus of the state in the transition and post-transition period. The last objective was at the forefront of policy deliberations throughout the mediation period and was a powerful argument in favor of a negotiated settlement. For an extended and drawn-out military conflict, Washington reasoned, correctly in hindsight, maximized the possibility of an eventual FSLN victory and the "loss" of both the regime and the state. Somoza, however, had his own, quite different agenda. It soon became apparent that he perceived mediation as an opportunity to reconsolidate his political and military hold on office.

Once the mediation began, Carter administration judgments divided over possible U.S. courses of action: NSC Advisor Brzezinski cautioned against precipitating a regime change in the absence of a suitable replacement and seriously doubted that the "acceptable" opposition elements were currently strong enough or sufficiently united to take over the reigns of government; others, notably Ambassador Bowdler and Assistant Secretary of State Vaky,

192 Interview with Viron Vaky.

assigned the first priority to getting rid of the dictatorship. "The mediation effort became a conflict," said one official, "between Bowdler and Vaky who really felt we should put maximum pressure on Somoza and get him out, and those people such as Brzezinski, and even Vance, who spoke of the constitutional issue – an American president cannot push a constitutional president from his perch."[193] Yet, for all its moralistic, non-interventionist rhetoric, the White House was not averse to specific forms of direct involvement in Nicaragua's internal conflict. During 1978, for instance, President Carter had no qualms about putting his signature to a "finding" that authorized covert CIA intervention in support of the "moderate" anti-Somoza forces.[194]

Increasingly convinced that popular support for the Sandinistas and widespread hostility toward Somoza were opposite sides of the same coin, Washington tried, without success, to get the Nicaraguan leader to voluntarily leave office before his term expired. The explanation for this lack of success was twofold. First was the administration's excessive forbearance toward the client's duplicitous behavior in order to keep him at the bargaining table and pacify the "Somoza lobby." There was also a reluctance to exploit the vulnerable economic pressure point: Initiatives here were limited to selective aid cutbacks, votes to postpone Nicaraguan loan requests to the IMF, and vague threats, not acted upon, to impose more far-reaching sanctions. While Deputy Assistant Secretary of State John Bushnell argued that the IMF votes "sent a clear message to Somoza that we were turning up the heat,"[195] American officials at the time insisted that these actions were based exclusively on economic and technical flaws in the submissions and did not constitute political pressure on the regime. Furthermore, those American commercial banks that decided to contract their exposure in Nicaragua were not encouraged to do so by Washington. On the contrary, it stemmed from their own perceptions about the future of the political-economic climate in Nicaragua.

Second, American policymakers underestimated the growing strength of the Sandinista movement as part of a broader failure to adequately sense the shifting nature of the political-military struggle. Their continuing belief that it was possible to achieve a negotiated solution that marginalized or excluded the FSLN offers no better illustration of this point. Even the most conservative opponents of the dictator – Washington's closest allies – declared that such an approach was totally unrealistic and could not succeed.

In seeking to accommodate Somoza's demands at almost every turn, the

193 Interview with Lawrence Pezzullo, New York, September 28, 1988. The respondent was American Ambassador to Nicaragua, 1979 to 1981.
194 See "A Secret War for Nicaragua," *Newsweek*, November 8, 1982, pp. 44, 48.
195 Interview with John Bushnell.

U.S. coopted, pressured and, ultimately, so compromised the non-radical opposition that it disintegrated as a significant political force. When Somoza's actions finally exceeded the limits of Washington's tolerance – signaling the collapse of the mediation track – the White House again revealed its opposition to a definitive political or economic break with the dictatorship by authorizing retaliatory measures that consisted of limited or "symbolic" sanctions only.

"We blinked on pushing hard to get Somoza out in late 1978 and blinked on getting the mediation proposals enacted," remarked a disillusioned State Department official. "That's when things fell apart."[196] The breakdown of the mediation – undermined by a combination of inadequate policy calculations and conflicts with the client dictator – led the U.S. government to discontinue its pressure on Somoza during the first quarter of 1979 in the apparent belief that the threat of mass insurrection had passed and the non-radical civilian opposition was incapable of bringing about a regime change. In late May, to Washington's considerable surprise, the Sandinistas detonated a new wave of insurrectionary struggle that in less than two months produced the very outcome the Carter White House had fought hardest to prevent: the military defeat of Somoza, the disintegration of the National Guard, and the FSLN capture of political and state power in Nicaragua.

196 Interview with Malcolm Barnaby.

6

Washington ruptures a historic relationship: Dumping the dictator to save the state

In May 1979, after more than four decades of support for the Somoza family dynasty in Nicaragua, the threat to the state posed by a popular revolutionary movement led by Sandinista guerrillas forced Washington to adopt a position in favor of supporting a regime change. This policy shift was inextricably linked to dramatic changes in the nature of the socio-political and military struggles.

After the September 1978 insurrectionary upheaval, the FSLN embarked on a concerted effort to broaden its political base, supporting the establishment of the United People's Movement (MPU) and, subsequently, the National Patriotic Front (FPN). The emergence of structured urban support networks, including armed militias, civil defense units, and neighborhood committees, complemented these moves. The Sandinistas further consolidated their hegemonic status among the anti-regime forces when the three "tendencies" (Proletarian, Prolonged People's War, and Insurrectional/ Tercerista) resolved their tactical and strategic differences, and established a unified high command. Within the space of nine months, the FSLN was transformed from an organization numbering approximately 600 active members[1] to unchallenged head of a mass social movement of wage workers, urban poor, peasants, students, property owners, and churchpeople, and their respective political, labor, and civic organizations. This severely complicated Washington's ability to gain control of events and shape their outcome in a manner compatible with U.S. permanent interests.

Between January and April 1979, the military conflict escalated from relatively small-scale, rurally based confrontations to major clashes in cities and towns. On March 8, for instance, American Embassy Chargé d'Affaires Frank Tucker reported that "fighting between the Guardia and increasingly

---

1 Central Intelligence Agency, Background Article, "Nicaragua: The Sandinista Guerrillas and Their International Links," December 6, 1978, DFOIA.

large groups of Sandinistas is intensifying in the northern mountains and in areas in the South, some within 20–30 miles of Managua."² Accompanying these developments was rising National Guard violence against civilian noncombatants "suspected" of supporting the FSLN. One American Embassy cable did not mince words: "Reports of [government] human rights abuse in the form of beatings, torture and deaths appear daily [in the local media]. . . . "³

In late May, the Sandinistas announced a new nationwide offensive to oust the ruling family from power. By mid-July, the FSLN controlled all major provincial cities and towns, and stood poised on the brink of military victory in Managua, leaving the Carter administration with one of two options: direct military intervention to safeguard U.S. "national security," or accommodation to the inevitability of a Sandinista military victory over a historic client regime *and* state in Central America.

When American policymakers first began to seriously contemplate the possibility of a political transition in Nicaragua, the survival of the National Guard, restructured and under new leadership, emerged as a fundamental strategic priority: "We wanted to split the National Guard from Somoza. If we could drive a wedge between Somoza and the National Guard, then we thought we could win over important elements of the Guard and keep it intact as an organization, and a new National Guard would be an agent for law and order under a new regime."⁴ Washington's efforts to pry the Guard loose from Somoza's iron grip, however, proved a formidable, and ultimately unattainable, goal. The dictator was able to retain the loyalty of his officer corp through an effective manipulation of professional ambitions and personal needs. "Somoza personally makes all decisions on promotions," a knowledgeable Nicaraguan commented at the time of the October 1977 Sandinista-led national uprising. "If one of them [officers] gets sick, he goes to Somoza for help. If he needs a loan, he gets it from Somoza."⁵ As a result, said a Pentagon official, "the military institution itself was secondary to the personal bonds between the officer corp and Somoza."⁶ The Nicaraguan leader also moved swiftly during 1978 and 1979 to purge Guard officers suspected of supporting Carter policy goals, making any White

---

2 Department of State Telegram, Confidential Managua 1207, American Embassy (Tucker) to Secretary of State, March 8, 1979, Subject: "(U) Post Differential," DFOIA.
3 Department of State Telegram, Managua 1720, American Embassy (Tucker) to Secretary of State, April 9, 1979, Subject: "Political Disturbances and Human Rights Situation March 25–April 6," DFOIA.
4 Confidential interview, Department of State official, Virginia, September 20, 1989.
5 Quoted in DeYoung, "Somoza's Nicaragua," p. A30.
6 Confidential telephone interview, Department of Defense official, Maine, September 26, 1989.

House effort to sever the Guard's allegiance to the regime that much more difficult.[7]

Post-mediation U.S. policy: Accommodating Somoza?

Throughout 1977 and 1978, Carter policy toward Nicaragua was based on manipulating a two-track approach: criticism of specific Somoza regime practices and declarations of support for segments of the opposition movement interspersed with concessions to the dictatorship. This had the practical effect of, at least temporarily, strengthening Somoza's position and confirming his belief that Washington was not committed to a confrontationist policy to force him from office.

During the brief interregnum between the collapse of efforts to negotiate a solution to the Nicaraguan conflict and the climactic military encounter in the summer of 1979, the Carter White House abandoned efforts to force Somoza to leave the presidency before May 1981. "It was not willing to apply maximum pressure to force Somoza out," complained a number of State Department officials. "It was basically reluctant to face up to telling Somoza he had to leave."[8] Assistant Secretary of State Vaky acknowledged that "the U.S. did deal differently with Somoza during this period" largely as a consequence of the mediation debacle. "It was a period in which there were no options there that made any sense. Policy was in disarray. The middle really broke up with the mediation. The effect was a belief that Somoza was really strong enough to probably finish out his term."[9] Ambassadors Pezzullo and Moss placed more emphasis on Somoza's armed forces buildup, which inclined Washington to think that the threat of mass insurrection had passed. At worst, the military conflict had devolved into "a kind of stalemate. Somoza couldn't defeat the Sandinistas and the Sandinistas couldn't defeat Somoza. Therefore, there was no great urgency to do anything drastic."[10] The "basic dilemma" U.S. policymakers faced in contemplating the possibility of a regime change remained what it had always been: "What could possibly take Somoza's place that would be in our interest?"[11] If the dictator had his way it would be "a handpicked successor"

7 Ambassador Mauricio Solaun, correspondence with Harold D. Sims, "Revolutionary Nicaragua: Dilemmas Confronting Sandinistas and North Americans," in Adelman and Reading, eds., *Confrontation in the Caribbean Basis*, p. 73.
8 Interview with Malcolm Barnaby, Washington, D.C., October 4, 1988; interview with David Newsom, Washington, D.C., October 6, 1988.
9 Interview with Viron Vaky, Washington, D.C., September 15, 1988.
10 Interview with Lawrence Pezzullo, New York, September 28, 1988; interview with Ambler Moss, Washington, D.C., September 21, 1988.
11 Confidential interview, Department of State official, September 20, 1989.

in 1981 who would allow him to retain "direct or predominant control over the NG [National Guard]."¹²

In late February, Somoza indicated a desire to "normalize relations with the U.S. and reinvolve the USG [United States Government] in seeking a political solution" to the internal conflict. Ambassador Solaun interpreted this overture as evidence that Washington's "measures of disassociation" were hurting the regime economically and politically.¹³ Secretary Vance agreed, terming proposed Nicaraguan government reforms nothing more than an attempt "to regain USG [United States Government] support for an underwriting of Somoza's policy." For Washington to take new diplomatic initiatives at the request of an autocratic leader who had deliberately sabotaged prior efforts, and at a time when he was "relatively strong," would only "discourage the opposition and project an image of U.S. identity with the GON [Government of Nicaragua]." The current climate was not conducive to "productive new initiatives," Vance wrote. Therefore, "our posture should be cool but correct...while we assess the internal correlation of forces and possible new opportunities."¹⁴

Even so, the White House could still not bring itself to forcefully pursue a regime change. Possible domestic political consequences of a U.S.-orchestrated transition ranked high on the agenda of concerns. First was the impact it might have on the president's reelection chances. "It was a shaky presidency already," said a senior foreign policy official. "The administration had to think what the ouster of Somoza by a liberal American president would do in the way of damage among many conservative constituencies in the United States."¹⁵ Second was its likely "fallout" on the Panama Canal treaties, the highest priority item on the White House Latin American agenda.

The prospect of razor thin majorities in both houses of Congress for passage of the Canal treaties posed a major problem for an executive branch attempting to formulate a Nicaragua policy without provoking the wrath of influential Somoza supporters on Capitol Hill. On March 16, the Senate ratified the treaties by the slimmest of margins – one vote more than the necessary two-thirds majority. Implementation, however, required the passage of companion legislation through the House as well as the Senate.

12 Department of State Telegram, Secret Managua 1016, American Embassy (Solaun) to Secretary of State, February 26, 1979, Subject: "(U) Ambassador's Analysis of the Political Situation," DFOIA.
13 Department of State Telegram, Secret Managua 1003, American Embassy (Solaun) to Secretary of State, February 23, 1979, Subject: "(S) GON Seeks Normalization and to Re-Involve USG," DFOIA.
14 Department of State Telegram, Secret State 064200, Secretary of State (Vance) to American Embassy, March 16, 1979, Subject: "GON Desire to Reinvolve the U.S.," DFOIA.
15 Confidential interview, Department of State official, September 20, 1989.

With the Congress almost evenly split between supporters and opponents, the "Somoza lobby" moved to exploit this opportunity in an attempt to gain more favorable U.S. treatment for the dictatorship.[16] Led by the chairman of the House Merchant Marine and Fisheries Committee (responsible for drafting the enabling legislation) John Murphy, the treaty opponents targeted the Panamanian government of General Omar Torrijos, which it accused of smuggling weapons to the Sandinistas. The day before the scheduled full House vote on the treaty implementing legislation (June 21), the dictator's allies forced the chamber to meet in secret sessions for the first time in 150 years to consider the accusations they were leveling against the Torrijos regime. The evidence submitted was so flimsy and lacking in credibility that it failed to convince more than a few legislators outside of the Somoza cabal. Nonetheless, President Carter had reportedly informed the Panamanian head of state Aristides Royo that Washington contemplated no new moves against Somoza prior to a favorable House vote on the Canal treaties.[17]

The administration's policy reversal on Nicaraguan loan applications to the International Monetary Fund (IMF) was also symptomatic of its post-mediation approach toward the autocratic regime. After the Fund, at White House urging, twice postponed a vote on a request for aid in late 1978, Managua had informed the country's overseas creditor banks that it could not maintain current payments schedules and asked for a debt restructuring. In December, the bankers turned down an initial request.[18] The following February, Nicaraguan Central Bank officials returned with a more detailed proposal, including a request for a new eight year $88 million loan, reportedly to enable the government to repay medium term debts falling due in late 1979. They told the creditor banks that the country "had a serious political problem but that they were taking care of the problem, and were trying to hold the flow of dollars by keeping liquidity at a minimum."[19] Although the smaller banks voiced reluctance to increase their exposure in such a politically volatile setting for what seemed (eight years) an inordinately long period, at least one of the larger banks was "in general...very receptive" to extending new lines of credit.[20]

While the creditors agreed to form a committee to discuss the Nicaraguan

16 Jorden, *Panama Odyssey* p. 670.
17 See ibid.; Carter, *Keeping Faith: Memoirs of a President*, p. 183; John Goshko, "More Pressure to Oust Somoza," *Washington Post*, June 13, 1979, p. A20.
18 See Karen DeYoung, "Nicaragua Asks Loan From IMF to Prevent Collapse of Economy," *Washington Post*, March 13, 1979, p. A11.
19 Telephone interview with Onofre Torres, Florida, October 4, 1989. Also see Department of State Telegram, Managua 0635, American Embassy (Solaun) to Secretary of State, February 5, 1979, Subject: "Central Bank Team Visits US," DFOIA.
20 Quoted in Edward P. Foldessy, "Nicaragua, Hurt by Financial Troubles, Asks Its Creditors for a New, 8-Year Loan," *Wall Street Journal*, February 20, 1979, p. 7.

request, one message came through loud and clear to the Somoza officials at the February meeting: The regime's chances of obtaining new loans would substantially improve if it reached an accord with the IMF, whom commercial lenders to the Third World had increasingly begun to view as the "enforcer" of economic development programs that gave the highest priority to countries meeting their international debt obligations. The Nicaraguan delegation had conferred with Fund officials in Washington. D.C. before meeting the private bankers in New York City where much of the talk, as suggested above, "centered around the effort Nicaragua was making to reach an agreement with the Fund."[21] That March, the dictatorship submitted a request to the IMF for three "stabilization" loans totaling approximately $65 million. An internal Treasury Department memorandum prepared for Secretary W. Michael Blumenthal said that the Fund response would significantly influence the country's prospects for successful debt refinancing and access to new large-scale foreign loans.[22]

Meanwhile, the creditor banks' dialogue about Nicaraguan lending revealed a widening rift between Citibank, the most exposed of all the private lenders, and its competitor institutions. The major disagreement was over the likely future of the regime. The response to Citibank's pessimistic assessment, presented at three prior mini-conferences, and a second meeting of all the creditor banks in the New York City office of Merrill Lynch in May, 1979, was decidedly frosty. Citibank's Managua branch manager Onofre Torres attended all four meetings: "The discussion [in May] was about when things were going to get better in Nicaragua. I was asked how serious was the threat to the Somoza government. I said there was absolutely no doubt it will be overthrown within the next 30 days and there was no way renegotiation will go through. There was no point in doing anything until the new government took over. I do remember feeling at these [four] meetings that Citibank was the bad guy and everyone wanted to dissociate themselves from us." They refused to heed Citibank's warning mostly out of ignorance of what was happening in Nicaragua: "The only contact with Nicaragua most of the foreign banks had, including the U.S. banks, was through their correspondent banks who basically told them that Somoza was dealing with the problem." A few banks' actions were predominantly shaped by their extensive financial ties with the regime. The most notable among these was the Swiss Bank Corporation, the bulk of whose $100 million exposure had been lent to enterprises owned by the ruling family.[23]

Over at the IMF, the Staff had presented its confidential report on the

---

21 Telephone interview with Onofre Torres.
22 Department of the Treasury Memorandum, Assistant Secretary Bergsten to Secretary Blumenthal, March 14, 1979, Subject: "Nicaraguan Request for IMF Standby Credit and Status of Negotiations to Refinance Commercial Debt," DFOIA.
23 Telephone interview with Onofre Torres.

Nicaraguan submission in late April – which seriously questioned whether the traditional criteria for Fund assistance to overcome a temporary external sector crisis could be met. The report found there was no case for providing Compensatory Financing Facility (CFF) funds because the value of exports declined only marginally ($4.6 million) in 1978, which was more than offset by a $168 million fall in import costs, producing a positive trade balance exceeding $38 million. Moreover, 1979 projections indicated an upward trend in exports ($118 million over 1978) and a further drop in imports, resulting in a trade surplus of $188 million and an overall surplus on the current account of more than $55 million. The fundamental cause of Nicaragua's financial crisis was not a severe temporary export shortfall or balance of payments deficit but massive capital flight. An estimated net outflow of private capital in 1978 totaling $280 million was deemed largely responsible for a fall in net international reserves of $223 million over the twelve month period. Financial mismanagement such as "the practice of using short-term commercial bank credits to cover budgetary outlays" was also targeted as a contributor to the economic downturn. The document concluded that Nicaragua's proposal " 'involves substantial risks.' "[24]

Despite this harsh assessment, there was widespread support among Fund members for proceeding with the applications, primarily because the Somoza regime had agreed to abide by IMF "standby" conditions and had already implemented the requisite measures. Commented the State Department's Richard Feinberg: "All the Europeans were in favor of the loan and were saying 'don't politicize this.' " Influenced by this argument, the White House decided to reverse its earlier stance. Those U.S. officials who continued to insist that "this was a narrow view of assessing the loan, that political and economic factors were intertwined and that the economy was not going to be able to live by these conditions" fought a losing battle.[25] Senior Treasury officials, in particular Assistant Secretary C. Fred Bergsten, were reportedly instrumental in convincing President Carter that recent American policy in the Fund had created a "negative reaction" threatening the institution's "integrity and ability to function smoothly."[26] But, as Caleb Rossiter pointed out, Washington's votes to postpone a decision on the earlier loan applications in no way constituted a challenge to the IMF's normal operating procedure. The U.S. merely "express[ed] its opposition in technical terms permissible under the IMF's rules."[27]

While U.S. representatives to the IMF were being instructed to "ease

24 Center for International Policy, *Background Paper: IMF Loan to Nicaragua* (Washington, D.C., June 21, 1979), 7pp.
25 Interview with Richard Feinberg, Washington, D.C., October 17, 1988.
26 Rossiter, *Human Rights: The Carter Record, The Reagan Reaction* p. 11.
27 Ibid.

up" on Nicaragua, State Department officials were busy castigating the Somoza regime for arresting five FAO leaders to preempt efforts by the civilian opposition to organize another general strike timed for early May. Such heavy-handed action, State feared, was most likely to benefit the radical, armed protagonists of the regime, namely the Sandinistas.

When the Fund's Executive Directors gathered to vote on the Nicaraguan requests, State and Treasury officials decided that the U.S. representatives would play "a low visibility role in discussion but will go along with the expected approval." On May 14, the Board unanimously approved all three loans and immediately released $22.3 million to the Nicaraguan Central Bank. Simultaneously, Secretary of State Vance cabled the American Embassy in Managua to explain to "key moderate opposition leaders" that Washington's action was based "solely on economic and technical criteria" and did not constitute any basic policy shift.[28] In justifying its vote, the administration argued that Nicaragua met the traditional criteria for IMF support: a balance of payments crisis due to a substantial fall in export income resulting from an abrupt collapse in world market prices for cotton and sugar.[29] "The difference between September and November 1978 and May 1979," insisted the NSC's Robert Pastor "was that Nicaragua had fulfilled the technical criteria."[30] Such assertions, however, were markedly at odds with the Fund's Staff report.

The most trenchant and incisive critique of the IMF's decision, and the Carter administration's concurrence, was offered by the influential chairman of the House Committee on Banking, Currency and Urban Affairs, Henry M. Reuss. In a letter to Treasury Secretary Blumenthal, he wrote that passage of the loans contradicted both the spirit and the letter of the Fund's technical criteria. First, it was unclear whether the balance of payments crisis stemmed from an export shortfall or from massive capital flight authored largely by Somoza family members and their crony capitalist supporters. Second, granted substantial export losses, to the degree that they resulted from disruptions caused by the nationwide social and military conflict, in what sense could such disruptions be characterized as temporary or the result of circumstances over which the member country had no control? Reuss contended that the IMF had "in effect render[ed] a political judgement that the Nicaraguan government is not responsible for the disarray

---

28 Department of State Telegram, State 121855, Secretary of State (Vance) to American Embassy, May 12, 1979, Subject: "Nicaraguan IMF Drawings," DFOIA; Department of State Telegram, Confidential State 122613, Secretary of State (Vance) to American Embassy, May 14, 1979, Subject: "Nicaragua IMF Drawings," DFOIA.
29 See Dan Morgan, "U.S. Supported a Loan by IMF to Somoza's Government in May," *Washington Post,* July 7, 1979, pp. A1, A3.
30 Telephone interview with Robert Pastor, Georgia, October 5, 1989.

within its borders." He continued with telling logic: "Is there a standard set of IMF instructions for technical adjustments to offset the economic effects of civil war? To the extent that the problem is political, how can the solution be other than political." That the Fund decision had automatically bolstered Somoza's political position seemed obvious: "There is no doubt that the recent loan will greatly strengthen the Somoza government at the expense of its adversaries. . . . "[31]

Treasury Secretary Blumenthal simply parried the Reuss criticism and reiterated the public White House argument for supporting the loans: The Nicaraguan request was in total conformity with the "operational standards and procedures of the IMF – the technical criteria [were] fully met. . . . "[32] To have acted otherwise, he subsequently warned, "could lead to the extreme politicization of the IMF."[33] The critical issue of whether the Nicaraguan government could successfully implement the program – which depended in large part, as State's Richard Feinberg observed, on a revival of private sector confidence in the regime – was ignored. Yet the IMF had decided to place its faith in a business community that had categorically turned its back on Somoza, instituted a capital "strike," and declared its intention to make no new investments even if the National Guard defeated this latest revolutionary challenge.[34]

In both the military and economic spheres, U.S. policy reflected an approach less intent on forcing Somoza from office and more preoccupied with containing the growth of Sandinista power. Through most of 1978, and into 1979, the White House and State Department maintained a constant pressure on Panamanian leader General Omar Torrijos to halt military assistance to the FSLN and prevent his country from being used as a "pass through" for such aid from other sources. In stark contrast to this aggressive effort to get Panama to sever its military links to the guerrillas, Washington took a remarkably relaxed view of Israeli arms shipments to Somoza during the last year of the dictatorship. The State Department only began actively to lobby Jerusalem on this matter less than two months before Somoza's overthrow. On June 13, Deputy Assistant Secretary Brandon Grove called in the Israeli Embassy's political counselor to discuss the Nicaraguan conflict. He told his visitor that in order to achieve a negotiated solution and prevent

31 Letter from Henry M. Reuss, Chairman, House Committee on Banking, Finance and Currency, to W. Michael Blumenthal, Secretary of the Treasury, May 23, 1979, DFOIA.

32 Letter from W. Michael Blumenthal, Secretary of the Treasury, to Henry M. Reuss, Chairman, House Committee on Banking, Finance and Currency, July 11, 1979, DFOIA.

33 Quoted in Hobart Rowen, "Blumenthal Supports Loan to Nicaragua," Washington Post, June 14, 1979, p. D1.

34 Richard Feinberg, "The International Monetary Fund and Basic Needs: The Impact of Stand-by Arrangements" in Margaret E. Crahan, ed., Human Rights and Basic Needs in the Americas (Washington, D.C.: Georgetown University Press, 1982), p. 229.

a regionalization of the struggle, the U.S. "[is] urging all outside suppliers to halt arms shipments of any kind to either Somoza or Sandinista forces."[35] Washington finally prevailed on its Mideast ally to halt all military aid to Somoza three weeks prior to his downfall.[36]

The U.S. government's seeming acceptance of Somoza rule until at least early 1981 was abruptly shattered by the Sandinista decision to launch another nationwide insurrection in late May 1979. Relatively unprepared for this turn of events, Carter policymakers struggled frantically to formulate an appropriate response. This new and increasingly definitive confrontation between a mass social movement led by radical guerrillas and a totally isolated client regime so alarmed Washington that even the specter of direct U.S. military intervention began to seep into the policy debate, fueled by intelligence reports attributing FSLN military victories to increased Cuban involvement on the side of the guerrilla forces.

Some officials conjured up the possibility of a rerun of the 1965 Dominican Republic crisis when President Johnson ordered thousands of marines to intervene in a civil war to prevent "another Cuba" in the hemisphere. On that occasion, a compliant Organization of American States (OAS) willingly gave its post facto "seal of approval" to the invasion. Opposition to the Somoza dictatorship, however, was so widespread that armed intervention would have incurred the wrath of almost the entire hemisphere – allies and enemies alike. Mexico, Brazil, Peru, Ecuador, Costa Rica, Grenada, and Jamaica had already severed diplomatic ties with Managua, and two high-level Mexican government missions were currently traveling around Central America and the Caribbean lobbying other countries to follow suit.[37]

Military intervention in Nicaragua: America proposes, the OAS disposes

The second mass revolutionary upheaval in less than a year had a dramatic impact on U.S. policymakers' perceptions of the Nicaraguan conflict. In Washington, Viron Vaky thought that "this was it, that the worst alternative was happening, that the Sandinistas were winning a military victory, and

---

35 Department of State Telegram, Secret State 166874, Secretary of State (Vance) to American Embassy, June 13, 1979, Subject: "Alleged Israeli Arms Shipments to Nicaragua," DFOIA.

36 See "Israel Agrees to Suspend Nicaraguan Arms Deliveries," *Washington Post*, July 1, 1979, p. A27.

37 See Alan Riding, "Mexico Presses U.S. to End Somoza Aid," *New York Times*, May 22, 1979, p. 13; Marlise Simons, "Mexico Leads Major Regional Effort to Isolate Somoza," *Washington Post*, May 23, 1979, p. A17.

that the only question now was how to deal with that and find ways to limit the ongoing consequences."[38] In Managua, Embassy officials responded similarly. "We realized right away that it was over," said Ambassador Lawrence Pezzullo. "The question was what comes after that and time is running out and the options available were very limited. We had to put policy together from scratch very quickly. There was a limited amount of time."[39] In the Department of Defense, alarm bells sounded "about the instability that would follow and the opening it would give for expanded Soviet influence in Nicaragua and throughout the region."[40]

The insurrection finally convinced senior Carter officials that Somoza "would not likely be able to serve out his term" and that urgent action was necessary to prevent a Sandinista capture of political power.[41] The client had finally outlived his usefulness. "The feeling," Malcolm Barnaby recalled, "was that as long as we were closely identified with Somoza and Somoza tried to hang on, our ability to create or deal with any alternative was practically nil. And if we were going to play a role, his departure was an essential prerequisite."[42] The more difficult problem was how to minimize FSLN involvement in a new government.

The shift in the correlation of military forces and the realization that the Sandinistas, backed by a mass social movement and armed popular militias, were capable of contesting National Guard firepower came as a major surprise to official Washington. Discussing this latest U.S. failure to "read" the trajectory of the political and military struggle, Deputy Assistant Secretary of State John Bushnell conceded that "we did not expect the Sandinistas to do as well against the National Guard as rapidly as they did."[43] In Ambassador Pezzullo's view, faulty intelligence reporting was still a major problem. Field operatives had continued to minimize both the growing strength of the guerrillas and the extent of Somoza's political isolation:

> There was an underestimation of what the Sandinista strength really was. First, the reporting of the strength of the Sandinista forces in early June demeaned their capability. Washington was visibly surprised when this thing grew. Washington didn't really understand the scope of the opposition to Somoza. It was still thinking in classic insurgency terms – the size of the band of guerrillas fighting the National Guard which

38 Interview with Viron Vaky.
39 Interview with Lawrence Pezzullo.
40 Confidential telephone interview, Department of Defense official, September 26, 1989.
41 Jeremiah O'Leary, "U.S. Sees Somoza Finished, Hopes for Exit to End Crisis," *Washington Star*, June 9, 1979, pp. A1, A7.
42 Interview with Malcolm Barnaby.
43 Interview with John Bushnell, Washington, D.C., September 8, 1988.

had bigger numbers. But you had the whole population against the government. But Washington didn't comprehend this.[44]

Part of the administration's problem in this area was self-inflicted: The policy of non-contact with the Sandinistas severely limited its ability to cultivate liaisons within the guerrilla movement. According to a Department of State official familiar with covert operations in Central America, the paucity of local "agents of influence" not just in the FSLN but throughout the Nicaraguan state and society was the root cause of the poor quality U.S. intelligence reporting: "There was a general erosion of human intelligence resources in Central America that began before the Carter administration but continued after it came into office. By 1978–79, there were very few human intelligence resources remaining in Central America, and especially in Nicaragua."[45]

Under the pressure of time constraints, policymakers debated how best to secure the kind of political transition in Nicaragua that would safeguard basic American interests. Simultaneously, the State Department began lobbying regional allies to involve themselves in the process. Special Ambassador William Bowdler conferred with a number of governments "on possible joint approaches in which the United States might participate."[46]

On June 11, the administration streamlined the policymaking process, establishing an interagency "Working Group on Nicaragua" under the formal direction of Assistant Secretary of State Vaky and the day-to-day leadership of Deputy Assistant Secretary Brandon Grove to study and evaluate policy options. That same day the Policy Review Committee (PRC) debated a proposal originating with its chairman, NSC Advisor Zbigniew Brzezinski, for a regional military "peacekeeping" force to intervene in the conflict, halt the fighting, and oversee a political transition. This idea had first surfaced nine months earlier at a meeting of the crisis management Special Coordination Committee (SCC) where it was raised by Deputy NSC Advisor David Aaron in connection with "reassur[ing] the National Guard and . . . keep[ing] the situation from being dominated by the Sandinistas." The PRC now recommended it to the President so long as it was coordinated with Somoza's ouster.[47]

The White House desired a regime change that included "preservation of existing [state] institutions, especially the National Guard" and a role for

---

44   Interview with Lawrence Pezzullo.
45   Confidential telephone interview, Department of Defense official, September 26, 1989.
46   John M. Goshko, "More Pressure to Oust Somoza Weighed," *Washington Post*, June 13, 1979, p. A20.
47   Pastor, *Condemned to Repetition*, pp. 86, 135. On U.S. intelligence reports that the National Guard would probably put down the insurrection, see Goshko, "More Pressure to Oust Somoza Weighed," p. A20.

"all elements of the GON [Government of Nicaragua] in establishing the new electoral process and procedures." To this end, President Carter "authorized explorations re the possibility of an Inter-American Military Peace Force to maintain peace and guarantee the transition process," and thereby eliminate "the potential for a Castroite take-over of Nicaragua."[48]

The State Department instructed regional embassies to exercise the greatest care in choosing local officials with whom to discuss the military "peacekeeping" proposal and specified the kinds of approaches most likely to succeed with different regimes. To convince the military dictatorships in Brazil, Argentina, Uruguay, and Chile, attention should be directed to the "real communist threat" in the absence of swift regional action; to assuage probable resistance among elected presidents in the Andean Pact countries, Mexico, and the Dominican Republic, State counseled its diplomats to stress the key role such a body could play in guaranteeing a democratic transition. Beyond specific appeals to individual governments, every Latin American capital should be left in no doubt that "a threat to the peace of the hemisphere" exists in Nicaragua and that only inter-American cooperation to produce a solution can defuse and eliminate this "threat."[49] On June 13, Secretary of State Vance told a press conference that failure to achieve a "political solution" to the conflict would almost certainly lead to a "radical solution" inimicable to U.S. interests.[50]

Washington also revived the idea of convening an OAS Foreign Ministers meeting on Nicaragua and Central America, which had been strongly resisted by a number of Latin governments when first broached in mid-February because they "believe[d] our interest now [was] vindictive since we were unable to pressure Somoza to take the actions encompassed within the [mediation team's] report and believed that the reconvening of the MFM [Ministers of Foreign Affairs] [was] primarily to pull our chestnuts out of the fire."[51] State instructed its diplomats to approach foreign ministers or presidents and make a case for such a conference on the basis that "the situation is getting out of control," raising the prospect of escalating violence, a more polarized society, growing Cuban involvement and "an eventual Marxist/Castroite take-over of power."[52]

---

48 Department of State Telegram, Secret State 153522, Secretary of State (Christopher) to All American Republic Diplomatic Posts, June 13, 1979, Subject: "OAS Action on Nicaragua," DFOIA.

49 Ibid.

50 Secretary of State Cyrus Vance, Press Conference, June 13, 1979, *State Department Press Release*, No. 154. Also see Graham Hovey, "U.S. is Said to Believe Somoza Must Resign to Pacify Nicaragua," *New York Times*, June 15, 1979, p. 7.

51 Department of State Memorandum, Confidential, From Irving G. Tragen, U.S. Permanent Mission to the OAS, February 16, 1979, Subject: "Reconvening of Meeting of Foreign Ministers (MFM) on Central America," DFOIA.

52 Department of State Telegram, Secret State 153522.

This regional diplomatic offensive coincided with a new round of feverish political activity in Nicaragua where the situation, in the words of a nervous Warren Christopher, was "evolving rapidly and dramatically. . . . "[53] Embassy officials met almost daily with local military leaders and "moderate [political] elements" in an effort to prepare the groundwork for the eventual establishment of a transitional "Government of National Reconciliation" acceptable to the Carter administration.[54]

On June 18, the White House requested an urgent OAS Foreign Ministers meeting to formulate a multilateral approach for dealing with the Nicaraguan crisis. This came hard on the heels of an announcement by the Sandinista leadership in Costa Rica that it had established a five-member provisional junta to act as a "Government of National Reconstruction" and supervise the post-Somoza transition process. The governments of Ecuador, Venezuela, Colombia, Bolivia, and Peru immediately recognized the FSLN as a "legitimate army" and thus eligible for assistance as a belligerent under international law. Some U.S. officials privately conceded that Washington's call for an OAS conference was intended not only to force Somoza's resignation and minimize the possibility of a Sandinista military triumph but also to forestall moves by other hemispheric regimes to accord the guerrillas belligerent status.[55]

By this time, the military confrontation between the National Guard and the FSLN had reached a critical point. An internal Pentagon briefing paper prepared for Secretary Harold Brown and the Chairman of the Joint Chiefs of Staff prior to a June 19 SCC meeting on Nicaragua described the Guard as being stretched "to the breaking point" and argued that only "an active, forceful US role [could] prevent a hard left, Marxist-Leninist government from coming to power." The paper assessed three possible options: a new attempt to get Somoza to resign in favor of a coalition regime acceptable to the FSLN and the National Guard; a request to the OAS to support the "peacekeeping" idea; or unilateral U.S. military intervention. The "peacekeeping" force was the "preferred solution" but it faced numerous obstacles including the certain lack of OAS majority support. Direct U.S. military intervention would demonstrate to Moscow and Havana the administration's resolve "to prevent communism in the hemisphere" and ensure Washington considerable "influence with whatever government emerges." But this option would almost certainly be opposed by most regional and global allies, pro-

53 Department of State Telegram, Secret State 156042, Secretary of State (Christopher) to Secretary Vance, June 16, 1979, Subject: "Nicaragua," DFOIA.

54 Department of State Telegram, Secret State 157388, Secretary of State (Christopher) to American Embassy, June 19, 1979, Subject: "Meeting With——[deleted]," DFOIA.

55 See John M. Goshko, "U.S. Seeks Meeting of OAS to Resolve Nicaraguan Crisis," *Washington Post,* June 19, 1979, p. A10; Karen DeYoung, "Andean Nations Provide Sandinistas a Diplomatic Opening," *Washington Post,* June 18, 1979, p. A20.

duce a forceful Cuban response, and encourage third parties to support the FSLN. Still, if the FSLN did triumph, the U.S. was obligated to project its military power in such a way as to prevent the spread of revolution to other countries in the area: "Primarily, the U.S. should undertake some actions/initiatives to neutralize Cuban and other external support to the insurgent groups."[56]

The interagency disagreements that surfaced over what to do about Nicaragua at this late stage centered around differing NSC and State Department assessments of the most efficacious means of achieving a consensual goal: a new civilian regime prepared to cohabit with the old Somoza state. The "peacekeeping" force idea provoked the most discussion. To mobilize support within the imperial state for the military option, the NSC had taken the lead in defining Central America as an area of strategic importance to the United States and arguing that a Sandinista victory in Nicaragua would have a broad destabilizing impact on the whole subregion, increase Cuban influence, and create the potential to severely damage the administration's reelection chances in 1980 by triggering a "who lost Nicaragua" debate.[57] The Pentagon, the CIA, and the other executive branch intelligence agencies supported this interpretation and advocated a renewal of military aid to the dictatorships in El Salvador, Guatemala, and Honduras to offset any "ripple effect" that might flow from a Sandinista triumph.

Senior State Department officials opposed this kind of thinking on the grounds that any military intervention in Nicaragua "would trigger an adverse reaction from the Latin Americans,"[58] thereby threatening to isolate the United States at the upcoming Foreign Ministers meeting. The Deputy U.S. representative to the OAS Irving Tragen had already informed Assistant Secretary Vaky of comments made by one regional Ambassador on this issue. Tragen was told that Washington "will run into a buzzsaw on intervention if we propose an external mediating force.... When I suggested an OAS Peace Force _____ commented that there aren't the votes...."[59]

Regarding the proposed spotlight on alleged large-scale Cuban military assistance to the Sandinistas, Assistant Secretary of State Patricia Derian cautioned that American policy goals might be better served by a more low-key approach: "to the extent that we play up Cuban involvement it can only

56 Department of Defense, Talking Paper for the Secretary of Defense and Chairman, Joint Chiefs of Staff, re Special Coordinating Committee Meeting, June 19, 1979, Subject: "Nicaragua, Secret," DFOIA.
57 See Graham Hovey, "Vance Asking O.A.S. to Aid in Nicaragua," New York Times, June 21, 1979, p. 13.
58 John M. Goshko, "OAS Weighs Nicaragua Move," Washington Post, June 23, 1979, p. A17.
59 Department of State Memorandum, Confidential, Irving G. Tragen, U.S. Permanent Mission to the OAS, to Viron Vaky, June 15, 1979, Subject: "17th MFM," DFOIA.

be a negative factor in our efforts on the Hill to seek support for the process of change in Nicaragua. Also, we reduce our own ability to work with those elements now and in the future. It is clear they are a diverse coalition – even the FSLN itself. Our best hopes are for recognizing the distinctions rather than submerging them in a "Marxist" cover."[60] Other U.S. diplomats questioned the benefits of any move to develop closer military ties with area dictatorships, contending that it would seriously weaken the credibility of the administration's human rights policy and complicate efforts to develop a normal working relationship with any future FSLN government.

On June 19, Brzezinski chaired a meeting of the SCC, attended by the Secretaries of State and Defense, and the CIA Director, to discuss Nicaraguan developments and make recommendations to the President. The "peacekeeping" issue, Somoza's ouster, and the nature of the political transition dominated proceedings. Brzezinski reaffirmed his enthusiastic support for the regional military option, arguing that what was occurring in Nicaragua was basically an extension of the East-West struggle. None of State's leading policymakers embraced this view. As far as they were concerned, the first order of business was still to get Somoza to relinquish power. Furthermore, there was no evidence of much, if any, Latin American support for the "peacekeeping" proposal. But, as one of their number acknowledged, "the NSC had the upper hand at this point."[61] The three recommendations to the White House testified to the Council's bureaucratic clout: that the administration accelerate efforts to convince the OAS to take a more active role in removing Somoza from office, stress the importance of a regional "peacekeeping" army to guarantee a stable political transition, and highlight Cuba's alleged role in the conflict, especially its military assistance to the FSLN.[62]

Although the SCC's advice was reportedly acceptable to President Carter, the final State Department draft of Secretary Vance's June 21 OAS speech – reviewed by Vance and Vaky before forwarding to the White House – included no mention of the "peacekeeping" force or Cuban military involvement in Nicaragua. Whereupon, Brzezinski interceded with Carter who subsequently decided to write into the Secretary's presentation specific mention of both subjects.[63]

In his address to the foreign ministers, Vance charged that there was

---

60 Department of State Memorandum, Secret, Patricia Derian, Human Rights, to Secretary of State, June 20, 1979, Subject: "Nicaragua," DFOIA.

61 Confidential interview, Department of State official, September 20, 1989.

62 See Pastor, *Condemned to Repetition*, p. 142; Bernard Gwertzman, "A Painful Decision for Carter," *New York Times*, June 22, 1979, pp. 1, 8. The June 21 murder of American television journalist Bill Stewart by National Guardsmen virtually ended any significant American opposition to the call for a regime change in Nicaragua.

63 See Lake, *Somoza Falling*, pp. 223–224.

"mounting evidence of involvement by Cuba and others in the internal problems of Nicaragua" and called for a "political solution" based on Somoza's replacement by an interim government of national reconciliation. To establish the requisite tranquility and order for a return to democratic rule, the OAS should dispatch a "peacekeeping" military force "to assist the interim government in establishing its authority. . . ."[64] According to Vaky, the aim of the speech was to convince the assembled delegates that only "a sharp break with the past" (Somoza's ouster) offered any possibility of a negotiated solution and that only direct hemispheric involvement was likely to "avoid radical control" of a post-Somoza government.[65] It was hoped that intervention would also serve the twin purposes of limiting the guerrillas' access to outside military aid and containing the struggle within the geographical boundaries of a single country. "The peacekeeping force," said Vaky, "was seen as a force that would insulate countries around Nicaragua from the effect of Nicaragua's troubles and possibly also reduce support from the outside for Sandinista elements in Nicaragua. It was not expressed at the OAS but that was certainly a part of the concept as far as Washington was concerned."[66] Ambler Moss was more succinct and to the point, describing the plan as an attempt to promote "an intervention without it being our intervention."[67] Not surprisingly, Vance's speech made no mention of the recently formed FSLN provisional junta.

The hemispheric response to the "peacekeeping" proposal was almost uniformly critical, whereas the reference to Cuba elicited comments ranging from skepticism to outright disbelief. Although a clear majority of OAS member governments supported an immediate regime transition in Nicaragua, not a single delegate spoke in favor of the military interventionist option. On the contrary, the most politically influential countries in the region (Mexico, Brazil, and the Andean Pact governments) denounced the idea as nothing more than a refurbished attempt to justify U.S. intervention in the internal affairs of a sovereign state.[68] Regarding Cuba, even democratic Latin governments were moved to publicly accuse the Carter administration of wildly exaggerating Havana's military assistance to the Sandinistas.

The case for Cuban involvement on the side of the FSLN derived from

---

64 Secretary of State Cyrus Vance, Statement before the Organization of American States, June 21, 1979, *State Department Press Release*, No. 158.
65 Statement of Viron P. Vaky, Assistant Secretary of State for Inter-American Affairs, in U.S. Congress, House, *United States Policy Toward Nicaragua*, p. 34; Letter from Viron P. Vaky to Lee H. Hamilton, Chairman, Subcommittee on Europe and Middle East, Committee on Foreign Affairs, September 8, 1979, in Ibid., p. 75 (Appendix 4).
66 Interview with Viron Vaky.
67 Interview with Ambler Moss.
68 See Graham Hovey, "U.S. Proposals on Nicaragua Crisis Meet Sharp Criticism From O.A.S.," *New York Times*, June 23, 1979, p. 3.

U.S. intelligence reports based on uncorroborated evidence obtained from Somoza and the National Guard charging that the Castro government was providing weapons, training expertise, and even military units to fight alongside the Sandinista forces – notwithstanding a May CIA report that stressed the limited nature of Cuba's military participation in the Nicaraguan struggle. Even before the conference ended, the White House was forced to admit that it had "no direct evidence of Cubans on the ground," and the Defense Department downgraded Cuba's alleged role to that of cooperating with Panama and Costa Rica to facilitate arms shipments to the Sandinistas.[69] The next day, Washington admitted that it could not even produce evidence to sustain this Pentagon claim. State Department spokesman Tom Reston acknowledged that the U.S. "is unable to prove the intelligence report that the three countries had been cooperating to arm the Nicaraguan rebels...."[70]

During Congressional testimony, Assistant Secretary of State Vaky termed the Nicaraguan struggle "fundamentally" indigenous in character and described Cuba as "not the only or even the most important of the supporters of the anti-Somoza rebellion."[71] Other American officials referred to the conflict as "essentially an internal rebellion."[72] The transparently fraudulent nature of the White House case against Havana was summarized by the *Washington Post*'s correspondent in Managua at the conclusion of the OAS meeting: "So far, Somoza has presented very little evidence of Cuban involvement, and the United States has provided none."[73] Bernard Died-

---

69 Quoted in Richard Burt, "U.S. Asserts Cubans are Supplying and Training Rebels in Nicaragua," *New York Times*, June 23, 1979, pp. 1, 3. Also see Karen DeYoung, "Guard Drive Against Rebels in Eastern Managua Slowed," *Washington Post*, June 26, 1979, p. A15; "Panama, Cuba Linked to Nicaraguan Strife," *Houston Post*, June 29, 1979, p. 10A.

70 Jeremiah O'Leary, "U.S. Protests to Cuba, Others on Sandinista Arms Running," *Washington Star*, June 30, 1979, p. A6.

71 Statement of Viron P. Vaky, in U.S. Congress, House, *United States Policy Toward Nicaragua*, p. 34.

72 Quoted in Don Bohning, "War in Nicaragua is Still 'Internal,' U.S. Says," *Miami Herald*, June 28, 1979, p. 25A.

73 DeYoung, "Guard Drive Against Rebels in Eastern Managua Slowed," p. A15. Most Sandinista arms purchases from abroad were made on black markets in the United States and Western Europe. See ibid. According to Eduardo Kuhl, the FSLN "Roving Ambassador in Europe," the Cuban government refused three separate FSLN arms requests during 1978 and 1979 "in order not to prejudice the independence of our revolution." Quoted in Department of State Telegram, Paris 24551, American Embassy, Paris (Chapman) to Secretary of State, August 1979, Subject: "Sandinista Rep Says Guerrillas Obtained Arms on U.S. Black Market," DFOIA. The Cuban leader's cautious and prudent approach was confirmed by Tercerista leader Edén Pastora who said that Castro responded to requests for military assistance in late 1978 or early 1979 with the comment that "The best help I can give you is not to help you at all." Quoted in Christian, *Nicaragua: Revolution in the Family*, p. 107.

erich's richly detailed account of the revolutionary struggle lends credence
to this assessment, revealing a minimal Cuban role until the final, decisive
confrontation "when [Havana] stepped up its arms delivery to the winning
side."[74]

For the first time since its founding in 1948, the OAS stood poised to
hand Washington a sizeable diplomatic defeat. As the State Department
later conceded, "most Latin delegations interpreted Secretary Vance's statement as part of a carefully designed U.S. plan to intervene in Nicaragua to
ensure the continuation of U.S. influence through a successor government
acceptable to [the] U.S., not necessarily to the Nicaraguan people."[75] Confronting widespread regional opposition to the military "peacekeeping"
force, the Carter White House forestalled any more embarrassment by withdrawing its proposal. Mexico and the Andean Pact governments offered a
substitute resolution calling for a rapid political transition "which will recognize the contribution that the various groups within [Nicaragua] have
made in seeking to replace the Somoza regime."[76] The U.S. delegation's
response was notably restrained. It endorsed the call for the "immediate
and definitive replacement" of the Somoza dictatorship and acknowledged
the futility of continuing efforts to promote the "peacekeeping" idea. But
the hegemonic power cautioned that no alternative plan could be implemented unless it was acceptable to the vast majority of OAS members that,
by implication, must include the United States.

Back in the White House, President Carter and senior administration
officials met throughout the day of June 22, then attended an emergency
SCC meeting the next morning to settle on a response to the Latin American
resolution as well as discuss broader U.S. policy concerns about Nicaragua.
Except for NSC Advisor Brzezinski, who continued to advocate some form
of direct military intervention to prevent a "second Cuba," the President
and the other committee members had accommodated themselves to the
need for more subtle and "low profile" interventionist strategies to achieve
the desired goals. The meeting reaffirmed the importance that Washington
attached to the survival of the National Guard during any transition process
(and to the U.S. role in ensuring that outcome) and discussed the approach
to be adopted toward the new FSLN provisional junta. Finally, the SCC
decided to seek amendments to the Latin American resolution "that would

74 Diederich, *Somoza and the Legacy of U.S. Involvement in Central America*, p. 282.
75 Department of State Telegram, Confidential State 168853, Secretary of State to All
American Republic Diplomatic Posts, June 30, 1979, Subject: "Outcome of Second Session of 17th MFM on Nicaragua," DFOIA.
76 Quoted in John M. Goshko, "OAS Votes for Ouster of Somoza," *Washington Post*, June
24, 1979, p. A13.

permit the United States some authority to negotiate a transition in Nicaragua."[77]

Warren Christopher, Viron Vaky, and Robert Pastor returned to the OAS on June 23 and successfully lobbied for changes in the substitute resolution. In its final form, the resolution was carried by a vote of 17 to 2 (Nicaragua, Paraguay) with 5 abstentions (the rightist pro-U.S. military dictatorships of Guatemala, Honduras, El Salvador, Uruguay, and Chile). Even though the document obliquely criticized the United States by requesting all governments "to scrupulously respect the principle of non-intervention and to abstain from taking any action incompatible with an enduring and peaceful resolution," it also identified the Somoza regime as the fundamental cause of the civil war, demanded its immediate replacement by an interim regime composed of representatives of the moderate opposition forces and the guerrillas, and called for the OAS to play an active role in facilitating a peaceful political settlement. Although the resolution lacked "the specificity we had originally desired," Deputy Secretary of State Christopher was satisfied that it "does permit, indeed it authorizes and encourages, constructive action by member countries."[78] Of course, for Washington to have cast a negative vote would have risked virtual isolation from the rest of the hemisphere.

The State Department instructed Ambassador Pezzullo to contact the Broad Opposition Front (FAO) leadership, provide it with a copy of the resolution, and emphasize that the latter offered "new opportunities" for prevailing on Somoza to resign and go into exile, thus opening the way for a dialogue between the principal opposition forces about the establishment of a "Government of National Reconciliation." In the event such a dialogue occurred, Pezzullo should urge "the moderate groups [to] position themselves to emerge as independent participants."[79] FAO leader Jaime Chamorro told an Embassy official that no decision had been taken over whether to adopt an independent posture or align with the FSLN provisional junta. To which the latter responded that Washington "had no official position" regarding the provisional junta, but that it preferred the FAO "maintain [its] independence."[80]

77 Pastor, *Condemned to Repetition*, pp. 148–149.
78 Organization of American States, *Meeting of Consultation of Ministers of Foreign Affairs*, OEA/Ser.F/11.7, June 23, 1979; Department of State Telegram, State 163598, Secretary of State to All American Republic Diplomatic Posts, June 23, 1979, Subject: "MFM-Resolution on Nicaragua," DFOIA.
79 Department of State Telegram, Secret State 163604, Secretary of State (Christopher) to American Embassy, June 24, 1979, Subject: "OAS Resolution Offers Opportunity for Dialogue," DFOIA.
80 Department of State Telegram, Secret Managua 2787, American Embassy (Tucker) to Secretary of State, June 24, 1979, Subject: "Message to the FAO," DFOIA.

Promoting an anti-Sandinista state and regime:
The failure of White House diplomacy

In April 1979, the U.S. Ambassador to Uruguay Lawrence Pezzullo accepted a State Department request to take over the vacant Managua Embassy following the departure of Mauricio Solaun in early Spring. According to Pezzullo, his predecessor "had just picked up and left, without authority, or so much as by your leave." Attending an early May conference of U.S. officials on Central American policy in San José, Costa Rica, the Ambassador-designate was surprised that "the report on Nicaragua basically focused on how we would convince Somoza to step down at the end of his term in 1981. [There was] not a whisper about impending civil war." Before leaving for Managua in late June, he participated in three weeks of policy discussions in Washington that did little to allay his concerns about the broad thrust of administration thinking: "[There were] almost daily meetings at NSC or elsewhere. Most of the discussions almost sounded like something about cleaning apartments, because everybody was talking about vacuums... what to do about the vacuums, and this vacuum, and that vacuum."[81]

The first U.S. attempt to communicate directly with the Sandinistas took place during the San José meeting. The State Department's Director for Central America Brewster Hemenway let it be known that he was interested in talking with the conservative Tercerista Edén Pastora – a request turned down by the FSLN leadership.[82] Although members of the U.S. delegation to the June OAS meeting on Nicaragua (Assistant Secretary Vaky, Ambassador Pezzullo) did confer with Miguel D'Escoto, the FSLN "Ambassador at Large," Washington steadfastly refused to acknowledge the existence of the newly formed provisional junta or sanction any formal contact between the United States and the Sandinista leadership. Senior officials still entertained hopes of devising and implementing a regime change that avoided a direct transfer of power to the junta and conceded only a limited, highly circumscribed, role to the Sandinistas within any interim government. This issue was at the root of a simmering bureaucratic disagreement between State and the NSC.

The FSLN announcement of a provisional junta in mid-June provoked two distinct responses within the executive branch. Viron Vaky explained: "The State Department position that we should accept a fait accompli and

81 Ambassador Lawrence A. Pezzullo, *oral history interview*, February 24, 1989, Association for Diplomatic Studies, Foreign Affairs Oral History Program, Lauinger Library, Georgetown University, Washington, D.C., pp. 13, 14.
82 See Warren Hoge, "Sandinista Chiefs Express Anger at U.S. for Not Making Contact," *New York Times*, June 28, 1979, p. 3.

be realistic and try to deal with that, and the White House, especially Brzezinski, arguing that there may be a vacuum so we must try to put something in Managua to negotiate with the junta."[83] The issue was high on the agenda of a June 25 SCC meeting on Nicaragua. Influenced by Brzezinski's forceful presentation on the importance of saving the Somoza state (especially the National Guard) in the event of the dictator's demise, the Committee decided that the U.S. should pursue a two-track strategy: apply pressure on the junta to moderate its political outlook and enlarge its membership with the addition of more conservative individuals, and explore the possibilities of establishing an alternative, non-Sandinista, transition junta. "We felt a need for a process", said one State official, "that had a chance of working, that involved people of prominence and political viability."[84]

That same day, a close associate of former Costa Rican President José Figueres visited the U.S. embassy in San José to report on a conversation with Washington's most "acceptable" Sandinista leader Edén Pastora. According to the envoy, Pastora desired American military assistance to enable the forces under his command to reach Managua ahead of the more radical Prolonged People's War faction. The Tercerista leader wanted the U.S. to "persuade" Somoza to use the National Guard to "block" the advance of the other Sandinista forces and facilitate the rapid movement of his own group toward the capital. Failing that, Pastora desired that "U.S.-controlled or Venezuelan-controlled aircraft" be employed to "soften" Guard defenses on the southern front (where Pastora's forces were mobilized) by "bombing." Informed that U.S. policy was to promote a cessation of hostilities and a negotiated political settlement, the Figueres' colleague Dr Jaime Gutiérrez announced his intention to take the matter up directly with Washington.[85]

When Lawrence Pezzullo arrived in Managua he did not present his diplomatic credentials to Somoza. This was one way, the State Department hoped, of "get[ting] the message" across that the administration had irrevocably decided to cast him adrift.[86] At their inaugural meeting on June 27, the new American Ambassador spelled out the administration's three major policy objectives: to ensure "that the Guardia not collapse"; to seek the formation of a transition government dominated by conservative and moderate opposition groups; and to marginalize, or preferably eliminate, the FSLN as a significant political force in the post-Somoza era. Their achieve-

83 Interview with Viron Vaky.
84 Confidential interview, Department of State official, September 20, 1989.
85 Department of State Telegram, Confidential San Jose 2691, American Embassy, San José (Weissman) to Secretary of State, For the Nicaraguan Working Group, June 25, 1979, Subject: "Figueres' Associate Suggests USG Aid Edén Pastora," DFOIA.
86 Quoted in Oswald Johnson, "U.S. Moves to End Nicaraguan Conflict, Sends Envoy to Press Somoza to Quit," Los Angeles Times, Part 1, June 28, 1979, p. 8.

ment depended in large part on a "clean break with the [Somoza] government" which included the dictator's resignation and exile. Otherwise, the fighting would continue, increasing the likelihood of "an extreme leftist takeover." He also emphasized the importance of the timing of Somoza's departure: "[It] had to be tailored with great precision to bolster moderate forces, preserve the institutional integrity of the GN [National Guard] and stop the bloodshed."[87] Among those touted by Pezzullo for possible inclusion in a transition regime were Edén Pastora and representatives from the Broad Opposition Front (FAO), the Nationalist Liberal Party (PLN), and the Conservative Party.

It would be impossible, he told Somoza, to "preserve the Guard" unless measures were taken to "rupture" the public perception of the organization as an extension of the ruling family. A change of this magnitude could not be achieved overnight. For that reason, it was critically important that the dictator leave the country well before the regime change occurred. There was no likelihood of major assistance to the Guard until some time after his departure because it "still remains associated in the minds of the people here as your Guard." The Ambassador then pointedly reminded Somoza that his political support had dissolved not only in Nicaragua but throughout the hemisphere as well. Somoza's response was measured rather than angry: He was prepared to leave office if the United States would "guarantee" roles for the National Guard and his PLN in the transition and post-transition period.[88] At this late stage, however, Washington was not prepared to give "assurances of that kind."[89]

Conferring again on June 28, the American envoy reiterated the fundamental objective of White House policy: "preserving some institutional structure and...preventing an extreme leftist solution" in Nicaragua. This meant, first and foremost, "preserv[ing] some segments of the Guard" even though the U.S. was "very vulnerable" to regional criticism on this issue as many governments were convinced it was simply trying to "impose another version of Somocismo." The success of the anti-FSLN strategy would, he reminded Somoza, depend on his willingness to allow the United States to dictate the timing of his departure. Maintaining a calm demeanor, Somoza acknowledged that his leaving was "an essential first step" and agreed that the planning process should begin as soon as possible.[90]

87 Department of State Telegram, Secret Managua 2857, American Embassy (Pezzullo) to Secretary of State, June 27, 1979, Subject: "Somoza – The First Visit," DFOIA.
88 Quoted in Somoza, *Nicaragua Betrayed*, pp. 334, 337–338, 342, 343, 345. Also see Alan Riding, "Somoza is Reported Ready to Quit, But on Terms Unacceptable to Foes," *New York Times*, June 29, 1979, pp. 1, 6.
89 Department of State Telegram, Secret State 165686, Secretary of State (Christopher) to American Embassy, June 27, 1979, Subject: "Nicaragua," DFOIA.
90 Department of State Telegram, Secret Managua 2886, American Embassy (Pezzullo) to

The first of the American-authored transition schemes floated by NSC Advisor Brzezinski, Pezzullo, and other officials during the last week of June involved the creation of what the State Department's Warren Christopher termed a "credible caretaker" government.[91] U.S. officials met secretly with Somoza to outline the proposal, which was predicated on his resignation and replacement by a yet to be designated PLN official who would remain head of state only long enough to appoint a five-member "executive committee" that would constitute a provisional government or "Government of National Unity." Membership of this "executive committee" would be confined to representatives of the National Guard, the PLN, the FAO, the Superior Council of Private Enterprise (COSEP), and the Catholic Church. Upon completion of the process, the Carter administration would extend immediate diplomatic recognition to the new government, which in turn would request the FSLN provisional junta to nominate two additional members – thus creating the illusion of a broad-based transitional regime capable of preparing the country for elections and the restoration of constitutional rule.[92]

Despite Ambassador Pezzullo's best efforts to interest "several potential candidates" in the scheme during this first 24 hours in Managua, he quickly concluded that there was "little if any chance of putting together an executive committee of any size. The opposition figures we identified have either openly supported the provisional junta or are fearful of playing an independent role."[93] Although Archbishop Obando Y Bravo, at the Ambassador's suggestion, agreed to "consider issuing a pastoral letter and other support for such an initiative", the President of the Red Cross and head of the Chamber of Industries Ismael Reyes spoke for most of the targeted "notables" approached by the Embassy when he told Pezzullo that "there are too many unknowns for his comfort."[94]

American policy was still operating on the assumption that a political

Secretary of State, June 29, 1979, Subject: "Somoza – Second Visit," DFOIA; Somoza, *Nicaragua Betrayed*, pp. 355, 356.

91 Department of State Telegram, Secret State 168715, Secretary of State (Christopher) to American Embassy (Pezzullo), June 30, 1979, Subject: "Nicaraguan Scenario," DFOIA.

92 The U.S. plan is discussed in Graham Hovey, "2 U.S. Diplomats Off to Nicaragua in Growing Bid to Replace Somoza," *New York Times*, June 28, 1979, p. 3; John M. Goshko, "U.S. is Pressing Somoza to Resign, Leave Nicaragua," *Washington Post*, June 28, 1979, pp. A1, A24; Riding, "Somoza is Reported Ready to Quit, But on Terms Unacceptable to Foes," pp. 1, 6.

93 Department of State Telegram, Secret Managua 2870, American Embassy (Pezzullo) to Secretary of State (Vaky), June 28, 1979, Subject: "The Current Scene," DFOIA.

94 Department of State Telegram, Confidential Managua 2884, American Embassy (Pezzullo) to Secretary of State, June 28, 1979, Subject: "Meeting with Archbishop," DFOIA; Department of State Telegram, Confidential Managua 2887, American Embassy (Pezzullo) to Secretary of State, June 29, 1979, Subject: "Meeting with Red Cross President," DFOIA.

transition could be fashioned that ignored the FSLN. This, notwithstanding the fact that the provisional junta had already been endorsed by the most conservative FAO factions as well as the influential private sector organization COSEP. In conversations with U.S. officials at the time, spokesmen for both the FAO and COSEP quickly disabused Washington of any groundswell of support in these quarters for the competing junta plan. Opposition political and business leaders not only reaffirmed their support for the provisional junta; they also warned against any political solution that envisaged a role for the National Guard and the PLN on the grounds that virtually the entire population was opposed and it would therefore only prolong the conflict. Ultimately, the United States could not overcome the refusal of its closest anti-regime allies to lend their names to a transition arrangement that denied the provisional junta a role commensurate with the Sandinista contribution to the anti-dictatorial struggle.[95] In a dispatch to the State Department on June 29, Ambassador Pezzullo reported that the possibility of creating "anything resembling a viable executive committee quickly" is so doubtful that it "appears to be a dead letter."[96]

Reflecting on the failed attempt to mobilize support for the establishment of a credible alternative to the provisional junta, Pezzullo singled out two interrelated problems in his encounters with opposition leaders: potential candidates' unease over "the lack of an assured security and support base" that could back up their decision to participate in the U.S. plan; and the fear of FSLN reprisals. In contrast to a junta with the backing of the Sandinista high command and the governments of Panama and Costa Rica, all the United States could offer anyone willing to join "a caretaker executive committee," he told Assistant Secretary Vaky, "was helpful words." The mediation experience, Pezzullo reported, had left a profound lack of "trust" among the civilian leadership of the anti-regime movement in Managua: "They had exposed themselves eight months before, when suddenly – when the moment of truth came, to get Somoza out, we couldn't deliver. I mean that's how they saw it, to put it in the bluntest terms. And they weren't about to expose themselves again in the middle of a civil war."[97]

Surprisingly, Pezzullo did not reject the "executive committee" strategy as flatly unattainable. The one glimmer of hope depended on the ability of

95 See Alan Riding, "Nicaraguan Moderates Reject U.S. Plan for Conservative Interim Regime," *New York Times*, June 30, 1979, p. 8; Stephen Kinzer, "Nicaraguans Resist U.S. Efforts to Shape New Government," *New York Times*, July 1, 1979, p. 27.
96 Department of State Telegram, Confidential Managua 2887; Ambassador Lawrence A. Pezzullo, *oral history interview*, p. 14.
97 Department of State Telegram, Secret Managua 2919, American Embassy (Pezzullo) to Secretary of State (Vaky), June 30, 1979, Subject: "Nicaragua Scenario," DFOIA.

the National Guard to survive a political transition with its prerogatives and power intact. The prospect "of attracting individuals to form part of the caretaker body" would be immeasurably improved "once it appears that a reconstituted GN [National Guard] can hold. . . . " He therefore urged the State Department to "move with haste to help select a new Guard commander so that he [can] begin putting a staff together, assuring that the rank and file of the GN [National Guard] will support him and offering support to a caretaker committee."[98] In the days that followed, the cable traffic between Managua and Washington referred again and again to the fundamental importance "of preserving enough of the GN [National Guard] to maintain order and to hold the FSLN in check after Somoza resigns." Failure to do so, Ambassador Pezzullo warned, can only lead to one other outcome: "the vacuum we all wish to avoid will be filled by the FSLN, with all the negative consequences that would bring."[99]

Amid these efforts to engineer an anti-Sandinista political transition, the Carter administration decided to establish official contact with the FSLN provisional junta. On June 27, Special Ambassador William Bowdler, accompanied by Ambassador to Panama Ambler Moss, met with junta members Daniel Ortega, Violeta Chamorro, Alfonso Robelo, and Sergio Ramírez in Panama City. "The first meeting," Moss recalled, "got down to particulars – elections, assurances of no reprisals against Somocistas. We talked about integrating the Guard within the Sandinista army."[100] Although both American diplomats avoided discussion of the "credible caretaker" plan, it did not pass unnoticed. After the meeting, junta member Ramírez spoke on behalf of his colleagues: "We consider the plan direct intervention in the affairs of the Nicaraguan people." Bowdler and Moss also confronted a good deal of junta skepticism over Washington's ability or willingness to control Somoza. This was most evident in the response to the Bowdler's statement that Ambassador Pezzullo would request Somoza's resignation the next day. "Mr. Bowdler seemed so sure it was going to work, but we said, 'Why? It's the same demand he's turned down before.' "[101] Partly as a gesture of goodwill toward the U.S., the junta announced at the conclusion of the meeting that a new Nicaraguan government would include an elected

98 Department of State Telegram, Confidential Managua 2887.
99 Department of State Telegram, Secret Managua 2914, American Embassy (Pezzullo) to Secretary of State (Vaky), June 30, 1979, Subject: "(S) National Guard Survival," DFOIA.
100 Interview with Ambler Moss.
101 Quoted in Warren Hoge, "Nicaraguan Rebel Leaders Reject U.S. Plan for Settling Civil War," *New York Times,* June 30, 1979, pp. 1, 8. Also see Foreign Broadcast Information Service, *Daily Report: Latin America,* July 2, 1979, p. 7; Karen DeYoung, "U.S. Envoy, Junta Leaders Talk," *Washington Post,* June 29, 1979, pp. A17, A19.

thirty-member legislative council drawn from all political parties, civic associations, trade unions, and business groups except those closely linked to the Somoza regime.

In Washington, meanwhile, the debate between State and the NSC over the credible caretaker/executive committee strategy flared anew during June 28 and 29 SCC meetings. The NSC and some White House officials challenged Pezzullo's cables about the alternative junta scheme. For the administration to resign itself to an FSLN victory would lead to the very outcome all foreign policy officials wanted to avoid: a Sandinista monopoly of political and state power. Representing the State Department, Viron Vaky and Warren Christopher dismissed the alternative junta idea as unrealistic and unworkable, arguing that the United States would be better placed to influence the provisional junta in government the sooner hostilities were terminated. In the end, the Committee agreed to persist with the two-track approach, continue efforts to reconstitute and strengthen the National Guard, and increase communications with the Sandinista leadership with a view to expanding the membership of the provisional junta and reaching agreement on a number of questions "which will give the moderates a fair opportunity to survive the power struggle that is bound to ensue." It also decided against setting a specific, fixed date for Somoza's departure, pending discussions between the Embassy and key civilian opposition leaders.[102] The timing was all important, as Pezzullo remarked again in a June 30 telegram, if Washington was to avoid a "vacuum that could be exploited by the extreme left...."[103]

On June 29, the American Ambassador detailed Washington's strategy for "prevent[ing] leftist domination [of Nicaragua]" to Somoza. It depended on the latter's resignation, the substitution of a "caretaker committee or person" to head the transition regime, "and the preservation of elements of the National Guard to prevent an FSLN takeover."[104] The next day, Deputy Secretary of State Christopher cabled the Embassy that it was also imperative to dissuade Somoza from any attempt to appoint his own transition government on the grounds that it would be rejected not only by the FSLN and the moderate opposition but also by virtually every OAS member state. He urged Pezzullo to "please continue to seek some coalescing of opposition elements willing to take up the baton" and reaffirmed the importance of

---

102 Department of State Telegram, Secret State 169011, Secretary of State (Christopher) to American Embassy, Caracas, Managua, Panama, San José, Bogotá, Guatemala, Lima, Quito, Tegucigalpa, June 30, 1979, Subject: "U.S. Strategy – Nicaragua," *DFOIA*. Also see Pastor, *Condemned to Repetition*, pp. 156–157.
103 Department of State Telegram, Secret Managua 2911, American Embassy (Pezzullo) to Secretary of State, June 30, 1979, Subject: "Somoza – The Third Meeting," DFOIA.
104 Department of State Telegram, Confidential Managua 2887.

preserving an effective, reconstituted National Guard presence so as to make certain the FSLN would not be the "only organized military force" in the post-Somoza era.[105] The Ambassador responded that any chance of success depended on the level of hemispheric support the Department could mobilize: An "essential element in building the confidence of a caretaker group and a reconstituted Guardia Nacional is support by Andean Group countries and other LA [Latin American] states."[106]

Washington's determination to fashion a political transition based on a reformist and restructured National Guard gave U.S. policy the distinct appearance of simply wanting to "hit at the top" rather than dismember the foundations of the old regime. Although the State Department repeatedly denied that it was negotiating with Somoza over the future of the Guard and the PLN, the importance it attached to the survival of the armed forces amid a regime change remained at or near the top of the policy agenda.[107] American officials actively encouraged Pentagon-trained junior Guard officers to remain at their posts in the hope of sustaining the institution's historic role as a bulwark against radical political rule and socioeconomic policies, and the guarantor of U.S. permanent interests.[108] The Carter administration scenario presupposed the demobilization and breakup of the Sandinista army and the incorporation of selected "moderate" guerrillas into the ranks, not the leadership, of a refurbished Somoza military organization.

In preparation for a July 2 SCC meeting, the Defense Department prepared a "talking paper" for Secretary Harold Brown and the Joint Chiefs of Staff reviewing U.S. policy toward Nicaragua in the light of recent developments. Commenting on the objectives agreed to at the June 29 meeting, the paper's author termed them unrealistic and virtually unattainable given the reluctance of the moderates to participate in any alternative "caretaker" government, American intelligence reports describing the National Guard as "demoralized" and ready to collapse when Somoza departs, and the growing likelihood of an FSLN military victory. The paper also challenged "some [of the] conventional wisdom propping up" U.S. objectives in Nicaragua. First, it cited Ambassador's Bowdler's reports indicating the low probability of achieving a military ceasefire. Second, it referred to pronounced divisions among administration officials over the National Guard's ability to survive a regime transition. Third, it criticized those policymakers

105 Department of State Telegram, Secret State 168715.
106 Department of State Telegram, Secret Managua 2919.
107 See, for example, Karen DeYoung, "Army is Crucial Issue in Nicaragua," *Washington Post*, July 9, 1979, p. A14.
108 See Karen DeYoung, "U.S. Trying New Move to Save Somoza's Guard," *Washington Post*, July 10, 1979, p. A2.

who expected an expanded provisional junta to "evolve into a power some-what friendly to U.S. interests" for failing to appreciate that "the elements with the most ideological cohesiveness and impetus are marxist-oriented [and that] they will dominate the eventual outcome in the absence of a viable National Guard." Finally, it cast doubt over the belief that "there is no realistic prospect of setting up an Inter-American peacekeeping force to separate the combatants and police a ceasefire. There are recent indications that some countries may now support such an effort." This remained the best and most "effective way of preserving the National Guard...." There-fore, Defense should recommend two courses of action: new approaches to Latin American governments to contribute "units and logistic support" for a multilateral "peacekeeping" force, and U.S. military assistance to the National Guard if the FSLN "presses for a complete military victory" after Somoza leaves the country, on the basis that this was "probably the only way to prevent a radical left dictatorship from coming to power."[109]

The July 2 meeting of Carter's senior foreign policy advisors was a "knock down, drag out" battle for the primacy of two competing strategies[110]: one that dismissed the alternative junta effort as futile and advocated support for a new National Guard commander and pressure on the FSLN provi-sional junta to moderate its program as offering the best chance, at this late stage, of salvaging an outcome that included the survival of the Somoza military institution (Bowdler, Vaky, Christopher); the other that still clung to the military "peacekeeping" idea as a viable option (Brzezinski) or insisted that the State Department approach was not the best way of saving the Somoza state (Brzezinski, his deputy David Aaron, Brown). Ambler Moss summarized the trajectory of the debate and its outcome:

> The tenor of the meeting was whether or not to cut a deal with the provisional junta in San Jose. The Brzezinski side said no, we mustn't make a deal with them because the Sandinistas will dominate the junta, they are communists, they won't make a deal. We must look for moderates. Pezzullo let loose a barrage of four letter words [to the effect that] there aren't any moderate elements, either make a deal with the provisional junta or there is no-one to make a deal with. The other side was still looking for the center. The decision was referred to the President who decided in favor of the Latin Americanists in the State Department and told Brzezinski to shut up.[111]

109 Department of Defense, Talking Paper for the Secretary of Defense and Chairman, Joint Chiefs of Staff, re Special Coordinating Committee Meeting, July 2, 1979, Secret, Subject: "Nicaragua," DFOIA.
110 Interview with Ambler Moss.
111 Ibid.; Pastor, *Condemned to Repetition*, pp. 160–161.

Having settled on a plan that included expanding the provisional junta, affecting a ceasefire, integrating the armed combatants into a new military institution, and exiling Somoza, the White House turned to Panamanian leader General Omar Torrijos to lobby the Sandinistas while it remained in the background. Carter told Torrijos this did not mean that Washington's role as a major player was about to diminish. On the contrary, the United States would remain active in seeking to shape the outcome of the Nicaraguan conflict but "without using its hands."[112] In this period of daily Sandinista gains on the battlefield, however, American prospects of derailing the guerrilla forces' momentum seemed bleak indeed.

The growing sense of urgency and foreboding among White House and State Department officials was understandable. By the first week of July, the FSLN completely controlled six major population centers including the key northern cities of León and Matagalpa.[113] A cable from the American Embassy said that the National Guard was "bombarding various provincial cities held by the Sandinistas."[114] As the insurgents gradually extended their authority to all parts of the country in preparation for the final assault on Managua, U.S. officials began to express concern over the possible regional multiplier effect of a revolutionary victory. "We're worried," Warren Christopher cabled regional embassies, "that the moderates throughout the area will wind up with their backs to the wall."[115] The Pentagon reviewed contingency invasion plans but stressed that no instructions had been received "to take planning actions."[116]

On July 6, Ambassador Pezzullo cautioned the State Department against applying pressure on Somoza to halt the Guard bombing of urban guerrilla strongholds in the absence of some kind of equivalent gesture by the FSLN: "Air power is the only effective force the GN [National Guard] has to combat the FSLN force which is capturing more towns daily and clearly has the momentum.... Our estimate is that the GN [National Guard] is close to the breaking point...."[117] Sandinista military victories limited Washington's ability to wrest political concessions from the FSLN. In the event that the warring parties agreed to negotiations, the guerrillas would

112 Ibid. p. 164.
113 See Foreign Broadcast Information Service, *Daily Report: Latin America,* July 2, 1979, p. 6; Alan Riding, "Pressure Mounting on Somoza to Quit," *New York Times,* July 5, 1979, p. 6.
114 Department of State Telegram, Confidential State 171293, Deputy Secretary of State (Christopher) to All American Republic Diplomatic Posts, July 2, 1979, Subject: "Nicaragua Working Group Sitrep No. 34–Situation in Nicaragua as of 1530 Hours," DFOIA.
115 Quoted in "Somoza's Last Stand?," *Newsweek,* July 2, 1979, p. 20.
116 Pentagon spokesman, quoted in Ibid., p. 22.
117 Department of State Telegram, Secret Managua 3033, American Embassy (Pezzullo) to Secretary of State, July 6, 1979, Subject: "Negotiations With FSLN," DFOIA.

be in a powerful bargaining position. "The trouble," as one Carter official acknowledged, "is that you cannot take away from the Sandinistas at the conference table what they have won on the battlefield."[118]

Of all the executive branch agencies, State was the strongest and most consistent advocate of the need to mobilize hemispheric support for the administration's policy. With time running out, it mounted another anti-Sandinista diplomatic offensive, targeting the FSLN's closest Latin American allies. The primary objective remained the fate of the National Guard; the secondary goal was to lobby for a more "ideologically and politically balanced" provisional junta in order to strengthen Nicaragua's "democratic forces" before a transition regime took power.[119] "Three of the five members are leftists," said one involved U.S. official. "We would like to see a balance of preferably a majority of moderates."[120] Washington's suggested "moderate" additions included General Julio Gutiérrez, Somoza's Ambassador to Japan, Ernesto Fernandez, finance secretary of the governing PLN, Emilio Alvarez, a Conservative Party politician, Mariano Fiallos, a Liberal Party lawyer and rector of the National University, and Jaime Chamorro, manager of the opposition newspaper *La Prensa*.

During the first week of July, senior State Department officials made lightning visits to at least eight regional capitals where support for the Sandinista cause was strongest, while Special Ambassador Bowdler held almost continuous meetings with the provisional junta in San José. Bernard Diederich splendidly conveys the frenetic nature of American diplomacy in the waning days of Somoza family rule:

> Bowdler met with the junta in San José in round-the-clock sessions on broadening the junta. Phone calls continued to the junta from a series of Latin American nations on behalf of the United States initiatives. American diplomats were active through Central and South America in hopes of twisting the Sandinista's arm. While Bowdler was in Costa Rica, Viron Vaky toured Venezuela, Colombia and the Dominican Republic, and American ambassador to Panama Ambler Moss dealt with Torrijos and [Panamanian President Aristides] Royo.[121]

118 Quoted in Jeremiah O'Leary, "U.S. Makes Contact With Somoza Forces in Effort to Oust Him," *Washington Star*, June 29, 1979, p. A3.
119 Department of State Telegram, Secret Managua 2915, American Embassy (Pezzullo) to Secretary of State (Vaky), June 30, 1979, Subject: "Revised Scenario – Nicaragua," DFOIA.
120 Quoted in Alan Riding, "U.S. Asks Nicaraguan Rebel Junta to Aid Moderates," *New York Times*, July 2, 1979, p. 3.
121 Diederich, *Somoza and the Legacy of U.S. Involvement in Central America*, p. 296. Also see Warren Hoge, "U.S. Keeping Up Pressures on the Nicaraguan Junta," *New York Times*, July 15, 1979, p. 11.

Until the results of this effort to " 'neutralize' the radical elements of the opposition" could be assessed one way or the other,[122] Ambassador Pezzullo was directed to obtain Somoza's resignation but await instructions regarding his actual exit from the country.

Attempting to exploit regional concerns about political instability in Central America, U.S. diplomats raised the junta membership issue at every opportunity arguing that "to broaden the junta would be a reflection of all the opposition to Somoza, it would damp down fears of radical change. Otherwise, the situation would continue to polarize."[123] To further induce Latin governments to apply pressure on the FSLN to expand the junta and guarantee the survival of the National Guard, they were not beneath resorting to crude scare tactics and even the threat of sanctions: A "second Cuba" would pose a serious problem for all Central American and Caribbean rulers, and those offering support to such a regime might suffer U.S. economic retaliation. Peter Tarnoff, who advised Secretary of State Vance on hemispheric matters, elaborated: "First, we said if there was going to be a radical pro-Cuban revolutionary regime on the mainland so to speak, everyone was going to pay very dearly for this. Second, was the impact on domestic politics. It would wreck the Carter administration in hemispheric affairs if some of our best partners became involved with such a regime. Hemispheric policies – aid, assistance – would be adversely affected."[124]

One of the biggest obstacles in the path of the roaming envoys was the widespread distrust of Washington assurances that, as Ambassador Pezzullo put it, "we would deliver Somoza, get him to step down. They were deeply doubted by most of the Latins because they saw what happened in the mediation effort and they thought Somoza was so much our man that we couldn't do it."[125] On July 7, however, a *New York Times* correspondent reported that "several Latin American governments have begun pressing a rebel-backed Nicaraguan provisional junta to make major political concessions in exchange for [Somoza's resignation]."[126] Costa Rica, Panama, and Venezuela, probably the Sandinistas most important political allies and/or sources of military assistance, all capitulated to U.S. entreaties. Having previously opposed the "alternative junta" scheme, they now threatened to withdraw political and military support for the FSLN unless the provisional junta "showed more flexibility."[127]

122   Alan Riding, "U.S. In Role of Key Nicaraguan Arbiter," *New York Times*, July 10, 1979, p. 3.
123   Interview with Viron Vaky.
124   Telephone interview with Peter Tarnoff, New York, September 19, 1988.
125   Interview with Lawrence Pezzullo.
126   Alan Riding, "Latins Pressing Nicaraguan Left For Concessions," *New York Times*, July 8, 1979, P. 1. Also see Riding, "U.S. in Role of Key Nicaraguan Arbiter," p. 3.
127   Karen DeYoung, "Somoza Agrees to Quit, Leaves Timing to U.S.," *Washington Post*,

Costa Rican President Rodrigo Carazo met personally with junta members to make sure they understood his endorsement of Washington's goals.[128] In the case of Venezuela (reportedly the original source of the "expanding provisional junta" idea) and Panama, the receptiveness of Presidents Carlos Andrés Pérez and General Omar Torrijos to U.S. arguments did not constitute major policy shifts. Although both leaders were prominent supporters of the Sandinista movement, they had always most closely identified with the conservative Tercerista Edén Pastora, believing "that ultimately Pastora would emerge on top." Lawrence Pezzullo insisted that Pastora's faction received "all of the money" the Venezuelan government provided to the FSLN.[129] According to Ambler Moss, Torrijos' attitude was influenced by his perception of the guerrilla as someone cut from the same mould as himself: "He saw Edén Pastora as a dashing kind of social democrat in uniform."[130] At the June OAS meeting on Nicaragua, the Panamanian leader revealed his political outlook and policy objectives when he urged the Sandinistas "not to become radicals and make the mistakes that are being committed ... by Somoza." At the time, Moss interpreted this statement as "in effect recogniz[ing] the concern of the U.S. about the ideological makeup of the Government of National Reconciliation [provisional junta]. . . . "[131]

The Carter administration's diplomatic "full court press" was directed toward a single overriding objective: to "contain extremist power" in Nicaragua and thereby eliminate a potential threat to U.S. permanent interests throughout Central America.[132] Once again, the United States was, for all practical purposes, seeking to assume its historic role as the ultimate arbiter of Nicaraguan political arrangements. This latest "outsider" strategy, however, suffered much the same fate as earlier efforts. Not only was it opposed by the FSLN leadership in San José and Panama City; it lacked almost any semblance of support inside Nicaragua. Washington's local allies, especially the moderate anti-Somoza business and political leadership, were simply unwilling to collaborate in any plan that could be interpreted as an ultimatum

July 7, 1979, pp. A1, A3. Also see Graham Hovey, "U.S. Envoys Press Drive for Peace in Nicaragua in Six Latin Capitals," New York Times, July 6, 1979, p. 3; Riding, "U.S. in Role of Key Nicaraguan Arbiter," p. 3.

128   See Riding, "Latins Pressing Nicaraguan Left for Concessions," p. 3.
129   Interview with Lawrence Pezzullo.
130   Interview with Ambler Moss.
131   Department of State Telegram, Confidential Panama 4791, American Embassy (Moss) to Secretary of State, June 27, 1979, Subject: "Torrijos Message to Sandinistas – Representatives of Government of National Reconciliation to Visit Panama," DFOIA.
132   Department of State Telegram, Secret State 179849, Secretary of State (Vance) to All American Republic Diplomatic Posts, July 12, 1979, Subject: "Nicaragua – Status Report," DFOIA.

to the FSLN, or sanction any of its members joining the provisional junta except at the express request of the Sandinista high command.[133]

Economic diplomacy complemented American political initiatives in the attempt to force the FSLN to broaden the junta's membership and moderate its political program. Irrespective of which forces inherited the political mantle from Somoza, the destruction wrought by the civil war would place a premium on swift access to large-scale reconstruction assistance. The Carter administration indicated its preparedness to use the promise of extensive financial support as a bargaining chip to wrest concessions from the provisional junta in government. "We made it very clear to them," State's John Bushnell recalled, "that the emergence of a democratic government respecting human rights in Nicaragua would bring further flows of assistance."[134] What the Sandinistas also had to understand, explained another U.S. official, was the relationship between foreign aid programs and domestic politics: "We can't be seen helping a bunch of radicals. The junta has to look moderate for us to be able to sell the package back home."[135]

As the political-military struggle in Nicaragua approached its climax, U.S. policymakers and diplomats continued efforts to shore up the National Guard, disassociate the institution from the Somoza family, and press for changes that would maximize its chances for survival during and after a regime transition. In early July, Ambassador Pezzullo informed the State Department that the time had arrived for the appointment of a new Guard Commander so that the individual chosen "can set in motion certain essential confidence-building actions which will help allay the fears of the middle and lower grade Guard officers, who are the ones who command the troops and will form the nucleus of the GN [National Guard] after Somoza," and upon whom the U.S. will be dependent "to prevent a FSLN sweep."[136] Secretary Vance agreed and further emphasized the importance of engineering "a total transformation of the Guard" as quickly as possible in order "to preempt the expected Sandinista propaganda assault. . . . These steps will enable [the] new Guard to assert control immediately Somoza departs."

The Carter administration was more than ever convinced that the fate of the moderates and the Guard were intertwined. "In your conversation with moderate leaders," Vance told his Ambassador, "you should make clear to

133 See Riding, "U.S. Asks Nicaraguan Rebel Junta to Aid Moderates," p. 3; Stephen Kinzer, "Nicaraguans Resist U.S. Efforts to Shape New Government," *New York Times,* July 1, 1979, p. 27.
134 Interview with John Bushnell.
135 Quoted in Alan Riding, "U.S. Presses Effort to Add Moderates to Nicaragua Junta," *New York Times,* July 6, 1979, p. 3.
136 Department of State Telegram, Secret Managua 2990, American Embassy (Pezzullo) to Secretary of State, July 5, 1979, Subject: "Somoza/The Fourth Meeting," DFOIA.

them that they will be making a mistake if they rely solely on the provisional junta to safeguard their rights. You may wish to consider urging them to establish contact with appropriate people in the National Guard. We expect that their only chance to hold their own after Somoza departs will depend on the extent they use the Guard to support their cause." Otherwise, the non-Sandinista forces will probably find themselves "isolated and vulnerable."[137] Between July 7 and 17, Pezzullo and his newly arrived Deputy Chief of Mission (DCM) Thomas O'Donnell took part in "about half a dozen meetings with Somoza to work out the succession.... The Ambassador's principal concern was to work out an arrangement for a transition that would preserve the so-called clean elements of the National Guard."[138]

Even at this late stage, American officials were not immune from making statements that indicated a continuing failure to accurately interpret current political and military developments. In a meeting with senior Embassy officials, for instance, the rightist FAO leader Adolfo Calero "lamented the apparent inability of the USG [United States Government] to resolve the situation and avert a Marxist victory." Assurances that a negotiated settlement "remained a strong possibility" failed to impress Calero, leading Ambassador Pezzullo to caustically remark: "Calero's attitude is representative of the doomsday view we get from most moderates in the capital."[139]

Amid the welter of diplomatic comings and goings, American activities in Costa Rica revived lingering concerns over whether the military interventionist option had been completely abandoned by the White House. On July 8, two U.S. Air Force helicopters and thirty-five marines landed at the Llano Grande Airport near the northern city of Liberia, about 52 miles from the Nicaraguan border and not far from a major Sandinista supply line for one of its largest fighting forces based in the area. According to Costa Rican officials, the Minister of Public Safety Juan José Echeverría bowed to a "humanitarian" request from U.S. Ambassador Marvin Weissman to allow the Air Force presence in case emergency measures were necessary to evacuate American Embassy personnel or other American citizens resident in Nicaragua. Upon their arrival, however, the marines proceeded to set up a highly sophisticated communications network, creating widespread local concern over the primary reason for their presence on Costa Rican territory.

137 Department of State Telegram, Secret State 176171, Secretary of State (Vance) to American Embassy (Pezzullo), July 7, 1979, Subject: "Nicaragua – National Guard," DFOIA.
138 Thomas J. O'Donnell, "Installation of the Government of National Reconciliation," in Binnendijk, ed., *Authoritarian Regimes in Transition*, p. 143.
139 Department of State Telegram, Confidential Managua 3096, American Embassy (Pezzullo) to Secretary of State, July 10, 1979, Subject: "Oppositionist Views – Adolfo Calero," DFOIA.

In granting a foreign military force permission to enter Costa Rica, the government acted without the constitutional authority to make such a decision, which is vested in the legislative branch. On July 9, bowing to overwhelming popular pressure, the Congress met in emergency session and voted 29 to 20 to request President Rodrigo Carazo to order the Americans to leave within 24 hours on the grounds that their presence constituted an affront to national sovereignty. Washington refrained from any urge it may have had to contest the expulsion order. For Carazo, the episode represented an embarrassing and humiliating diplomatic defeat.[140]

Against the backdrop of the Somoza regime's deteriorating military position, Washington renewed direct negotiations with the FSLN's provisional junta in yet another attempt to "save" the National Guard and enhance the position of its local civilian allies. Before the talks got underway, Ambassador Pezzullo counseled the State Department to remain sensitive to the possibility that the FSLN "may drag out the negotiations in the knowledge that time is on their side." Moreover, although such discussions offered the hope of a political settlement that created "opportunity" for the moderate forces, it was imperative to have a contingency strategy ready "to prevent the FSLN from dominating the post-Somoza political scene." Pezzullo even offered his own scenario: first, Somoza's resignation; second, the designation of a high profile political figure such as Foreign Minister Julio Quintana as temporary president with responsibility for establishing a Government of National Reconciliation; third, the transition leader appoints a new National Guard commander in preparation for negotiating an armistice with the FSLN. Pezzullo believed that it was absolutely vital to identify the transitional head of state in the public mind with Somoza's ouster because this would "sap an unknown, though perhaps considerable, amount of FSLN support" and substantially improve the prospects of the non-Sandinista forces. The latter, as well as the United States, would receive a further boost if the Carter administration was also perceived "as an instrument" of the dictator's political demise. The Ambassador conceded that the success of this plan "would smack somewhat of Somocismo sin Somoza" but this was a secondary consideration beside the fact that it would be widely hailed as "a break with the past."[141]

On July 11, Special Ambassador William Bowdler met with the provisional junta in San José, Costa Rica. Their colloquy ranged over Somoza's

---

140   See Warren Hoge, "Costa Ricans Expel U.S. Air Force Unit," *New York Times*, July 11, 1979, p. 7; William D. Montalbano, "Costa Rica Orders U.S. Copters Out," *Miami Herald*, July 11, 1979, p. 1A; "Nicaragua is an Impasse," *Central America Report*, July 16, 1979, p. 218.
141   Department of State Telegram, Secret Managua 3032, American Embassy (Pezzullo) to Secretary of State (Vaky), July 6, 1979, Subject: "Contingency Possibilities," DFOIA.

resignation, the composition of the junta, an orderly transfer of power, the structure of a transition regime, the fate of the National Guard, and the protection of the rights of Somoza officials and supporters from indiscriminate reprisals. The twin issues of Somoza's departure and the makeup of the junta soon emerged as sticking points. Despite Bowdler's assurances "that the U.S. was willing to make a major effort to get Somoza out," the problem was that the junta "never really believed that."[142] On the membership issue, it simply rejected any change as an unwarranted concession. Viron Vaky elaborated: "The FSLN just kept throwing back the main argument put forward by Bowdler, saying that it was already a big problem to get the junta formed and now you are asking us to go through a new disequilibria and we can't do it again."[143]

On July 13, with key issues relating to the transition process still unresolved, the junta announced the cessation of talks and made public its own plan, which offered two concessions to Washington: a willingness to incorporate those National Guardsmen who agreed to an immediate ceasefire and returned to their barracks after Somoza's departure into a new national army; and guarantees of safe passage out of the country for all government officials and military personnel "not found involved in crimes against the people."[144] The State Department criticized the lack of prior consultation, the failure to address the membership question, and what it perceived as a subordinate role for the Guard within a Sandinista-dominated military institution. Secretary Vance instructed regional embassies to approach host government foreign ministers and encourage them to continue a dialogue with the provisional junta "with a view to broadening and moderating the basis of [its] program" so that the "moderate elements" might survive and flourish in post-Somoza Nicaragua.[145] Significantly, though, the White House also approved an SCC recommendation to establish direct contact with Edén Pastora "to explore future possibilities for cooperation."[146]

The collapse of the Somoza state and regime

The same day the San José discussions ended, and with the FSLN poised to begin its assault on Managua, Ambassador Pezzullo cabled the State

142   Interview with Lawrence Pezzullo.
143   Interview with Viron Vaky.
144   Quoted in Warren Hoge, "Nicaraguan Rebels Soften Stand on National Guard," *New York Times*, July 12, 1979, p. 14; Karen DeYoung, "Sandinistas Advance Transition Plan, Await U.S. Response," *Washington Post*, July 13, 1979, p. A27. Also See Karen DeYoung, "Nicaraguan Rebels Reach Some Agreements with U.S.," *Washington Post*, July 12, 1979, p. A21.
145   Department of State Telegram, Secret State 179849.
146   Pastor, *Condemned to Repetition*, p. 173.

Department with the news that a timetable for Somoza's departure had finally been drawn up and that it must be executed before the epicenter of the military struggle shifted to the nation's capital. The result, hopefully, would be the blunting and rapid collapse of the Sandinista offensive due to widespread celebrations over Somoza's exit. The assumption behind Pezzullo's excessively optimistic prediction was that popular sentiment desired changes primarily at the level of the regime, not in the state and economy. On the other hand, he warned, "once the [FSLN] attack begins in Managua, the departure of Somoza [then] will appear to have been the result of a military defeat [rather] than a negotiated settlement." In that case, "the benefits we derive from orchestrating his departure will slip from our hands and the survivability of any element of the GN [National Guard] will be unlikely."[47]

Secretary Vance needed no convincing. The Nicaraguan leader must understand that his failure to leave the country within the next 48 to 72 hours "will render our capacity to establish an orderly change impossible by radicalizing the situation still further...." Accompanying this warning should be an implied threat that any delay "complicates the question of your arrival in the U.S."[48] Somoza "appeared to accept this argumentation," Pezzullo wrote, while restating his concern over the lack of "guarantees" for the future of the National Guard and the Nationalist Liberal Party (PLN).[49] Although "saving the Guard" was at the top of the U.S. agenda, the administration had already reconciled itself to the fact "that the PLN will play no role in a transitional government."[50]

True to form, the client continued to pursue his own agenda whether or not it conflicted with U.S. objectives and timetables. Determined to exhaust all possible options, he made a secret trip to Guatemala on July 13 in an unsuccessful attempt to convince the other members of the Central American Defense Council (El Salvador, Honduras, Guatemala) to send troops to fight the FSLN and enable the dictatorial regime to hold onto political

---

147 Department of State Telegram, Secret Managua 3141, American Embassy (Pezzullo) to Secretary of State, July 13, 1979, Subject: "The Urgency of Somoza Leaving Quickly," DFOIA. Also see Department of State Telegram, Secret Managua 3159, American Embassy (Pezzullo) to Secretary of State, July 13, 1979, Subject: "Opposition Views on Current Situation," DFOIA; Department of State Telegram, Secret Managua 3179, American Embassy (Pezzullo) to Secretary of State, July 14, 1979, Subject: "Somoza's Departure Date," DFOIA.

148 Department of State Telegram, Secret State 181058, Secretary of State (Vance) to American Embassy (Pezzullo), July 13, 1979, Subject: "Nicaragua – Next Meeting with Somoza," DFOIA.

149 Department of State Telegram, Secret Managua 3178, American Embassy (Pezzullo) to Secretary of State, July 14, 1979, Subject: "Meeting with Somoza – July 13, 1979," DFOIA.

150 Department of State Telegram, Secret Managua 3039, American Embassy (Pezzullo) to Secretary of State, July 7, 1979, Subject: "Congress Is Ready for Somoza's Resignation," DFOIA.

power.[151] When word leaked of the visit, State's patience reached breaking point. An angry Vance informed Somoza that the fate of the non-Sandinista opposition was tied to "your prompt departure and the designation of a successor and a new Guard commander." Any refusal to leave the country post haste would almost certainly guarantee a military solution to the conflict that would not "permit the moderate elements to survive and compete with extremists."[152] A number of officials were convinced that the Secretary's letter "blew [Somoza] out of the water," destroying, once and for all, any thoughts he might have still harbored about postponing his exile.[153]

There was renewed optimism in Washington when the provisional junta and Ambassador Bowdler resumed discussions in San José on July 15. Since their last tete-à-tete, the junta had named an eighteen-member cabinet containing only one Sandinista member. Moderate businessmen and technocrats were appointed to the key economic posts and a former National Guard colonel Bernardino Larios was put in charge of the Defense Ministry. It was later revealed that the FSLN originally intended to give the military post to Sandinista commandante Humberto Ortega but agreed to substitute Larios under considerable U.S. pressure.[154] Cabinet nominees also included four members of the liberal "Group of Twelve" or Los Doce.

This time around, Bowdler did not raise the contentious membership issue, presumably reflecting State's determination that it was a non-starter and would only stalemate the negotiations, thereby prolonging military hostilities and weakening the position of the Guard. Instead, the talks focused on military-related questions and the fate of Somoza officials during and after the transition period. Secretary Vance expressed particular satisfaction with the "progress in defining modalities for a ceasefire, a [military] standstill, and the eventual integration of the opposing military forces into a new Nicaraguan army."[155]

But while these negotiations continued, there still remained the unresolved question (for the Carter administration) of who to appoint as the new National Guard commander. The State Department backed Colonel Ino-

151 See Foreign Broadcast Information Service, *Daily Report: Latin America*, July 17, 1979, p. 34. Somoza's trip to Guatemala is also discussed in Karen DeYoung, "Somoza Reportedly Meeting Latin Allies," *Washington Post*, July 14, 1979, pp. A1, A11.

152 Department of State Telegram, Secret State 183243, Secretary of State (Christopher for Vance) to American Embassy (Pezzullo), July 14, 1979, Subject: "Somoza's Departure," DFOIA.

153 Quoted in Don Oberdorfer, "Somoza's Plea to Carter was Squashed by Vance," *Washington Post*, July 18, 1979, p. A14.

154 See Christian, *Nicaragua: Revolution in the Family*, p. 129.

155 Department of State Telegram, Secret State 183745, Secretary of State (Vance) to All American Republic Diplomatic Posts, July 15, 1979, Subject: "Nicaragua Status Report," DFOIA. Also see "Nicaragua Rebels Say U.S. is Ready to Back Regime Led by Them," *New York Times*, July 16, 1979 pp. 1, 3.

cente Mojíca on the grounds that he had "credibility" with the officer corp, the provisional junta, and foreign governments most closely associated with the Nicaraguan conflict. The Embassy had solicited names of eligible individuals from Somoza but unequivocally rejected his two favored suggestions – General Humberto Sanchez or Lieutenant Colonel Alberto Moreno – as undermining Washington's basic objective: the survival of the Guard based on a restructuring of the chain of command and the projection of a more acceptable public image. Moreno was characterized as "a good soldier [who] lacks the prestige and polish of Mojíca" while Sanchez was dismissed as a worse liability, "an old Somoza war-horse [and] a corrupt deadbeat who would seriously prejudice the survivability of the Guard." Ambassador Pezzullo cabled State that he would do his best "to convince Somoza...that Mojíca is the best candidate to protect the GN's [National Guard's] interests...."[156]

Two days later, Somoza took a major step toward addressing U.S. concerns about the structure of the Guard. He retired almost 100 senior officers, including all the generals and most of the colonels and lieutenant colonels. This decision eliminated one stumbling block to a ceasefire and at least potentially improved Washington's chances of recreating a new Nicaraguan army within which the FSLN would play a subordinate role. American policymakers hoped that when the provisional junta arrived in Managua it would confront a National Guard whose senior posts were held by younger, professional officers less tainted than their predecessors by any association with the dictatorship.[157] The question of a new commander was also settled when both the U.S. and Somoza agreed on the appointment of Colonel Federico Mejía, selected from a new list of potential candidates prepared for Ambassador Pezzullo by the CIA Station head, to the posts of Guard Director and Chief of Staff – with the reported intention of offering one of the positions to Edén Pastora at a later date.[158]

On July 17, Somoza resigned from office, beginning a transition scenario worked out between the outgoing dictator, officials of his government including Francisco Urcuyo, a senior PLN member and president of the Chamber of Deputies, the FSLN's provisional junta, civilian opposition figures, and American officials in Washington and Managua. Urcuyo was

156 Department of State Telegram, Secret Managua 3204, American Embassy (Pezzullo) to Secretary of State (Vaky), July 14, 1979, Subject: "New Guard Commander," DFOIA. Also see Department of State Telegram, Secret State 176619, Secretary of State (Vance) to American Embassy, Guatemala, Info American Embassy, Managua, July 8, 1979, Subject: "Colonel Mojíca," DFOIA.

157 See Alan Riding, "Somoza Retires 100 Senior Officers Amid Signs His Resignation Nears," *New York Times*, July 17, 1979, pp. 1, 9.

158 See Lake, *Somoza Falling*, p. 252; Somoza, *Nicaragua Betrayed*, p. 383; Christian, *Nicaragua: Revolution in the Family*, p. 131.

appointed interim president for no longer than 72 hours with instructions to arrange a meeting between Colonel Mejía and the Sandinista commanders to negotiate a military ceasefire and standstill, and begin discussions on the structure of the proposed new integrated national army – preparatory to the junta's arrival in the capital city to assume the reigns of political power.[159] The agreement also included a Sandinista pledge of no reprisals against Somoza supporters and Guard officers.

Unbeknownst to the White House, however, the exiled dictator had apparently not completely given up hope of regaining his former power and authority. Without warning, interim President Urcuyo reportedly ordered Colonel Mejía not to establish contact with the FSLN military leadership. When Pezzullo and O'Donnell called on Urcuyo in Somoza's "bunker" and suggested in the presence of Mejía that the new Guard leader "fly to the Costa Rican border and open negotiations with Humberto Ortega, Urcuyo forbade it."[160] He also told the diplomats that he was "not prepared to surrender power to the Junta."[161] The interim president frustrated at least two meetings arranged by American officials to implement a ceasefire and standstill agreement. Also, Somoza had deliberately neglected to brief senior Guard officers about the transition formula. At the "bunker" conference, Mejía informed the two Embassy officials "he had understood that once Somoza left, the United States would actively support the National Guard. Apparently Somoza had told the senior Guard officials [this]. . . . "[162] State Department officials vehemently denied that any such promise had ever been made. Whether or not Somoza consciously deceived his Guard colleagues and Urcuyo, it is not beyond the realm of possibility that individual Pentagon officials may have encouraged him to believe that such military assistance would be forthcoming, or that the Department would strongly push for it after his departure. Indeed, the agency had previously indicated it favored rearming the Guard once the new regime took power.

Within hours of the formal termination of Somoza family rule, Urcuyo issued a statement calling on the Sandinistas to voluntarily demobilize, making no reference to the ceasefire process or any of the transition agreements to which he was a party, and then notified Ambassador Pezzullo that he

159 See Karen DeYoung, "Somoza's Successor Seeks to Hold Power," *Washington Post*, July 18, 1979, pp. A1, A14; Alan Riding, "Somoza Yields Power and Arrives in U.S.; Fighting Continues," *New York Times*, July 18, 1979, p. 18; Bernard Gwertzman, "U.S. Hails Departure of Somoza, Deplores Decision of Successor," *New York Times*, July 18, 1979, pp. 1, 3.

160 O'Donnell, "Installation of the Government of National Reconciliation," p. 144.

161 Department of State Telegram, Secret Managua 3250, American Embassy (Pezzullo) to Secretary of State, July 17, 1979, Subject: "(S) GON Backs off from Agreement," DFOIA.

162 O'Donnell, "Installation of the Government of National Reconciliation," p. 144.

intended to remain in office. After receiving Pezzullo's report of his meeting, which lasted into the morning of July 18, the State Department concluded that it was no longer possible to negotiate "reasonably" with Urcuyo. The Ambassador and most of the Embassy staff were recalled "for consultation."[163] In a communique to Latin American diplomatic posts, Secretary Vance excoriated Urcuyo for sabotaging "the transition of power." Although "personally involved" in the "intensive negotiations" that produced the transition of which he "clearly approved," the interim president simply refused to abide by his commitments. He ignored the 72 hour deadline for handing over office to the provisional junta, failed to request the armed combatants to arrange a ceasefire, obstructed planned meetings between the two military leaderships, and "indicated his intention to retain power indefinitely."[164] The next day, Vance expressed the hope that other Central American governments would pressure Urcuyo to relinquish control "so that elements of the Guard will be preserved" and so that a "bloodbath can be avoided."[165]

From the outset of this evolving debacle, Washington strongly suspected that Somoza had encouraged Urcuyo's ambitions. In Secretary Vance's opinion, he acted "presumably with Somoza's backing or acquiescence...."[166] The State Department publicly expressed "grave concern" over the turn of events and pointedly reminded Somoza that he, like Urcuyo, had "plainly and clearly" agreed that there would only be "a short interim" before the transfer of power to the provisional junta.[167] Declared one outraged U.S. official: "In Latin American eyes, it was extremely important that we immediately disassociate ourselves from the son of a bitch [i.e. Somoza]."[168] Deputy Secretary of State Warren Christopher telephoned the

163 Department of State Telegram, Confidential State 184507, Secretary of State (Vance) to All American Republic Diplomatic Posts, July 17, 1979, Subject: "Nicaragua Working Group Sitrep No. 49–Situation in Nicaragua as of 0600 Hours (EDT) – July 17, 1979," DFOIA; Department of State Telegram, Secret State 185838, Secretary of State (Vance) to All American Republic Diplomatic Posts, July 18, 1979, Subject: "Nicaragua Status Report," DFOIA.

164 Department of State Telegram, State 185481, Secretary of State (Vance) to All American Republic Diplomatic Posts, July 18, 1979, Subject: "Statement by Department Spokesman on Nicaragua," DFOIA.

165 Department of State Telegram, Secret State 186183, Secretary of State (Vance) to American Embassy, Tegucigalpa, July 19, 1979, Subject: "Nicaragua – Conversation with——," DFOIA.

166 Department of State Telegram, Secret State 185838.

167 Quoted in Oberforder, "Somoza's Plea to Carter Was Squashed by Vance," p. A1. Also see "U.S. Puts Blame on Somoza for Urcyuo Threat to Peace," Miami Herald, July 20, 1979, p. 22A; Gwertzman, "U.S. Hails Departure of Somoza, Deplores Decision of Successor," pp. 1, 3; DeYoung, "Somoza's Successor Seeks to Hold Power," pp. A1, A14; Don Oberdorfer, "U.S. Uses Hard Pressure in Nicaragua Changeover," Washington Post, July 19, 1979, p. A31; Don Bohning, "Next to Somoza, U.S. May be Biggest Loser," Miami Herald, July 19, 1979, p. 18A.

168 Quoted in "Life Without Somoza," Newsweek, July 30, 1979, p. 45.

exiled dictator at his Miami Beach residence on four separate occasions during the morning of July 18. His words were short, blunt, and the implication unmistakable: Unless Urcuyo abided by the original understandings, Somoza risked extradition back to Nicaragua.[169] Employing the more sedate language of diplomacy, Department spokesman Hodding Carter said Christopher urged the former client to play "a positive role in seeing that the agreements are honoured...."[170] With little room to maneuver, an apparently reluctant Somoza contacted Urcuyo and other political allies in Nicaragua and told them: "Let's be realistic and keep our word in this matter."[171] Urcuyo promptly fled the country, but not before presiding over what the Carter administration feared above all else: the complete dismembership and dissolution of the National Guard.

During the final moments of the dictatorship, National Guard forces in the major provincial cities either surrendered to the FSLN or began fleeing to Honduras and other Central American countries. The Sandinista leadership dismissed the machinations of Somoza and Urcuyo in their last desperate attempt to retain power and demanded the total capitulation of the Guard. The combination of guerrilla military victories and the collapse of the Somoza coercive apparatus presented the new Guard commander Colonel Mejía with only one realistic option: to hand over power to the provisional junta when it entered Managua, thus ensuring that the FSLN would not only be the politically hegemonic force in the post-Somoza era but also the new military apparatus of the Nicaraguan state.

Conclusion

U.S. policy toward the prospect of a political transition in Nicaragua during 1979 centered around the goal of securing a regime change in order to ensure the continuity of the state. Washington was willing to sacrifice a longstanding client and accommodate a regime change as long as the state structure (or, at a minimum, its coercive branch) survived the process intact. The fundamental strategic objective of the Carter White House was to prevent the Sandinistas from emerging as the military apparatus of the post-Somoza state, thereby creating an uncontested internal basis for political, socioeconomic, and foreign policy initiatives antagonistic to basic U.S. interests in Nicaragua and Central America. Consequently, how to preserve

---

169 See ibid.; Somoza, *Nicaragua Betrayed*, p. 390.
170 Quoted in Graham Hovey, "U.S. Exerting Pressure, Say Nicaragua Peace Plan Is Taking Hold," *New York Times*, July 19, 1979, p. 4.
171 Quoted in "Somoza Planning to Leave U.S. for Three Month Trip," *Miami Herald*, July 20, 1979, p. 20A.

the National Guard institution was an agenda item at every executive-branch meeting on Nicaragua between October 1978 and July 1979.[172] Washington's reluctance to break with the Guard, despite criticism of its "excesses" and a willingness to accept changes in its command structure and personnel, indicated that in the order of priorities, defeating anti-regime and anti-system forces (avoiding a Sandinista victory) was paramount over and above political-socioeconomic reforms (ousting Somoza).

In the aftermath of the mediation collapse, the U.S. government seemed to concede that Somoza had weathered another crisis and was likely to survive in office until his current term expired in 1981. Encouraged in this belief by a relative hiatus in the military conflict and persistent doubts about the capacity of the elite-led, non-FSLN opposition forces to change the regime, policymakers were manifestly unprepared for the revolutionary upheaval of late May 1979. "What we fatally misjudged," the State Department's Richard Feinberg admitted, "was the speed of the Sandinista reorganization. The administration felt it had more time."[173] Arriving in Washington to take part in the Nicaragua policy debate in early June, the newly appointed U.S. Ambassador Lawrence Pezzullo discovered "an administration that was putting policy together from scratch. There was no consistent sense of what to do, the policy was being put together very quickly."[174]

In this period of rapidly narrowing opportunities, a major diplomatic offensive was initiated both inside and outside Nicaragua. The former attempted to develop a center-right "credible caretaker" government as an alternative to the FSLN's provisional junta. It failed primarily because those moderate political and business groups supported by Washington refused to collaborate in any transition scenario that denied the Sandinistas a role that reflected their contribution to the anti-dictatorial struggle. On a regional level, State Department officials waved the specter of radical nationalist guerrillas taking over the Nicaraguan government and state in an effort to mobilize support, especially among pro-FSLN heads of state, for pressuring the insurgents to expand the junta membership, moderate their political program, and accept the continued existence of a reformed and restructured National Guard.

Interagency deliberations over Nicaragua, in the words of an involved Pentagon official, revealed no "differences over goals, only over the timing of actions and things like that."[175] Within a framework of common objec-

172 See Pastor, *Condemned to Repetition*, p. 145 and passim.
173 Interview with Richard Feinberg.
174 Interview with Lawrence Pezzullo.
175 Interview with Franklin Kramer, Washington, D.C., September 26, 1988. Kramer was Special Assistant to the Assistant Secretary of Defense (International Security Affairs),

tives, debate focused on such questions as the durability of the dictatorship, estimates of what strategies would achieve the best results, and the timing of Somoza's departure. State representatives, for instance, argued that American policy objectives were better served by forcing the recalcitrant client out of office as soon as possible, whereas their colleagues in Defense and the NSC were reluctant to approve this course of action in the absence of an acceptable successor regime.

Throughout this period, Washington kept its options open, including consideration of at least symbolic displays of U.S. military power as one means of pressuring the Sandinistas. "Nobody discussed a bunch of B52s dropping bombs," said John Bushnell, "but one could send jets to fly low in formation over Nicaragua and get attention, big ships off the shore, a show of force. Those sort of things were discussed."[176] According to both State and Defense officials, "there was no serious discussion of direct intervention beyond the normal contingency kinds of planning."[177] Nonetheless, the President himself did not rule out intervention per se, having originated the proposal to seek OAS approval for a multilateral military "peacekeeping" force to halt the conflict and prevent a Sandinista victory.

The failure of the "peacekeeping" gambit reflected one particularly powerful conjunctural constraint within which U.S. policymakers were forced to operate. Historically, Washington has been enormously successful in using the Organization of American States to fashion a regional bloc to legitimate military and other forms of intervention against selected targets in Latin America. On this occasion, however, it was unable to secure regional support for a military solution. This dictated the shift to a more flexible political approach in pursuit of desired objectives.

On July 17, the Carter administration was forced to come to terms with the worst possible transition outcome (from its perspective): the total collapse of the Somoza regime *and* state, and the accession to power of a mass revolutionary movement hegemonized by Sandinista guerrillas. Its policy lay in ruins, not only a casualty of diplomatic setbacks, unexpected regional adversaries, and the posture adopted by Nicaraguan allies, but of other factors as well. First, by May 1979 the revolutionary process had advanced too far, the radical forces had already assumed undisputed hegemony, and no credible split-off from the opposition movement was available. Second, a conflict emerged between Somoza, who perceived his relations with the

Department of Defense, 1977 to 1979 and Principal Deputy Assistant Secretary to the Assistant Secretary (International Security Affairs), Department of Defense, 1979 to 1980.
176   Interview with John Bushnell.
177   Interview with David McGiffert, Washington, D.C., October 7, 1988. Similar sentiments were expressed by Assistant Secretary of State Viron Vaky. Interview with Viron Vaky.

United States in strategic terms, and the changing tactical policies of Washington, which viewed Somoza as expendable. This conflict led the client to adopt an intransigent position, refusing to leave office until it was too late, thus delaying the regime change and endangering the state. Finally, the United States faced the particularly difficult task of effecting a political transition in circumstances where the client regime was tightly connected with the state, all the more so because the client dictator had built up strong political loyalties in the armed forces that resisted pressure from the outside. Washington could not isolate the regime from the state, to sacrifice the former to save the latter.

Having exhausted all its options, the White House announced that it expected to maintain "continuing" diplomatic relations with Nicaragua,[178] and immediately began to formulate new strategies for confronting the FSLN in power. Even before the collapse of the National Guard, a number of U.S. diplomats, anticipating a Sandinista victory, had turned their attention to the task of how to promote the interests of the center-right forces after Somoza's demise. Only days before, the Ambassador to Costa Rica Marvin Weissman recommended that State organize a briefing for "a representative group of Nicaraguans who are now in the U.S. for the purpose of encouraging them to return . . . to Managua to strengthen ranks of the moderates and help them form a real counter-weight to the radical Sandinistas."[179] Lawrence Pezzullo cabled the Department "strongly endors[ing]" the suggestion and proposed that Francisco Aguirre, a former Guard colonel resident in Washington, D.C., be included in the group.[180]

178 Quoted in Tom Fiedler, "U.S. Expects to Continue Relationships with New Regime, Raps Interim Chief," *Miami Herald,* July 18, 1979, p. 12A.
179 Department of State Telegram, Secret San José 3082, American Embassy (Weissman) to Secretary of State, American Embassy, Managua, July 15, 1979, Subject: "Suggestion for Bolstering Moderate Influence," DFOIA.
180 Department of State Telegram, Secret Managua 3194, American Embassy (Pezzullo) to Secretary of State, July 15, 1979, Subject: "(S) Suggestion for Bolstering Moderate Influence," DFOIA.

7

The Carter administration and revolutionary Nicaragua: Containing Sandinista power

Introduction

The response of U.S. policymakers to the forces of political and economic nationalism in Latin America has not always been consistent or uniform. Toward some nationalist regimes the attitude has been hostile and conflictive; toward others, Washington has adopted a more accommodative posture and attempted to manage or negotiate outstanding differences. A framework for explaining imperial state behavior must take account of those factors that executive-branch officials view as pivotal in devising policy for dealing with these kinds of regimes.

First, what sectors of the new nationalist government are dominant and, therefore, likely to direct the process of political and socioeconomic change? Where radical guerrillas predominate, the potential for a structural transformation is seen to increase; where civilian political and business leaders take charge, the likelihood of containing the process of change within "acceptable" limits is similarly reinforced.

Second, what forces control the state, especially the coercive institutions? Given that U.S. policymakers have traditionally viewed the military and police apparatuses as the ultimate guarantors of American permanent interests in these societies, the survival of "collaborator" armed forces during periods of political transition assumes the highest priority within the foreign policy bureaucracy. Its replacement by a guerrilla force with no external linkages (to the Pentagon) evokes maximum alarm over the nature and scope of the change process.

Third, how will the new government's policies affect the distribution of political power and class relationships? Washington is likely to be less sympathetic toward a regime intent on changing the existing distribution of political power and pursuing socioeconomic programs that favor workers and peasants at the expense of traditional elites with historic ties to imperial state power centers.

Fourth, do the nationalist regime's economic measures represent an effort to constrain or restructure capitalism, to modify the existing capitalist economy or fundamentally transform it? American officials pose a number of questions that focus on the kind of changes proposed and the context within which they are likely to take place. For instance, if local and foreign-owned properties are nationalized, will "adequate and effective" compensation be paid? Is the takeover of private property to be confined to one industry or economic sector or does the new regime envisage the ultimate socialization of all the means of production (sectoral vs. structural)? What role will foreign investment actually play in the new economic order? How will the process of change affect the country's trade ties with the capitalist world? Will the United States retain its traditional access to strategic raw materials? Will the nationalist regime accept the country's international economic obligations (for example, foreign debt) inherited from the previous government(s)? To what extent will economic decisionmaking be influenced by pressure "from below" for rapid and large-scale change rather than determined "from above" and based on incremental and sectoral adjustments?

There is no more critical index of the nature and content of overall change than the question of property compensation. A regime that compensates satisfactorily does so because it is prepared to pursue further economic relations with the United States. Moreover, where such nationalization is also limited in scope, this usually leads the White House and State Department to adopt a policy of accommodation because it signals that there is no intention to confront and challenge the dominant imperial power – but to simply tackle perceived problems within a discrete area of the economy.

Fifth, and finally, what kind of foreign policy will the new regime pursue? Will it form new alliances and break old ones? More concretely, if the old government was a close American ally, policymakers will look for indications or signals from the new regime that it intends to maintain this relationship and not become more non-aligned in international affairs, leading (pre-late 1980s) to expanded political and economic relations with the socialist bloc.

In summary, when an incoming nationalist regime upholds the continuity of existing political and state structures (particularly the institutional integrity of the armed forces), rejects large-scale socioeconomic changes and transformations of the class structure, develops policies favorable to foreign investors, accepts responsibility for foreign debts accumulated by prior governments, harbors no thoughts of a major shift in foreign policy positions, limits mass mobilization politics, and contains the radical left, the United States is likely to accommodate this kind of political change. On the other hand, where such transitions are based on high levels of social mobilization, the active participation of the radical or guerrilla left, redistributionist economic policies, dismantled state institutions (especially the traditional armed forces), shifts in political and class power, and a move toward more diversified international ties, the United States is likely to be less tolerant and more disposed to a policy of confrontation, defining the new regime as a threat to its permanent interests (local, regional, and/or global).

Strategic fears: Washington debates the regional implications of Sandinista rule

Revolutionary upheavals and the overthrow of Third World client regimes eroded the power and influence of the human rights bureaucracy and produced a shift toward a more interventionist American foreign policy during the last two years of the Carter presidency. Identifying these political transitions with alleged Soviet-Cuban expansionism, influential administration officials such as National Security Council (NSC) Advisor Zbigniew Brzezinski concluded that only a reassertion of U.S. military power abroad could forestall new defeats of U.S. allies and safeguard American strategic and economic interests. Whereas Secretary of State Cyrus Vance preferred negotiation over confrontation, Brzezinski "took the realpolitik view that threats, force, and the threat of force were highly effective ways to gain successes for the United States."[1] In the Third World, which he identified as the key arena of superpower competition for allies and influence, Washington should seek to aggressively pursue its interests, support its allies, resist nationalist or revolutionary challenges for political and state power, and be prepared to augment diplomacy with military measures if the situation demanded. The first step toward reactivating American global military power was the failed June 1979 effort, spearheaded by Carter and Brzezinski, to secure passage of an OAS resolution creating an inter-American "peacekeeping" force to intervene in Nicaragua to prevent a Sandinista victory.

This policy shift received its formal enshrinement with the enunciation of the so-called Carter Doctrine in January 1980. Triggered by the December 1979 Soviet invasion of Afghanistan, the Doctrine extended the definition of American "national security" interests to cover the entire Third World and gave warning that the White House would respond with force,

---

1   Barry Rubin, *Secrets of State: The State Department and The Struggle over U.S. Foreign Policy* (New York: Oxford University Press, 1987), p. 174. Also see Gaddis Smith, *Morality, Reason & Power: American Diplomacy in the Carter Years* (New York: Hill & Wang, 1986), pp. 35–40.

if necessary, to secure threatened U.S. interests.[2] "After the Soviet invasion of Afghanistan," a senior Defense Department official commented, "the Carter administration became more hardnosed and viewed the Soviets in a more traditional threat mode."[3]

The Nicaraguan revolution of July 1979 signified a watershed in U.S.-Central American relations. It directly challenged the longstanding policy based on alliances with oligarchies and generals, and the assumption that Central America was, and would always be, a subordinate element in Washington's regional and global designs. Given the common historical experiences, social structures, economic models, and political regimes, the Nicaraguan experience had the potential of becoming an example for other broad-based social movements challenging similar regimes and structures in the subregion.

The likely strategic consequences of the Sandinista victory generated a vigorous debate among senior Carter policymakers. The Department of Defense was particularly alarmed by the Nicaraguan outcome. Only two weeks earlier, at the July 2 Special Coordination Committee (SCC) meeting, Secretary Harold Brown expressed the firm view "that the Sandinistas were dominated by hardcore Marxist-Leninists."[4] For the Pentagon, the subsequent turn of events constituted the "horrible worst case scenario." Officials were "stunned" by the collapse and disintegration of the National Guard.[5] The message coming from the inter-American affairs section, a senior advisor to the head of United States Southern Command (SOUTHCOM) in Panama General Wallace Nutting recalled, was that the Sandinistas were nothing but "a bunch of communist firebreathers."[6] With the FSLN capture of political power, officials became fearful this would lead to increased external support for local guerrilla movements, thereby facilitating greater Cuban-Soviet involvement in the area. The U.S. Air Force's John Pustay,

---

2 See Melvin P. Leffler, "From the Truman Doctrine to the Carter Doctrine: Lessons and Dilemmas of the Cold War," *Diplomatic History*, Vol. 7, No. 4, Fall 1983, pp. 258–259; Raymond L. Garthoff, *Detente and Confrontation: American-Soviet Relations from Nixon to Reagan* (Washington, D.C.: The Brookings Institution, 1985), pp. 971–982; Zbigniew Brzezinski, *Power and Principle: Memoirs of the National Security Adviser 1977–1981* (London: Weidenfeld and Nicolson, 1983), pp. 426–469.
3 Telephone interview with John Pustay, Virginia, September 15, 1989. The respondent was Assistant to the Chairman of the Joint Chiefs of Staff (United States Air Force), Department of Defense, 1979 to 1981.
4 Interview with Ambler Moss, Washington, D.C., September 21, 1988.
5 Interview with Viron Vaky, Washington, D.C., September 15, 1988; interview with John Bushnell, Washington, D.C., September 8, 1988.
6 Confidential telephone interview, Department of Defense official, Maryland, October 9, 1990. The respondent was attached to the U.S. Army School of the Americas in Panama, 1978 to 1980, and a senior advisor to General Wallace Nutting, Commander-in-Chief, United States Southern Command (SOUTHCOM), 1980 to 1981.

an assistant to the Chairman of the Joint Chiefs of Staff, summed up the dominant mood: "Now we have a Cuba on the continent proper and the Soviets are going to use it as a launching pad to support Central American guerrilla movements. This is a target of opportunity for Havana and Moscow. It is closer to Central America than Cuba, not an island, and it can do more mischief there."[7] Defense located the "danger" posed by Sandinista rule within a global context as well: "There was concern about the implications of a thoroughly Marxist-Leninist government in Nicaragua in terms of the strategic importance of the Caribbean Basin to the United States. The major supplies to NATO in the event of an attack on Europe would pass through the sea lanes there."[8]

The coercive agency was not alone in voicing ideological concerns and fear that the Nicaraguan upheaval might trigger the "export of revolution" or result in "the domino process being carried to Central America."[9] The entire foreign policy bureaucracy agreed on the strategic uncertainty posed by the Sandinista victory, not least the possibility that Moscow and Havana might conclude "that significant political and strategic gains were possible at little or no cost."[10] Like the Pentagon, "the idea that the Sandinistas were a beachhead for the Cubans was a very active theme in the NSC, certainly with Brzezinski."[11] And the State Department was "just as concerned about the possible strategic implications of a Sandinista victory."[12] Indeed, as a Sandinista victory loomed in early July, State appointed former Under Secretary Philip Habib to monitor Cuban activities in Central America and the Caribbean. Within days of Somoza's overthrow, Secretary Vance cabled sub-regional embassies describing Nicaraguan developments as a "major trauma" and informing the ambassadors that "we shall be consulting with you soon so that we can cooperate jointly to avoid the potential threat of a Communist expansion in Central America with all that would mean to all of us."[13] The interagency SCC decided to send State's Viron Vaky "to

7 Telephone interview with John Pustay.
8 Telephone interview with Frederic Chapin, Washington, D.C., September 22, 1988. The respondent was Deputy Assistant Secretary, Department of Defense, during the last half of 1980.
9 Interview with David Newsom, Washington, D.C., October 6, 1988.
10 John Bushnell, quoted in "Cuban Connections," Newsweek, August 6, 1979, p. 20.
11 Confidential interview, Department of State official, Washington, D.C., October 3, 1990. The respondent was a senior Latin American specialist on the Policy Planning Staff, 1978 to 1979.
12 Interview with David McGiffert, Washington, D.C., October 7, 1988; interview with Viron Vaky.
13 Department of State Telegram, Secret State 186183, Secretary of State (Vance) to American Embassy, Tegucigalpa, July 19, 1979, Subject: "Nicaragua – Conversation with——," DFOIA.

undertake consultations on Central America, specifically on El Salvador and the Northern tier."[4]

Within the framework of a common strategic objective – to contain and limit the sub-regional impact of the Nicaraguan revolution – there emerged divergent tactical approaches to the "threat" posed by the Sandinistas. The hardliners in the NSC, the Pentagon, and the intelligence agencies, for example, tended to give the greatest weight to the specter of "falling dominos" and "more Cubas" in order to press their case for immediate increases in U.S. military assistance to dictatorial clients threatened by mass-based opposition movements in El Salvador and Guatemala. Defining a Sandinista-led Nicaragua as a fundamental challenge to American regional hegemony, they argued that any realistic response must include military initiatives. The State Department was also receptive to the "defending allies" arguments: "We had to make sure that these governments had the wherewithal to support themselves. We had to build up the defenses of those countries whose domestic insurgencies might be actively supported by the new Nicaraguan government."[5] At the same time, a desire to minimize any possibility of replicating the Nicaraguan outcome produced opposition to reversing policy on military aid to the ruling generals in El Salvador and Guatemala – considered to be among the worst human rights abusers in Latin America.

Pentagon officials such as John Pustay believed that the diplomats' resistance to increased military involvement in El Salvador was related to the still formidable shadow cast by the 'Vietnam syndrome': "The Pentagon was pushing for more direct involvement than the State Department and the White House. But these things were being curbed [for example, setting limits on the number of advisors] and rejected. Their concern was too much involvement with an unpopular conflict. If it escalates and the U.S. is sucked in, it could mean we start reliving Vietnam."[6] But the State Department was also more sensitive to the possible negative domestic and regional political "fallout" of rearming the military regimes: It quite likely would antagonize hemispheric allies supportive of Washington's Nicaragua objectives and provoke powerful Congressional opposition at home.[7]

As the agency charged with primary responsibility for the management

---

14 Department of State Telegram, Confidential State 189724, Secretary of State (Vaky) to American Embassy, San Salvador, Tegucigalpa, Panama, Bogotá, Caracas, Mexico, July 21, 1979, Subject: "Consultations on Central America," DFOIA.
15 Telephone interview with Peter Tarnoff, New York, September 19, 1988.
16 See John M. Goshko, "U.S. Debates Aid to Latin Rightists to Bar Takeovers," *Washington Post*, August 2, 1979, p. A16.
17 Telephone interview with John Pustay.

of Nicaragua policy in the post-Somoza era, State quickly set about convincing Latin American governments to provide economic and military aid to the Sandinista regime "in order to encourage the moderate elements within it [and] constrain Cuban involvement."[18] Even before the fall of the dictatorship, other Central American governments were being encouraged to start thinking about "what will happen after Somoza leaves," and how they might contribute to defusing Sandinista radicalism and strengthening the power of the moderates in the new regime. On occasion, the directives to embassy officials were quite specific. Ambassador Moss in Panama was instructed "to try to get General Torrijos to focus more on the post-Somoza military situation in Nicaragua."[19]

Nicaragua was high on Secretary Vance's agenda for a series of meetings with Latin American foreign ministers and heads of state at the August 11, 1979, inauguration of newly elected Ecuadorian president Jaime Roldos in Quito. State hoped the Andean governments would play a key role in ensuring the Sandinista regime "does not become Castroite."[20] The relevant briefing paper prepared for the Secretary outlined three major objectives: "1) [to] encourage the Andean Pact countries to be active in assistance [to] moderate elements in Nicaragua and elsewhere in Central America, 2) [to] develop an overall strategy to prevent the spread of Castroist/Communist influence and control in Central America, and the polarization which threatens to plunge the northern tier into violence, and 3) to coordinate our actions and planning to maximize their effect, including systematizing consultative procedures." To limit Cuba's role, the paper suggested that these allies should be probed about their willingness to provide aid to Nicaragua, "particularly military assistance, the area in which Cuba is concentrating" and asked whether they would consider a joint approach to Castro "in an effort to moderate Cuban influence." The subsequent discussions between Vance, Assistant Secretary Vaky, NSC staffer Robert Pastor, and the Andean foreign ministers focused on three interrelated issues: Nicaragua's economic problems, the measures necessary "to assure effective coordination" of a multilateral aid program, and "possible military and/or police assistance" to the new regime.[21]

18 Department of State, Confidential Briefing Papers for Secretary of State Vance's August 1979 Trip to Ecuador, Bilateral Papers: Dominican Republic (Meeting with Foreign Minister Jiménez), Costa Rica (Meeting with President Rodrigo Carazo).
19 Department of State Telegram, Secret State 169011.
20 Department of State, Confidential Briefing Papers for Secretary of State Vance's August 1979 Trip to Ecuador, Bilateral Papers: Dominican Republic, Costa Rica.
21 Department of State Telegram, Confidential State 211259, Secretary of State (Vance) to All American Republic Diplomatic Posts, August 13, 1979, Subject: "The Secretary's Meeting with Andean Foreign Ministers: 1. Reconstruction Aid for Nicaragua," DFOIA.

After the Quito meetings, the State Department sent Special Ambassador William Bowdler to El Salvador, Honduras, and Guatemala to explain U.S. policy toward Nicaragua, confer with "key leaders in [the] private sector... who are disposed and in a position to be supportive of moderates in Nicaragua,"[22] and dissuade these governments from any contemplated hostile action, such as the use of military force, against the Sandinista regime. "There was a concern in Washington," explained Viron Vaky, "that somebody might do something in order to bring us in."[23] The administration was fearful that any move of this kind would destabilize the subregion and "radicalize the revolutionary process in Nicaragua," thereby delivering a catastrophic blow to those groups whom Washington supported.[24] The Quito briefing papers for Secretary Vance's meetings with the foreign ministers of El Salvador and Guatemala had stressed the importance of convincing these governments to "avoid counter-revolutionary activities that would play into the hands of the extremists." Military intervention in Nicaragua was not only "the quickest way to further Cuban influence in Central America," but would also undermine the already precarious position of the "moderates" in the new regime.[25] "We wanted to explain to these governments what we were doing," said State's John Bushnell. "Not that we had suddenly fallen in love with the Sandinistas, but we were trying to play a role to strengthen the moderate forces in Nicaragua. Part of our effort was to explain the game plan and solicit their help in strengthening the more moderate groups."[26]

From the beginning, Washington placed great store on the role of neighboring governments in seeking to moderate changes inside Nicaragua; it saw proliferating relationships between them and the Sandinistas as critical to defusing "the revolutionary fires" certain to be ignited by Somoza's ouster. Ambassador Pezzullo wrote in an early August cable that if the northern tier Central American countries were "to play a positive role in preventing [regional] radicalisation, [they] should be urged to build bridges

Also see John M. Goshko, "Vance To Meet With Latin Leaders to Strengthen Ties," *Washington Post*, August 4, 1979, p. A18.

22   Department of State Telegram, Secret State 234736, Secretary of State to American Embassy, Tegucigalpa, Guatemala, San Salvador, September 6, 1979, Subject: "Informing the Private Sector about U.S. Policy toward Nicaragua," DFOIA.
23   Interview with Viron Vaky.
24   Alan Riding, "U.S. Wary After Rebellion in Nicaragua, Weighs How to Act in El Salvador as Violence There Mounts," *New York Times*, September 17, 1979, p. 8.
25   Department of State, Confidential Briefing Papers for Secretary of State Vance's August 1979 Trip to Ecuador, Bilateral Papers: El Salvador (Meeting with Foreign Minister José Antonio Rodríguez), Guatemala (Meeting with Foreign Minister Rafael Castillo Valdéz).
26   Interview with John Bushnell.

to the GRN [Government of National Reconstruction]."[27] To prevent or minimize any potential "spillover" impact, the administration pressed allies to institute the necessary political and economic reforms "to avoid another Nicaragua." In Tegucigalpa, for example, a political officer in the U.S. Embassy recalled a "sense that after Somoza fell Honduras came on the front line because the stakes had gotten higher." Ambassador Bowdler raised the question of "what can we do to insulate Honduras from what had happened in Nicaragua" with the ruling armed forces. Diplomatic pressures to force a return to civilian rule increased during 1979 and into 1980: "We kept telling them to get the military out, have elections, resuscitate the social programs. We would say Nicaragua is the alternative. The State Department cable traffic equaled 'Nicaragua avoidance.' Encourage developments that would avoid a replication of Nicaraguan events."[28]

If the "explosion in Nicaragua" generated concern about Honduras, it produced close to alarm over El Salvador "where social and political pressures were really building.... "[29] Bowdler's assessments of the political situation in each country he visited reportedly concluded that El Salvador was the most vulnerable to a popularly based revolution.[30] Irrespective of their differences over military aid programs, neither State nor Defense "wanted a situation where the government of El Salvador was overthrown."[31] The problem was how to get military dictator General Carlos Romero, who had frustrated all past diplomatic entreaties of this kind, to implement even minor reforms. "Carter and Brzezinski thought that the country was going to have a revolution," said U.S. Ambassador Robert White, "and they wanted to prevent that from happening. So they said 'look, the military must get out of the front seat.' "[32]

The State Department decided to try secret diplomacy. Assistant Secretary Vaky was instructed to meet with Romero and apprise him of the risks he was courting in the absence of reforms:

> I talked to Romero about avoiding El Salvador reaching the point Nicaragua had reached. There was a serious succession problem. The problem was one of social reforms and political freedom. If he would take care of the reform question, then he can deal with the insurgency.

27 Department of State Telegram, Secret Managua 3549, American Embassy (Pezzullo) to Secretary of State, August 6, 1979, Subject: "Need for Bridges Buildup," DFOIA.
28 Confidential interview, Department of State official, Maryland, October 10, 1990. The respondent was a political officer in the American Embassy, Honduras, 1977 to 1980.
29 Interview with Thomas O'Donnell, Maryland, September 27, 1989.
30 See Riding, "U.S. Wary After Rebellion in Nicaragua, Weighs How to Act in El Salvador as Violence There Mounts," p. 8.
31 Interview with Franklin Kramer, Washington, D.C., September 26, 1988.
32 Interview with Robert White, Washington, D.C., September 23, 1988. The respondent was American Ambassador to El Salvador, 1979 to 1981.

In private conversation with Romero, I suggested that he do something dramatic such as advancing the date of the elections. I didn't tell him to step down and turn it over. There was a similar concern in El Salvador as in Nicaragua about the center disintegrating and the resulting conflict between the army and the guerrillas. In that situation the army would have lost any popular base of support.[33]

El Salvador, Vaky testified before a Congressional committee in mid-September 1979, was in some respects, even more polarized than Nicaragua at the time of Somoza's ouster because "political, economic, and social rigidities under successive regimes have not allowed a sufficient outlet for rising frustration and dissatisfaction." Without rapid political and economic reforms it might be impossible to avoid "widespread insurrectional violence."[34]

Political and socioeconomic change in Nicaragua: The basis for negotiated conflict

The Carter administration was dismayed by the outcome of the Nicaraguan conflict. Influential segments of the foreign policy bureaucracy perceived the Sandinista-dominated regime as a potential danger to American allies and interests in Central America. Somoza's overthrow revived Washington's obsession with preventing a "second Cuba" in the sub-region. Nonetheless, the White House bowed to those officials who argued that a willingness to adapt to the transition and a flexible, non-confrontationist approach offered the best possibility of containing the process of change within "manageable" boundaries. When Secretary Vance conferred with Junta member Violeta Chamorro and Foreign Minister Miguel D'Escoto in Quito, a Department briefing paper wanted him to stress that the United States seeks "friendly relations of mutual respect" while noting concern over "Cuban interference."[35]

One of the most ardent proponents of "going the diplomatic route" was Ambassador Lawrence Pezzullo, who counseled against "forming mindsets about the new figures and currents we have to deal with here...." The more appropriate response to what he characterized as a "disorganized

33 Interview with Viron Vaky.
34 U.S. Congress, House, Committee on Foreign Affairs, Subcommittee on Inter-American Affairs, *Central America At The Crossroads*, 96th Congress, 1st Session, September 11 and 12, 1979 (Washington, D.C.: U.S. Government Printing Office, 1979), pp. 5, 35.
35 Department of State, Confidential Briefing Papers for Secretary of State Vance's August 1979 Trip to Ecuador, Bilateral Paper: Nicaragua (Meeting with Junta member Violeta Chamorro and Foreign Minister Miguel D'Escoto).

government" was to "be patient" and, above all, refrain from "jump[ing] into this in an ideological fashion and reacting viscerally to some of the more strident [Sandinista] statements, postures and activities."[36] To the State Department, this approach also offered the distinct advantage of placing the onus on Nicaragua for any future breakdown in relations. "The Nicaraguans," said Viron Vaky, "had to prove it wouldn't work. You had to try it and if it didn't work, then it proved something."[37]

The decision to subordinate the politics of hostility to conditional accommodation and negotiated conflict was substantially influenced by a realistic appraisal of the limited options available to the United States to reverse the outcome of the Nicaraguan upheaval – short of direct military intervention.[38] Likely collaborator groups or individuals lacked the necessary popular support to contest Sandinista power. "We didn't have too many cards to play for a major confrontation with the Sandinistas," said State's David Newsom. Washington also felt the need to be "sensitive to Central American opinion."[39] Regional allies in Venezuela and Panama who were just as committed to supporting the Nicaraguan moderates and preventing a "second Cuba" thought "that it was worth trying to cultivate the new government."[40] No less important were domestic political considerations: U.S. officials wanted to avoid any confrontations that might trigger a radical revolution with disastrous consequences for the President's reelection prospects.

A White House approach based on minimizing conflict and maximum flexibility was influenced by internal Nicaraguan factors as well: the personnel appointments to senior and mid-level posts within the new government and the state; the Sandinista's publicly-declared commitment to a mixed economy development "model"; and the belief that serious inherited economic problems and the consequent need to maintain access to traditional sources of foreign financing would act as a sufficient constraint on any radicalizing tendencies within the FSLN leadership.

In a July 30, 1979 cable to regional embassies discussing the basic thrust of U.S. policy, Secretary of State Vance explained that reaching a modus vivendi with the Sandinistas was part of a longer-term strategy to build a

36 Department of State Telegram, Secret Managua 3420, American Embassy (Pezzullo) to Secretary of State, July 31, 1979, Subject: "Military Assistance," DFOIA; Department of State Telegram, Confidential Managua 3598, American Embassy (Pezzullo) to Secretary of State, August 8, 1979, Subject: "Humanitarian Assistance," DFOIA; interview with Lawrence Pezzullo, New York, September 28, 1988.
37 Interview with Viron Vaky; interview with John Bushnell.
38 See John M. Goshko, "U.S. Walking Softly," *Washington Post*, July 25, 1979, p. A16.
39 Interview with David Newsom.
40 Telephone interview with Peter Tarnoff. Also see Juan de Onis, "Democratic Latin Countries Seek to Block "2d Cuba" in Nicaragua," *New York Times*, July 20, 1979, p. 4.

political base within the new regime to enable Washington to contain or reverse the revolutionary process:

> [Ambassador Pezzullo's] principal objective will be to reinforce the moderate individuals and currents within the GRN [Government of National Reconstruction] and the FSLN. Given the suspicion with which we are viewed, he will have to move with care to avoid damaging moderates by too open an association. [The Embassy will also] encourage [_____] moderate elements outside the government [_____] to pressure the GON [Government of Nicaragua] to protect their interests.[41]

The State Department expressed guarded optimism about the appointment of leading moderates and conservatives to key government posts, including membership of the Junta of the Government of National Reconstruction (JGRN). Said one State Department official: "There were people in the first phase of the Sandinista government that we had known – the Chamorros in particular, Arturo Cruz [Central Bank president] and so on – and therefore there were people we felt we could possibly work with."[42] In the first cabinet, business "notables" known to the international financial community were placed in charge of the key economic ministries (finance, planning, industry, and agriculture) as well as the Central Bank, and a former National Guard colonel who participated in an abortive 1978 coup against Somoza was appointed Defense Minister. Only two Sandinistas – Tomás Borge (Interior) and Ernesto Cardenal (Culture) – received cabinet level posts.

American officials were similarly heartened by the JGRN proposal to share legislative powers with an interim (preelection) national assembly or Council of State, especially as the formula established for membership – representatives from the FSLN, the National Patriotic Front, the Broad Opposition Front, the Superior Council of Private Enterprise, the National University, and the National Association of Clergy – virtually assured the bourgeois forces a majority of seats. Ambassador Pezzullo thought the Council would probably be "subject to junta veto" and have the "net effect" of consolidating the power of the ruling body.[43] But this was not sufficient reason to boycott its activities. "In our discussion with political figures," he wrote in mid-October 1979, "we continue to support the convening of the

---

41 Department of State Telegram, Secret State 197562, Secretary of State (Vance) to All American Republic Diplomatic Posts, July 30, 1979, Subject: "Nicaragua Policy," DFOIA.
42 Interview with David Newsom.
43 Department of State Telegram, Managua 3613, American Embassy (Pezzullo) to Secretary of State, August 8, 1979, Subject: "State Council Begins to Emerge," DFOIA.

Council of State, pointing out its positive advantages of lending an element of popular will to the government process and giving non-FSLN groups a political stake in the GRN [Government of National Reconstruction]."[44]

In the economic sphere, the JGRN outlined a development program based on a mix of public, private and joint enterprises, limited (sectoral) nationalization confined largely to Somoza family-owned properties, and explicit guarantees to property holders. In addition, it promulgated a series of measures directly benefiting the private sector. These included the availability of new credits at reasonable interest rates, tax concessions, the ability to purchase foreign currency from the Central Bank, asset revaluation, guaranteed profits from joint ventures with the state, wage controls, and a commitment to give priority to stimulating increases in productivity.[45] JGRN member and conservative industrialist Alfonso Robelo also announced that the regime would aggressively seek to attract new foreign investment into the economy.[46] Although the government instituted redistributive programs (rent reductions, housing projects, food subsidies, social welfare improvements, and so on) to consolidate and expand its social base of support among wage and salaried workers, the urban poor, and the peasantry, the basic emphasis was on selective and modest changes not antagonistic to private property, American investors, and Western financial and monetary institutions, or intended to move Nicaragua out of the capitalist economic orbit. U.S. Embassy reports characterized the junta's economic policy pronouncements as "relatively moderate and accommodating."[47]

The Sandinista's nationalization policies provided further confirmation of the moderate nature and scope of the envisioned economic transformation. Except for three foreign-owned mining companies, the state targeted domestic enterprises only, and confined its interventions to selected economic sectors: banks and insurance companies; natural resources; foreign trade; and the agricultural, industrial, and commercial properties belonging to the Somoza family and its closest associates. In the early months of the revolution, the U.S. Embassy did receive a number of complaints from American citizens over property "confiscations that do not seem to conform to GRN [Government of National Reconstruction] policy." The Ambassador, however, counseled Washington to refrain from any knee-jerk response, sur-

---

44 Department of State Telegram, Confidential Managua 5022, American Embassy (Pezzullo) to Secretary of State, October 18, 1979, Subject: "(U) More Slippage on Council of State," DFOIA.

45 See Henri Weber, *Nicaragua: The Sandinista Revolution* (London: New Left Review, 1981), p. 89.

46 See Patricia Alisau, "Nicaragua Seeking Return of Business," *Journal of Commerce*, August 9, 1979, p. 28.

47 Department of State Telegram, Managua 3346, American Embassy (O'Donnell) to Secretary of State, July 26, 1979, Subject: "GRN Junta Views of Economic Policy," DFOIA.

mising that such actions were probably instigated at the behest of local Attorneys General or over-zealous agrarian reform officials. In any event, he noted that the central government had begun to address the problem in September when it returned a "confiscated" rice farm to its former American owner.[48]

Amid official statements of support for property rights, the business sector, and foreign investment, the locally owned banking system was taken over by the state in late July 1979. The Central Bank President and the Treasury Minister both stressed that the decision to nationalize the banks was made on pragmatic, not ideological, grounds. The domestic financial system was bankrupt and "the GON [Government of Nicaragua] could not justify using its limited resources to save private companies."[49] According to junta member Robelo, the five local banks had debts to international financial institutions of around $180 million but net assets totaling no more than $80 million. Nationalization, he contended, was therefore a way of extending state guarantees to citizens' savings deposits. "In a sense, the junta is protecting the banks through nationalization." remarked a local banker. "They're facing up to the reality that this $180 million will eventually have to be restructured and repaid. The private banks are broke, and the state is assuming their debt."[50]

The government's takeover of the financial system would also enable it to increase the amount of credit facilities available for agricultural development, fund improvements in food distribution networks, create more employment opportunities in rural areas, and pursue other socioeconomic objectives.[51] Ambassador Pezzullo conceded that the bank nationalization decree was "in general a popular measure even among some members of the private sector," not least because it was directed against two bastions of the traditional economic oligarchy – the Banco de Nicaragua (BANIC) and the Banco de América (BANAMERICA).[52]

Citibank, Bank of America, Wells Fargo, and the other foreign-owned financial institutions operating in Nicaragua were exempted from state intervention but were directed to halt all savings-deposit activities as part of

---

48 Department of State Telegram, Managua 5003, American Embassy (Pezzullo) to Secretary of State, October 17, 1979, Subject: "Return of Rice Farm Las Lajas to its Rightful Owner," DFOIA.

49 Department of State Telegram, Managua 3346; Department of State Telegram, Managua 3407, American Embassy (Pezzullo) to Secretary of State, July 30, 1979, Subject: "GRN Nationalizes Private Banking System," DFOIA.

50 Quoted in "Local Banks Nationalized," *This Week: Central America & Panama*, July 30, 1979, p. 227.

51 See Karen DeYoung, "Junta Nationalizes Nicaragua's Private Local Banks," *Washington Post*, July 26, 1979, p. A25.

52 Department of State Telegram, Managua 3407.

the new development program. In future, they could no longer accept deposits from Nicaraguan nationals; they would function principally as conduits for foreign capital entering the country in the form of loans or export-import financing. This change did not particularly agitate the overseas banking fraternity. Commenting on the decree, one U.S. banker said: "It looks like the junta wants to restrict the international banks to international finance, and we function quite successfully in other countries with similar rules...."[53]

In mid-August, Pezzullo met with senior representatives of Citibank, Bank of America, Standard Brands, and Rosario Mining and was struck by "the sophisticated, pragmatic approach being followed by these [American] firms in their diverse fields. None of the firms are panicked ... All are hopeful that they will be able to continue their operations in Nicaragua and indicated their willingness and flexibility to work out reasonable arrangements with the new GRN [Government of National Reconstruction]."[54] The next day, Embassy officials conferred with a delegation of Citibank executives. Pezzullo opened the proceedings by noting that the Sandinistas "had shown a predominantly pragmatic streak [and that] the quality of the economic team was very high." Citibank Vice-President William Rhodes affirmed his regard for Central Bank president Arturo Cruz and stated his institution's desire to maintain its operations in Nicaragua "if the GRN [Government of National Reconstruction] made it worth their effort."[55]

Not long after, however, the Central Bank provoked some consternation when it decided to terminate the practice of allowing the foreign banks to use cordoba credit, instead of dollars, to cover withdrawals. What this meant, displeased Bank of America officials explained to U.S. diplomats, was that foreign banks would henceforth be required to make a dollar time deposit with the Central Bank as a guarantee for any local currency loan. But Ambassador Pezzullo was less perturbed, refusing to interpret the measure as part of an attempt "to discourage the foreign banks from working in Nicaragua." Acute financial problems and increased demands on scarce economic resources were more likely reasons: "...the Central Bank may have felt that the available cordoba financing could be better used elsewhere and that they could also obtain much needed foreign exchange by this measure. Perhaps they also felt that in these difficult times, foreign banks

---

53 Quoted in "Local Banks Nationalized," p. 228.
54 Department of State Telegram, Confidential Managua 3771, American Embassy (Pezzullo) to Secretary of State, August 16, 1979, Subject: "Mood in Managua – August 15, 1979," DFOIA.
55 Department of State Telegram, Managua 3778, American Embassy (Pezzullo) to Secretary of State, August 16, 1979, Subject: "Citibank's View of its Future in Nicaragua," DFOIA.

should help carry some of the burden." Pezzullo observed that if the Nicaraguans were intent on giving a "stronger signal" that foreign banks were no longer welcome, they could have done so simply by insisting that all withdrawals from these institutions be completed within 30 days.[56]

Following a visit to Nicaragua by a group of American bankers and businessmen under the auspices of the Council of the Americas in the first week of October, Ambassador Pezzullo again addressed the issue of the status of the American private banking subsidiaries in a telegram to the State Department. Conceding that Citibank and the Bank of America "have been placed in [a] difficult situation by GRN [Government of National Reconstruction] actions," the Embassy believed that the Sandinistas "[were] not purposely creating a hostile environment" in an attempt to force these institutions to cease operations. Nonetheless, he concurred with the banks' opposition to a government request that future activities be confined to maintaining representative offices only. Embassy officials and members of the visiting U.S. delegation raised this issue with the Sandinista National Directorate (DNC) and JGRN at every opportunity. Pezzullo remained optimistic that this particular disagreement could be solved to the satisfaction of both sides. "There is," he wrote in a communique to State, "still room for maneuver."[57]

The regime move to assume control over natural resource exploitation did not, in contrast to the financial sector, exempt foreign-owned enterprises. In November, the U.S.-controlled Neptune Mining Corporation and Rosario Mining Company operations, and the Septentrio Mining company, a joint venture established between the Somoza state and the giant Canadian multinational, Noranda, were nationalized under the terms of the official decree. This action was again justified on economic rather than ideological grounds – in this case, the need to revitalize a depressed mining industry. Although the Carter administration response was quite restrained, it simultaneously put Managua on notice that bilateral relations would be severely affected in the absence of satisfactory payments. Prior to a November meeting at the State Department with Deputy Assistant Secretary John Bushnell, an Embassy AID official briefed Nicaragua's Minister-Director of the Fund for International Reconstruction Alfredo César "on [the possible application of [the] Hickenlooper Amendment if U.S. mining property nationalized by [the] GRN [Government of National Reconstruction] is not

56 Department of State Telegram, Confidential Managua 4697, American Embassy (Pezzullo) to American Embassy, Caracas, Info Secretary of State, September 29, 1979, Subject: "U.S. Banks in Nicaragua," DFOIA.
57 Department of State Telegram, Confidential Managua 4833, American Embassy (Pezzullo) to Secretary of State, October 8, 1979, Subject: "U.S. Banks in Nicaragua," DFOIA.

promptly and adequately compensated." Ambassador Pezzullo suggested that it might be "worthwhile for Bushnell to reinforce [this] issue with César and have him bring [the] message back to [the] GRN [Government of National Reconstruction]."[58]

The Sandinistas were clearly intent on avoiding any kind of confrontation with the affected mining companies. "They didn't accuse the company of anything," an executive of Neptune's parent company (ASARCO) acknowledged. "They went as far as asking us if we could continue to manage the mines for a while. We reached an agreement for the staff to stay for six weeks or so." Furthermore, they accepted the mining company's objection to a new law basing compensation on the book value of an enterprise on the grounds that it contradicted an existing bilateral agreement "that said the government would have to pay the going concern value and we insisted on that."[59] Compensation negotiations were instituted by the Ministry of Justice and continued into the first Reagan presidency, when satisfactory agreements were signed with Neptune Mining in December 1982 and Rosario Mining in September 1983.[60]

The JGRN nationalized foreign trade and commerce in the hope of achieving a number of interrelated objectives: increased exports and export revenues, adequate returns to producers, reduced production and marketing costs, and more investment capital for development priorities. In a related effort aimed at resolving the fiscal crisis bequeathed by Somoza, the Minister of Planning Roberto Mayorga announced new import-export controls, particularly on luxury purchases from abroad.[61] Although multinational corporations operating in the export sector were told they would be required to sign marketing contracts with the state, a number of American companies, including Castle & Cook's banana exporting subsidiary, Standard Fruit & Steamship, continued to operate without government interference well into 1980.

The prime targets of the nationalization policy were those enterprises belonging to the Somoza family and its cronies. In the agricultural sector alone, this amounted to 2,200 farms, 65 agro-industrial companies, and 25

58 Department of State Telegram, Managua 5648, American Embassy (Pezzullo) to Secretary of State, November 20, 1979, Subject: "National Mines and Application of Hickenlooper," DFOIA.

59 Confidential telephone interview, American business executive, New York, September 11, 1989. The respondent is a senior official of ASARCO, with major responsibilities for its Latin American operations. Neptune Mining Company was a subsidiary of ASARCO prior to its nationalization by the Sandinista government in 1979. The respondent was closely involved with Neptune Mining during the Somoza and Sandinista periods.

60 See Stuart Auerbach, "Nicaragua Compensates U.S. Firms," *Washington Post*, September 29, 1983, p. B3.

61 See "Nicaragua: Restructuring the Economy," *Central America Report*, August 6, 1979, p. 242.

related service companies.[62] At the outset, senior officials publicly, and repeatedly, declared that there would be no economic offensive against the non-Somoza agricultural or manufacturing sectors. They stressed the government's basic commitment to private property, and offered guarantees and incentives to the local business community to encourage it to actively participate in the new development program. Foreign property-holders were treated little differently from their local counterparts. With the exception of the mining companies, overseas investors were viewed not as obstacles to national economic development but as valued participants in the reconstruction period and beyond.

One of the striking features of early Sandinista economic policy was its willingness to subordinate large-scale redistribution of wealth and income to the imperatives of reconstruction and production – and to deal harshly with advocates of a more rapid and profound socioeconomic transformation. During the first week of October, the FSLN high command stepped up its attack on the "ultra left," arresting Marxist labor leaders and purging radicals from the Ministry of Labor. Public statements accused these individuals of "stirring up the masses with impractical demands for wage increases and property seizures." The Sandinista bywords were patience regarding economic improvements, and increasing production in order to revitalize the economy. Ambassador Pezzullo wrote approvingly of Interior Minister Tomás Borge "[taking] a page from [American economist Paul] Samuelson in one of his speeches to explain why the economy cannot support wage increases now."[63] The Sandinista Workers Central (CST) supported government policy, "labell[ing] as irresponsible" union demands for higher wages, reduced working hours, and other benefits that conflicted with economic reconstruction objectives.[64]

Although the state's share of Gross Domestic Product increased from 15 percent in 1978 to 41 percent in 1980, Sandinista economic policy did not create a basis for U.S. hostility.[65] Almost all foreign-owned properties in

62 See Inter-American Development Bank, *Nicaragua: Credit Program for the Revival of Agriculture and Fisheries* (NI-0093), Loan Proposal, attached to an Internal Memorandum from The Secretary to the Board of Executive Directors, Subject: "Nicaragua. Proposed Loan for an Agricultural Recovery Credit Program," PR-1083, November 25, 1980, p. 6.
63 Department of State Telegram, Confidential Nicaragua 4825, American Embassy (Pezzullo) to Secretary of State, October 8, 1979, Subject: "FSLN Continues to Seek Middle Ground, Cracks Down 'Ultra Left,' " DFOIA.
64 Department of State Telegram, Managua 5177, American Embassy (Pezzullo) to Secretary of State, October 25, 1979, Subject: "CST Analyzes Worker-Employer Relations," DFOIA.
65 George Irvin, "Nicaragua: Establishing the State as the Center of Accumulation," *Cambridge Journal of Economics*, Vol. 7, No. 2, June 1983, p. 127; David F. Ruccio, "The State and Planning in Nicaragua," in Rose J. Spalding, ed., *The Political Economy of Revolutionary Nicaragua* (Winchester: Allen & Unwin, 1987), p. 66. For a discussion of the early de-

Nicaragua were excluded from the nationalization decrees, and those affected local enterprises were basically restricted to the Somoza empire and economic sectors in severe financial difficulties. The primacy of the capitalist mode of production was not threatened. On the contrary, the nationalization of the banks, mines, foreign trade and commerce, and Somoza-owned properties was part of a development strategy that sought to encourage foreign investment in other sectors of the economy. This absence of a more profound social and economic transformation, whether statist or socialist, minimized the likelihood of conflict between the United States and Nicaragua's revolutionary regime.

Of all the factors that shaped the Carter policy of conditional accommodation with the Nicaraguan Revolution, perhaps none was more important than the perception that the new regime's daunting economic problems would temper any inclination to rupture ties with the international capitalist system – particularly with its most important prospective aid donor. Washington fully expected to use its enormous potential leverage in this area to influence the pace and scope of change.

The Sandinistas assumed control of an economy devastated by a prolonged civil war. The United Nations's Economic Commission for Latin America estimated the cost of war-related damage to the nation's economic infrastructure between January 1978 and June 1979 at $580 million.[66] According to the President of the Superior Council of Private Enterprise (COSEP), the conflict left industry and commerce "totally bankrupt."[67] Manufacturing output plummeted by more than 30 percent, and the construction industry ground to a complete halt between 1978 and 1979 (contributing to a 30 percent under and unemployment rate among the urban labor force). Agricultural production was similarly disrupted by the political and military struggle: Export earnings declined by $219 million from 1978 to 1980 (over 47 percent in real terms), notwithstanding unusually high 1980 world market prices for Nicaragua's leading coffee, sugar, and cotton exports. The overall economic growth rate fell from 6.3 percent in 1977, to −7.2 percent in 1978, to −24.8 percent in 1979.[68]

velopment program, also see Elizabeth Dore, "Nicaragua: The Experience of the Mixed Economy," in Jonathan Hartlyn and Samuel A. Morley, eds., *Latin American Political Economy* (Boulder: Westview Press, 1986), pp. 319–350.

66 Don Casey, "Somoza Debt Stinging Nicaragua, Study Says," *Miami Herald*, September 5, 1979, p. 3B.

67 Quoted in "Nicaragua: Private Sector's Pips Squeak," *Latin America Regional Reports: Mexico & Central America*, November 16, 1979, p. 3.

68 World Bank, Latin America and the Caribbean Regional Office, *Nicaragua: The Challenge of Reconstruction.* Internal Document, Report No. 3524-NI, October 9, 1981, pp. 2–3; United Nations, Economic Commission for Latin America, *Economic Survey of Latin America 1979* (Santiago, Chile, 1981), p. 384; Weeks, *The Economies of Central America*, pp. 156, 158.

The Sandinistas not only inherited a debilitated economy but also had to deal with two other burdensome legacies of the last decade of Somoza rule: large-scale foreign borrowings and massive capital flight. The former (totaling $1.6 billion, of which $380 million was contracted during the last two years in the form of short-term supplier credits at steep commercial interest rates[69]) gave Nicaragua the dubious distinction of having the highest per capita foreign debt of any country in Latin America. The latter reached a peak during the last year of the dictatorship when an estimated $1.5 billion left the country for overseas banking or investment destinations.[70]

During the 1970s, the Somoza dictatorship had increasingly resorted to foreign financing, especially private multinational bank loans, to offset persistent balance of payments deficits (exacerbated by oil price rises and export shortfalls) to keep the economy afloat and growing. A large portion of these funds, however, found their way into the private coffers of members of the dynastic family, regime officials, and business cronies, or were siphoned off to satisfy the weapons needs of the National Guard – instead of being used to expand the economy's productive capacity. The systematic looting of the public treasury for personal gain or to ensure the survival of the regime continued unabated up until the Sandinista victory. In the months preceding his downfall, Somoza began agressively milking funds from his own companies through such schemes as mortgaging the enterprises to government banks and channeling the acquired funds into overseas bank accounts. On the eve of his ouster, he personally owed the state $23 million.[71] When the provisional junta arrived in Managua it discovered a paltry $3.5 million in foreign exchange reserves (sufficient to pay for approximately two days worth of imports) even though the regime had borrowed $33.1 million from the IMF only six weeks earlier. The state, in the words of newly appointed Central Bank president Arturo Cruz, "had almost no international liquidity left." To make matters worse, it faced the problem of where to find approximately $660 million in debt interest payments due by the end of the year.[72]

69   Figures provided by Junta member Alfonso Robelo. See A. Koffman O'Reilly, "World Awaits Action on Nicaraguan Debts," *Journal of Commerce*, October 3, 1979, p. 11.
70   Richard Stahler-Sholk, "Foreign Debt and Economic Stabilization Policies in Revolutionary Nicaragua," in Spalding, ed., *The Political Economy of Revolutionary Nicaragua*, p. 155.
71   Alan Riding, "Nicaragua: A Delicate Balance," *New York Times Magazine*, December 2, 1979, p. 82.
72   *Interview with Arturo Cruz*, Washington, D.C., October 5, 1990. Also see Greg Conderacci, "IMF Asked to Investigate Possible Theft of Loan Funds by Ex-Nicaraguan Aides," *Wall Street Journal*, August 6, 1979, p. 18; "Somoza Left a Well-Stripped Cupboard for His Successors," *New York Times*, August 27, 1979, p. E3; Alan Riding, "Nicaragua After Somoza," *New York Times* (International Economic Survey, Section 12), February 3, 1980, p. 62. Foreign exchange reserves fell by $60 million in 1977, by $200 million in 1978,

In a conversation with officials of the American Embassy in El Salvador only days after the Sandinista victory, the President of that country's Supreme Court, Rogelio Chávez, "stressed the importance of the USG [United States Government] extending economic assistance without political strings to the GRN [Government of National Reconstruction] as being a possibly crucial factor in insuring that Nicaragua did not turn to Cuba or the Soviet Union." This advice to Washington to concentrate on its "economic rather than political leverage" to influence the process of change in Nicaragua found a receptive audience among senior Carter administration officials.[73]

Deradicalizing the revolution: The foreign aid debate

Under the operational direction of the State Department, American policy toward Nicaragua during the initial period of Sandinista rule emphasized diplomacy and dialogue as it searched for ways of strengthening the power of the "moderates" in the new regime, state, and society. The transition from client dictatorship to revolutionary power constituted a profound setback but Washington remained hopeful that it could still play a role in shaping the political, social, and economic structures that would ultimately define post-Somoza Nicaragua. Assistant Secretary Vaky described the prevailing mood in State: "The worst alternative took place but maybe it was still a ball game. The options were not good, but there were other options that were bad and worse. There was no feeling that it was all through and it was time to circle the wagons. [The prevailing consensus was] what can we do to influence events in Nicaragua from here on out."[74]

On August 12, less than a month after the victorious guerrilla forces entered Managua, Secretary Vance drafted another communique to U.S. Ambassadors in Latin America "sketch[ing] the broad outlines of our policy toward Nicaragua and Central America in the post-Somoza era." In Nicaragua, he wrote, there are "a variety of political currents" and the "ultimate direction" of the regime "may not be established for some time to come." Although power has momentarily shifted "toward the more radical elements, moderates occupy positions of strength in the key areas of economic policy

and possibly by as high as $750 million in 1979. See Weeks, *The Economies of Central America*, p. 158. The debt interest payment figure was given by Central Bank President Cruz. See Casey, "Somoza Debt Stinging Nicaragua, Study Says," p. 18.

73 Department of State Telegram, Confidential El Salvador 4056, American Embassy, San Salvador (Devine) to Secretary of State, July 20, 1979, Subject: "(C) Reaction of President of Supreme Court to Recent Events in Nicaragua," DFOIA.

74 Interview with Viron Vaky.

and are beginning to show important vital signs in the private sector." The goal must be to shore up these groups in every possible way: "It is in our interest to identify and strengthen moderate elements in the GNR [Government of National Reconstruction], the private business sector, the church, the media, labor and elsewhere who are able and willing to work toward keeping the revolution on a left-of-center course and to unite to resist efforts of the radical left to monopolize key activities in areas such as security, propaganda and education." Finally, Vance wished "to dispel concerns over allegedly competing policy lines between State and the NSC."[75] Correspondence between NSC Latin American specialist Robert Pastor and his boss Zbigniew Brzezinski seemed to confirm the absence of any major bureaucratic dispute over Nicaragua policy. Evaluating weekly reports on the country's mass media during August and September, Pastor concluded that "the political situation is still quite fluid." Sandinista and non-Sandinista newspapers and radio stations operated freely and the latter were "permitted ... to criticize the government."[76]

Appearing before the prestigious Foreign Policy Association in September, Secretary Vance declared that the United States had nothing to gain from confrontation: "We cannot guarantee democracy will take hold there. But if we turn our backs on Nicaragua, we can almost guarantee that democracy will fail."[77] Only by adhering to a flexible, gradualist approach – a "boring from within" strategy – could Washington achieve, or come as close as possible to gaining, its primary objective: a weakening of the revolutionary impulse.

In pursuit of its deradicalizing goal, the administration looked to Latin American and Western Europe to financially support the Nicaraguan reconstruction effort. Regional embassies were instructed to "encourage" host governments on "appropriate occasions ... to respond generously" to Junta needs. "Moderate tendencies in the GRN [Government of National Reconstruction] can be strengthened," wrote Deputy Secretary of State Warren Christopher, "by effective cooperation from [a] wide range of European and hemispheric governments."[78] The positive and rapid response by Latin

75 Department of State Telegram, Secret State 210125, Secretary of State (Vance) to American Embassy, London, Info All American Republic Diplomatic Posts, August 12, 1979, Subject: "U.S. Central American Policy," DFOIA.

76 National Security Council Memorandum, Robert Pastor to Zbigniew Brzezinski and David Aaron, September 20, 1979, Subject: "The State of the Media – Nicaragua," White House Country Files, Box CO-47, Folder CO 114 8/1/79–1/20/81, Jimmy Carter Presidential Library.

77 Address to the Foreign Policy Association, New York, September 27, 1979, reprinted in *Department of State Bulletin*, Vol. 79, No. 2032, November 1979, p. 15.

78 Department of State Telegram, Confidential State 223250, Secretary of State (Christopher) to American Embassy, San José, Info American Embassy, Managua, August 25,

America, Western Europe, and other capitalist governments, as well as international banks and regional financial institutions, to Nicaragua's plight (emergency aid, signing economic agreements) buoyed Washington's hopes that it could influence the direction of post-revolutionary developments.[79]

Military assistance

For the Carter administration, military aid to the Sandinista state was a thorny and problematic issue. In late July 1979, Nicaragua's Interior Minister Tomás Borge first broached the subject with Ambassador Lawrence Pezzullo.[80] At the August 11 inauguration of Ecuadorean president Jaime Roldos, he raised the question with American officials again, emphasizing Nicaragua's commitment to a non-aligned foreign policy and the government's preference for obtaining arms from the United States and Western Europe rather than the socialist bloc countries. However, should it be forced to seek defense needs from Eastern Europe, Borge wanted it understood that "this would not necessarily signify that we are aligning ourselves with them politically. . . ."[81]

Secretary Vance outlined the official State Department position as one of being "prepared in principle to provide military assistance and to discuss specific needs quickly."[82] A number of senior officials in the Bureau of Inter-American Affairs, as well as Ambassador Pezzullo, hoped this would translate into a "more imaginative approach" than they feared might be forthcoming in practice.[83] As for the human rights activists, they opposed all weapons sales. With a touch of sarcasm, Deputy Assistant Secretary John Bushnell ascribed their position to "the 'clean hand' syndrome. That is, it

1979, Subject: "U.S. Cooperation with Costa Rica and Panama on Nicaraguan Assistance," DFOIA.

79   See "Nicaragua: Moving Forward," *Central America Report*, September 24, 1979, p. 298; Jim Morrell and William Jesse Biddle, *Central America: The Financial War*. (Washington, D.C.: Center for International Policy, March 1983), p. 7; Weeks, *The Economies of Central America*, p. 164; Peter Kornbluh, *The Price of Intervention* (Washington, D.C.: Institute for Policy Studies, 1987), p. 97.

80   See Charles A. Krause, "Nicaraguans Ask the United States for Military Aid," *Washington Post*, July 30, 1979, pp. A1, A18; "Nicaragua: Cool Operators," *Latin America Political Report*, August 3, 1979, pp. 234, 236.

81   Quoted in Richard J. Meislin, "Nicaraguan Says Red Bloc Won't Be Asked for Arms," *New York Times*, August 13, 1979, p. 3. Also see Warren Hoge, "Nicaragua Official Warns U.S. on Arms," *Washington Post*, August 12, 1979, p. A17.

82   Department of State Telegram, Secret State 197806, Secretary of State (Vance) to American Embassy, July 30, 1979, Subject: "Meeting with Interior Minister Borge," DFOIA.

83   Department of State Telegram, Secret Managua 3420.

was bad if the United States sold guns to shoot people, but it was less bad to sell trucks that carried the soldiers who fired the guns."[84]

In the Defense Department, officials pondered the sub-regional impact of U.S. arms sales to a guerrilla-led regime. Would it heighten existing tensions throughout the sub-region, or defuse a potential strategic threat by exerting a moderating influence on the Sandinistas while simultaneously preventing Moscow and Havana from gaining a second military foothold in America's traditional sphere of influence? At least the majority apparently thought it might be preferable to establish an assistance program, not excluding weapons purchases, and thus avoid any possible development of a long-term military relationship with the Soviet Union. But whatever the differences in emphasis or approach, there was unanimity regarding the overriding purpose of any aid program: to moderate the Nicaraguan regime's policies "in other fields."[85]

Neither President Carter nor his Secretary of State desired the United States to play other than an ancillary role in the provision of foreign military assistance to the Sandinistas. "We were interested," Ambassador Pezzullo said, "in other regional countries becoming involved. We tried to energize the Colombians, the Brazilians, and others to form military assistance groups."[86] This objective was repeated time and again in the confidential briefing papers Secretary Vance received in preparation for his August 1979 meetings in Ecuador with Latin presidents and foreign ministers. For instance, it was suggested that he encourage Colombia "to assist with security enhancement activities, including military assistance" and in conversation with Venezuelan President Luis Herrera "ascertain what [the] GOV [Government of Venezuela] will do in Nicaragua and urge both military and economic assistance."[87]

Washington expressed interest in a proposal floated by Panama's Omar Torrijos for "a joint [U.S.-Panamanian] military assistance presence."[88] American Ambassador Ambler Moss, accompanied by a Pentagon colonel stationed in Panama, visited Nicaragua in late July "to test the waters with the Junta concerning the idea of a survey/assistance mission which might

84   Interview with John Bushnell.
85   Quoted in "Nicaragua: IDB, IMF Help Nicaraguans," *This Week: Central America & Panama*, August 13, 1979, p. 245.
86   Interview with Lawrence Pezzullo.
87   Department of State, Confidential Briefing Papers for Secretary of State Vance's August 1979 Trip to Ecuador, Bilateral Papers: Colombia (Meeting with President Julio César Turbay), Venezuela (Meeting with President Luis Herrera).
88   Department of State, Confidential Briefing Papers for Secretary of State Vance's August 1979 Trip to Ecuador, Bilateral Paper: Panama (Meeting with Foreign Minister Carlos Ozores).

include U.S. and PN [Panamanian National] military personnel."[89] In Managua, the colonel held talks with Humberto Ortega and other Sandinista leaders "about upgrading the military and what training we might provide."[90] Before he left, Ambassador Pezzullo arranged for three U.S. army Latin specialists from the Southern Command (SOUTHCOM) to be posted to Nicaragua to liaise with the FSLN military high command. One of the military officials chosen for the task commented that both Pezzullo and the head of SOUTHCOM General Wallace Nutting "had a similar orientation about Nicaragua – to try and return to normal relations as soon as possible. This included helping to establish military to military contacts with the Sandinista regime."[91] In early August, Secretary Vance indicated that the United States was willing to discuss equipment needs with the DNC and dispatch "a survey team to help match specific needs to our availabilities," even though the Department's preferred response to the "informal GRN [Government of National Reconstruction] request[s] for U.S. military assistance" was a "coordinated approach with Panama."[92]

Although the White House was reluctant to contemplate any significant military relationship with the Sandinistas, it wanted to avoid unnecessarily complicating bilateral relations over this issue until the "dust had settled" and the direction of change became clarified. Therefore, it settled on a two-track military sales policy. On the one hand, it said no to weapons purchases while announcing that this decision was subject to "periodic review."[93] State Department officials justified the ban with reference to "legislative opposition to any direct sale of U.S. military equipment to the Sandinistas." Or, as one of their number bluntly put it, "arms requests for Nicaragua wouldn't get anywhere in the U.S. Congress."[94] Human rights factors also played a part as did a concern to avoid possible serious friction between the United

89 Department of State Telegram, Confidential Panama 5735, American Embassy (Moss) to Secretary of State, July 26, 1979, Subject: "Visit to Managua," DFOIA.
90 Interview with Thomas O'Donnell.
91 Confidential interview, Department of Defense official, Washington, D.C., October 2, 1990. The respondent was attached to the United States Southern Command (SOUTHCOM) in Panama. In July 1979, he was assigned to the American Embassy. He remained in Nicaragua until May 1980.
92 Department of State Telegram, Secret State 202619, Secretary of State (Vance) to American Embassy, Panama (Moss), August 4, 1979, Subject: "Military Assistance to Nicaragua," DFOIA; Department of State Telegram, Secret State 207938, Secretary of State (Vance) to American Embassy, Panama (Moss), August 9, 1979, Subject: "Military Assistance to Nicaragua," DFOIA.
93 State Department official, quoted in "U.S. Says No to Arms for Nicaragua," *This Week: Central America & Panama*, September 3, 1979, p. 226. Also see "U.S. Resists Arms Sale to Nicaragua," *Washington Post*, August 30, 1979, p. A20.
94 Interview with David Newsom; second U.S. official quoted in Karen DeYoung, "U.S., Nicaragua Easing Mutual Suspicions," *Washington Post*, December 1, 1979, p. A14.

States and its Central American allies, especially the autocratic regimes in El Salvador and Guatemala.

On the other hand, the administration exempted "non-lethal" weapons such as trucks, jeeps, medical supplies, and engineering equipment from the sales embargo, and indicated it would not oppose JGRN efforts to acquire light arms and ammunition from other sources. Remarked a Pentagon official: "Basically we said we wouldn't put any diplomatic pressure on other countries not to sell."[95] State was particularly "concerned not to further exacerbate our relations with the new government of Nicaragua by trying to institute a global embargo on arms sales."[96] In late August, a high-level official mission left Managua on an arms buying trip to a number of West European and Latin American capitals.[97]

The Sandinistas, according to a SOUTHCOM officer advising Ambassador Pezzullo, wanted "guns and bullets" because they were already "fixated on the counterrevolutionaries. They knew it was coming, that they were going to have to arm themselves to fight these people who would be aided by the United States."[98] During a September 1979 visit to the White House, members of the ruling junta held discussions with senior NSC and State Department officials on a range of issues, including the military aid question. Despite some pockets of bureaucratic support for the "if we don't provide them with arms, the Cubans will" argument,[99] the dominant sentiment among Carter advisors opposed any policy shift. High on the list of concerns was avoiding any dispute with Congress that might interfere with the larger "deradicalizing" strategy. And one development guaranteed to upset the legislators would be reports of American arms to Nicaragua finding their way to the guerrilla movement in El Salvador.

The administration also pursued a two-track approach in its efforts to diffuse the radical tendencies within the Sandinista armed forces leadership. One was a willingness to at least discuss the possibility of reestablishing a bilateral military relationship. The other aimed at promoting ties between the Nicaraguans and the rest of the hemisphere's armed forces. A SOUTH-COM officer transferred to the Managua Embassy to help "establish military to military contacts" explained the thinking behind the regional initiative:

95 Interview with David McGiffert.
96 Interview with David Newsom.
97 See Charles A. Krause, "Nicaraguan Defense Minister Sets Off on Arms Trip," *Washington Post*, September 1, 1979, p. A19.
98 Confidential interview, Department of Defense official, October 2, 1990.
99 Quoted in Robert Matthews, "The Limits of Friendship: Nicaragua and the West," *NACLA Report on the Americas*, Vol. XIX, No. 3, May/June 1985, p. 26.

Between August and November 1979, there was a sense in both State and the Pentagon, and the mission in Managua that we had the capability of coopting not the ideological foundations on which the revolution was based but the pragmatic or day to day execution of the recovery operation of Nicaraguan society. That is, if we could only get in and demonstrate that we did not want to topple the Sandinista revolution but only mould Nicaragua into a productive society, then we could in fact integrate the victorious military organization into the regional militaries and, through this process of integrating it, get the army away from its doctrinaire ideological orientation and we would not end up with another Cuba or a Soviet Union toehold on the continent.[100]

On October 20, the Chairman of the Joint Chiefs of Staff, declaring support for Ambassador Pezzullo's attempt to develop a military relationship with the Sandinista government, extended an invitation to the head of the armed forces, Humberto Ortega, to attend the Conference of American Armies (CAA) in Bogotá, Colombia in early November. Secretary of State Vance termed the Chairman's initiative "one step in the strategy endorsed by the President to build links in a relationship between the GON [Government of Nicaragua] and the rest of the hemisphere."[101] But Washington was not willing to insist on Nicaraguan participation over the opposition of the region's generals. During late November CAA committee meetings, a clear majority of delegates voiced support for a Brazilian proposal to change attendance regulations in such a way as to effectively exclude Sandinista participation at future conferences. Although the U.S. delegation argued against the rule change, on the final vote it chose not to antagonize the majority and, in Vance's words, "destroy the positive dialogue which had been created."[102]

Pentagon efforts to cultivate better relations with the Sandinista armed forces were not limited to the CAA invitation. Although an offer to train military personnel at the U.S. Army School of Americas in Panama was rejected because of the institution's historic association with the Somoza National Guard, a mid-November tour of American military bases on the East Coast arranged by the Defense Department for six Sandinista officers, including the army chief of staff Joaquín Cuadra, went ahead without any serious hitches. "We exposed them to training establishments," said the

100   Confidential interview, Department of Defense official, October 2, 1990.
101   Department of State Telegram, Confidential State 277334, Secretary of State (Vance) to All American Republic Diplomatic Posts, October 24, 1979, Subject: "Nicaraguan Participation in Conference of American Army Commanders," DFOIA.
102   Department of State Telegram, Confidential State 308180, Secretary of State (Vance) to American Embassy, Bogotá, Info American Embassy, Managua, November 29, 1979, Subject: "Conference of American Army Commanders," DFOIA.

SOUTHCOM official accompanying the delegation, "in the hope that they would see something there they would want to be part of. Initially they were very encouraging. They talked about sending people up to this course, we can do something here, and so on."[103]

But there was no follow-up by the Nicaraguans. The U.S. Embassy reported at the end of January 1980 that efforts to obtain "definitive guidance" from the Sandinista military leadership regarding the kinds of training programs it was prepared to accept "have not met with success other than repeated assurances that they are in fact still interested."[104] The only subsequent development of any note was an April agreement "to install a [U.S.] military liaison group" in Managua.[105] The Pentagon was in no doubt as to why the early positive indicators came to nought: "it all sort of changed with the large influx of Cuban advisors into Nicaragua."[106]

Economic assistance

During early interagency discussions to forge a policy for dealing with the Sandinistas in office, the State Department countered some of the more gloomy, pessimistic pronouncements from the Pentagon and the intelligence agencies by insisting that Nicaragua was not "lost" to the victorious guerrillas and the "extreme left." The "carrot" of badly needed economic assistance presented the United States with a real opportunity to make its presence felt: to bolster the political moderates inside and outside the regime, thereby containing the process of change within "acceptable" limits and preventing the emergence of a "second Cuba" in the Central America-Caribbean region. In mid-August, an Embassy official wrote that the private sector "remains one of the main bulwarks that will be able to help shape the ultimate nature of the new government and its policies [and it] looks to the U.S. government for guidance and assistance...."[107] The predominant sentiment in State was that "we were seeing a mixed economy emerging in Nicaragua and we hoped there would be moderate change that would let

---

103 Confidential interview, Department of Defense official, October 2, 1990.
104 Department of State Telegram, Confidential Managua 0426, American Embassy (O'Donnell) to Secretary of State, January 29, 1980, Subject: "FY 80 IMET for Nicaragua," DFOIA.
105 Department of State Telegram, Confidential Managua 01692, American Embassy (Pezzullo) to Secretary of State, April 9, 1980, Subject: "(U) Proposed Consolidation of DADS and MILGPS," DFOIA.
106 Confidential interview, Department of Defense official, October 2, 1990.
107 Department of State Telegram, Managua 3662, American Embassy (O'Donnell) to Secretary of State, August 11, 1979, Subject: "Financing for Nicaraguan Private Sector Reconstruction," DFOIA.

the private sector go on and prosper. If we can get to these guys [the Sandinistas] and get them working with us, they will back off from any silly ideas they might have. Our economic support can help."[108] Such aid would have the added result, wrote Viron Vaky, of ensuring that the country's financial system remained "tied to the West's political economy."[109]

Responding to President Carter's interest "in encouraging private U.S. institutions and U.S.-assisted private Nicaraguan groups," the Agency for International Development (AID) moved swiftly on a number of fronts. First, it supported the activities of the Wisconsin-based Partners of the Americas, whose president visited Nicaragua for the purpose of "assessing needs and discussing project ideas" with local private sector groups. Second, it approved a grant to the Partners to finance a visit to the United States by a delegation of Nicaraguan businessmen chosen by the U.S. Embassy for discussion with their opposite numbers on private sector cooperation and American investment in Nicaragua. Third, it began funding the regional anti-communist American Institute for Free Labor Development (AIFLD) and stayed "in close touch with them on labor union assistance possibilities."[110] Ambassador Pezzullo was a strong advocate of "an expanded AIFLD program" to counter the aggressive organizing of the Sandinista Workers' Central (CST).[111] Fourth, AID provided a $500,000 grant to the Nicaraguan Development Foundation (FUNDE) – a business organization it helped to establish in the early 1960s.

In mid-August, the administration decided to release approximately $35 million worth of public health, education, and agriculture loans to Nicaragua approved by Congress prior to Somoza's downfall but not disbursed.[112] Simultaneously, AID officials began drafting a fiscal 1980 supplemental aid package for presentation to Congress. Ambassador Pezzullo hinted that the Nicaraguans could expect a "fairly generous" amount of funds.[113] On Sep-

108 Interview with Ambler Moss.
109 Viron P. Vaky, "Hemispheric Relations: 'Everything is Part of Everything Else,' " *Foreign Affairs* ("America and the World 1980"), Vol. 59, No. 3, 1981, p. 622.
110 National Security Council Memorandum, Rutherford Poats to Zbigniew Brzezinski, August 11, 1979, Subject: "Involvement of Private US Institutions in Nicaragua's New Era," White House Country File, Box CO-47, Folder CO 114 8/1/79–1/20/81, Jimmy Carter Presidential Library; memorandum attached to above from Stephen F. Dachi, ICA/AR, to Robert Pastor, September 14, 1979, Subject: "USICA [International Co-operation Administration] Report on Nicaragua, September 5–11," Ibid.
111 Department of State Telegram, Confidential Managua 4087, American Embassy (Pezzullo) to Secretary of State, August 29, 1979, Subject: "(C) AIFLD Program," DFOIA.
112 Between July 17 and September 30, the U.S. government delivered $23.5 million of a promised $26 million in emergency assistance, about half of which was in the form of food aid. See "Nicaragua: US Aid Package Better Late Than Never," *Latin America Weekly Report*, December 7, 1979, p. 70.
113 Quoted in Richard Meislin, "U.S. Planning Loans and Other Aid for Nicaragua," *New York Times*, August 17, 1979, p. 8. The State Department officials involved in drafting

tember 11, Deputy Secretary of State Christopher and Assistant Secretary Vaky appeared before separate House subcommittees at the start of a powerful lobbying effort to "sell" the proposed aid strategy on Capitol Hill. Christopher testified in support of a White House proposal to reprogram $8.8 million of unused fiscal 1979 foreign assistance funds for Nicaragua. With the exception of a $23,600 military grant, the rest was earmarked for economic reconstruction and price stabilization purposes. He argued that the new regime was "moderate and pluralistic" and committed "to respect for private property." Although major changes had taken place "the situation in Nicaragua remains fluid," the private sector and non-Sandinista politicians are well represented at the highest levels of the government, and opportunities remain for coopting and influencing the process of change in a direction compatible with basic U.S. interests: "We would do well to... try to take advantage of change, to try to move it in our direction...." Only by playing "a constructive role" in the short term (via diplomacy and economic assistance), Christopher concluded, could Washington hope to produce a result in Nicaragua that "is agreeable to us in the longer term."[114] The Foreign Aid Appropriations subcommittee approved the request by a seven to three vote.

Assistant Secretary Vaky, the Department's highest ranking Latin American affairs official, presented an almost identical brief to the House Inter-American Affairs subcommittee. The ruling junta was composed of "moderate pluralistic tendencies," the cabinet and the bureaucracy harbored a diversity of ideological outlooks, and "many outcomes or scenarios [political and economic] are still possible within the framework of the Sandinista revolution."[115] In a letter to the subcommittee chairman, Vaky characterized the situation in Nicaragua as "confused... with a good deal of definition and resolution of power struggles yet to come."[116]

The aid strategy was not confined to legislative funding sources. In early October, senior NSC and State Department officials told the acting chairman of the quasi-government Export-Import (Exim) Bank that the administration was intent on "giving maximum support to the moderate democratic

the economic assistance proposal were AID Director Lawrence S. Harrison and Deputy Assistant Secretary Sidney Weintraub.

114   Quoted in U.S. Congress, House, Committee on Appropriations, Subcommittee on Foreign Operations and Related Programs, *Foreign Assistance and Related Programs Appropriations for 1980, Part 7*, 96th Congress 1st Session, 1979 (Washington, D.C.: U.S. Government Printing Office, 1979), pp. 44, 52, 77, 100. Also see Karen DeYoung, "House Unit Votes $9 Million in Aid for Nicaragua," *Washington Post*, September 12, 1979, pp. A1, A20.
115   Quoted in U.S. Congress, House, *Central America at the Crossroads*, pp. 3, 4.
116   Quoted from Letter, dated September 8, 1979, by Assistant Secretary of State for Inter-American Affairs Viron P. Vaky, reprinted in U.S. Congress, House, *United States Policy Toward Nicaragua*, p. 79.

elements" in Central America which, in the case of Nicaragua, meant economic assistance, including "Exim financial support," to the private sector. They emphasized the need for rapid funding to a war-torn economy heavily dependent on imports to maximize production, especially in the key agricultural sector: "If financing for the imports is not made available quickly to get the private sector going, the country is likely to turn to an authoritarian solution that inevitably will become Marxist in orientation." Bank officials concurred but explained that the institution was currently "shut down" in Nicaragua only because of its "inability to perceive a reasonable assurance of repayment in the light of present arrearages and [in the] absence of a debt rescheduling."[117] However, within days of his appointment as the new Central Bank president, Arturo Cruz had "expressed [a] desire to renegotiate debts with EXIM," which currently amounted to $1.7 million in short-term insurance payments and an additional $2 million under the guarantee, insurance, and direct credit programs.[118] The Exim's acting chairman told his executive branch visitors that the Bank would almost certainly be prepared to authorize new loans to Managua if it received "reasonable assurances of repayment" from the Sandinista government.[119]

In late November, the administration unveiled the centerpiece of what Ambassador Pezzullo described as a "full court press" to deradicalize the Nicaraguan revolution: a $75 million supplemental aid proposal, the majority of the funds targeted for the private sector.[120] The major goal of the package, in the words of one State Department official, was "to try to encourage those Sandinistas who were the economic leaders in the first period. They turned out to be moderate. To the extent that we strengthened these people, they could carry the burden of development and it would come out on a range satisfactory to us. We hoped that by strengthening them we would tip the balance in the contest."[121]

The White House and the State Department requested rapid Congressional passage of the aid request on three main grounds. First, the funds

---

117 Department of State Telegram, Confidential State 269771, Secretary of State (Vance) to American Embassy, October 16, 1979, Subject: "Exim Involvement in Nicaragua," DFOIA. The discussants were NSC Latin American specialist Robert Pastor and the State Department's John Bushnell.

118 Department of State Telegram, Managua 3372, American Embassy (Pezzullo) to Secretary of State, July 28, 1979, Subject: "Nicaraguan Government Debts to EXIM Bank," DFOIA.

119 Department of State Telegram, Confidential State 269771.

120 Quoted in U.S. Congress, Senate, Committee on Foreign Relations, *S.2012*, 96th Congress, 1st Session, December 6 and 7, 1979 (Washington, D.C.: U.S.Government Printing Office, 1980), p. 88. The private sector was designated to receive 60 percent of the $70 million loan part of the request. The remaining $5 million was to be in the form of a straight-out grant.

121 Interview with John Bushnell.

were intended to benefit primarily the business community and small rural property owners. Second, the political direction of the regime was still undecided, the moderates exercised "strong influence" within the policymaking process, and decisions were being made on a very pragmatic basis. Third, insisting that "the ball game is still on," Carter officials were convinced that economic aid offered the best possibility of restoring U.S. "credibility" and "influence" in Managua, and shoring up the non-Sandinista forces within the government, state, and economy.[122]

The biggest obstacle to a successful outcome was the fact that a large number of members in both the House and the Senate had already concluded that Nicaragua was lost to "a Marxist-dominated government.... By taking this large gamble, the odds are that instead of fostering moderate leadership, we will be providing the necessary support to solidify FSLN leadership."[123] In an effort to defuse this opposition, the administration pressed Managua to clarify its economic program. John Bushnell told the International Reconstruction Fund director Alfredo César that prospects for passage of the funds would be substantially enhanced if the Nicaraguan leadership publicly "pledged itself to preserving a mixed economy with a vigorous private sector."[124]

The Senate debate on the aid bill was extremely divisive and bitter as supporters attempted to counter "totalitarian state" assertions by reminding the chamber that the proposed funds would assist Nicaragua's political moderates and the private sector, thereby diminishing the likelihood of "radical solutions."[125] In late January 1980, the bill passed by a relatively divided

122 Deputy Assistant Secretary of State for Inter-American Affairs John Bushnell, quoted in U.S. Congress, House, Committee on Appropriations, Subcommittee on Foreign Operations and Related Programs, *Foreign Assistance and Related Programs Appropriations for 1981, Part 1*, 96th Congress, 2nd Session, February 26, 1980 (Washington, D.C.: U.S. Government Printing Office, 1980), p. 298; Assistant Secretary of State Warren Christopher, testimony before U.S. Congress, Senate, *S.2012*, p. 76; Assistant Secretary of State for Inter-American Affairs Viron P. Vaky, quoted in U.S. Congress, House, Committee on Foreign Affairs, Hearing and Markup, *Special Central American Economic Assistance*, 96th Congress, 1st Session, November 27 and December 11, 1979 (Washington, D.C.: U.S. Government Printing Office, 1980), pp. 5, 6, 42, 51. Also see "Carter Wants $75 Million in Aid to Avoid Marxism in Nicaragua," *Washington Post*, November 28, 1979, p. A19.

123 Quoted in U.S. Congress, House, Committee on Foreign Affairs, *Special Central American Act of 1979*, Report No. 96–713, 96th Congress, 1st Session, December 18, 1979 (Washington, D.C.: U.S. Government Printing Office, 1979), pp. 14, 15, 18. Also see U.S. Congress, House, *Special Central American Economic Assistance*, p. 96.

124 Department of State Telegram, Confidential State 308312, Secretary of State (Vance) to American Embassy, November 29, 1979, Subject: "Conversation with Alfredo César [on November 21, 1979]," DFOIA.

125 Senator David Durenberger, quoted in "Debate on Special Central American and Caribbean Security Assistance Act of 1979," *Congressional Record-Senate*, Vol. 126, No. 11, 96th Congress, 2nd Session, January 29, 1980, p. S526.

vote of 54 to 35 and was sent to the House, where debate promised to be just as conflictive.

The anti-aid coalition in the House of Representatives couched its arguments in the traditional rhetoric of Cold War politics: Nicaragua was "already a mini-Cuba" or controlled by a regime "already under Communist control and outside Communist influence" bent on exporting revolution and threatening the security of its neighbors.[126] Believing the country was "lost" to the "totalitarian forces of the extreme left," these legislators saw "no reason to contribute aid to make Marxism work in Nicaragua."[127] House proponents of the aid bill, on the other hand, were more concerned with whatever advantage could be gained from a still fluid political situation. Their arguments mirrored those of the White House: Economic assistance offered the best, and perhaps only realistic, chance of limiting the process of change and avoiding a complete erosion of U.S. influence in post-revolutionary Nicaragua. To deny aid "would be to walk away and concede victory to the Cuban and Soviet surrogates." Moreover, it was not only important to strengthen the moderate forces in the government, private sector, and society but also to ensure that Nicaragua maintained its economic links to the West – a point well understood by America's allies, including West Germany, Spain, Venezuela, and the Netherlands.[128]

Prior to the House vote, President Carter wrote a letter to Daniel Inouye, the chairman of the Senate subcommittee on Foreign Operations Appropriations, warning of "serious foreign policy problems" if Congress failed to pass the fiscal year 1980 foreign aid bill, which included the $75 million Nicaragua request. He complained that when he submitted the bill in the fall of 1979 its passage was labeled "urgent". Yet five months later it was still slowly winding its way through the committee system. Any decision to delay the entire bill "until later in the year would be very dangerous." The Nicaraguan funds were among the most "critical" in terms of foreign policy goals, and unless disbursement was commenced prior to the upcoming growing season, the prospects were for food shortages, a worsening eco-

---

126 Representative Edward J. Derwinski, quoted in Graham Hovey, "Never Popular, Foreign Aid is Even More on the Ropes," *New York Times*, April 6, 1980, p. E3; "Debate on Special Central American Assistance Act of 1979," *Congressional Record-House*, Vol. 126, No. 31, 96th Congress, 2nd Session, February 27, 1980, p. H1368.

127 Quoted in ibid., p. H1366; "Debate on Special Central American and Caribbean Security Assistance Act of 1979," *Congressional Record-House*, Vol. 126, No. 28, 96th Congress, 2nd Session, February 22, 1980, p. H1176. Also see "Special Aid for Nicaragua Sought by Carter Delayed by House Conservatives," *Congressional Quarterly Weekly Report*, Vol. 37, No. 50, December 15, 1979, pp. 2849–2850, 2864.

128 Quoted in "Debate on Special Central American and Caribbean Security Assistance Act of 1979," *Congressional Record-House*, February 22, 1980, p. H1174. Also see "Debate on Special Central American Assistance Act of 1979, *Congressional Record-House*, Vol. 126, No. 30, 96th Congress, 2nd Session, February 26, 1980, p. H1285.

nomic situation, "demoralization of private business," and a likely mass migration of the "middle-class Nicaraguans" upon whom Washington was placing most of its future hopes for moderating the revolution.[129]

On February 27, the House approved the supplemental aid package by the paper thin margin of 202 to 197 votes but only after a number of unprecedented conditions were attached to the bill. Funding would be terminated if the administration concluded that the Sandinista regime was engaged in large-scale and systematic human rights or political and civil liberties abuses, or if the White House determined that foreign military forces stationed in Nicaragua constituted a "national security" threat to the United States or any of its Latin American allies. The President was directed to pressure the Nicaraguan leadership to hold national elections and to certify to Congress, before the aid was released, that the regime was not involved in regional "subversion" or "terrorist activities." Finally, the House bill required that 60 percent of the monies be earmarked for the private sector, that no funds be allocated for educational institutions involving Cuban personnel, that loans be tied to the purchase of U.S. goods and services, and that as much as 1 percent of the total amount be used to publicize this example of American generosity throughout Nicaragua.

The most revealing feature of the Congressional debate thus far was the broad-based consensus on the need to undermine Sandinista political power, limit the socioeconomic transformation process, and contain the regional impact of the revolution. Within this common framework, the legislators diverged over the possibility and means of achieving these goals. The liberals set greater store on the instruments of diplomacy and economic aid to revive U.S. influence and bolster Nicaraguan allies. The conservatives were convinced that the Sandinistas had already achieved political hegemony and that only a confrontationist U.S. posture, including political and economic sanctions, held any hope of undermining their authority.

In mid-May, the House version of the aid bill went back to the Senate floor. The subsequent debate was largely a rerun of the January divisions and arguments. Loan advocates insisted that the $75 million was necessary "to undermine the economic conditions of radicalism" and prevent the private sector from being "overwhelmed." Senator Edward Zorinsky posed the following question: "... is the United States prepared to compete in the Nicaraguan case or is it prepared to sit on its hands and do nothing more than rant and rave about the Cuban presence in Nicaragua? Do we wish to

---

129 Letter, Jimmy Carter, White House, to Daniel K. Inouye, Chairman, Subcommittee on Foreign Operations, Senate Appropriations Committee, February 25, 1980, White House Country File, Box CO-47, Folder CO 114 8/1/79–1/20/81, Jimmy Carter Presidential Library.

suck our thumbs and sit it out or do we wish to stay in the game and play to win." Other aid proponents raised the specter of a radicalized Nicaragua "destabiliz[ing] the whole region and challeng[ing] remaining U.S. interests" if the administration request was denied. One of the bill's most vociferous Senate critics, Robert Dole, a conservative Republican, repeated the assertion that Nicaragua was "lost" and that Somoza's overthrow had ushered in "the first of a series of destabilizing coups and revolutions in Central America" likely to produce Cuban-backed regimes.[130]

Although a majority of Senators favored deleting some of the House amendments to the final bill, the chamber agreed, albeit reluctantly, to passage of the House version when it became clear that the House would refuse to consider any compromise proposal. On May 19, the Senate passed the bill, with its attached restrictions and prohibitions, and forwarded it to the White House for the President's signature. Although Carter expressed reservations over the House amendments, he signed the bill into law in the knowledge that the only alternative was the total collapse of the Nicaragua aid program.[131]

Addressing the Council on Foreign Relations on May 28, Deputy Secretary of State Christopher bemoaned the fact that while Cuba and other countries were able to speedily organize economic aid programs for Nicaragua, proposed U.S. funds remained stalled for months, hostage to Congress's determination that the Sandinista regime "passes ideological muster."[132] That same day, over the objections of the executive branch, the House of Representatives voted by 267 to 195 to delete a $5.5 million military assistance request (foreign military sales credits and training program monies) from the fiscal 1981 foreign aid authorization to the accompaniment of speeches accusing the new Nicaraguan government of having subordinated itself to "communist control."[133]

Managua was not oblivious to the scope and significance of Congressional hostility, and the need to do something to mollify or neutralize these concerns. At the beginning of June, the country's Central Bank president and newly appointed junta member Arturo Cruz visited Washington, D.C. to

130 Quoted in "Debate on Special Central American Assistance Act of 1979," *Congressional Record-House*, Vol. 126, No. 81, 96th Congress, 2nd Session, May 19, 1980, pp. S5546–S5577.
131 See "House Version of Nicaragua Aid Bill Accepted by Senate," *Congressional Quarterly Weekly Report*, Vol. 38, No. 21, May 24, 1980, pp. 1395–1396.
132 *Resources and Foreign Policy*, Address to the Council on Foreign Relations, New York, May 28, 1980, Current Policy No. 185, Department of State, Bureau of Public Affairs.
133 See "House Rejects Military Aid Request for Nicaragua," *Congressional Quarterly Weekly Report*, Vol. 38, No. 22, May 31, 1980, p. 1519; Graham Hovey, "Foreign Aid Measures Face Hard Fight," *New York Times*, June 5, 1980, p. 3.

address a special Organization of American States' meeting and hold discussions with officials of the Carter administration and the multilateral development banks. In an effort to reassure Capitol Hill about the policies and intentions of his government, Cruz extended his schedule to include meetings with several key legislators and apparently succeeded in convincing them that Nicaragua was not a "Cuban satellite."[134] Also, the Sandinistas were realistic enough not to reject the House aid 'conditions,' however distasteful, for to do so would have sunk the bill, in turn sending the wrong kind of message to the international banking community from whom they hoped to receive large-scale financial assistance.

On July 8, the fiscal 1980 supplemental appropriations bill that included the $75 million Nicaraguan aid package finally reached President Carter's desk. But Congress had succeeded in attaching one last amendment stipulating that the Nicaraguan funds could not be disbursed prior to October 1, which provoked a sharply worded missive from Ambassador Pezzullo "expressing grave concern about the possible consequences – both political and economic" of such a decision. "We have already paid major political costs for the inordinate delay in appropriation of the package," he observed, and any further holdup "will seriously damage the credibility of the United States" in its dealings with the Sandinista government.[135]

Despite anti-aid sentiments emanating from the NSC, the CIA and other parts of the intelligence community, all of whom targeted Nicaragua as a conduit for Cuban and Soviet military activities in Central America, and an active supporter of revolutionary movements in El Salvador and Guatemala, the White House remained firmly supportive of the State Department approach. The day the supplemental aid bill became law, the new Secretary of State Edward Muskie said that any reduction in foreign aid to the Third World would only "help the Soviets exploit internal stability in Nicaragua, in El Salvador and in many other places."[136] Discussing the importance of the Nicaraguan component of the bill in relation to the country's private sector "and the moderate forces friendly to the United States," another

---

134 Quoted in "Nicaragua: Cruz Visits Washington," *This Week: Central America & Panama*, June 9, 1980, pp. 171–172. Also see Cynthia J. Arnson, *Crossroads: Congress, The Reagan Administration, and Central America* (New York: Pantheon Books, 1989), p. 44.

135 Department of State Telegram, Confidential Managua 3241, American Embassy (Pezzullo) to Secretary of State, July 11, 1980, Subject: "Possible Delay in Disbursements from $75 Million Package," DFOIA.

136 Speech to the Foreign Policy Association in New York City, quoted in Peter Kihss, "Muskie Stresses Aid to Protect Nations From Soviet Threat," *New York Times*, July 8, 1980, p. 1. Vance resigned as Secretary of State on April 28. Also see John M. Goshko, "Aid for Nicaragua the Focus of Fierce Internal Policy Dispute," *Washington Post*, August 8, 1980, p. 2.

leading diplomat emphasized that "only by playing an active role in Central America can we compete with the Cubans and others who are intent upon pursuing their own interests in the area."[37]

The administration's 1981 foreign aid request for Nicaragua included $45 million in economic assistance, as well as the previously mentioned $5.5 million in military funds, which was ultimately rejected by both the House and the Senate. In late July, the State Department notified Ambassador Pezzullo that this economic package was also running into trouble on Capitol Hill "because of the failure of the GRN [Government of National Reconstruction] to comply with its promise to announce a date for municipal elections on July 19." Pezzullo relayed the message to junta member Arturo Cruz, who responded that the government was still committed to elections "but that other priority matters make it impossible to announce a timetable at this juncture." The Ambassador termed this statement "hardly convincing" and likely to reinforce anti-Sandinista sentiments in Congress and increase skepticism that elections would ever be held. After conferring with junta colleagues Sergio Ramírez and Daniel Ortega, Cruz reported back to Pezzullo that they "were sensitive to the vote in Congress, but were equally concerned about pressure being brought to bear on the government on this issue." The latter answered that he was merely "reflecting the reality in the Congress and the consequences of a negative vote on Nicaragua."[38]

One of the special conditions attached to release of the 1980 Nicaraguan aid package was a Presidential certification that the Sandinista government was not "aiding, abetting, or supporting acts of violence or terrorism in other countries."[39] In August, U.S. intelligence reports began to surface accusing Nicaragua of acting as a "pass through" country for Cuban military assistance to Central American guerrilla movements. Although the State Department challenged these allegations on the basis of insufficient hard evidence,[140] the bureaucratic opponents of Nicaraguan aid interpreted them as vindicating their position. Aware that the White House did not want the Republicans to make this a major presidential election issue in November,

---

137 Department of State, Letter from J. Brian Attwood, Assistant Secretary for Congressional Relations, to Hon. J. Bennet Johnston, United States Senate, July 20, 1980, DFOIA.

138 Department of State Telegram, Confidential Managua 3455, American Embassy (Pezzullo) to Secretary of State, July 23, 1980, Subject: "The Election Issue and its Effects on Congress," DFOIA.

139 U.S. Congress, Select Committee on Intelligence, Subcommittee on Oversight and Evaluation, *U.S. Intelligence Performance on Central America: Achievements and Selected Instances of Concern,* Staff Report, Committee Print, 97th Congress, 2nd Session, September 22, 1982 (Washington, D.C.: U.S. Government Printing Office, 1982), p. 5.

140 See Juan de Onis, "U.S. Aid to Nicaragua Now Facing Election Hurdle," *New York Times,* September 5, 1980, p. 6.

these forces seized upon the intelligence reports to block disbursement of the $75 million until Nicaragua's ties with Cuba and El Salvador's guerrilla movement could be thoroughly investigated.

On September 12, 1980, President Carter issued the requisite certification and then invoked "national security reasons" to circumvent the prohibition on disbursement of any funds before October 1 in order to release $45 million borrowed from fiscal year 1979 monies appropriated for Egypt. The President conceded "that there was "substantial evidence" to indicate that Nicaraguan territory was being used in support of the [Salvadoran] insurgents and that members of the Sandinista Front were probably involved." But the case for direct government involvement was termed sufficiently inconclusive to give it the benefit of the doubt.[141] The intelligence community registered its vigorous dissent from this White House interpretation of the reporting on Nicaragua. The CIA's analysis of the same data concluded "there is a very high likelihood that such activities [training of, and supplying weapons to, the Salvadoran guerrillas] are occurring and that they represent official FSLN policy."[142] Aware that President Carter was treading a fine line on this issue, the State Department instructed Ambassador Pezzullo to make vigorous representations to the Nicaraguan government "to take measures to stop any transit of arms and personnel to the Salvadoran terrorist groups."[143]

Later that month, Deputy Assistant Secretary of State James Cheek, accompanied by Ambassador Pezzullo and senior Embassy officials, met with DNC[143a] members Bayardo Arce, Humberto Ortega and Jaime Wheelock for discussions which "dealt principally with [the] terrorism amendment of the $75 million aid program, the current situation in El Salvador, and the future of our bilateral relations." Reflecting the administration's continuing nervousness about the alleged Salvadoran connection, Cheek was at pains to stress the potential this issue had for inflaming bilateral relations. Although the evidence of official Nicaraguan involvement with the Salvadoran guerrillas was "not strong enough" for the White House to consider

141 Department of State Telegram, Confidential State 242714, Secretary of State (Muskie) to American Embassy, September 12, 1980, Subject: "Certification Signed for the $75 Million," DFOIA.
142 U.S. Congress, Select Committee on Intelligence, *U.S. Intelligence Performance on Central America: Achievements and Selected Instances of Concern*, p. 7. The "substantial evidence" of Nicaraguan government and non-governmental involvement with the Salvadoran guerrillas was included in U.S. Department of State, *Communist Influence in El Salvador*, February 23, 1981. For a critique, see James Petras, "White Paper on the White Paper," *The Nation*, March 28, 1981, p. 370.
143 Department of State Telegram, Confidential State 242714.
143a Sandinista National Directorate.

reevaluating the aid program, U.S. intelligence reports "raised serious questions" about the precise nature of Managua's ties with the neighboring insurgents. "Elaborating on our concerns, he said that Nicaragua must bear them in mind...."[144]

Washington's economic diplomacy was intended to limit the process of transformation inside Nicaragua and avoid a revolutionary multiplier, thus obstructing the aspirations of Havana or other external powers seeking to expand their influence in Central America. Secretary of State Muskie called the multi-million dollar aid package "an essential element in our efforts to bolster moderate forces, and counter Cuba's growing influence [in Nicaragua]."[145] But other officials sounded a more pessimistic note. For them, the long, drawn-out aid struggle had significantly undermined the basic objective due to what they perceived as its "radicalizing impact" on the Sandinistas – precisely the outcome the economic strategy was designed to prevent.[146]

American multinational capital in Nicaragua: Adapting to the revolutionary milieu

Historically, U.S. investment and banking capital in Central America has worked closely with the imperial state and its rightist authoritarian clients. This convergence has not been incompatible with the appearance of differences in moments of political crisis and regime transition, especially when the imperial state has lost its capacity to impose its will. At these times, capitalist interests have shown themselves capable of developing a variety of positions relative to the particular regime – from accommodation to outright opposition.

Confronted by a popularly based regime hegemonized by radical nationalist guerrillas in July 1979, American economic interests in Nicaragua adopted a general posture that was more cooperative than confrontationist, more prudent than hostile. This cautious and relatively pragmatic response reflected a desire on the part of the bankers and multinational corporations not to pursue policies that might be counterproductive and lead to radical

---

144 Department of State Telegram, Confidential Managua 4660, American Embassy (Pezzullo) to Secretary of State, September 27, 1980, Subject: "(U) DAS Cheek Meeting with FSLN Political Committee," DFOIA.
145 Department of State Telegram, Confidential State 244698, Secretary of State (Muskie) to American Embassy, September 13, 1980, Subject: "Temporary Reallocation of 45 million dol[lar]s in ESP Earmarked for Egypt," DFOIA Also see White House officials quoted in Lee Lescaze, "President Approved Aid for Nicaragua," *Washington Post*, September 13, 1980, p. A1.
146 Quoted in ibid.

socioeconomic changes involving a repudiation of the foreign debt and the disintegration of the private sector – especially in circumstances where the U.S. government lacked the capacity to pressure the Sandinista leadership in directions favorable to foreign capital. Such flexible behavior was also shaped by a belief that the imperatives of underdevelopment (accentuated by the economic devastation wrought by the civil war) would eventually force the revolutionaries to come to terms with the demands and requirements of overseas investors.

The response of U.S. investors

Multinational corporation strategies in Third World countries are dictated by a number of factors, including the type and amount of investment, its size and profitability in relation to other overseas subsidiaries, and whether the internal market is expanding or contracting. Those corporations most likely to adapt to a new nationalist operating environment, or at a minimum seek a basis for doing so, are enterprises with large fixed investments not easily uprooted and relocated elsewhere. By contrast, foreign property holders most immediately – and negatively – affected by the regime's policies tend to advocate the most extreme solutions in meetings or correspondence with U.S. government officials. As a general rule, investor attitudes are largely shaped by perceptions of reaching an accommodation with the new government and their ability to adjust to the revised "rules of the (economic) game" without sacrificing profitability levels.

For the American business community, Somoza's Nicaragua had always been "a pretty good place to do business."[147] When difficulties arose, companies had virtually unlimited entree to the appropriate government agencies and officials. Neptune Mining's experience was typical. "We had easy access to labor and mining authorities in Nicaragua to deal with problems," a senior executive of the parent corporation remembered.[148] Not surprisingly, many U.S. investors were scornful of the Carter decision to target the Somoza dictatorship as a major Third World human rights violator. It was unlikely to have much political effect, they charged, but almost certain to worsen the climate for foreign business and profitmaking. One executive of an American multinational corporation with investments in Nicaragua asserted that "nobody in the business community liked Mr. Carter's policy. They thought he was a first class idiot. The feeling was that the man was dangerous from a commercial standpoint. He was going to ruin business if he kept doing what

147 Interview with James Hammond, Washington, D.C., October 15, 1988. The respondent
     was a Director of the Council of the Americas, 1976 to 1980.
148 Confidential telephone interview, American business executive, September 11, 1989.

he was doing. The United States should export its products not its morality. Don't let politics interfere with commerce."[149]

The January 1978 Chamorro assassination and general strike produced among the American business community "no great concern that anything really horrendous was going to happen." The dictator's military strength was sufficient to withstand any opposition challenge, now or in the future: "Nobody thought that the Sandinistas could knock Somoza over. The business community felt that Somoza could ride out the storm." Thus, the dominant attitude toward the internal conflict was one of non-involvement: " 'Let's not rock the boat. Somoza is a tough cookie, he's greedy, but we can work with him.' "[150]

Investor confidence in the Somoza regime did not waiver until September 1978 when the national insurrection and its aftermath created "a definite perception that the status quo was not going to last." American companies were particularly "nervous" about the emergence of the Sandinistas as a growing force within the anti-dictatorial movement.[151] According to Westinghouse Corporation's Director of International Operations, Peter Strolis, everyone was convinced "the business environment would deteriorate" if this trend carried over into the post-Somoza era. Above all, the upheaval punctured Nicaragua's image as a stable environment for long-term capital accumulation. It induced "a fear of the unknown, not knowing what was going to happen," said Strolis. "We had no fixed investments but companies with fixed investments were very pessimistic about how things would work out. We all were."[152]

As the level of political and class struggle increased, U.S. investors became more and more disenchanted over the perceived lack of decisive and resolute action by the Carter White House to impose a solution that would avoid a radical outcome. The administration "was not tough enough," exclaimed Chad Engler, head of the Monsanto Chemical Company's Latin American operations. "Something had to be done and was not being done by the U.S. government. Basically it was rather obvious that Somoza was polarizing the country and that the situation was getting out of hand. There was concern over an explosion. We wanted Somoza removed in one way or another without leading to a revolution. But Carter let it fester too long and it got out of hand."[153]

The political and military collapse of the family dynasty in mid-July 1979 triggered a mixed response among the U.S. business community: relief that

149 Telephone interview with Peter Strolis, Pennsylvania, September 23, 1988.
150 Interview with James Hammond.
151 Ibid.
152 Telephone interview with Peter Strolis.
153 Telephone interview with Chad Engler, Missouri, September 13, 1988.

the civil war, which resulted in widespread destruction of physical plant and equipment and the closure of enterprises, had ended, combined with anxiety over what would follow in its wake. Monsanto's Engler described "a lack of pessimism rather than a great deal of optimism."[154] Much of the apprehension, said a U.S. oil executive, was over "the unclear political intentions" of the new government.[155] James Hammond, a director of the influential New York-based Council of the Americas, whose membership accounted for over 90 percent of U.S. corporate investments in Latin America, described the immediate post-transition period as "a critical time because we were suddenly confronted by a new ball game. Somoza goes and in comes a new group of unknown people, policies and intentions. There was tremendous anxiety trying to find out who these people were and what was on their minds."[156] Edward Piernick, in charge of the U.S.-based Borden Company's regional activities, was more succinct. Discussing the future of the company's glue and resin factory in Managua, he told a reporter for the *Wall Street Journal:* "We aren't sure what we're dealing with in Nicaragua."[157]

Potentially, the dependent nature of Nicaragua's economy, in the context of large-scale war-related damage to physical plant and communication networks, offered considerable opportunities for overseas investors, bankers, traders, and technological rentiers to increase their earning power during the reconstruction period. The country's agricultural and industrial infrastructure functioned largely on the basis of continued access to foreign (primarily U.S.) machinery, spare parts, raw materials, and technology, as well as capital, to sustain production levels at maximum operating capacity. Furthermore, the Sandinistas' intention to accord the state a greater economic role through nationalization while simultaneously pursuing a development model based on a mixture of public and private capital suggested new openings for joint ventures with a regime lacking both capital resources and skilled managerial and technical personnel.

The American corporate community was reluctant to consider new investments pending the Sandinista government's clarification of its economic policies and future relations with Washington. "It clearly represented a dark moment," said the Council of the Americas James Hammond, "but this was no reason to throw the towel in right away. There was nobody who said 'this is the ballgame.' " The majority attitude was one of "prudence, wait

154 Ibid.
155 Quoted in Beth Nissen, "U.S. Firms in Nicaragua Are Reopening, Despite Uncertainty of Regime's Politics," *Wall Street Journal,* September 27, 1979, p. 16.
156 Interview with James Hammond.
157 Quoted in Nissen, "U.S. Firms in Nicaragua Are Reopening, Despite Uncertainty of Regime's Politics," p. 16.

and see, let's not be overly hasty. The new government people have not declared themselves and have made no quick embrace of the United States." At the same time, there were few expressions of concern that Nicaragua would be a rerun of Cuba in the early 1960s. Because of the country's massive economic problems, the Sandinistas could not afford to alienate overseas investors: "There was certainly a belief that the Sandinistas would have to come to terms with foreign capital."[158] One consequence of this attitude was a relative lack of concern over the possibility of state intervention. The president of the international division of Nabisco, Inc., for example, which was scheduled to reopen its Managua factory in October, cavalierly dismissed nationalization as a "threat [that] just comes with the territory."[159] Among the factors that promised to be decisive in influencing the actions of present and prospective U.S. investors was the pace of economic reconstruction, the ability to repatriate capital to the imperial center, and the ease of access to foreign exchange on a regular basis.[160] This latter concern was to pose an immediate problem for a number of overseas corporations with subsidiaries in Nicaragua.

The Sandinistas took control of a war-devastated, debt-burdened economy, and a central bank almost totally bereft of funds in a period of declining export revenues. The new bank president Arturo Cruz also accused "Somoza and his supporters of taking blank checks from the Central Bank with them" when they fled the country.[161] "We knew" said one American business executive, "that there was no hard currency in the country, no reserves, so we knew that we would have problems getting debts paid."[162] To fund critically needed infrastructure purchases from abroad, the government instituted "stringent allocations of scarce foreign exchange that immediately reduced the amount of exchange available to multinationals' operations." The inability of some MNC subsidiaries to obtain sufficient foreign exchange to import products, raw materials, or spare parts soon led to market share losses, the scrapping of expansion plans, and problems maintaining equipment in maximum working order.[163]

Executives of foreign firms in Nicaragua surveyed during the first six weeks of Sandinista rule by *Business Latin America* offered a mixed, but not necessarily unfavorable, picture of the new emerging business climate: Dis-

---

158 Interview with James Hammond.
159 Quoted in Nissen, U.S. Firms in Nicaragua Are Reopening, Despite Uncertainty of Regime's Politics," p. 16.
160 See "Survey of Firm's Operations Reveals Shattering Effects of Nicaraguan Civil War," *Business Latin America*, July 11, 1979, pp. 223–224.
161 Interview with Thomas O'Donnell.
162 Telephone interview with Chad Engler.
163 James E. Austin and John C. Ickis, "Managing After the Revolutionaries Have Won," *Harvard Business Review*, Vol. 3, May/June 1986, p. 104.

crete concerns over securing financing, transportation problems, labor relations, and bureaucratic disorganization coexisted with a general
acknowledgment of the government's flexibility and willingness to provide
financial support to encourage firms to continue operations. For example,
most enterprises affected by the regime's freeze on overseas bank accounts,
especially those attempting to meet back payrolls or in need of large amounts
of capital to finance start-up operating costs, reported that the revolutionary
regime "has been helpful in this respect, particularly with money for wages."
Companies severely affected by the war such as Ralston Purina, which lost
warehouses, raw materials, finished products, and financial records, were
"offered operating capital loans" to help them rebuild and resume operations.

The appearance of a more organizationally and politically powerful working class demanding changes in labor-capital relations, including greater
participation in decision-making processes, did create temporary problems
for some foreign-owned subsidiaries. One U.S. chemical company was
forced by its employees to unionize "almost overnight." Another American-
owned manufacturing enterprise was pressured by its newly elected union
leadership to sack the general manager, but "things returned to normal once
this was done." However, labor practices in a large number of foreign firms
changed little, if at all, under Sandinista rule because their work forces had
already been unionized during the Somoza era.

Despite the changed environment for capital accumulation and expansion,
few American or other executives of overseas companies viewed the Sandinista economic program as likely to create an intolerable environment for
foreign investment and private sector operations. Although many of the
international firms surveyed by *Business Latin America* were critical of the
difficulties encountered "in contacting the right government people," such
irritants – which typically accompany any large-scale process of political
transformation – were not a cause for immediate concern. In general, there
was little sense of panic that Nicaragua "[would] repeat the Cuba experience...." Most of the respondents told *Business Latin America* that their
firms "planned to remain in the country at least for the time being."[164]

The majority of U.S.-owned enterprises that revived their operations
following the cessation of hostilities were those that suffered minimal physical plant damage, those with large fixed investments that could only be
terminated at great financial sacrifice, and those (for example, Nabisco,
Pillsbury) with little or no war-related losses (usually confined to offices,

inventory, and records) – especially if the economic stake were relatively limited. The H.B. Fuller Company, which owned two factories in Managua, only partially fitted into this latter category, and adopted a more complex strategy. It reopened a plastic products plant that had suffered only minor damage but kept its seriously fire-damaged paint factory closed "until we know more about the government's economic policies."[165] Those American corporations least able to easily "pull up stakes" and relocate, particularly if their subsidiaries survived the conflict more or less intact, remained optimistic, hoping to accommodate the economic changes and continue profitable operations. The Hercules Chemical Corporation typified this attitude: "Hercules, which had a huge complex, were in a situation where they had no alternative. Their plant was not destroyed so they had to make the best of it. If you were Hercules and have a $20 million or $30 million plant in Nicaragua, you are going to be pragmatic."[166]

The Intercontinental Hotel in Managua, a joint venture involving Pan American World Airways and the Somoza government, took the regime change in its stride. The building sustained no damage from the military conflict and operated more or less uninterruptedly during the political transition, even though majority control (52 percent of shares) was now vested in the Junta of the Government of Revolutionary Nicaragua (JGRN). The public intervenor, however, had no interest in running the hotel; nor would he recommend that it be nationalized. Furthermore, the JGRN agreed to respect the existing management contract, which still had ten years to run. Less than three weeks after the Sandinista victory, Intercontinental's Manager and Vice-President for Finance Ben White told a U.S. Embassy economic officer that the hotel "is enjoying a healthy cash flow which it appears will continue as Managua continues to receive a steady stream of visitors interested in the reconstruction effort." Consequently, the hotel's new majority shareholder, Compañía Hotelería de Nicaragua, was likely "to have no problem in working out some reasonable repayment schedule" with Bank of America regarding an outstanding $73,000 loan.[167]

One group of overseas investors was accorded more deferential treatment than most. Even investors critical of the regime's attitude toward the private sector acknowledged that those foreign-owned industrial and agricultural enterprises (petroleum, herbicides, and so on) deemed central to economic recovery were "treated pragmatically and fairly."[168]

---

165 Fuller Executive David Croonquist, quoted in Charles Roberts, "Nicaragua: The Unfolding Scene," *Multinational Monitor*, Vol. 1, No. 2, March 1980, p. 20.
166 Telephone interview with Bruce Cuthbertson, Florida, October 17, 1988.
167 Department of State Telegram, Managua 3517, American Embassy (Pezzullo) to Secretary of State, August 3, 1979, Subject: "OPIC Guarantee – Intercontinental Hotel," DFOIA.
168 Telephone interview with Chad Engler.

The petroleum industry was dominated by the giant American multinationals Exxon and Texaco. The former's subsidiary, Esso Inter-América, ran the country's only refinery, while the latter sold Esso's petroleum products to about sixty local service stations. In late July, Esso's refinery decided to temporarily halt production because all storage tanks were full and company officials estimated that the existing stock could easily satisfy the current relatively low level of demand until September, when operations would start up again. Initially, the JGRN was skeptical about the reason given and ordered the gasoline stations to sell oil on a priority basis. But this concern quickly evaporated. On July 28, an Esso official reported to the American Embassy that the government had intervened in the refinery but only "to check on and ensure deliveries to the government. . . . The gasoline stations are now selling gas to all customers as the GRN [Government of National Reconstruction] is apparently convinced that there is sufficient gas and that the refinery will start up when demand is sufficient to justify it. . . ."[169] Testifying before a Congressional subcommittee in February 1980, Ambassador Pezzullo commended the Sandinistas' favorable attitude toward foreign investment, noting the example of Exxon's dealings with the nationalist regime. The parent corporation, he assured the legislators, "is perfectly happy" with a recent marketing and production agreement negotiated between the JGRN and its Nicaraguan subsidiary.[170]

Both Exxon and Texaco subsidiaries consciously sought to maintain a low profile, their executives "shrug[ging] off Nicaragua's politics as none of their business."[171] To cement good relations with the new regime, Esso even provided financial assistance to a Central Bank strapped for funds to tackle the country's most pressing, short-term problems. The Nicaraguan manager of Esso Inter-América arranged with Central Bank president Arturo Cruz to lend the government $30 to $40 million in credits. "Arturo," a U.S. Embassy official remembered, "was able to use this with the Sandinistas to demonstrate there was goodwill and a willingness to cooperate among the foreign business sector."[172]

The Monsanto Chemical Corporation's subsidiary, which operated a herbicide formulation plant producing insecticides to spray on the cotton (export) crop, began receiving respectful treatment from the Sandinistas in the midst of the civil war. The FSLN leadership directed its forces not to attack the plant or disrupt its operations in any way. "One of the areas of heavy

169 Department of State Telegram, Managua 3373, American Embassy (Pezzullo) to Secretary of State, July 28, 1979, Subject: "Esso Refinery and Nicaraguan Fuel Supplies," DFOIA.
170 Quoted in U.S. Congress, House, *Foreign Assistance and Related Programs Appropriations for 1981, Part 1*, p. 310.
171 Quoted in Nissen, "U.S. Firms in Nicaragua are Reopening, Despite Uncertainty of Regime's Politics," p. 16.
172 Interview with Thomas O'Donnell.

fighting was León where our plant was located," recalled a senior company executive. "The Sandinistas had standing orders not to shoot or destroy anything around the Monsanto insecticide plant in León. The insecticide plant was critically important for the cotton crop and employment in León. So everyone understood the orders that it was not part of the play." When Somoza fell, Monsanto requested an immediate meeting with the country's new leaders to discuss a $4 million debt owed by the dictatorship, in the knowledge that they would be bargaining from a position of relative strength: "We knew we had some value in the economy. Basically the country needed to have our plant operations and the raw materials to spray the cotton crop. We were in a strong position."[173] The Sandinistas agreed to honor the debt. Reflecting on the corporation's experience in Nicaragua during the first five years of revolutionary rule, the Director of Monsanto's Latin American Division Richard Vance could only say that "the Sandinistas have been very friendly to us."[174]

The Standard Fruit & Steamship unit, which operated sixteen banana plantations in northwestern Nicaragua, also reached a swift and amicable accommodation with the JGRN. In mid-August 1979, Ambassador Pezzullo met with a group of the company's executives and was informed that "Standard has not experienced any serious problems in dealing with the new GRN [Government of National Reconstruction]. In fact, its relations with the local community in Chinandega are so good that the local FSLN commanders pushed them to accept guards on all of their trucks carrying bananas to Corinto for export." Despite increasing militancy among an already unionized labor force, the company remained confident "[it] would be able to work with even communist unions as they have in other countries."[175] A number of other American companies who counted the government among its major customers, such as IBM's subsidiary, expressed similar sentiments about the climate for business under the Sandinistas and voiced few or no complaints about their own operations.[176]

The appointment of individuals with credible reputations among the international financial community to head the economic ministries was one factor that exercised a powerful positive influence on American capitalists in Nicaragua. Visiting U.S. executives of four of the largest banks and businesses operating in the country, for instance, told Ambassador Pezzullo that

173 Telephone interview with Chad Engler.
174 Quoted in Jason Adkins, "Taking Care of Business in Nicaragua," *Multinational Monitor*, Vol. 6, No. 4, April 1985, p. 3.
175 Department of State Telegram, Managua 3754, American Embassy (Pezzullo) to Secretary of State, August 15, 1979, Subject: "Standard Fruit Registers First Exports from the New Nicaragua," DFOIA.
176 See Adkins, "Taking Care of Business in Nicaragua," p. 3.

their contacts "with the members of the GRN [Government of National Reconstruction] economic team have left them encouraged."[177] The general manager of the Hercules Chemical Company subsidiary and Vice-President of the American Chamber of Commerce of Latin America, Walter Duncan, spoke in quite glowing terms of the "centrist thinking, pragmatic people" in positions of ministerial and bureaucratic authority: "The new government is definitely headed by and spoken for by some of the best that Nicaragua has. We can vouch for the qualification and character of the top economic team and they have been fortunate in the quality of people they have been able to recruit for the second level of those ministries and institutions."[178]

U.S. enterprises in post-revolutionary Nicaragua were further buoyed by Sandinista and JGRN statements that foreign capital had an important role to play in the process of economic revival and development – especially in the critical agricultural sector. Responding to a query from the president of the Oliva Tobacco Company in Tampa, Florida, about future prospects for its Nicaraguan operations, Ambassador Pezzullo stressed the government's pro-investment attitude and calls to respect private property to accelerate the economy's return to maximum production levels, as well as its decision to confine property takeovers largely to Somoza-owned investments.[179] Appearing before the Senate Foreign Relations Committee, Hercules' Walter Duncan was just as encouraged by recent developments: "The Cabinet and, let us say, the junta on balance are in favor of the introduction of foreign technologies, foreign investments, and I would say are definitely in favor of promoting private investments."[180]

A delegation of U.S. banking and business executives visiting Managua in October 1979 was pleasantly surprised by their discussions with Sandinista officials about the country's economic direction. The Council of the Americas James Hammond, the group's leader, touched on the reasons: "The Sandinistas say they recognize their foreign debts and will try to pay them. They also intend to work with the market system, though with greater emphasis on joint state enterprises. They talk about limiting profits and remissions of earnings abroad, but the Junta says it welcomes foreign investment."[181] On one occasion, the delegation met with the three Sandinista National Directorate (DNC) members responsible for domestic affairs (Bayardo Arce, Henry Ruiz, Victor Tirado) who affirmed the revolution's com-

177 Department of State Telegram, Confidential Managua 3771.
178 Quoted in U.S. Congress, House, *Central America at the Crossroads*, p. 40.
179 Department of State Telegram, Managua 3667, American Embassy (O'Donnell for Pezzullo) to Secretary of State, August 11, 1979, Subject: "Oliva Tobacco Company," DFOIA.
180 Quoted in U.S. Congress, Senate, S.2012, p. 67.
181 Quoted in "Nicaragua: U.S. Business Visit Nicaragua," *This Week: Central America & Panama*, October 15, 1979, p. 318.

mitment to economic development and reconstruction in which the private sector and foreign investment had a role to play. "The FSLN members," in the words of Ambassador Pezzullo, "came across as confident, realistic, and pragmatic. The U.S. businessmen were surprised and impressed by the moderate tone of their views...."[182] By the end of the trip, the executives agreed that Nicaragua was, in James Hammond's words "definitely an undefined situation. We would have to keep looking at it and keep a finger on the pulse. They all appreciated the idea that it was important to establish contacts and build bridges so that future contacts could be made." But there were still few prospects of new investments at least "until the smoke clears in Nicaragua and political visibility improves."[183]

During 1980, Sandinista pragmatism in its dealings with the multinational business community was increasingly in evidence. First, except for the mining sector, foreign companies were excluded from the nationalization program. Additionally, the takeover of the predominantly Somoza-owned or controlled properties involved only a change in ownership; it did not lessen their traditional dependence on overseas capital, technology, and goods. Although the state assumed a greater role in the economy, the scarcity of funds, machinery, and skilled managerial and technical expertise provided new opportunities for American entrepreneurs to develop lucrative ties with this expanded public sector. Second, the regime entered into compensation discussions with the two affected U.S. enterprises that reached successful conclusions during 1982–83, and at no time during the extended negotiations did the mine owners see fit to badger the Carter (or Reagan) administration to apply diplomatic or economic pressure on Managua to wrest a satisfactory outcome.

Third, new foreign investment controls in the agricultural export sector were not always applied to the letter of the law, and on occasion were even revoked when targeted multinationals threatened retaliation that promised to seriously disrupt the nation's trade. One such case involved Nicaragua's major banana exporter, the Standard Fruit & Steamship unit owned by the Honolulu-based Castle & Cooke, which purchased approximately $24 million worth of bananas annually for sale abroad. In December 1980, the Ministry of Agriculture announced that all banana marketing and production functions were being taken over by the state. The American multinational indicated that Nicaragua risked losing a valuable source of foreign exchange if it implemented such a policy. In a show of strength, it forced the gov-

182 Department of State Telegram, Managua 4900, American Embassy (Pezzullo) to Secretary of State, October 11, 1979, Subject: "FSLN Views on the Economy and the Private Sector," DFOIA.

183 Interview with James Hammond; quoted in Nissen, "U.S. Firms in Nicaragua are Reopening, Despite Uncertainty of Regime's Politics," p. 16.

ernment to back down. "We diverted our banana boats," said Robert Cook, vice-president and chief financial officer. "We didn't go in there to pick up fruit for two weeks."[184] Instead of retaliating in kind, the Sandinistas, through Ambassador Pezzullo, offered to negotiate. Junta member Sergio Ramírez told the Ambassador that every effort would be made "to keep them here" less for economic than political reasons. United Fruit and other companies had expressed an interest in marketing the bananas but the government feared that "the political impact of Standard leaving at this juncture, in the face of a fragile economy and GRN [Government of National Reconstruction] efforts to attract private investment and maintain a positive international image, 'would be devastating.' "[185] The new five-year contract worked out between Agriculture Minister Jaime Wheelock and the company differed little, if at all, from the previous one negotiated with the Somoza regime.[186]

Fourth, the imperatives of increasing productivity and exports produced a shift in Sandinista labor policy away from legitimizing strikes, factory takeovers, and workplace demands to support for measures to contain union militancy (strikes) and a willingness to impose wage restraints. In the process, the regime became more involved in mediating and resolving labor-capital disputes. One of these involved the Texaco subsidiary, where in June 1980, after seven months of fruitless negotiations with the Union of Petro-chemical Workers, the employees suspended talks and occupied the plant (but kept it operating), demanding salary increases and participation in the management of the distributorship. Even American Embassy cables noted the persistent regime efforts to "control these labor disputes and strikes [by] appealing to the revolutionary duty of each worker to raise production and forego immediate salary increases in favor of the greater needs of Nicaragua."[187]

The pragmatic or "wait and see" approach displayed by a large majority of American and other foreign firms during the first twelve to eighteen

184 Quoted in "Castle & Cook Unit and Nicaragua Agree on Banana Production," *Wall Street Journal,* January 13, 1981, p. 16.
185 Department of State Telegram, Secret Managua 0103, American Embassy (Pezzullo) to Secretary of State, January 9, 1981, Subject: "(C) Conversation with Junta Member Sergio Ramírez," DFOIA.
186 Kenneth A. Rodman, *Hegemonic Decline, Multinational Corporations, and U.S. Economic Sanctions Since the Pipeline Case,* Paper presented to the annual conference of the American Political Science Association, Washington, D.C., September 1–4, 1988, p. 12.
187 Department of State Telegram, Managua 1093, American Embassy (O'Donnell) to Secretary of State, March 4, 1980, Subject: "(U) Labor Strife Continues – GRN Sends Mixed Signals," *DFOIA.* Also see Rodman, *Hegemonic Decline, Multinational Corporations, and U.S. Economic Sanctions Since the Pipeline Case,* p. 13; James E. Austin and John C. Ickis, "Management, Managers, and Revolution," *World Development,* Vol. 14, No. 7, July 1986, p. 783.

months of Sandinista rule was, nonetheless, accompanied by gloomier, more pessimistic, and occasionally hostile pronouncements from some sectors of the overseas business community. For a minority of American investors, the transition from a more or less unregulated economy to one in which the state assumed a greater control over the processes of capital accumulation was in itself an unacceptable development. "Somoza was a free trader," said one. "He allowed you to run your business the way you wanted to. The Sandinistas had their priorities and foreign investment wasn't one of them."[188] Bruce Cuthbertson, President of the American-Nicaraguan Chamber of Commerce and secretary-treasurer of a group of construction companies with majority Nicaraguan ownership, accused the Sandinistas of "pursuing an active policy to weaken and eliminate the private sector" by encouraging labor unions to make unreasonable demands and through the state's control of the financial system and foreign exchange earnings.[189] In his opinion, Washington was also partly to blame. Instead of the Carter administration "giving them money" in the hope "that would moderate their point of view," it should have either totally ruptured relations or pursued a strategy "that pressured them in some way. I think we could have changed them if we had pressured enough and pressured consistently. The only policy likely to work would have been a tough line immediately in order to moderate them."[190]

Opposition to the state's more intrusive role in the economy was also accompanied by a conviction that the government's sectoral nationalization of mainly locally owned properties was a harbinger of a major offensive against foreign enterprises along the lines of the Cuban revolution. They thought they were witnessing "a tremendous sense that the noose would tighten fast like Cuba" and that Nicaragua would experience "a more sophisticated rerun of the Cuban example."[191] These individuals and companies perceived a change process that was irreversible and for the worse. "When the nationalizations occurred," said Monsanto's Chad Engler, "you knew that any investment opportunities Nicaragua might have encouraged were gone." This, combined with the frictions created by the new economic controls and Sandinista demands for private sector concessions, explained the low level of new American investments:

188 Telephone interview with Chad Engler.
189 Quoted in A. Koffman O'Reilly, "Confidence Ebbs in C. America," *Journal of Commerce*, May 1, 1980, p. 1. Also see U.S. Congress, House, Committee on Foreign Affairs, Subcommittee on Inter-American Affairs, *Assessment of Conditions in Central America*, 96th Congress, 2nd Session, April 29 and May 20, 1980 (Washington, D.C.: U.S. Government Printing Office, 1980), pp. 24–27.
190 Telephone interview with Bruce Cuthbertson.
191 Interview with James Hammond; telephone interview with Bruce Cuthbertson.

The new government was out of money and was being forceful, saying it was sacrificing a lot and it thought we should do the same. For example, we should provide long term credits, carry our outstanding debt for 10 or 15 years, sell products [to the government] that year on 365 day terms, everything up front. The government purchased all the inputs and had price controls on anything produced in Nicaragua. The state controlled the prices and then looked at operations and only allowed 8 percent over total cost, so we couldn't control labor costs. It was a very tightly controlled economy, which had a strong impact on business.[192]

A handful of American enterprises suffered major property losses during the anti-dictatorial struggle and simply decided that the risks or costs of reviving their operations outweighed any prospective benefits. Bruce Cuthbertson recalled a meeting of the American-Nicaraguan Chamber of Commerce at the Intercontinental Hotel sometime between August and October 1979 attended by executives of "a lot of American businesses in Nicaragua. I remember speaking to the American Cynamid Company people whose $1.5 million laminated plastic sheets factory was totally destroyed and the question was should they rebuild it. Their concern was if they invested the money to rebuild would the atmosphere be stable enough to allow them to rebuild. They took eight months to decide no. American Standard and Quaker Oats also decided to do nothing."[193]

For some foreign companies, though, the decision to leave had little or nothing to do with Sandinista policy. Booth Fisheries, the local subsidiary of Consolidated Foods of Chicago, which exported between $14 and $16 million worth of shrimp to the United States annually, fell into this category. The parent company's decision to close down its Nicaraguan operations stemmed exclusively from events surrounding the arrest and imprisonment of its local manager because of his involvement in air attacks on Sandinista troops during the anti-Somoza struggle. The effort to get him released consumed headquarters' time and personnel way out of proportion to the corporation's $3.4 million investment stake. Once the U.S. Embassy finally convinced the government to free him, explained Deputy Chief of Mission Thomas O'Donnell, "the corporation said they had had it. They didn't have any problem with the Nicaraguan government but they were a multi-million organization and had the whole of the Chicago corporation management tied up for months over this. But there were more important problems than this."[194]

Still, most American multinationals operating in Nicaragua toward the

192 Telephone interview with Chad Engler.
193 Telephone interview with Bruce Cuthbertson.
194 Interview with Thomas O'Donnell.

end of 1980 expressed a measured confidence in the future direction of the government's economic policies. *Business Latin America* attributed their "cautious optimism" to three main factors: the shift from a "radically leftist" to a pragmatic approach to economic management; an end to references to property nationalizations in official statements; and the regime's decision to negotiate with the growers' associations over price supports for key agricultural crops.[195] The measure of confidence was not a function of any particular policy but derived from the perception of a regime committed to maintaining a substantial private sector, encouraging foreign investment, and retaining the country's traditional ties to the international capitalist economy.

Irrespective of government restrictions, bureaucratic disorganization, and the like, there were still substantial profits to be made from Nicaraguan trade and investment. A mid-1980 study prepared by the American Embassy catalogued the revolutionary regime's need for U.S. management skills, technical expertise, and agricultural and industrial products. Discussing the latter, it noted that apart from "normal imports of agricultural inputs and industrial raw materials, there is now a large market for spare parts and new agricultural and industrial machinery." Furthermore, the demand for construction equipment and materials, and basic foodstuffs like wheat and powdered milk, would remain at their current abnormally high levels until agricultural production returned to traditional pre-revolutionary levels.[196]

As 1980 drew to an end, the Sandinistas continued to extend a hand to the foreign investment community. Delegations from the Council of the Americas and the Inter-American Committee of the New York City Bar Association were invited by the JGRN to advise the government on a proposed new foreign investment law. Afterward, a member of one of these groups remarked that "all evidence indicated that the Nicaraguans are relatively pragmatic and willing to listen."[197] In early January 1981, junta member Sergio Ramírez told Ambassador Pezzullo that negotiations were proceeding with ASARCO, the American owners of the nationalized Neptune Mining Company, and Managua "was hopeful an agreement could be reached shortly, under which ASARCO would continue to operate the mines" based on a joint-venture arrangement.[198] Although the long-term direction of economic policy had not yet been clarified to the overwhelming satisfaction of many within the American business community, this early

195   "Nicaragua Gravitates to Moderate Course One Year After Upheaval," *Business Latin America*, August 6, 1980, p. 249.
196   U.S. Department of Commerce, International Trade Administration, *Foreign Economic Trends and Their Implications for the United States*, Prepared by the American Embassy, Managua, Nicaragua, June 1980, p. 7.
197   Quoted in Purcell, "The Perceptions and Interests of U.S. Business in Relation to the Political Crisis in Central America," p. 107.
198   Department of State Telegram, Secret Managua 0103.

period of Sandinista rule nonetheless witnessed a substantial growth in the total U.S. investment stake (from $121 million in 1978 to $160 million at the end of June 1980[199]) – a partial acknowledgement of the revolution's economic "pragmatism."

The response of U.S. banks

During the 1970s, the Nicaraguan economy was severely buffeted by rising oil import costs, falling export prices, contracting markets, and two global recessions. To offset these economic setbacks, Somoza resorted to large-scale overseas borrowings, especially from private banks. Despite more onerous terms and scaled back exposure by a few banks, most notably Citibank (down from $128 million in mid-1977 to around $90 million at the time of Somoza's ouster[200]) the regime was able to obtain substantial amounts of new capital from these sources during its final years.

When the Sandinistas achieved political power in July 1979, they inherited a $1.6 billion foreign debt, the bulk of which was owed to these multinational financial institutions. Of the $618 million in principal and interest payments due before the end of 1979, $444 million was owed to the foreign private banks, with American banks accounting for approximately three-quarters of this amount.[201] Washington and the international banking community both viewed the new Nicaraguan government's attitude toward public and private debt rescheduling as a critical indicator of its willingness to maintain the country's traditional links with the capitalist world economy. Ambassador Pezzullo lobbied the Sandinistas hard on this point. Discussing "the importance of early contacts with the financial communities in the U.S. and Europe" with junta members in mid-August, he strongly advised "that a responsible businesslike image presented to the financial communities in New York and London would do much to restore the confidence of the international banking community in the new GRN [Government of National

---

199 See Purcell, "The Perceptions and Interests of U.S. Business in Relation to the Political Crisis in Central America," p. 114; *New York Times*, July 9, 1980, p. 10; Tom Barry, Beth Wood, and Deb Preusch, *Dollars and Dictators* (New York: Grove Press, 1983), p. 250.

200 Telephone interview with Onofre Torres, Florida, October 4, 1989.

201 See Alan Riding, "Nicaragua Tries Economic Cure," *New York Times*, November 27, 1979, p. D1. Most of the rest of the total ($126.5 million) was owed to the multilateral development banks. Ibid. The biggest U.S. bank lenders were Citibank ($52 million), Bank of America ($38 million), First National Bank of Chicago ($35 million), Wells Fargo Bank ($22 million), and American Express ($17 million). *Facts on File*, October 5, 1979, p. 753.

Reconstruction]."[202] The overwhelming message to Managua was that the level of new foreign funding hinged on the attitude adopted toward its creditor banks and governments.

Tracking the evolving relationship between the U.S. private banks and the revolutionary regime not only offers insights into the former's investment policies but also into the nature of bankers' ties to Washington policymakers.

On September 14, 1979, Deputy Assistant Secretary of State Charles Meissner held separate meetings with First National Bank of Chicago's "Latin American trouble-shooter" Stephen Thomas and Citibank Vice President Richard Valelly to discuss Nicaragua's financial plight. Burdened by relatively large foreign debt obligations on the one hand and likely to receive only modest amounts of external funding on the other, it was obvious to the administration "that the public sector would not, of itself, be able to provide financial stability nor the resources necessary to improve the economic situation of the middle class and business class in Nicaragua." In this circumstance, Meissner told the bankers, the position taken by their institutions would be "extremely important" in facilitating Washington's efforts to "reestablish political stability" and avoid the growth of a "leftist dictatorship."[203]

While enlisting the banks' support for the goal of moving the Sandinistas "to the political center," American officials simultaneously took advantage of every opportunity to "push Nicaragua to negotiate its private debt."[204] During a September 25 White House meeting attended by Daniel Ortega, Alfonso Robelo, and Sergio Ramírez, most of the discussion centered around Nicaragua's debt problems, and at one point "the President emphasized to them [the Junta members] the importance of dealing with the IMF and the banks."[205] In October, prior to a meeting between Sandinista government officials and a group of prominent American bankers and busi-

202 Department of State Telegram, Confidential Managua 3443, American Embassy (Pezzullo) to Secretary of State, August 12, 1979, Subject: "(C) Credentials Ceremony Conversations with Junta – Economic Topics," DFOIA.

203 Department of State, Memorandum of Conversation, Confidential, September 14, 1979, Subject: "Nicaragua and the Private Banks," Participants: Deputy Assistant Secretary Charles Meissner, First National Bank of Chicago Vice-President Stephen Thomas, DFOIA; Department of State, Memorandum of Conversation, Confidential, September 14, 1979, Subject: "Nicaragua and the Private Banks," Participants: Deputy Assistant Secretary Charles Meissner, Citibank N.A. Vice-President Richard Valelly, DFOIA.

204 Interview with John Bushnell.

205 Telephone interview with Henry Owen, Washington, D.C., October 2, 1989. The respondent was a senior foreign economic policy official in the Carter White House. Also see John M. Goshko, "Three From Nicaragua Get Red-Carpet Welcome Here," *Washington Post*, September 25, 1979, p. A6 U.S. pressure on the Sandinista government to negotiate with the IMF is discussed in Pastor, *Condemned to Repetition*, pp. 206–207.

ness executives, Ambassador Pezzullo cabled the State Department that this was a timely moment for the Embassy, as well as the bankers in the delegation, to drive home "the importance to the GRN [Government of National Reconstruction] of dialogue with creditor banks...."[206]

Within the revolutionary regime and the American overseas banking fraternity, the predominant sentiment favored an amicable settlement of the debt issue. The Bank of America and Citibank (the two largest private bank claimants) said they would approach any negotiations with a flexible and pragmatic attitude. Vice-President William Rhodes spoke of Citibank's prior experience with Third World "rescue operations," most recently in Peru and Jamaica, at a meeting with U.S. Embassy officials, and could foresee no major problem in the case of Nicaragua with one proviso: "[The banks] have to know the rules of the game." But one potential stumbling block was the banks' enthusiasm for International Monetary Fund (IMF) involvement in such negotiations, given the latter's historic relationship with Somoza. "[The banks] are willing to accept something that the GRN [Government of National Reconstruction] can live with," said Rhodes, "but feel that international institutions must also participate such as [the] IBRD [Inter-American Development Bank], and IMF or it would not stand up."[207]

Initial Sandinista pronouncements about the foreign debt were not totally devoid of the kind of ambiguous statements guaranteed to produce some unease among creditor banks. Speaking before the United Nations General Assembly in late September, Daniel Ortega, the head of the JGRN and DNC member, proposed that the international community, in particular those nations "who supported Somoza with [public and private] credits," should assume responsibility for Nicaragua's debt. Quick to allay any fears of a possible default, JGRN member Alfonso Robelo issued a clarifying statement to the effect that the government had no intention of repudiating its debt obligations. He downplayed Ortega's comments as political rhetoric to highlight the country's parlous economic situation. The government formally announced it would honor all old foreign debts with the exception of monies owed to Argentina and Israel for arms purchases made by the Somoza dictatorship. An American banker observed at the time that a comprehensive debt disavowal would have instantly turned Nicaragua into a global economic pariah: "Any unilateral cancellation would not only destroy Nicaragua's credit standing with the private banks but would also dry up

206 Department of State Telegram, Confidential Managua 4872, American Embassy (Pezzullo) to Secretary of State, October 9, 1979, Subject: "Nicaragua Official Debt Rescheduling," DFOIA.
207 Department of State Telegram, Managua 3778. Also see Department of State Telegram, Confidential Managua 3771.

loan sources in the international finance institutions, such as the IMF, the World Bank and the Inter-American Development Bank."[208]

Among the foreign banks with exposure in Nicaragua, there was no consensus about what the Sandinistas might do. Richard Weinert, the American investment banker advising the Nicaraguan government on the debt negotiations, found a very tense and uneasy group of bankers contemplating the possibility of a "worst case scenario":

> They were terrified, terrified, very concerned about the possibilities of debt repudiation. This was partly because this was a revolutionary government self-described and other revolutions have disavowed their foreign debts and there was a fear that Nicaragua would too. Second, there was concern because many of the banks had been involved in questionable dealings and were concerned that that would also provide justification for repudiation. They were also very concerned about the precedent that anything they did in Nicaragua would have for other debt negotiations with Third World governments in similar situations.[209]

Some bankers' belief that the Sandinistas "would go the way of Cuba in 1959 and repudiate all foreign loans incurred by the previous regime" was reinforced by skepticism over the capacity of a war-devastated economy to recover sufficiently to enable the regime to repay past debts. Doubts were voiced about how "serious" the Sandinistas were in wanting to renegotiate their foreign debt. A number of the creditor banks were "very surprised" when Nicaragua announced its desire to begin talks.[210] Swiss Bank's Tony Spicijaric attributed the JGRN decision to abide by tradition to the "non-Sandinista economic officials in the government who influenced the process."[211] Whatever the reason, it was termed a "good sign" by one U.S. banker because it signaled an acceptance of the country's debt obligations "which means that they're not opting out of the Western economy."[212]

208 All quotes in "Nicaragua: Talk Now, Explain Later," *This Week: Central America & Panama*, October 8, 1979, pp. 306, 308.

209 Interview with Richard Weinert, Washington, D.C., September 26, 1989. The respondent was hired by Nicaraguan Minister for Reconstruction Alfredo César in December 1979 to advise the Sandinista government on debt negotiations with the country's private foreign creditor banks.

210 Quoted in "Nicaraguan Debt Accord Offers Promising Signs of Government's Course," *Business Latin America*, October 29, 1979, p. 351; Purcell, "The Perceptions and Interests of U.S. Business in Relation to the Political Crisis in Central America," p. 108.

211 Telephone interview with Tony Spicijaric, New York, October 3, 1989. The respondent is an executive with Swiss Bank Corporation which had the largest exposure of any European bank in Somoza's Nicaragua. He was a participant in the 1979–1980 Nicaraguan debt negotiations.

212 Quoted in Alan Riding, "Nicaragua Debt Talks Are Opened," *New York Times*, December 15, 1979, p. 35.

In mid-December 1979, representatives of seventy-two creditor banks and the Nicaraguan government's senior economic officials (Head of the International Reconstruction Fund Alfredo César, Minister of Finance Joaquín Cuadra, Minister of Planning Roberto Mayorga, and Central Bank President Arturo Cruz) assembled in Mexico City for the inaugural round of negotiations. Arturo Cruz summarized the Nicaraguan team's message to the bankers: "[Nicaragua] wanted to renegotiate, but there was one basic thing they had to take into account: the country's economic reality."[213] Alfredo César's main presentation was generally well-received, notwithstanding his announcement that the government would be unable to make interest payments on $1.26 billion of its total external debt during 1980 and 1981. Said one prominent creditor bank executive: "It was quite an impressive performance...their presentation was realistic and thorough, there was almost no revolutionary rhetoric, and they showed that they are ready, even anxious, to sit down and negotiate."[214] But there was still a residue of mistrust about the Sandinista's real intentions: "Some banks were concerned about whether Nicaragua was going to recognize its debt obligations and were somewhat skeptical whether they were for real."[215]

At Mexico City, the creditor banks established a twelve-member steering committee (eight of whom were American, including Citibank, Bank of America, First National Bank of Chicago, and Wells Fargo Bank) to conduct future negotiations with the Nicaraguans on behalf of all the participating institutions. There were banks represented on the committee "willing to sign anything" to avoid drawn-out bargaining, which they feared might precipitate a Sandinista walkout; others, led by Citibank, insisted on repayment of all loans and past-due interest, and Nicaragua's acceptance of standard commercial terms for any new loans.[216] A Citibank official who had helped run the Managua branch between 1977 and 1979 explained the rationale for headquarters' "hardline" approach: "We were there to do business and if they [the Sandinistas] wanted to posture don't waste our time. The tough stance was sending a message to the Nicaraguan government to get serious."[217]

Mexico City sharply focused the basic contours of the debate: Nicaragua wanted debt repayments linked to the country's "ability to pay"; the banks were united in demanding acknowledgment of the principle and practice of

213 Quoted in Steve Downer, "Nicaragua: The Recovery is Only Just Beginning," *Euromoney*, December 1980, p. 129.
214 Quoted in "Nicaragua: Taking on the Debt," *This Week: Central America & Panama*, December 24, 1979, p. 395.
215 Interview with Richard Weinert.
216 Steering Committee member, quoted in Purcell, "The Perceptions and Interests of U.S. Business in Relation to the Political Crisis in Central America," p. 107.
217 Telephone interview with William Dewey, Florida, October 17, 1988.

commercial loan interest rates. According to a Citibank official, the debtor provoked a near crisis when it proposed "a fixed interest rate of 7 percent and 30 years to pay or something like that. The banks were absolutely shocked. No country had ever laid down lending conditions before."[218] The creditors' steering committee was determined to avoid any precedent setting arrangement with the Sandinistas that questioned the inviolability of standard commercial rates. The Nicaraguan delegation was left under no illusion that a refusal to concede on this issue would have devastating consequences for the government's ability to obtain new loans and credits, not just from private banks but also from multilateral development institutions and foreign governments.[219] Although all indications pointed to very difficult and extended negotiations, most participants returned from this opening session in an optimistic frame of mind. Reports filtering back to the American Embassy in Managua said "the meeting in Mexico City went very well and the presentation made by the GRN [Government of National Reconstruction] was thoughtful and professional."[220]

Although the steering committee members were initially divided over Sandinista intentions, they agreed on the need "to maintain a united front. As a negotiating strategy they didn't want to reveal divisions." But this public appearance of unity masked divergent outlooks, which Richard Weinert attributed to individual banks' financial strength or the nature of their exposure in Nicaragua during the Somoza period:

> There were "clean" banks and "dirty" banks in the sense of banks that had done business in Nicaragua but had stayed away from corrupt practices and other banks deeply involved in payoffs, etc. The "clean" banks included Citibank, Manufacturers Hanover, and Bankers Trust. The "dirty" banks included First National of Chicago. It is probably more accurate to divide them into financially stronger (mostly "cleaner") and the financially weaker (more "dirty") banks. This was probably the most important division. The weaker tended to be less aggressive in the debt negotiations. At the same time, Manufacturers Hanover which was one of the cleanest of the banks and didn't lend to the government or to Somoza was one of the more accommodating, softer-line banks on debt policy matters because it was in a very weak financial position.[221]

218 Telephone interview with Onofre Torres.
219 See "Nicaragua Makes Peace with Bankers over Somoza's Unpaid Debts," *Latin America Weekly Report*, September 12, 1980, p. 1; "Nicaraguan Debt Accord Offers Promising Signs of Government's Course," p. 350.
220 Department of State Telegram, Managua 6173, American Embassy (Pezzullo) to Secretary of State, December 20, 1979, Subject: "GRN Has First Meeting on Rescheduling of the Private Bank Debt," DFOIA.
221 Interview with Richard Weinert.

The mood of the bankers turned more pessimistic after the January and March 1980 discussions between the committee and Nicaraguan officials failed to make much headway. Ambassador Pezzullo reported that the March meetings "were cordial but the positions of the two sides remain far apart on everything from interest rates to IMF participation."[222] However, one ray of hope was a Nicaraguan proposal to repay $490 million of the outstanding debt, a figure based on what Alfredo César termed "economic limitations" likely to persist until at least 1991. The steering committee "neither accepted nor rejected" the submission but promised a response when the delegations reconvened in Mexico City in late April.[223]

The nub of the problem remained that of narrowing the veritable chasm between the rescheduling proposals each side put forward at the start of the negotiations. The banks sought repayment of all debts over a 7-year period (plus 2-3 years grace) and past due interest ("commercial terms"); Managua proposed a 25-year repayment period, capitalization of all past due interest, and the deferral of all interest payments without interest. Some creditor bank executives began to express doubts over Managua's ability or willingness to meet its financial obligations. "Until the debt renegotiation efforts produce some results," announced one, "credit lines to Nicaragua are being held in abeyance. We are not making any new money available to Nicaragua and are doing our best to reduce our exposure through existing credit lines to manageable levels."[224] Between June 1979 and June 1980, the total exposure of eight of the largest U.S. banks declined from $265.9 million to $221.8 million.[225]

Although both sides remained at odds over a starting date for the resumption of interest payments, a more serious sticking point was what, if any, role the IMF should play in shaping Nicaragua's economic reconstruction agenda. The creditor banks set a relatively high priority on an IMF "seal of approval" and pressured the Sandinistas to negotiate with the Fund for an austerity stabilization loan. This insistence was traceable to the problems a number of them encountered following a 1976 decision to restructure Peru's foreign debt without forcing a resistant military government to first negotiate a Fund loan: "The lesson the banks [the majority of whom had exposure in Nicaragua], and especially [the second] steering committee

222   Department of State Telegram, Confidential Managua 1465, American Embassy (Pezzullo) to Secretary of State, March 27, 1980, Subject: "GRN, Foreign Bankers Meet to Discuss Debt Rescheduling," DFOIA.
223   Quoted in "Nicaragua: Payment Plan is Big Secret," *This Week: Central America & Panama*, March 31, 1980, p. 102.
224   Quoted in A. Koffman O'Reilly, "Nicaragua Debt Talks to Resume," *Journal of Commerce*, May 9, 1980, p. 10.
225   Purcell, "The Perceptions and Interests of U.S. Business in Relation to the Political Crisis in Central America," p. 114.

chairman William Rhodes of Citibank, learnt from the Peruvian experience of 1976 was that they should rely on the IMF more and more in this kind of process."[226]

To the Sandinistas, however, the conditions attached to such loans (public spending cutbacks, wage and salary reductions, lifting of price controls, and so on) prefigured unacceptable economic as well as political consequences. Typically, the burden of IMF austerity measures fell most heavily on those groups or classes in society (workers, urban poor, peasants) that constituted the revolutionary regime's major social base of support.[227] Moreover, Fund lending to Somoza, not least the May 1979 multi-million dollar loan, had generated "enormous resentment and hatred among the Sandinistas," such that "the idea of doing something with the IMF under any circumstances was not a politically discussible subject."[228] Although the new regime indicated it would remain a member of the institution in good standing and scrupulously maintained the country's schedule of quota payments, there was no thought "at this stage" [of] "get[ting] involved in an [IMF] austerity program."[229] Thus when the banks again floated this option at the March round of talks, Alfredo César answered that his government was "not willing to meet" the Fund's loan conditionality requirements.[230]

The failure to achieve a rapid settlement not only exacerbated tensions between the bankers and Managua but also within the steering committee itself. The most exposed institution, Citibank (owed approximately $80 million) voiced increasing frustration over what it perceived as a lack of dynamic and aggressive leadership:

> Initially, First National Bank of Chicago's Steve Thomas headed the committee. Citibank felt that because Steve continued to run First Chicago's large Mexico City regional office (with its $750 million plus portfolio), he was not as available as Bill Rhodes [Citibank Vice-President and committee representative] felt he should be and didn't take upon himself the leadership mantle aggressively enough. Citibank

---

226 Interview with Richard Weinert. For a discussion of the Peruvian debt negotiations, see Barbara Stallings, "Peru and the U.S. Banks: Privatization of Financial Relations," in Richard R. Fagen, ed., *Capitalism and the State in U.S.-Latin American Relations* (Stanford: Stanford University Press, 1979), pp. 237–240.

227 On the impact of IMF "stabilization" loans, see James Petras and Howard Brill, "The IMF, Austerity and the State in Latin America," *Third World Quarterly*, Vol. 8, No. 2, April 1986, pp. 425–448.

228 Interview with Richard Weinert.

229 Quoted in William Chislett, "Banks in Nicaragua Debt Talks," *Financial Times*, March 18, 1980, p. 27.

230 Quoted in "Nicaragua: Payment Plan is Big Secret," p. 102.

wanted a group of people on the steering committee who would do nothing else but this.[231]

Thomas was subsequently replaced by Citibank's William Rhodes, a shift one participant in the talks claimed had more to do with major financial losses sustained by First National than anything else: "Shortly after negotiations started, First National was reporting great losses and Steven Thomas was eventually removed from the chair of the steering committee because of this weakness."[232]

But unity continued to remain the byword among committee members. Tony Spicijaric of Swiss Bank, the largest European creditor, stressed that "everybody wanted the best rescheduling" at the same time as "there was still a lot of distrust of the Nicaraguans' intentions, what they were doing, and whether they really wanted to negotiate with the banks and not simply hold discussions for public relations reasons only." He rejected suggestions that Citibank was demanding the harshest possible settlement terms: It was "not the most hardline institution but was simply setting the tone. All of the banks were more or less on the same wavelength so that when differences did arise within the committee it was easy to reach a consensus."[233] And on one issue there was never any inkling of a split: Any Sandinista refusal to accept a "commercial solution" would trigger the breakup of the steering committee and the collapse of negotiations.[234]

Although the negotiations appeared to have more or less stalled over a range of issues, Alfredo César described the fourth meeting "as cordial and positive as progress was made in narrowing differences,"[235] In a cable to the State Department at the end of May, the Embassy's DCM Thomas O'Donnell wrote that "there appears to be a generally favorable disposition in the GRN [Government of National Reconstruction] to work out an agreement with the banks and get the negotiation behind them." At the same time, he expected the negotiations to "go on for several months yet" simply because the JGRN has all along proceeded in a careful and deliberate fashion, refusing to allow itself to "be rushed on this...."[236] All along, the Sandinistas received encouragement and support from their closest regional allies, notably Cuba, to reach a solution if possible. At the first anniversary

231 Telephone interview with William Dewey.
232 Interview with Richard Weinert.
233 Telephone interview with Tony Spicijaric.
234 See Terri Shaw, "Cuba's Debt Mistakes: A Lesson for Nicaragua," *Washington Post*, October 5, 1980, p. G7.
235 Department of State Telegram, Confidential Managua 2541, American Embassy (O'Donnell) to Secretary of State, May 30, 1980, Subject: "Rescheduling Negotiations," DFOIA.
236 Ibid.

celebrations in Managua, Fidel Castro told William Rhodes "that Cuba had made a mistake breaking off financial relationships with the rest of the world and has advised Nicaragua to honor its foreign debts."[237] Nor were the banks themselves any less committed to a rescheduling agreement. As Richard Weinert cogently put it, each side had its own reason for desiring a satisfactory outcome: "The Sandinistas were saying they wanted to make peace with the international financial community and be integrated into the Western system. The banks wanted to prove that they were able to relate to Third World countries in difficulties and to do so without betraying commercial principles."[238]

In July 1980, as the negotiations sputtered along with no end in sight, representatives of a small number of the creditor banks attended an informal luncheon in New York City with Nicaraguan Foreign Minister Joaquín Cuadra to hear a new Sandinista proposal aimed at addressing the banks' refusal to budge on "the so-called Tranche D capitalization of interest" and the "Nicaraguans saying they cannot pay interest at all and that the banks had to capitalize everything."[239] Nicaragua would "recognize" a commercial rate of interest if the credit institutions would accept part payment of the past-due interest and capitalize the rest until some future specified time period. The bankers expressed interest and agreed to refer the proposal to the whole steering committee. A group of U.S. banks on the committee termed it "an interesting idea but one that wouldn't work because it would violate accounting and regulatory principles."[240]

The Nicaraguan team went to Mexico City on July 22 for the fifth round of talks "with high expectations that a basic agreement would finally be reached...." Since April, Alfredo César and JGRN member Arturo Cruz "had worked hard to convince the [JGRN and the DNC] to agree to pay commercial rates" in return for a debt rescheduling.[241] César also "saw good signs on the part of the banks to try to understand Nicaraguan economic reality and the payment capacity of the revolution."[242] Once discussions got under way, it was evident that such optimism was misplaced, at least temporarily.

The Nicaraguans proposed a rescheduling based on a gradually rising

237 James L. Rowe Jr. and Caroline Atkinson, "Citibank's Superman Juggles Latin-American Loans," *Washington Post*, August 21, 1983, p. F4.
238 Interview with Richard Weinert.
239 Telephone interview with Tony Spicijaric.
240 Interview with Richard Weinert.
241 Department of State Telegram, Confidential Managua 3681, American Embassy (Pezzullo) to Secretary of State, August 5, 1980, Subject: "(U) GRN Debt Negotiations with Private Bankers," DFOIA.
242 Department of State Telegram, Managua 3347, American Embassy (Pezzullo) to Secretary of State, July 17, 1980, Subject: "GRN Debt Rescheduling," DFOIA.

interest rate, payments spread over 10 to 12 years, capitalization of part of
the interest due, and the relending of approximately half the payments to
the government at commercial interest rates. The "hard line" banks were
unimpressed: They apparently wanted to re-lend less than half while insisting on a large "up front" payment by Managua at the time an accord
was signed.[243] Citibank also pushed the Sandinistas to agree to annual debt
service payments equivalent to 30 percent of export revenues, ignoring the
pleas of César and the other "moderate" ministers that any figure in excess
of 15 percent would jeopardize the economic recovery effort. Finally, the
banks were decidedly cool to the capitalization of interest idea. The Nicaraguans argued they were asking for no more than what many of these same
banks had offered the Chrysler Corporation in recently completed debt
restructuring negotiations. Some 400 U.S. banks, including the largest New
York-based institutions, agreed to renegotiate a $4.4 billion debt using a
formula that "included the capitalization of interest for a while." On that
note, said Richard Weinert, the discussions "broke down."[244]

An exasperated César accused Citibank and two other banks of inflexible
negotiating postures and "holding out to squeeze more out of Nicaragua
than it could afford to pay. . . . " American Embassy officials agreed. " . . .
our perception here," wrote Ambassador Pezzullo, "is that the GRN [Gov-
ernment of National Reconstruction] offer is reasonable and that Nicaragua's economic outlook at this point does not leave much room for carrying
a heavier burden of debt payments."[245]

Not long after the conclusion of the fifth round, the steering committee
decided to reconsider the capitalization of interest proposal. The resulting
debate exposed lots of disagreement "over whether to do it and how to do
it, and over how long to reschedule interest payments for. Our first proposal
to the Nicaraguans was that they should pay ten percent and everything that
accrues over ten percent should be capitalized. Nicaragua countered with
five percent and five percent. Then we reached an agreement on seven
percent." The negotiations over the rescheduling of interest payments involved just as much give and take. The banks ultimately agreed on 12 years
"although a number of banks wanted six or seven or eight years."[246]

In early September, both sides tentatively agreed to renegotiate $582

243 Department of State Telegram, Confidential Managua 3681.
244 Interview with Richard Weinert. The Chrysler Corporation negotiations are discussed
     in Reginald Stuart, "Debt Restructuring for Chrysler is Set," *New York Times*, June 21,
     1980, pp. 1, 38.
245 Department of State Telegram, Confidential Managua 3681. Also see "Nicaragua: For-
     eign Debt Talks Run Aground," *Latin America Regional Reports: Mexico & Central America*,
     August 15, 1980, p. 5; "Nicaragua: Banks Hold Out for Tough Terms in Debt Nego-
     tiations," *Latin America Weekly Report*, August 15, 1980, p. 3.
246 Telephone interview with Tony Spicijaric.

million in principal and interest payments (over 60 percent of which was held by American banks, the rest divided among Canadian, British, European, and Japanese financial institutions). All creditor banks had to approve the accord by December 15 for it to take effect.[247]

The compact was the result of nine months of negotiations and eight formal sessions. To achieve it, the Sandinistas accepted a 12 (instead of a proposed 25) year period for repayment of the debt plus five years grace on the principal, agreed to recognize debt interest that accrued during the Somoza period, dropped the distinction between "good" and "bad" loans, and accepted responsibility for the entire private debt as well as all past-due interest, relented on the bank's demand for acceptance of commercial, as distinct from fixed, interest rates, and acquiesced to the banks' request for a $20 million past-interest payment on December 15 (approximately 20 percent of the overdue interest). Most banks had received no payments for at least 18 months. Citibank's William Rhodes, a major player in the final negotiations, commented: "We were very insistent on that [last] point."[248]

In return, the creditor banks agreed to what was still an exceedingly generous payments schedule (12 years) by Third World debt negotiating standards. This was accompanied by two concessions that were precedent-setting: the deferral of interest payments (half would not fall due before 1990); and an agreement to capitalize most of the past-due interest rather than insist on the traditional procedure of payment at the time of signing. The banks made these decisions with the greatest of reluctance. "We decided to accept the seven percent fixed interest rate," said one creditor bank participant, "but it was hard to swallow. The final deal was that they would pay a fixed rate of seven percent plus libor and a floating rate above seven percent, the difference to be capitalized. The banks had never done that before. We didn't like it. Nobody liked it."[249] Finally, the private creditors bowed to Nicaragua's refusal to involve the IMF, apparently concluding that the Sandinistas were unmoveable on this point and that it was not so important an objective that it should be allowed to undermine the possibility of a settlement. In Richard Weinert's words: "The banks perceived correctly that there would be no agreement if they continued to insist on an IMF standby, so they backed off."[250]

The bankers support for this compromise solution derived from shifting

247 See Ann Crittenden, "Nicaragua Renews Debt, Gaining 'Lenient' Terms," *New York Times*, September 9, 1980, p. D9.
248 Quoted in Downer, "Nicaragua: The Recovery is Only Just Beginning," p. 129.
249 Confidential telephone interview, Citibank executive, New York, September 18, 1989. The respondent was a participant in the 1979–80 Nicaraguan debt negotiations.
250 Interview with Richard Weinert.

perceptions of the Sandinistas' intentions and authority. They eventually realized that the revolutionaries were determined to negotiate an agreement, were willing to be flexible and pragmatic (make concessions) in order to reach that goal, and were firmly in control of political and state power. Of course, the fact that negotiations were conducted with the regime's pro-capitalist economic ministers helped immeasurably. An involved Citibank official went so far as to say that "if they didn't have Arturo Cruz and Alfredo César we would never have moved."[251] To another U.S. banker, they were an effective counterweight to any thought of debt default within the FSLN leadership: "Some members of the Sandinista Front felt the Cuban role on repudiation might have been the right way but the technical people were in favor of the traditional way."[252] The steering committee also conceded the uniqueness of Managua's case – the combination of a war-devastated economy and a regime with broad-based, cross-class support. Moreover, the risks of a debt default "were weighted more heavily [especially by the American banks] than the risks of accepting a precedent in a clearly exceptional case." Utilizing the "exceptional case" argument, they believed "that they could hold the line" against other Third World debtors regarding the special interest payment concessions offered the Nicaraguans.[253] Finally, Swiss Bank's Tony Spicijaric emphasized the creditor institutions "wanted a deal. We all wanted that Nicaragua resume payment of interest before the end of 1980. Some banks were desperate to get payment of interest restored by the end of 1980. We were also eager to get into the second and third round of debts."[254]

Although a minority view among the creditor banks held that the Sandinistas' debt rescheduling was based on "very lenient" terms, First National Bank of Chicago's Stephen Thomas expressed the most widely held sentiment: "The Nicaraguans have made a sacrifice, there is no doubt about it, with regard to paying commercial rates."[255] Richard Weinert termed the

251 Confidential telephone interview, Citibank executive, September 18, 1989.
252 Quoted in Shaw, "Cuba's Debt Mistakes: A Lesson for Nicaragua," p. G7.
253 Rodman, *Hegemonic Decline, Multinational Corporations, and U.S. Economic Sanctions Since the Pipeline Case*, p. 11. The American private banks with exposure in Nicaragua were particularly concerned to avoid any possibility of a debt default. For this reason, a number of them individually lobbied Congress to pass the administration's $75 million economic aid package for Nicaragua in the belief that a favorable vote would indicate U.S. government confidence in the stability of the Sandinista regime. Defeat of the legislation was viewed as having the potential to undermine the debt negotiation process. Many foreign bankers were confident that passage of the aid request would release as much as $500 million in multilateral development bank assistance. Remarked one London banker: "With a yes vote from the U.S. world money ought almost to pour in to Nicaragua." Quoted in Beth Nissen, "Nicaragua Aid Victory in House Hailed by State Department but Others Skeptical," *Wall Street Journal*, February 29, 1980, p. 25.
254 Telephone interview with Tony Spicijaric.
255 Richard M. Bliss, chairman, American Express International Banking Corporation,

final outcome for his client "a good deal for both sides. Nicaragua gets five good years to rebuild the economy.... The banks got a complete recognition of the debt and agreement to pay a commercial rate of interest."[256] Senior Carter policymakers also welcomed the agreement. Assistant Secretary of State Viron Vaky wrote that it "locked Nicaragua into the private money market, and that Nicaragua's willingness to do so was a significant move toward a pragmatic, pluralist course."[257]

The creditor banks were subjected to a good deal of "subtle pressure" from Washington, other Western capitals, and the Inter-American Development Bank to reach an agreement based on Nicaragua's unique problems. Much of the pressure carried with it the implied threat that they risked "isolat[ion]...had they taken an uncompromising stand."[258] Throughout the course of negotiations, the U.S. government maintained close contact with the steering committee, encouraging it to pursue a strategy similar to the approach being taken in dealing with that part of Nicaragua's debt owed to American public agencies. Deputy Assistant Secretary of State John Bushnell played a key role in keeping the bankers appraised of the administration's preferred approach:

> On three occasions, I held talks with William Rhodes and the negotiating team of the private banks and told them they need to play the same game we did. They didn't want to lend new money to Nicaragua. We told the banks that we supported a favorable deal but that it had to be regularized. The gist of what I told the steering committee was this: I explained our policy – insisting on the principles but then being very liberal. Given the nature of the Nicaraguan economy, I thought their best tactic should be similar – refuse to forgive the debt and violate principle, and within that contract be as liberal as the public creditors.[259]

The NSC's Robert Pastor likewise remembered "speaking to one of the American bankers and telling them to be as flexible as possible."[260]

On December 15, 1980, representatives of 182 foreign private banks and the Nicaraguan government rescheduled payment on $492 million in debt principle and approximately $100 million in past-due interest. The

quoted in Crittenden, "Nicaragua Renews Debt, Gaining "Lenient" Terms," p. D1; Steven Thomas, quoted in Downer, "Nicaragua: The Recovery is Only Just Beginning," p. 129.

256 Richard Weinert, quoted in Terri Shaw, "Cuba's Debt Mistakes: A Lesson for Nicaragua," *Washington Post*, October 5, 1980, p. G7.
257 Vaky, "Hemispheric Relations: 'Everything is Part of Everything Else,' " p. 621.
258 Richard S. Weinert, "Nicaragua's Debt Renegotiation," *Cambridge Journal of Economics*, Vol. 5, No. 2, June 1981, p. 193.
259 Interview with John Bushnell.
260 Telephone Interview with Robert Pastor, Georgia, October 5, 1989.

bankers received their promised $20 million in "up front" interest pay-
ments, and Washington seemed reassured that the Sandinistas were not
intent on rupturing the country's historic links to the international capitalist
economy.[261]

The successful debt restructuring, however, did not induce the multinational banking community to offer substantial new lines of credit to the
economically hard-pressed Nicaraguan regime. According to a representative of one creditor bank, potential lenders were holding off until Managua
reached a settlement of its "second category" commercial debt: loans contracted by Somoza-owned companies and local banks that had been nationalized, and loans contracted by other private businesses (insurance firms,
manufacturing enterprises, and so on). These debts were estimated at $200–
250 million.[262]

In reality, though, the banks had little or no intention of increasing their
loan exposure in Nicaragua. They still remained enormously distrustful of
the new regime, including its willingness to stand by commitments given.
Tony Spicijaric explained: "We were telling the Nicaraguans that it was
in their interest to strike a deal with the banks, that it would open up
flows to Nicaragua which never eventuated. In fact, the banks had no trust
in what they were doing. They were not convinced that the Nicaraguans
would honor the agreement they had reached."[263] A number of American
banks privately confided to State's John Bushnell that "they were not
prepared to give new money to Nicaragua because their policy was not
to lend to Communist governments and in their view that is what the
Nicaraguan government was."[264] Employing more diplomatic language, a
Citibank official justified this stance on the grounds that the situation
"kept deteriorating politically."[265] Not surprisingly, the Central American
country was soon transformed into a net exporter of capital to these
institutions: between July 1979 and July 1983, new loans totaled a paltry
$11 million, debt interest payments a massive (for a small, resource poor
economy) $160 million.[266]

---

261 See Juan de Onis, "Lenders Now Consider Nicaragua a Good Risk," *New York Times*,
     December 25, 1980, pp. 35, 39; Terri Shaw, "Nicaragua's Sandinistas Adopt Reassuring
     Stance," *Washington Post*, December 28, 1980, p. G1; "Nicaragua: Government Signs
     Debt Accord," *This Week: Central America & Panama*, December 15, 1980, p. 389.
262 See "Happy Ending in Sight for Debt Rescheduling," *Financial Times*, September 16,
     1980, p. 24.
263 Telephone interview with Tony Spicijaric.
264 Interview with John Bushnell.
265 Confidential telephone interview, Citibank executive, September 18, 1989.
266 Central American Historical Institute (Georgetown University), *Update*, No. 8, Novem-
     ber 5, 1982; "US Pressure on Lenders Blamed for Liquidity Crisis," *Latin American
     Markets*, No. 63, August 1, 1983, p. 12.

Washington and Nicaragua's official debt: Promoting the IMF solution

The Sandinistas were bequeathed a substantial foreign public debt, which further complicated their efforts to establish credibility with the international financial community and gain access to fresh sources of overseas funding for development programs. In November 1979, Nicaragua owed debts to the governments of the United States, Japan, Spain, and West Germany totaling approximately $250 million plus an additional $48 million in outstanding interest payments due by the end of the year.[267] "The debt issue was never a major bilateral issue between the United States and Nicaragua," observed one involved U.S. diplomat. "It was never a great irritant, always something manageable."[268] Still, it generated some friction, adding to Washington's growing unease during 1980 over the direction in which the revolution was moving.

Within weeks of the regime change, the Carter administration indicated that a prompt rescheduling of Nicaragua's foreign public debt would be an urgent priority in its dealings with the new government. American officials in Washington and Managua sought to impress upon the Sandinista leadership the importance of renegotiating this portion of the debt first "because the [creditor] governments are likely to be more forthcoming and thus a precedent would be established."[269] Furthermore, a swift rescheduling offered the possibility of large-scale bilateral economic assistance in return. Ambassador Pezzullo confidently predicted "that the GRN [Government of National Reconstruction] will give prompt attention to the reorganization of the official debt."[270]

But neither the government nor the moderates nominally charged with running the economy had the authority to formulate policy on what the DNC viewed as fundamentally a political issue. When Embassy officials pressed Central Bank President Arturo Cruz and JGRN member Alfonso Robelo in mid-September on "the advantage of moving quickly to reschedule the official debt," the latter responded that this was a DNC matter and a final decision would be announced "in the context of an overall policy."[271]

267 Alan Riding, "Nicaragua Tries Economic Cure," *New York Times*, November 27, 1979, p. D1.
268 Interview with Lawrence Pezzullo.
269 Department of State Telegram, Confidential State 223290, Secretary of State (Christopher) to American Embassy, Paris, August 25, 1979, Subject: "Nicaraguan Debt Negotiation," DFOIA.
270 Department of State Telegram, Confidential Managua 3935, American Embassy (Pezzullo) to Secretary of State, August 21, 1979, Subject: "Nicaraguan Debt Negotiation," DFOIA.
271 Department of State Telegram, Managua 4425, American Embassy (O'Donnell) to Secretary of State, September 15, 1979, Subject: "Paris Club Debt Rescheduling," DFOIA.

Regardless, Washington continued to apply subtle and not so subtle pressures on the ruling junta to produce a quick result. The State Department went so far as to raise the specter of a possible aid cutoff under the Brooke Amendment to the 1979 Foreign Assistance Act, which mandated the automatic suspension of economic assistance to any country more than 12 months in arrears on Agency for International Development (AID) or Foreign Military Sales (FMS) payments. From Managua, Ambassador Pezzullo cabled that a visiting delegation of American business executives in October "afforded frequent opportunities to bring up [the] question of debt rescheduling with GRN [Government of National Reconstruction] officials...."[272] At the request of Secretary Vance, he told the Sandinista leadership that prospects for congressional passage of the $75 million supplemental economic aid request for Nicaragua were "obviously dim" in the absence of a speedy rescheduling of the official debt.[273]

The Sandinistas' reluctance to incur new debts, or establish any kind of loan precedent, prior to the formulation of "an overall policy" largely explained their decision to reject a $10 million Wells Fargo Bank loan offer to the Nicaraguan Development Bank, 75 percent guaranteed by the Export-Import Bank, to finance the purchase of much-needed agrichemicals from American producers. The offer would have been rejected in any event because the terms of the proposed loan were unacceptable: 14 percent interest was deemed excessive, and a one-year repayment period was considered too short.[274] During the September meeting with Central Bank President Cruz and Junta member Robelo, Embassy officials indicated that Washington was unhappy over this decision and hoped the Nicaraguans understood the difference between normal commercial financing for the private sector (for example, supplier credits) and debts directly accumulated by a government, often on concessionary terms. The Wells Fargo offer "of doing normal business in Nicaragua was positive and a rejection of it carried a cost." Cruz and Robelo appreciated the distinction but said that "the Sandinistas have other criteria."[275]

Initially, the Carter administration was no less insistent than the foreign bank creditors on the need for IMF participation in the economic recon-

272 Department of State Telegram, Confidential Managua 48720, American Embassy (Pezzullo) to Secretary of State, October 9, 1979, Subject: "Nicaragua Official Debt Rescheduling," DFOIA.
273 Department of State Telegram, Confidential State 261974, Secretary of State (Vance) to American Embassy, October 5, 1979, Subject: "Nicaragua Official Debt Rescheduling," DFOIA.
274 Department of State Memorandum, August 28, 1979, Subject: "Eximbank Approval Guarantee for Nicaragua," DFOIA; Department of State Telegram, Managua 4424, American Embassy (O'Donnell) to Secretary of State, September 14, 1979, Subject: "GRN Reject Wells Fargo Line of Credit," DFOIA.
275 Department of State Telegram, Managua 4425.

struction program. Although all forms of bilateral and multilateral aid foster the development of "a climate of confidence" that reassures private investors, Secretary Vance wrote to all regional embassies, "of paramount importance will be Nicaragua's relationship with the IMF. . . . Agreement with the IMF on an economic stabilization program would be a strong signal to all that the GON [Government of Nicaragua] is working toward long-term financial stability."[276] Another Department official dismissed any criticism of this call for Fund involvement with a Third World debtor, terming it merely standard operating procedure: "This was a normal condition. No Paris Club [Western governments] renegotiation without an IMF agreement. We were trying to be forthcoming, to treat them like everybody else. So it behooved them to make these arrangements."[277]

From the outset, as previously noted, relations between the revolutionary regime and the Fund were clouded by the latter's favorable vote on a stabilization loan to the Somoza dictatorship in May 1979 – two months prior to its downfall. One of the Sandinistas first official acts was to cancel the loan (which had already been partly disbursed) on the grounds that the economic and financial dislocation caused by the war rendered compliance with the IMF "austerity" conditions an impossible task. But demonstrating its desire to maintain ties with the Fund and not provoke any unnecessary confrontation, the new government then applied for an IMF Special Drawing Rights (SDR) $17 million Compensatory Financing Facility (CFF) loan ($22.1 million) to offset an expected 40 percent drop in fiscal year 1979 export earnings.[278] Central Bank president Arturo Cruz stated emphatically that Nicaragua had no intention of leaving the Fund: "We are fully aware we have to work with the IMF and submit to a certain discipline. We don't want to be the mavericks of the world."[279]

On August 22, the National Advisory Council on International Monetary and Financial Policies (NAC), the interagency executive branch committee responsible for advising the Secretary of the Treasury on U.S. policy in the international financial institutions, decided to support the Sandinista CFF request because it met the basic IMF criteria: Nicaragua was experiencing

---

276 Department of State Telegram, State 24088, Secretary of State to American Embassy, Bogotá, Info all American Republic Diplomatic Posts, September 14, 1979, Subject: "Nicaragua Relations with IMF and IBRD," DFOIA.

277 Interview with John Bushnell

278 Department of the Treasury, Office Memorandum, U.S. Executive Director (Sam Y. Cross) to The Secretary, National Advisory Council, August 21, 1979, Subject: Nicaragua – Use of Fund Resources – Compensatory Financing Facility; Confidential Memorandum, "Nicaragua: State of the Economy and IMF Stabilization Program" prepared by Brian Zipp, IDN, September 7, 1979, DFOIA. Also see "Nicaragua IMF Loan of $22.1 Million Set; Larger Credit Voided," Wall Street Journal, August 29, 1979, p. 21.

279 Quoted in Marlise Simons, "Nicaragua Ready to Accept IMF Aid," Washington Post, August 19, 1979, p. A20.

a balance of payments crises; the export shortfall was attributable to forces largely beyond the government's control; and Managua had provided "reasonable" technical/economic calculations to bolster its case. The NAC also deemed Managua's request for cancellation of the May 1979 stabilization loan "reasonable under the circumstances," especially in view of the regime's intention to retain Somoza's 43 percent currency devaluation and enter into funding discussions with the IMF at some future date. This constituted strong evidence that the regime was "treating its relations with the IMF seriously." NAC officials said that when a new agreement was signed it would contribute immeasurably to the country's financial stability and "establish the new government's creditworthiness" with the major capitalist world lending institutions.[280] Treasury Secretary W. Michael Blumenthal agreed and instructed the Fund's U.S. Executive Director to vote accordingly. The IMF's governing board concurred with the NAC recommendations.

In early September, an internal Treasury Department memorandum argued for renewed pressures on the ruling junta "to quickly negotiate a financial program supported by the IMF" in order to put to rest "a number of uncertainties about the GRN's [Government of National Reconstruction] new economic policies...."[281] The State Department had no major objections but was willing to make a limited concession to the Nicaraguans by ignoring the "normal requirements for having [an] IMF agreement in place before reaching [the] first stage of [the] multilateral agreement on [the] official debt reschedule."[282] Other creditor governments, however, such as the West Germans, were prepared to simply waive the normal requirement that a country seeking to renegotiate its Paris Club debt first enter into a stabilization loan agreement with the IMF. Washington refused to contemplate any such dramatic gesture. "The U.S. position," Secretary Vance declared, "is that implementation of bilateral agreements with creditors will be linked to [the] successful completion of [an] agreement between [the] IMF and [the] GRN [Government of National Reconstruction] on [an] economic stabilization program"[283] The Department's "Seventh Floor" was not swayed by Ambassador Pezzullo's implicit plea for a flexible approach on

280 Department of the Treasury, Inter-Office Memorandum, Confidential, Acting Deputy Assistant Secretary Pelikan to Assistant Secretary Bergsten, August 23, 1979, Subject: "Nicaragua – Request for IMF Compensatory Financing Facility," DFOIA.

281 Department of the Treasury, "Nicaragua: State of the Economy and IMF Stabilization Program".

282 Department of State Telegram, Confidential Managua 5228, American Embassy (Pezzullo) to Secretary of State, October 26, 1979, Subject: "Nicaraguan Debt Rescheduling," DFOIA.

283 Department of State Telegram, State 290937, Secretary of State (Vance) to American Embassy, November 7, 1979, Subject: "Nicaraguan Debt Rescheduling," DFOIA.

this issue given that the Sandinistas were making a genuine attempt to "overcome strained relations with the IMF," witness the CCF loan request, and official invitations to the Fund for a delegation of senior officials and a technical mission to visit the country before the end of 1979.[284]

In an October dispatch to the American Embassy, Vance conceded that the U.S. insistence on a multilateral rather than a bilateral rescheduling of Paris Club debts was "caus[ing] the GRN [Government of National Reconstruction] problems due to the nature of some debts owed to other countries (Israel, Spain)."[285] The Sandinistas refused to honor debts accumulated by Somoza as a result of weapons purchases or corrupt regime practices. The most notable cases involved more than $7 million owed to Israel ($4.1 million) and Argentina ($3.2 million) for military acquisitions and a $28 million commission to the dictator's family that was part of a $160 million credit provided by Spain's Foreign Trade Bank (in 1976–77) to finance the purchase of trucks and jeeps. Speaking of the former, Daniel Ortega insisted that "not one cent [of the $5.5 million still owed on the contracts] will be paid." Regarding the latter, Alfredo César said that it could only be settled on the basis of some kind of "special arrangement" agreed to by Madrid.[286] In each case, the symbolic significance of the debt weighed far more heavily with the Sandinista leadership than the actual, rather modest, amount of funds involved. Amid a wide-ranging discussion in late November, State's John Bushnell reminded César of the danger of Nicaragua contravening the Brooke Amendment if it failed to meet its debt obligations on Foreign Military Sales (FMS) credits by January 3, 1980. Otherwise the Central American country would be ineligible for any new loans or credits from U.S. government agencies.[287]

Although the outstanding FMS payments totaled less than $700,000, Ambassador Pezzullo reported the delay was due to the fact that "it is basically a political decision...."[288] On December 5, Reconstruction Min-

284 Department of State Telegram, Confidential Managua 5445, American Embassy (Pezzullo) to American Embassy, Bonn, Info Secretary of State, November 7, 1979, Subject: "Nicaraguan Official Debt Rescheduling," DFOIA.

285 Department of State Telegram, Confidential State 269771, Secretary of State (Vance) to American Embassy, October 16, 1979, Subject: "Exim Involvement in Nicaragua," DFOIA.

286 Ortega quoted in Karen DeYoung, "Junta Nationalizes Nicaragua's Private Local Banks," *Washington Post*, July 26, 1979, p. A25; César quoted in Department of State Telegram, Confidential Managua 5445. Also see Patricia Alisau, "Nicaragua Won't Honor Somoza Debts," *Journal of Commerce*, August 7, 1979, p. 9.

287 Department of State Telegram, Confidential State 308312, Secretary of State (Vance) to American Embassy, November 29, 1979, Subject: "Conversation with Alfredo César," DFOIA.

288 Department of State Telegram, Confidential Managua 5859, American Embassy (Pezzullo) to Secretary of State, December 3, 1979, Subject: "Nicaraguan Official Debt Rescheduling," DFOIA.

ister César told Embassy officials that although the Sandinistas had "political problems with paying the military debt" they "did not want to harm the cordial relationships" that had developed between the two countries over recent months.[289] An announcement on official debt rescheduling could be expected before the end of the year. Such assurances did not stop repeated pronouncements by Carter officials linking prospects for new loans to an acceptance of all debts incurred before mid-July 1979. On December 12, Deputy Secretary of State Warren Christopher telegrammed the Managua Embassy to make sure the governing junta "understand[s] clearly that [the] USG [United States Government] expects that all direct and guaranteed debts will be repaid. Repudiation of any debt to [the] USG [United States Government] will make new assistance virtually impossible."[290] At a meeting with junta and Sandinista officials to discuss the FMS debt, Sergio Ramírez informed Ambassador Pezzullo that the regime had a "political problem," having publicly announced its refusal to accept responsibility for any of Somoza's military debts. Well and good, replied Pezzullo, but the White House was bound by legislation "specifically prohibit[ing] any act which would have the effect of relieving creditors of making payment to the U.S. government."[291]

Subsequent efforts to reschedule the $250 million official debt at Paris Club meetings in October and November 1980 foundered on Washington's continued insistence that Nicaragua enter into a stabilization loan agreement with the IMF as the price for an accord. The Nicaraguans refused and initiated discussions with West Germany and Spain on the possibility of reaching separate bilateral settlements.[292]

In December, Nicaraguan Finance Minister Joaquín Cuadra traveled to Washington, D.C. to sign development loans from the World Bank and the Inter-American Development Bank totaling $70 million. During the visit he stressed, on more than one occasion, that Managua had no intention of severing its ties with the IMF, even though the Sandinistas were convinced that the Fund austerity programs made meaningful social and economic reforms difficult to pursue. Nicaragua would remain a member in good

---

289 Department of State Telegram, Confidential Managua 5944, American Embassy (O'Donnell) to Secretary of State, December 6, 1979, Subject: "Nicaraguan Official Debt Rescheduling and Late Payments Problem," DFOIA.

290 Department of State Telegram, State 320155, Secretary of State (Christopher) to American Embassy, December 12, 1979, Subject: "FMS Arrearages," DFOIA.

291 Department of State Telegram, Confidential Managua 6214, American Embassy (Pezzullo) to Secretary of State, December 22, 1979, Subject: "Nicaraguan FMS Arrearages," DFOIA. According to JGRN member Sergio Ramírez, the Argentine government had offered to write off Nicaragua's approximately $3 million military debt.

292 See de Onis, "Lenders Now Consider Nicaragua a Good Risk," p. 39; Shaw, "Nicaragua's Sandinistas Adopt Reassuring Stance," p. G4.

standing, keep up its quota payments, and make use of those Fund facilities for which it was eligible. Cuadra also held out an "olive branch" in the form of an invitation to the IMF to send a mission to Nicaragua in mid-1981.[293]

Creating a non-permeable state and regime: American policy and the consolidation of Sandinista hegemony

In the absence of a direct challenge to foreign investors and a willingness on the part of the Sandinista government to encourage a revival of multi-national corporate activity, as well as promote a mixed economy that allocated the private sector an important role, economic considerations were not critical in the shaping of early Carter administration policy toward Nicaragua. Of more immediate concern were the strategic implications of a revolution in America's traditional "sphere of influence" and the fate of local allies or collaborator forces within the new regime, state, and society. From Washington's perspective, the lack of countervailing pressures in the form of non-Sandinista elements capable of imposing a moderating influence on the process of change kept on the agenda the possibility of a future shift of a longstanding Central American client out of the U.S. political and economic orbit. During late 1979 and 1980, a number of developments in the domestic and foreign policy spheres appeared to give substance to Washington's public and private concerns about the direction in which the revolution might be, or was, moving.

American policymakers were initially buoyed by the fact that formal governmental authority was vested in the politically eclectic Junta of the Government of National Reconstruction (JGRN) and that moderates nominally controlled the key economic and defense ministries. Yet, substantial bourgeois visibility within the upper reaches of the new regime did not reflect the actual power realities. The nine-member Sandinista National Directorate (DNC) reigned supreme in the political and economic decisionmaking process, and exercised unfettered control over the armed forces and foreign policy. The first social and economic reforms were implemented by DNC decree, not by the economic ministries; key international economic policies (for example, foreign debt) were formulated by the DNC; a new military command structure, a popular army, and security and police forces were established by Sandinista edict, without regard to the opinions of Defense Minister Bernardino Larios and his advisors.[294]

---

293 See ibid., p. G1.
294 See Warren Hoge, "Sandinistas to Draft New 'Popular' Army," *New York Times*, July 30, 1979, p. 3.

To establish a greater congruence between state and regime, the Sandinista leadership mandated a number of key cabinet changes at the end of 1979: DNC member Humberto Ortega was appointed Defense Minister, replacing Larios; another Sandinista commandante, Henry Ruiz, took over as Planning Minister from the technocrat Roberto Mayorga; and the Directorate's Jaime Wheelock added the Ministry of Agriculture to his position as head of the Agrarian Reform Institute, ousting Manuel José Torres, a conservative Christian Democrat and wealthy livestock rancher. The elevation of Humberto Ortega to the top job in the Defense Ministry produced most concern at the White House. When the original ministry was being chosen in July, President Carter had signaled that Ortega's appointment to this position was not acceptable to the United States. With Sandinista commandante Daniel Ortega as head of the JGRN, these cabinet changes further cemented the interlock between state and regime.

As part of its multitrack attempt to counter this ominous trend, the White House authorized a CIA political-action program in support of anti-Sandinista political, labor, and media forces. The basic objective, John Bushnell explained, was to sustain "the moderate factions" in the hope that they might be able to contest Sandinista political hegemony at some future time: "La Prensa and the political organizations were being squeezed, so if we didn't provide support they would cease to exist. In the same way as we supplied support to the economic leaders [in the government], we were supporting other forces that had the possibility of changing the [political] balance over time, and the only mechanism to do that was the CIA."[295] Administration officials were also determined to prevent a repeat of the early period of the Cuban revolution when the bourgeois opposition, lacking the wherewithall to contest the Castro forces, migrated in large numbers, in the process fatally weakening the internal counterrevolutionary option: "We didn't want another Cuba where all the opposition resigns and comes to the U.S. That was no use. We didn't want the opposition to leave. So, what can we do to keep them there and support them."[296]

A second, interrelated, objective of the covert funding initiative was to develop a new group of "human intelligence sources." The old network of CIA agents had disintegrated along with the Somoza regime; most were "eliminat[ed]" after the FSLN captured the dictator's intelligence files.[297]

295 *Interview with John Bushnell.* Also see Bob Woodward, *Veil: The Secret Wars of the CIA 1981–1987* (New York: Simon & Schuster, 1987), p. 113; Scott Armstrong and Malcolm Bryne, *The Chronology: The Documented Day-by-Day Account of the Secret Military Assistance to Iran and the Contras* (New York: Warner Books, 1987), p. 3.

296 Confidential interview, Department of State official, Washington, D.C., September 18, 1989. The respondent was a senior official in the Bureau of Inter-American Affairs, 1979 to 1981.

297 Woodward, *Veil: The Secret Wars of the CIA 1981–1987,* p. 113.

Establishing liaisons within the DNC and other Sandinista power centers promised to be no easy task given that "the U.S. had no network of agents built up with the Sandinistas before the revolution," said a Defense Department official involved with Central America. "Therefore, it had no agents with ties to the new government officials or the new armed forces."[298]

DNC-authored changes in the membership of the proposed Council of State appeared likely to further consolidate Sandinista hegemony while simultaneously undercutting American attempts to foster a viable and organized political movement capable of contesting Sandinista policy formulations. The original decision (July 1979) to establish a 33-seat Council to share legislative responsibilities with the JGRN until national elections could be held allocated the largest bloc of seats to the non-Sandinista political, business, educational, and religious parties and organizations. In April 1980, however, the Junta's Sergio Ramírez, also a DNC member, announced that the number of Council seats was being expanded to 47 to provide representation for the newly created labor unions and mass organizations linked to the Sandinista movement. Those seats originally assigned to organizations no longer functioning were withdrawn. These changes guaranteed a clear Sandinista majority in the Council at its inaugural May meeting.[299]

The decision to restructure membership of the Council of State had reverberations in Managua and Washington. The two most prominent non-Sandinistas on the ruling junta – Violeta Chamorro and Alfonso Robelo – submitted their resignations. Whereas the political moderate Chamorro cited health and family reasons, the conservative industrialist Robelo blamed the proposed Council changes and accused the Sandinistas of reneging on previous commitments to restore political democracy to Nicaragua.[300] To Washington, Robelo's words were further evidence of the growing consolidation of revolutionary power. In a cable to the Secretary of State, Ambassador Pezzullo suggested that the official public statement on the resignations should emphasize that this was but one of a series of recent developments in Nicaragua that "raises questions about the direction of the

298 Confidential telephone interview, Department of Defense official, September 26, 1989.
299 The expansion and reorganization of the Council of State is discussed in Richard Sholk, "The National Bourgeoisie in Post-Revolutionary Nicaragua," *Comparative Politics*, Vol. 16, No. 3, April 1984, p. 258.
300 See Christopher Dickey, "Sandinistas Act to Keep Business Sector's Favor," *Washington Post*, April 29, 1980, p. A12; "Nicaragua: Robelo Goes as the Revolution Moves On," *Latin America Regional Reports: Mexico & Central America*, May 2, 1980, p. 6. All the media outlets, government and opposition, accepted Chamorro's reasons for leaving the junta at face value and did not see them as "calculated to achieve a political goal." Department of State Telegram, Managua 1879, American Embassy (Pezzullo) to Secretary of State, April 21, 1980, Subject: "Doña Violeta Resignation – Press Reaction," DFOIA.

revolution" combined with a blunt warning to Managua that a continuation of this perceived negative trend "will have [a] major influence on the nature of our bilateral relations."[301] The Department followed the envoy's advice. On Capitol Hill, the influential speaker of the House of Representatives, liberal democrat Thomas (Tip) O'Neill Jr., turned the pressure up a notch with the announcement that further action on the administration's $75 million Nicaragua aid package would be delayed until "moderates" had been named to fill the two vacant Junta seats.[302]

Concerned to avoid a major breach with Washington and an irrevocable split with the local bourgeoisie, the DNC mounted a swift damage control operation. Official statements by Sandinista leaders reaffirmed the government's commitment to a mixed economy and political pluralism, and "held open a door to dialogue with the private sector...."[303] The American Ambassador agreed to a request to act as mediator in talks between the DNC and representatives of the Superior Council of Private Enterprise (COSEP). The Sandinistas agreed to replace Chamorro and Robelo with individuals acceptable to the private sector, offer new assurances to property owners so long as "they work within the legal framework of the revolution," terminate property takeovers, decree a new law guaranteeing the owners of nationalized enterprises the right to legal redress through the courts, lift the state of emergency that only days earlier had been extended until April 1981, and announce an election timetable in the near future. These political and economic concessions temporarily healed the rift and were sufficient to ensure the attendance of COSEP representatives at the first Council of State meeting on May 4.[304]

The two additions to the ruling Junta were Rafael Córdova Rivas, a Conservative Party politician and member of the Supreme Court, and Arturo Cruz, President of the Central Bank and a former official of the Inter-American Development Bank. Interviewed prior to his appointment, Cruz

301 Department of State Telegram, Managua 1904, American Embassy (Pezzullo) to Secretary of State, April 23, 1980, Subject: "Suggested Press Guidance on Chamorro/Robelo Resignations from Junta," DFOIA. Also see "Nicaragua: Consolidating the Power," *This Week: Central America & Panama*, April 28, 1980, p. 124.

302 Quoted in Alan Riding, "2 Moderates Named to Nicaragua Junta to Calm Fears of a Leftist Drift," *New York Times*, May 20, 1980, p. 14.

303 Department of State Telegram, Confidential Managua 1929, American Embassy (Pezzullo) to Secretary of State, April 23, 1980, Subject: "(U) Robelo Resignation Statement; GRN/FSLN COSEP Reaction," DFOIA.

304 See Dickey, "Sandinistas Act to Keep Business Sector's Favor," p. A12; Christopher Dickey, "Sandinistas, Businessmen Said to Reach Accord Ending Crisis," *Washington Post*, May 5, 1980, p. A28; Riding, "2 Moderates Named to Nicaraguan Junta to Calm Fears of a Leftist Drift," p. 14; Alan Riding, "Nicaragua's Junta Makes a Modest Turn to the Center," *New York Times*, May 25, 1980, p. E5; "Nicaragua: Reconciliation with Private Enterprise," *Central America Report*, May 12, 1980, p. 37.

declared that the government was "definitely not" interested in eliminating the private sector or following the Cuban road to socialism.[305]

Cruz's statement and Sandinista concessions notwithstanding, the local capitalist class remained jittery over the medium and long-term economic climate.[306] Ambassador Pezzullo wrote that "few business leaders have much faith in Sandinista assurances and are not likely to consider compromises acceptable on a piecemeal basis."[307] In late July, less than a week after the DNC-COSEP negotiations concluded, COSEP Vice-President Jorge Salazar declared that private enterprise "has been marginalized by the revolution." Alfonso Robelo thundered that the country was "in the hands of totalitarians. . . . "[308] Given that the efforts to accommodate the private sector had gone hand in hand with a policy limiting the socioeconomic demands of its own political constituency, such statements were, to put it mildly, not well received by the DNC.

The Sandinista-private sector conflict flared anew in late August with the announcement that elections would be postponed until 1985. COSEP accused the DNC of wanting to retain power indefinitely and interpreted the statement on elections as evidence of a growing radicalization of regime policies. To emphasize its disillusionment, the Nicaraguan bourgeoisie (COSEP, three political parties, two labor federations) withdrew its representatives from the Council of State.[309] Relations worsened dramatically following the death of Salazar in a November 1980 confrontation with Sandinista security officials.

By year's end, the Sandinistas had consolidated their hold on governmental (as well as state) power. Stephen Gorman provides an excellent summary of why their strategy was so effective in marginalizing its political opponents:

> By neither excluding private sector representatives from government, nor allowing them to acquire control of key political institutions, the DNC avoided premature political polarization between right and left, and legitimized the new regime. The Sandinista Front was able to contain bourgeois political participation in the government by moving

305 Quoted in Alan Robinson, "Nicaragua Welcomes Private Sector," *Journal of Commerce*, May 16, 1980, p. 11.

306 See Steve Frazier, "Nicaragua Business Still Has Jitters," *Wall Street Journal*, July 31, 1980, p. 21.

307 Department of State Telegram, Confidential Managua 2016, American Embassy (Pezzullo) to Secretary of State, April 29, 1980, Subject: "(C) GRN Answers Two Cosep Demands, Moves Forward Council of State," DFOIA.

308 Quoted in "Nicaragua: One Year After the Fall," *Central America Report*, July 28, 1980, p. 21.

309 See Dennis Gilbert, *The Bourgeoisie and the Nicaraguan Revolution.* Paper presented at the Latin American Studies Association Meeting, Mexico City, October 1983, p. 16.

quickly to secure exclusive control of the military and preempt political leadership of the mobilized masses. Most important, the delay in creation of the Council of State, coupled with the absence of elections, deprived the traditional political parties of both a possible independent political base in the new government and a public forum for policy debates.[310]

Nor did the failure of CIA efforts to gain entree into the Sandinista political and military leadership help the cause of the bourgeoisie. Upon his appointment as agency Director by President Reagan in early 1981, William Casey "discover[ed] that the CIA [still] had virtually no good intelligence penetrations or human resources among the Sandinistas."[311]

In the economic sphere, the participation of the private sector in formulating the 1980 national reconstruction program, and Sandinista efforts to limit worker demands that conflicted with the goals of increasing production and maintaining the confidence of the domestic capitalist class could not prevent a gradual worsening of relations. The government did not endear itself to the business community with its occasional direct intervention to solve labor disputes in situations where striking workers had taken over firms to support wage demands or prevent capital flight and production slowdowns. The American Embassy reported that "in at least some cases the government appears to be using labor disputes to extend its control over selected private businesses."[312] At the same time, it also acknowledged the Sandinistas' willingness to crack down on left-wing threats to the basic objectives of the economic program. One example was the closure of the independent radical leftist daily *El Pueblo*, taken partly on the grounds that it "had been egging on labor agitators...."[313] Another was the arrest of Communist Party members for encouraging workers to demand wage increases.[314]

In practice, the Sandinistas were manifestly reluctant to automatically legitimate each and every pressure "from below" during 1980 because of the twin concerns with reconstruction and a desire to minimize bourgeois opposition to its policies. They failed to introduce an agrarian reform law, refused to sanction spontaneous peasant land takeovers, subordinated changes in land tenure relations to increasing productivity on existing farms,

310 Stephen M. Gorman, "Power and Consolidation in the Nicaraguan Revolution," *Journal of Latin American Studies*, Vol. 13, No. 1, 1981, p. 148.
311 Woodward, *Veil: The Secret Wars of the CIA 1981–1987*, p. 113.
312 Department of State Telegram, Managua 1093.
313 Department of State Telegram, Confidential Managua 0406, American Embassy (Pezzullo) to Secretary of State, January 28, 1980, Subject: "GRN Cracks Down on Ultra-Left," DFOIA.
314 See "Junta Rallies Home Support," *Latin America Regional Reports: Mexico & Central America*, November 28, 1980, p. 2.

and kept a tight control on wage demands, so much so that real wages of urban and rural workers in Nicaragua declined by approximately 20 percent.[315] In early December, the regime postponed long-promised labor code reforms that "did not dovetail with economic reactivation plans."[316]

The measures to restrain lower-class power – individually or in toto – failed to impress the country's leading business organization, COSEP, which preferred to emphasize the expanding public sector and new regulations affecting privately owned firms. But much of its hostility was directed toward a specific target: what it perceived to be an increasingly militant, Sandinista-dominated trade union movement willing to pressure the owners of capital for improved wages and working conditions, and not reluctant to demand of the government itself that it spend more on rural services and redistribute nationalized and unused land. By mid-1980, approximately 80 percent of the more than 450 urban unions were affiliated with the Sandinista Workers' Central.[317]

Economic developments in post-revolutionary Nicaragua produced far less disquiet in Washington than either the political changes or the new regime's developing external ties, principally its expanding relations with Havana and Moscow. Within days of the FSLN victory, Secretary of State Vance instructed the American Embassy in Managua to "closely monitor Cuban and Soviet bloc activities."[318] Having "lost" a strategic regional client in the Middle East (Iran) six months earlier, the outcome of the Nicaraguan conflict, together with the December 1979 Soviet invasion of Afghanistan, accelerated the shift toward a more aggressive, confrontationist, anti-communist foreign policy. Developments in Managua were viewed through the prism of the revived East-West conflict. As Sandinista relations with Cuba and the Soviet Union deepened, it fueled the White House perception that the country was becoming a site for Cold War competition.

Cuba's support for the Nicaraguan revolution was "more of a concern" to senior administration policymakers than the Soviets. Reconstruction aid, bilateral agricultural agreements, and the provision of large numbers of teachers and health-care workers was one thing; what "particularly dis-

315 Richard Feinberg, "Central America: No Easy Answers," *Foreign Affairs*, Vol. 59, No. 5, Summer 1981, pp. 1127–1128. Also see Gilbert, *Sandinistas*, p. 90.

316 Department of State Telegram, Managua 5933, American Embassy (Pezzullo) to Secretary of State, December 12, 1980, Subject: "Bi-Weekly Roundup," DFOIA.

317 See "Nicaragua Private Sector Baulks at Reconstruction Plan," *Latin America Weekly Report*, December 21, 1979, p. 85; Department of State Telegram, Managua 0841, American Embassy (O'Donnell) to Secretary of State, February 20, 1980, Subject: "ATC [Association of Rural Workers] Stages Rally," DFOIA; Department of State Telegram, Managua 1093; Marifeli Perez-Stable, "The Working Class in the Nicaraguan Revolution," in Walker, ed., *Nicaragua in Revolution*, pp. 138–139; Gilbert, *Sandinistas*, pp. 14, 111.

318 Department of State Telegram, Secret State 197562.

turbed" Washington was the presence of Cuban military and security personnel – and their role in consolidating the Sandinistas' hold on state power.[319] Ambassador to Panama Ambler Moss recalled how "the Cuban intelligence apparatus moved immediately into Somoza's bunker and set up shop."[320] A Southern Command (SOUTHCOM) officer in Managua described the Cubans as being "heavily into the Sandinista military down to the regiment level. Once they got in there we simply lost the ability to influence the government. We were overwhelmed."[321] To the Defense Department and the CIA, these developments raised "great concern;" to the NSC they were "ominous;"[322] to Ambassador Pezzullo "it wasn't too long before it became clear that the Cubans had an in that nobody was going to compete with."[323]

Carter officials were not only miffed by the Sandinistas' refusal to accommodate American concerns on this issue but also by their failure to heed criticism from sympathetic subregional governments. When Panamanian General Staff officers were dispatched to help rebuild Nicaragua's military intelligence capabilities, they found "that the Cubans had filled all the important military advisory positions, leaving Panama with only the police."[324] Encouraged by Washington, a disappointed President Torrijos agreed to allow members of his National Guard to participate in creating a new Nicaraguan police force, hoping that this might provide a "backdoor" for eventual Panamanian involvement in the military and security spheres as well. Between August and October, over 170 Nicaraguan police attended training courses in Managua or Panama City.[325] But the Panamanians "reached the conclusion before we did," said an involved U.S. military official, "that they were not going to be able to prevent the Cubans from running this show or coopt this revolution."[326] Unable to contain his "distaste for the extent of the Cuban presence," Torrijos recalled the Guard contingent from Managua.[327]

319 Confidential interview, Department of State official, Washington, D.C., October 3, 1990; confidential interview, Department of State official, September 20, 1989.
320 Interview with Ambler Moss.
321 Confidential interview, Department of Defense official, October 2, 1990.
322 Interview with Ambler Moss; Robert Pastor, Latin American Director on the National Security Council Staff, quoted in WGBH Television, Boston, *Crisis in Central America: Revolution in Nicaragua*, Transcript of Frontline #313, April 10, 1985, p. 15.
323 Ambassador Lawrence A. Pezzullo, *oral history interview*, p. 35.
324 "A Revolutionary Friendship Turns Sour," *Latin America Weekly Report*, December 21, 1979, p. 92.
325 Ibid.; Steve C. Ropp, *Panamanian Politics* (New York: Praeger Publishers, 1982), p. 129.
326 Confidential telephone interview, Department of Defense official, Maryland, October 9, 1990.
327 Department of State, Confidential Briefing Papers for Secretary of State Vance's August 1979 Trip to Ecuador, Bilateral Paper: Panama.

Although the Venezuelan government declined a request "to train the Sandinista air force" also because of "Cuban involvement,"[328] it was the Torrijos decision, said Ambler Moss, that "had the most significant impact on American policy. In the view of Washington, the Sandinista regime now really began to define itself as looking more in the Cuban direction."[329] If State and Defense Department officials tended to exaggerate the actual numbers of Cuban military and security personnel,[330] there was no dispute about the key role these individuals played in helping to build a non-permeable state structure (to external manipulation "from the outside"), thereby ensuring the long-term survival prospects of the revolution.

The Soviet connection with the Nicaraguan revolution had a less profound but nonetheless significant impact on administration diplomacy: Although "the Cuban presence was of more concern, we didn't like the expanding relations with the Soviet bloc at all."[331] The actual quantities of Soviet bloc military and economic assistance during the first 18 months of the Nicaraguan revolution were remarkably small. Total military assistance in 1980, for example, was between $6 million and $7 million – less than one-fifth the amount of authorized U.S. military aid to its Central American allies. Economic assistance increased between 1979 and 1980, but not dramatically. Rising oil import costs, an almost empty treasury, and U.S. Congressional footdragging on passage of the aid bill made it doubly imperative that the Sandinistas find new overseas funding sources. In March 1980, the revolutionary regime signed a number of economic cooperation agreements with the Soviet Union, the forerunner of additional pacts negotiated with other Eastern European countries.

Soviet bloc credits in 1980 ($100 million) amounted to only 19 percent of total foreign credits, which was less than the combined Latin American figure of 22 percent. The value of Nicaragua's exports to the bloc markets that year was also insignificant (3 percent of the value of its total exports) whereas the equivalent figures for imports from these sources totaled a minuscule $2 million or 0.1 percent.[332] But Carter administration policymakers were less interested in the levels of aid and trade than in the pro-

328 Matthews, "The Limits of Friendship: Nicaragua and the West," pp. 26–27.
329 Interview with Ambler Moss.
330 See, for example, U.S. Department of State, *Soviet Attitudes Towards Aid to and Contacts with Central American Revolutions*. Prepared by C.G. Jacobsen, June 1984, pp. 16–18; Marc Edelman, "Lifelines: Nicaragua and the Socialist Countries," *NACLA Report on the Americas*, Vol. XIX, No. 3, May/June 1985, p. 50.
331 Interview with John Bushnell.
332 See Matthews, The Limits of Friendship: Nicaragua and the West," p. 20; Edelman, "Lifelines: Nicaragua and the Socialist Countries," pp. 38, 43, 49–50; Ruben Berrios, "Relations Between Nicaragua and the Socialist Countries," in Augusto Varas, ed., *Soviet-Latin American Relations in the 1980s* (Boulder: Westview Press, 1987), pp. 144–173.

liferating economic ties themselves. Each new agreement was interpreted "as a little negative chip."[333]

The establishment of diplomatic, economic, and/or military relations with Cuba and the Soviet bloc countries, and membership in the non-aligned movement, were all part of a deliberate Sandinista policy to diversify Nicaragua's relations with the rest of the world. While one government delegation was in Moscow in March 1980, for instance, another was touring Western European capitals in search of aid donors. To the United States, however, the existence of a former longtime dutiful collaborator in world affairs now actively pursuing an independent foreign policy could not be allowed to go unchallenged. Apart from the Soviet-Cuba connection, Washington and Managua clashed over a number of regional and global issues – including Nicaragua's abstention on the United Nations resolution to condemn the Soviet invasion of Afghanistan, Sandinista support for the Salvadoran guerrillas and criticism of the U.S. role in El Salvador, and American hostility toward other nationalist and socialist governments (Jamaica, Grenada, Cuba) in the Central America/Caribbean region.

In his memoirs, President Carter described the major thrust of U.S. policy during his final months in office as that of "trying to maintain our ties with Nicaragua, to keep it from turning to Cuba and the Soviet Union."[334] The growing ideological tone of policy formulation paralleled the closure of the Nicaraguan state and regime to the hegemonic power's influence and was accompanied by increasing official rhetoric about alleged Sandinista attempts to export their revolution to the rest of Central America. Despite administration criticism of Congress over the time taken to pass the $75 million economic aid package, only $60 million was actually disbursed between September 1980 and early January 1981, when the Farabundo Martí National Liberation Front (FMLN) guerrillas in El Salvador launched a nationwide insurrection against a repressive military-controlled civilian regime allied to Washington.

Intelligence reports on the Salvadoran upheaval received by the White House presented what NSC Latin American specialist Robert Pastor termed "conclusive proof" and U.S. Ambassador to El Salvador Robert White called "compelling and convincing" evidence of large-scale Nicaraguan aid to the insurgents.[335] According to Pastor, the "most convincing information"[336] was not made public until September 1985 when the State

---

333 Interview with Lawrence Pezzullo.
334 Carter, *Keeping Faith: Memoirs of a President*, p. 585.
335 Pastor, *Condemned to Repetition*, p. 225; White quoted in "Guerrilla Offensive Sweeps El Salvador as U.S. Renews Aid, Accuses Nicaragua," *Latin American Index*, January 15, 1981, p. 1.
336 Pastor, *Condemned to Repetition*, p. 357.

Department released *"Revolution Beyond Our Borders": Sandinista Intervention in Central America* (hereafter *Report*) which purported to present a comprehensive, airtight case for Nicaragua's role as a major supplier of arms to the FMLN since late 1980.

The *Report*'s discussion of the Carter period (the "evidence" of "Sandinista intervention") centered on a wildly muddled account of a single arms shipment from Nicaragua to El Salvador just before the Salvadoran guerrillas' military offensive. Initially, the Soviet Union was supposed to have referred the Salvadorans to the Vietnamese, who promised to ship them 60 tons of arms. Then, the figure in the *Report* jumps to 120 tons of military equipment waiting in Nicaragua to be shipped to El Salvador. Then the source of the arms (now alleged to be 300 to 400 tons) shifted to Cuba where, the *Report* claimed, they awaited transfer "to Nicaragua and then to El Salvador" in mid-November 1980. Next, the *Report* quoted a Salvadoran defector, Luis Alvarado Saravia, who provided yet another version of what arms were shipped to El Salvador during this period. They included 2,200 rifles, 2 radio transmitters, ammunition, grenades, more than 15 rocket launchers, 4 machine guns, 125 boxes of TNT, and 10 grenade launchers. Finally, the *Report* offered evidence provided by another Salvadoran, Napoleón Romero, that differed substantially from that of Saravia: "[Romero] described the first such delivery as consisting of 300 weapons infiltrated at the end of 1980 in preparation for the January 1981 'final offensive.' " What was most striking about these figures was the small quantities of military aid involved and how the total amount dropped as the source shifted from the State Department to the defectors. This strongly suggested that the arms were being relayed to El Salvador through a Salvadoran network in Nicaragua acting independently of the Sandinistas.

Paradoxically, the *Report* itself substantiated the existence of a Salvadoran support network with no links to Managua. Referring to the testimony of the defector Saravia, it noted: "He detailed how the Nicaraguan Government provided food, transportation, and false documents to enable him to train in Cuba. He also described movements of guerrillas and arms from Nicaragua into El Salvador days prior to the January 1981 offensive." In this and other statements about the period, Saravia did not tie the Sandinista regime to the arms movements but only to transfers of "food, transportation, and false documents." Further, they revealed only that weapons moved from Nicaragua to El Salvador through unspecified, non-government, channels. Likewise, Napoleón Romero, Washington's other key informer source, did not mention the involvement of a single Nicaraguan government official or agency in the "logistical network" that funneled the 300 rifles from Nicaragua to El Salvador.

Offering no solid evidence of Nicaraguan government involvement in arms trafficking to El Salvador, the *Report* advanced more information to support the Salvadoran network thesis: "In mid-January 1981, Honduran security forces intercepted a trailer truck in Comayagua that was part of an arms supply network run by the FPL [a Salvadoran guerrilla group, the Popular Liberation Forces] guerrillas working through Nicaragua." The operative terms in this statement – "arms supply network run by FPL guerrillas" and "working through Nicaragua" – implied not Sandinista intervention in El Salvador but the existence of Salvadorans organizing and supplying themselves through their own networks in Nicaragua.[337]

However, in contrast to the *Report's* unconvincing and inflated claims, there is other more convincing documentation that does reveal that the Sandinista government was actively involved in arms smuggling to the Salvadoran guerrillas. On the basis of an exhaustive review of intelligence and State Department reports, and information gathered from other U.S. government agencies, CIA analyst David MacMichael concluded that there was "credible evidence" of stepped-up supplies of Nicaraguan government military assistance to the FMLN during late 1980 and early 1981, but not thereafter: "It didn't come in any more after the beginning of 1981, February or March."[338]

Among the most persuasive evidence is captured FMLN documents that indicate the guerrillas' annoyance at the on-again, off-again nature of the Sandinistas military aid program. During meetings with Nicaraguan officials, including DNC member Bayardo Arce, in July 1980, a delegation of the Salvadoran Guerrilla Joint General Staff complained about the regime's decision to halt all weapons shipments until it could assess the FMLN's general military plan. The delegation implored the Sandinistas to "approve the shipments without political conditions...." The following September, the Sandinistas placed a one-month embargo on arms deliveries in response to U.S. protests over such activities. In early November, a senior Salvadoran guerrilla leader criticized the FSLN's failure to adequately coordinate its arms delivery program with the shifting requirements of the struggle. He attributed this to a continuing Sandinista refusal "to take more into consideration the opinions and plans prepared here [in El Salvador]...." Two weeks later, as it geared up for the January 1981 "final offensive," an anxious FMLN high-command instructed its representative in Managua to emphasize to the Sandinistas "the difficulties which would result from abrupt suspension of the shipments now when time can make a crucial difference.

---

337 U.S. Department of State, *"Revolution Beyond Our Borders": Sandinista Intervention in Central America*, Report No. 132, September 1985, pp. 7–11.
338 Quoted in Richard Bernstein, "Latin Arms Trade Detailed in Court," *New York Times*, September 17, 1985, p. 9. Also see Philip Taubman, "In From the Cold and Hot for Truth," *New York Times*, June 11, 1984, p. B6.

...Unilateral decisions [regarding arms shipments] will only harm our cause."[339]

Additional confirmation of Sandinista complicity in arms smuggling to the Salvadoran guerrillas comes from two of the leading players themselves. At the August 1987 Esquipulas summit of Central American presidents, Daniel Ortega made an admission to this effect in talks with José Napoleón Duarte; more recently, the FMLN's top field commander Joaquín Villalobos also conceded that his forces received weapons assistance from the FSLN in the months prior to the failed January 1981 offensive.[340] But what is indisputable is that Carter policymakers vastly inflated the amount of this aid *and* its significance in affecting the trajectory of the Salvadoran conflict.

Convinced of the Sandinista government's direct involvement in the flow of arms across Nicaraguan territory to the insurgents in neighboring El Salvador, the White House moved swiftly to suspend all further economic assistance. The president then approved a Special Coordination Committee (SCC) recommendation eliminating the ban on military assistance to the Salvadoran regime – ignoring its continuing reputation as one of the worst human rights abusers in the Third World. That the Bureau of Humanitarian Rights and Human Affairs played no part in this decision underlined the diminished importance of morality in the Carter foreign policymaking process.[341] On January 17, 1981, the President authorized an emergency $5.6 million package of lethal military assistance (including grenade launchers, rifles, ammunition and helicopters) to avoid the possibility of another mass social movement with deep national roots overthrowing a U.S.- supported regime in Central America.

Conclusion

Between September 1978 and July 1979, Washington promoted a regime change in Nicaragua in order to preserve the existing state. Confronted by a longstanding client that had lost all legitimacy and was threatened by a mass popular movement, U.S. policymakers resorted to the strategy of a

339 Transcripts of the documents are reprinted in Walter Poelchau, ed., *White Paper Whitewash* (New York: Deep Cover Books, 1981), Appendix A, pp. A41, A43, A53–54, A82, A86.

340 One report implies that Esquipulas was not the only time Ortega acknowledged the Sandinista's involvement. See James LeMoyne, "Salvador Rebels: Where Do They Get Their Arms?,'" *New York Times*, November 24, 1988, p. 14.

341 Department of State Memorandum, Assistant Secretary of State Derian to Acting Secretary, December 31, 1980, Subject: "Resumption of Military Assistance to El Salvador," DFOIA.

"negotiated transition" based on the cohabitation of a center-right civilian government with authoritarian state institutions. But this effort to manipulate and influence the outcome of the anti-dictatorial struggle proved inadequate to the task: The Carter administration was forced to come to terms with the reality of a historic sub-regional ally now controlled by guerrilla forces intent on re-creating the regime and state to serve new political, economic and foreign policy agendas. At least potentially, the nature of the transition constituted a fundamental challenge to U.S. permanent interests in Nicaragua and Central America.

In the absence of any viable alternative, the White House adopted a policy of conditional accommodation with the Sandinistas and set about formulating strategies to contain the revolution within one country and limit the scope of the domestic transformation. Interagency debate was confined to arguing over how best to achieve these consensual objectives (for example, whether or not to renew military funding to rightist Central American allies).

The administration decision to concentrate its energies on promoting a political base within the new regime that could eventually challenge the Sandinista-dominated state testified to the continuing centrality of the state/regime distinction in policy deliberations about Nicaragua. This "regime against state" or "boring from within" strategy, instead of resorting to costly (direct or indirect) military intervention, was partly dictated by the unfolding Sandinista economic development program based on a mixture of public, private, and foreign investment. The composition of the first cabinet included moderate appointees to the key economic posts; property nationalizations were largely confined to Somoza family interests and the takeover of selected foreign-owned enterprises were justified on economic, not ideological, grounds; and the regime's rhetoric accorded as much importance to economic reconstruction and increasing productivity as to redistributive measures. Taking these factors into account, U.S. policymakers concluded that the political and socioeconomic direction of the revolution had not yet jelled, and that opportunities still existed to mobilize support within the regime to push it in an "acceptable" direction.

The Sandinista attitude toward the American investment community in Nicaragua further reinforced the belief among senior Carter policymakers that a non-confrontational strategy offered the best chance of gaining fundamental objectives at minimal cost. Foreign capital viewed the Somoza ouster with a mixture of relief over the end of hostilities tempered by some anxiety about the future "rules of the economic game." Nonetheless, most U.S. multinationals showed considerable political flexibility in dealing with the new regime, encouraged by initial Sandinista policies (sectoral nationalization, pro-foreign investment rhetoric, an emphasis on wage restraint and increasing productivity, and so on), which gave no indication of any emerging intolerable situation for the private sector. Despite a growing public sector, new regulations on private business, and increased labor militancy, the development "model" gave Washington little or no pretext for any reversion to a policy of hostility.

Contrary to the notion that Third World revolutions are necessarily "bad for business," the Nicaraguan experience suggests that they may well be quite compatible with foreign capital given not only the constraints imposed by the historical development of their economies (for example, excessive dependence on foreign imports and markets) but also the typical array of inherited problems such as low levels of foreign exchange, big external debts and massive capital flight. The economic/development context within which the Sandinistas came to power offered potential rewards for those overseas investors and traders capable of adapting to the new set of demands established by the revolutionary regime.

The "engine" of the White House-State Department "regime against state" strategy was economic diplomacy. It consisted of an aid program intended to bolster the fortunes of the private sector (and their political supporters inside the regime); and demands that the Sandinistas rapidly conclude new debt restructuring agreements with the country's public and private creditors, thus forcing the revolutionaries to reaffirm, and deepen, Nicaragua's ties to, and dependence on, the major lending institutions of the capitalist world.

Much to the administration's consternation, the economic strategy was not all plain sailing. The request for Congressional passage of the pivotal $75 million aid package triggered highly divisive House and Senate debates that dragged on for months before reaching a successful conclusion – but only after the White House was compelled to accept a number of House-imposed conditions. The other economic pressure point, the country's foreign debt, which Minister of Planning Henry Ruiz described as "a needle in the spine which must be faced up to,"[342] was also the subject of long, drawn-out negotiations. American officials badgered and pressured the Sandinistas to reach rapid settlements with their overseas creditors. The United States and other multinational bank lenders were able to extract important concessions from the Sandinistas en route to a restructuring of the private debt in late 1980. But promised new loans were not forthcoming. The bankers subsequently admitted that their public rhetoric belied their private conviction that no such funds would be forthcoming: They believed the Sandinistas, irrespective of the outcome of the debt negotiations, were al-

---

342 Quoted in Department of State Telegram, Managua 3160, American Embassy (Pezzullo) to Secretary of State, July 8, 1980, Subject: "Minister of Planning Comments on Debt Rescheduling," DFOIA.

ready beyond the ideological pale. Although efforts to achieve a multilateral rescheduling of the much smaller public debt owed to Western governments (the so-called Paris Club) ultimately collapsed over Washington's insistence that Nicaragua negotiate a stabilization loan with the IMF beforehand, it did not undercut the relative success of this aspect of the U.S. aid strategy.

The consolidation of Sandinista political and state power, and the regime's evolving foreign policy, rather than economic factors, were responsible for the deterioration in bilateral relations that occurred during 1980. It did not take long for U.S. policymakers to realize that the "regime against state" strategy was not working. The takeover of key cabinet posts by FSLN commandantes, the restructuring of the newly established Council of State legislative assembly, which ensured a future Sandinista majority, and the proliferation, and increasing political weight, of Sandinista mass organizations testified to its ineffectiveness. Instead of a visible increase in political influence wielded by the "moderates," the trend was in the opposite direction. To counter this growing institutionalization of revolutionary power, the White House authorized a covert political-action program to shore up the opposition forces in government, the economy and the society.

Even more central to explaining the downturn in Washington-Sandinista relations during the twilight of the Carter presidency was United States hostility to aspects of Nicaragua's external relations: the close links with Fidel Castro's Cuba, especially in the military and security spheres; the new diplomatic, aid, and market ties with the Soviet Union and Eastern Europe; and renewed allegations of military aid to Salvadoran guerrillas. To U.S. officials, this combination of political shifts and foreign policy developments seemed ominous indicators of the direction in which the revolution was moving.

8

Conclusion

The shifts and changes in American policy toward Nicaragua were dictated largely by movements in the level of the sociopolitical and class struggle between Somoza and his domestic adversaries. Between the 1950s and mid-1970s, U.S. policymakers accommodated a family dictatorship that firmly controlled the polity and state, and unquestionly supported Washington's global and regional goals. Throughout the Nixon-Ford era, neither protests by sectors of the local bourgeoisie nor lower-class discontent had any significant impact on the bilateral relationship. Washington was unmoved by this relatively low-level, uncoordinated opposition, which posed no serious challenge to the power of the client. The limited policy shift that occurred during the last year of the Ford presidency was primarily a response to increasing Congressional concern over human rights abuses in Nicaragua, which forced the administration to at least make private diplomatic efforts to encourage Somoza to halt National Guard "excesses."

During the first 18 months of the Carter presidency, a groundswell of anti-regime sentiment manifested itself in two failed attempts to oust Somoza from power: a guerrilla-led insurrectionary challenge in October 1977 and a general strike organized by the civilian opposition in January 1978. In response, the administration stepped up criticism of Somoza's repressive rule and lack of tactical flexibility on the one hand; and expanded ties with the anti-regime civilian leadership as part of an effort to promote some kind of power-sharing arrangement with the dictatorship, and limited reforms, on the other. But the White House indicated no desire to move beyond censuring aspects of the client's authoritarian governance; senior officials did not, for example, contemplate any fundamental rupture in economic and military aid programs. The power of the National Guard, together with the lack of an acceptable and effective political alternative, dictated an approach based on pursuing reforms "through Somoza" and marking time until his term of office expired in May 1981. This strategy was shattered by the failure of another bourgeois-led general strike to topple the regime in late August 1978 and the first revolutionary wave of early September.

Against the background of a worsening economic crisis, this nationwide upheaval writ large the extent of the ruling dynasty's political isolation. The appearance of a broad-based, polyclass opposition force potentially threatening both the regime and the state, and therefore U.S. permanent interests in Nicaragua, galvanized Carter policymakers to action. Two interrelated issues dominated the bureaucratic debate: how to ensure the survival of the National Guard *and* prevent the most radical elements of the anti-dictatorial movement (the Sandinistas) from hegemonizing any political transition. Washington's strategy of a negotiated solution ("mediation") ultimately foundered on Somoza's intransigence and refusal to make any substantive concessions to the "acceptable" anti-regime civilian groups. Although U.S. officials pressured their bourgeois allies to make one concession after another to keep the dictator at the bargaining table, the latter was all the time pursuing his own agenda – exploiting this "space" to reconsolidate his political and military authority.

After the collapse of the mediation talks in January 1979, U.S. policy, based on a perception that Somoza had indeed strengthened his position, reverted to a more accommodative approach – seemingly reconciled to the dictator's leaving office on his own timetable. The lull in the military conflict, however, was deceptive and short-lived. At the end of May, the rural insurgents detonated a second revolutionary wave, setting the stage for a climactic confrontation with the coercive state.

Acknowledging that Somoza's demise was now inevitable, Washington proceeded to do all within its power to bolster the standing of the "acceptable" opposition leadership, all the while encouraging it to forge an alliance with the National Guard to block a Sandinista-dominated regime change. The survival of the Guard was the highest priority because the administration, in the words of American Ambassador to Nicaragua Lawrence Pezzullo, "felt that we needed some way of preventing the extreme left from dominating the political spectrum."[1] The White House also tested the degree of regional support for direct military intervention to prevent a guerrilla victory only to discover a marked lack of enthusiasm in the Organization of American States for any power projection "from the outside." Unwilling to act unilaterally, it renewed diplomatic efforts in a last ditch attempt to weaken the power of the anti-regime, anti-system forces. This involved a two-track approach: establishing a credible alternative to the FSLN's provisional junta, and pressuring the Sandinistas directly and through other

1   Interview with Lawrence Pezzullo, New York, September 28, 1988.

hemispheric governments, to make changes in the junta's membership and political program. Neither succeeded – partly the result of a dramatic shift in the correlation of military power.

Throughout these final months of dictatorial rule, American policymakers continued to display a limited understanding of the shifts and changes (the "dynamics") of the unfolding conflict as it sped toward its denouement. Nowhere was this more evident than in the persistent belief, until almost the eve of Somoza's overthrow and despite contrary advice from Nicaraguan and regional allies, that it was possible to marginalize the Sandinistas from the centers of political power following a regime change.

Ambassador Pezzullo has argued that the National Guard could have been preserved in some form "if Somoza had played the game" and not continually attempted to obstruct and undermine American policy objectives.[2] But this interpretation fails to take account of Washington's failure to develop horizontal ties with the Guard officer corps, which in no small measure prevented it from reshuffling the regime in a manner consonant with U.S. permanent interests. Moreover, the reason for this failure, according to one disillusioned Pentagon official, was not so much a lack of opportunity to cultivate these subordinate military officers as it was a manifest absence of initiative within the imperial state: "There was no desire on the part of the U.S. to detach the Guard from Somoza. I never saw anything approaching the effort by the U.S. to separate the PDF [Panamanian Defense Forces] from [General Manuel] Noriega [during the late 1980s]. This was not something attempted in Nicaragua."[3] By monopolizing all ties with the U.S., Somoza was able to effectively maintain hierarchical discipline over the Guard and block any U.S.-organized coup.

What the Nicaraguan outcome illustrates is that it cannot be assumed that what U.S. governments "will" they can "realize" – that Washington has an omnipotence that allows it to pull whatever trigger, whenever it chooses.

In the aftermath of the Sandinista political and military victory, the foremost issue confronting Carter policymakers was how to come to terms with the collapse of a historic ally and preserve U.S. permanent interests in this Central American country. The White House decided to elaborate a new strategy based on a conditional acceptance of Sandinista power and maintenance of normal diplomatic ties with a view to exploiting its access to the regime and the economy to apply pressure on the state. Aware that revolutionary power was concentrated in the state, the objective in supporting

---

2 Ibid.
3 Confidential interview, Department of Defense official, Washington, D.C., October 2, 1990.

the moderate and conservative forces inside and outside the new regime and channeling funds to the private sector was to weaken and divide the target forces to the point where they would relinquish state power. The rationale for the aid program was to prevent a "Cuban solution," which Deputy Secretary of State Warren Christopher asserted was the most likely outcome in the absence of "our refusal to help.... "[4] Such "help" also extended to the covert funding of non-Sandinista political, media and labor organizations.

Despite the moderate character of the new economic program (for example, sectoral nationalization, advocacy of foreign investment, no agrarian reform law, renegotiating the foreign debt), growing Sandinista dominance within the state and regime during 1980, and the accompanying decline in political influence of the U.S. and its internal allies, served to heighten imperial state anxieties over the ultimate direction of the Nicaraguan revolution. Sandinista foreign policy – its ties with Cuba and the Soviet Union, and its purported role as a major weapons supplier to the guerrillas in El Salvador – accelerated the downward spiral in bilateral relations as the Carter presidency drew to a close.

From Carter to Reagan

In *Confronting Revolution: Security Through Diplomacy in Central America,* Blachman et al. argue that although the Carter and Reagan administrations shared the same "hegemonic strategic vision," there were "vast differences" in the methods used to pursue common strategic objectives in the subregion. In seeking to impose anti-nationalist, anti-left political outcomes compatible with "American national interests," the "moderate" hegemonists (Carterites) preferred to employ political/diplomatic pressures and economic diplomacy in contrast to the "hard" hegemonists (Reaganites) who advocated the immediate resort to military force when confronted by Central American regimes deemed to be "security threats" to the United States. These contrasting "operational policies" reflect the divergent ideological outlooks that exist between liberal Democrats and conservative Republicans. In the final analysis, Blachman et al. contend, it was these ideological differences that accounted for the dramatic turnabout in American policy toward Nicaragua in the transition from Carter to Reagan.[5] Although the distinction between

4 Address by Deputy Secretary of State Warren Christopher, American Bar Association, Honolulu, August 4, 1980, reprinted as *Human Rights and the National Interest,* Current Policy No. 206, Bureau of Public Affairs, Department of State.
5 See Morris J. Blachman et al, eds. *Confronting Revolution: Security Through Diplomacy in Central America* (New York: Pantheon Books, 1986), pp. 313, 329–337.

"moderate" and "hard" hegemonists is a useful analytical tool, the explanatory power attributed to ideological differences in the case of Nicaragua seems excessive – insofar as it understates the continuities and overlapping approaches that suggest a much less fundamental shift in policy took place after January 1981 than Blachman et al. are willing to concede.

The Reagan military interventionist policy grew out of the failure of the Carter "boring from within" approach to change the Nicaraguan regime and state; it was the outcome of a search for a more effective way of pursuing the common "hegemonic" goal. But the argument for a sharp break between the "soft" Carterites and the "hard" Reaganites is further blurred if consideration is given to (a) the shifts in Carter global policy during 1979–80, (b) the involvement of conservative members of both the executive and legislative branches in efforts to create the foundations of a contra force within weeks of the Sandinista victory, and (c) the ties of the contra political and military leadership to the Carter administration.

As early as the fall of 1979, the Carter White House began to shift toward a more interventionist foreign policy. Contrary to earlier human rights pronouncements, global arms sales and the overall military budget embarked on a new upward spiral. Among the primary recipients of the expanded "security assistance" programs were an array of military and autocratic regimes in Latin America and other parts of the Third World that had previously been criticized for widespread human rights violations. Simultaneously, efforts were stepped up to create a 100,000 strong Rapid Deployment Force (RDF) capable of intervening within hours in any part of the globe where American interests were threatened. This period was also notable for a White House attempt to fabricate a Soviet military threat in Cuba, which was so transparently fraudulent that even the Washington political establishment was soon forced to reject it. Nonetheless, it was part of a singular bellicose pattern – a drift toward "direct action." Indeed, out of the non-threat of Soviet troops in Cuba, the White House was able to establish a Caribbean Joint Task Force in Florida to police the area and prepare for possible interventionary actions.

The ideology of "national security" became the basis for this post-Vietnam mobilization of military resources and public opinion to defend imperial interests, culminating in the January 1980 unveiling of President Carter's "new doctrine" of unilateral U.S. military intervention in the event of any attempt to limit American access to the Persian Gulf and its oil fields.[6] But Congressional testimony on the RDF revealed what Melvin Leffler called "the global, amorphous, and imprecise definition of American national se-

6 See Hedrick Smith, "The Carter Doctrine," *New York Times*, January 24, 1980, p. 1.

curity interests let loose by the Carter Doctrine."[7] Under Secretary of Defense Robert Komer quickly dismissed any suggestion that RDF activities would be confined to the Persian Gulf region: "To the contrary, the rapid deployment force will be capable of being used wherever American interests are threatened."[8] The Doctrine also unleashed a massive global weapons sales program: The total value of conventional arms transfers in 1980 reached $15.3 billion, only $500,000 below the record 1975 figure.[9]

In the case of Nicaragua, having found it impossible to weaken revolutionary state power utilizing the strategy of "boring from within" (the regime), the Carter White House began targeting the Sandinista's relations with the Soviet Union and Cuba as the basis for future conflict. With the framework and climate for a new Cold War foreign policy firmly in place, political power in the United States passed to a set of policymakers even more ideologically committed to an aggressive projection of American military power abroad in support of "national security" interests, especially in the Third World.

The active involvement of right-wing elements within the Carter foreign policy bureaucracy in developing an anti-Sandinista military option also weakens the argument about a profound change in Nicaragua policy following Reagan's election. Beginning in late 1979, a number of Pentagon officials established contact with former National Guard colonel and Nicaraguan military attaché to the United States Enrique Bermúdez to explore possible avenues for reversing the Sandinista revolution. The head of the Air Force's Western Hemisphere Division subsequently introduced Bermúdez to interested CIA officials. By mid-1980, the Nicaraguan "was on the CIA payroll" and being groomed by the covert agency to serve "as the point man for the Agency's most ambitious project in Latin America since the Bay of Pigs."[10] Bermúdez also became a leader of the September 15 legion, a group of exiled Somocista Guardsmen who, together with other anti-Sandinista groups, received funds and counterinsurgency training from the Argentine armed forces.[11] Although none of these groups received pub-

---

7 Leffler, "From the Truman Doctrine to the Carter Doctrine: Lessons and Dilemmas of the Cold War," p. 259.
8 Quoted in ibid.
9 "U.S. Overseas Arms Sales Hit Near-Record in 1980" *Washington Post*, January 1, 1981, p. A2.
10 Sam Dillon, *Commandos: The CIA and Nicaragua's Contra Rebels* (New York: Henry Holt, 1991), pp. 63, 65.
11 See ibid., pp. 63–64; Edgar Chamorro, *Packing the Contras: A Case of CIA Disinformation* (New York: Institute for Media Analysis, 1987), p. 6. Recruited by the CIA in November 1982, Chamorro served as FDN public relations director. He was dismissed from this position in December 1984 after publicly conceding that the contras had committed major human rights abuses.

lic or covert U.S. aid, the CIA was certainly able to fund Bermúdez's organizing activities from its "political budget under the terms of its annual intelligence authorization that allowed the Agency to channel funds to the Sandinista's opponents...."[12] In any event, Pentagon and CIA officials, conservative legislators (in particular, Senator Jesse Helms and his senior aide John Carbaugh), Honduran military officers and Nicaraguan exiles "operated along parallel tracks" throughout 1980 to establish "the groundwork" for the subsequent Reagan decision to support the contra military option.[13]

Perhaps even more suggestive of the lack of any profound "break" in Nicaragua policy between Carter and Reagan are the key roles played by many of the same Nicaraguan political and military figures in operationalizing the "contrasting" policy approaches. The Carter White House "moderate" strategy – initially to prevent a Sandinista victory, then to undermine revolutionary state power – aligned itself with a number of prominent anti-Somoza civilian "influentials" whom the "hard" hegemonists of the Reagan administration later recruited to head the military and political wings of the contra movement.

Francisco Aguirre, an influential figure in the Nicaraguan exile community, whom Ambassador Lawrence Pezzullo identified as one of those the State Department should involve in any initiative to "bolster the moderates" after the Sandinista victory, had extensive contacts within the CIA and State, and played an instrumental role in getting the Reagan White House to fund the contra mercenaries.[14] Enrique Bermúdez, the former ex-Guard officer who became a CIA operative in 1980, was considered by Carter officials as a possible candidate to head a refurbished Somoza military institution. In August 1981, he became the military commander of the Nicaraguan Democratic Forces (FDN), the largest of the contra organizations, and remained in charge of military operations in northern Nicaragua throughout the Reagan years. Edén Pastora, the one Sandinista leader upon whom U.S. officials passed favorable judgments during 1978–79, established a contra-military force in Costa Rica in 1983 funded and armed by the CIA.

Among the anti-Somoza civilian leadership, Alfredo César, Alfonso Robelo, and Arturo Cruz Sr. were lauded by Carter officials as "responsible" and "moderate" opponents of the dictatorship and their appointments to leading positions in the new government were deemed vital to maintaining the Sandinista's political and economic credibility abroad. Yet each willingly

---

12 Dillon, *Commandos: The CIA and Nicaragua's Contra Rebels*, p. 341.
13 Roy Gutman, *Banana Diplomacy: The Making of American Policy in Nicaragua 1981–1987* (New York: Simon & Schuster, 1988), p. 39.
14 See ibid., pp. 19–51; Chamorro, *Packaging the Contras: A Case of CIA Disinformation*, pp. 5–6.

transferred his allegiance to the Reagan military strategy. After holding the posts of Reconstruction Minister and Central Bank president, César went into exile in 1982. Three years later, he helped found the Southern Opposition Bloc (BOS) which merged with the United Nicaraguan Opposition (UNO) in 1987 to become the Nicaraguan Resistance Directorate (RN). Alfonso Robelo, a wealthy businessman and one of the leaders of the U.S.-supported Broad Opposition Front (FAO) during the 1978 mediation talks, was appointed by the Sandinistas to the first revolutionary junta. He resigned from the governing body in April 1981 and within a year had established his own opposition party in exile, the Nicaraguan Democratic Movement (MDN). Later he joined forces with Edén Pastora in Costa Rica to become political coordinator of the Democratic Revolutionary Alliance (ARDE). In June 1985, he became one of the leaders of the UNO; in May 1987 he was elected a member of its successor political contra organization, the RN.

Arturo Cruz Sr., identified by Assistant Secretary of State Viron Vaky in September 1978 as one of two "moderates" (the other was Robelo) Washington thought capable of exercising political power in a post-Somoza Nicaragua, held a number of important positions under the Sandinistas: head of the Central Bank, member of the governing junta (replacing Robelo), and Ambassador to the United States. In 1983, however, he joined the exile opposition, soon after became a paid asset of the CIA and, in February 1985, was transferred to a payroll controlled by National Security Council official Oliver North. In June of that year, he was named a director of the UNO.

Another prominent civilian oppositionist from the Carter period who ended up in the Reagan contra camp was rightist politician and businessman Adolfo Calero. The head of the Conservative Party and active in the FAO during the mediation process, he favorably impressed U.S. Embassy officials, who described him as a "moderate". According to U.S. government sources, Calero "had been a CIA asset well before he left Managua" at the covert agency's urging in December 1982 to become leader of the FDN directorate.[15] He served with Cruz and Robelo on the UNO directorate, worked closely with Oliver North to raise arms, funds, and Congressional support for the contras, and remained in the forefront of contra political activities until mid-1989.

The new Reagan administration, like its predecessor, defined the state as the locus of power in Nicaragua and acknowledged its domination by the revolutionary forces. But unlike Carter, Reagan was completely uninterested in questions of democracy, elections, human rights, and political pluralism under Sandinista rule. His singular objective, at first unstated, later publicly

---

15 Gutman, *Banana Diplomacy: The Making of American Policy in Nicaragua 1981–1987*, p. 152.

declared, was to overthrow the revolutionary state by force and change the regime. As a result, the Carter "regime against state" strategy was jettisoned in favor of economic warfare, and the recomposition of the Somoza state, specifically former National Guardsmen, as a counterrevolutionary army – in alliance with dissident moderate and conservative civilian politicians. In the process, Reagan policy belatedly constructed the prototype of the regime that Carter unsuccessfully promoted in the last days of the dictatorship: a civilian-military apparatus compatible with U.S. permanent interests in Nicaragua.

"Saving the state": Concluding remarks

This study attests to the centrality of the state/regime distinction in American foreign policy deliberations about how to respond to Third World political transitions. As with Cuba in the 1950s, Vietnam in the 1960s, El Salvador in the late 1970s and early 1980s, and Guatemala and the Philippines in the 1980s, White House policy toward the Nicaraguan state during the Carter presidency remained constant; toward the regime, variable. It supported a shift from dictatorship to civilian rule as part of an effort to weaken anti-system groups that had emerged to challenge a client regime and state, in the process facilitating the ascendancy of those political forces disposed to coexist with the strategic institutional structures that underpinned the Somoza dynasty. The failure to broker such an outcome in this case did not serve to invalidate the traditional U.S. view of Third World political systems; nor did it weaken policymakers' belief that Washington's ability to exert maximum leverage in support of U.S. permanent interests is dependent, in the final analysis, on the continuity of state structures with historic linkages "to the outside."

Although past American policy has alternated between support for democracies and dictatorships in the Third World, its response to the issue of rulership since the Nicaraguan revolution indicates a sustained preference for working with popularly elected regimes so long as they are compatible with existing state structures, able to control and limit the influence of anti-system forces, and willing to defend U.S. permanent interests. This is particularly evident in the case of Latin America.

Since the early 1980s, the U.S. has fashioned a complex and coherent regional strategy based on its formidable military and ideological power: promoting civilian regimes receptive to "free market" economic doctrines and willing to cohabit with existing military structures. These electoral transitions from authoritarian to elected presidents, with U.S. officials often playing the role of "broker," have nowhere attempted to challenge the power of the armed forces or the entrenched socioeconomic elites. Regarding the former, these new civilian regimes have typically legitimated the role of the military, largely through laws granting impunity and amnesty for major human rights abuses committed in office (for example, Chile); accepted a continuing high degree of military violence as the price they must pay for survival in office (for example, Guatemala); and/or provided the legal cover for an increasing U.S. military presence in these societies—whether in the guise of fighting the anti-drug war or combating "subversion" or for the "common defense" (for example, Peru).

Nonetheless, although U.S. policymakers welcomed and encouraged the return to electoral politics throughout the hemisphere, if circumstances arise where the democratic regimes pose a threat to the state or begin to decay (triggering the revival of anti-system groups and mass mobilization politics), then Washington will likely revert to supporting a more authoritarian kind of rulership in order to reestablish political "stability" and eliminate "threats" to state structures. The Bush administration's response to the overthrow of Haiti's first democratically elected government in September 1991 illustrated the continuing order of priorities.

In December 1990, campaigning on a platform of socioeconomic changes and reforming key state institutions, including the armed forces, Jean-Bertrand Aristide was elected president of Haiti with an overwhelming 67 percent of the popular vote. On assuming office, however, he confronted two active centers of resistance: a local economic elite that branded him a "Bolshevik" and "the devil" and a military leadership that opposed his efforts to reform the institution and implement existing constitutional provisions affirming civilian authority over the armed forces.

Aristide's presidency lasted a mere nine months; in September 1991 it was terminated by a military coup. Initially, Washington joined with other regional governments in denouncing the junta and calling for the reinstatement of the ousted Haitian leader; days later, however, the Bush administration started to back away from unqualified support for the deposed president's return with all his former powers intact. This policy shift was linked to a concern over Aristide's populist orientation. The White House was ambivalent about supporting an elected leader who was committed to empowering a largely peasant population through changes in the economy, the regime, *and* the state. And as the policy unfolded, it soon became clear that support for Aristide's return was predicated on the latter's willingness to accept specific limitations on his presidential powers, not least because his efforts to democratize the Haitian state were perceived as a potential threat to U.S. permanent interests.

For all its professed aversion to the military *golpistas*, the United States dragged its feet on endorsing an Organization of American States trade embargo of Haiti, and subsequently (February 1992) exempted American-owned assembly plants and other businesses from its provisions. Then it sought to broker an "acceptable" political compromise: Under intense pressure from Washington, Aristide agreed to sign an accord with Haitian parliamentarians appointing an interim Prime Minister and establishing a timetable for his return as little more than a figurehead president at some future, unspecified, date. After the parliament, bowing to military opposition, failed to approve the accord, Washington quickly revealed a disposition to tolerate the existing political arrangements. In July 1992, it encouraged Aristide to negotiate with the new military-imposed Prime Minister, Marc Bazin, a former World Bank official and U.S.-backed candidate in the December 1990 elections in which he received only 14 percent of the total vote. This further emphasized the conditional nature of Bush's support for the restoration of Aristide's presidency: It had to be acceptable to Haiti's military and economic elite.

In the late 1970s and 1980s, Washington confronted non-elected client regimes in Latin America whose policies and behavior were viewed as endangering state institutions. But this is no guarantee against a policy reversal in the future – an accommodation with a new cycle of military coups and authoritarian dictatorships if the electoral experiments falter and collapse. During the 1980s and early 1990s, U.S. governments elaborated a regional political strategy based on promoting democratic rule; simultaneously, they also consolidated ties with the region's armed forces as insurance against the civilian regimes losing control of their populations or "free market" economies disintegrating to the accompaniment of popular uprisings incorporating large anti-system elements wanting to change regimes *and* states.

Bibliography

Interviews

This study is based partly on personal interviews conducted with U.S. executive branch officials who participated in the making and execution of U.S. policy toward Nicaragua during the Nixon, Ford, and Carter administrations, and with representatives of U.S. corporations and banks with investments or financial exposure in Nicaragua during this same period. Most of these interviews were "on the record" but a small number were conducted on an understanding of strict confidentiality. I also quote from the transcripts of Oral History Interviews, Association for Diplomatic Studies, Foreign Affairs Oral History Program, Lauinger Library, Georgetown University, Washington D.C., and the transcript of a program presented by WGBH Television, Boston, Massachusetts entitled "Crisis in Central America: Revolution in Nicaragua," Frontline #313, April 10, 1985, which included interviews with Carter administration officials involved in Nicaragua policymaking.

Unpublished U.S. government documents

Perhaps the single most important source of primary data was the U.S. government's Freedom of Information Act (FOIA). A large number of classified documents were released to the author as a result of mandatory declassified review requests. Additional unpublished government documents were obtained from The National Security Archive, Washington, D.C., the National Archives, Washington, D.C., the Richard M. Nixon Presidential Materials, Alexandria, Virginia, the Gerald R. Ford Presidential Library, Ann Arbor, Michigan, and the Jimmy Carter Presidential Library, Atlanta, Georgia.

Unpublished manuscripts

Center for International Policy. *Background Paper: IMF Loan to Nicaragua.* Washington, D.C., June 21, 1979.
Gilbert, Dennis. *The Bourgeoisie and the Nicaraguan Revolution.* Paper presented at the Latin American Studies Association Meeting, Mexico City, October 1983, 36pp.
Inter-American Development Bank. *Nicaragua: Credit Program for the Revival of Agriculture and Fisheries* (NI-0093). PR-1083. November 25, 1980.

Padula Jr., Alfred. *The Fall of the Bourgeoisie: Cuba, 1959–1961.* PhD dissertation, University of New Mexico, 1974.

Rodman, Kenneth A. *Hegemonic Decline, Multinational Corporations, and U.S. Economic Sanctions Since the Pipeline Case.* Paper presented to the annual conference of the American Political Science Association, Washington, D.C., September 1–4, 1988, 48pp.

World Bank, Latin America and the Caribbean Regional Office. *Nicaragua: The Challenge of Reconstruction.* Internal Document, Report No. 3524-NI, October 9, 1981.

Published U.S. government documents: Executive branch

Agency for International Development. *U.S. Overseas Loans and Grants and Assistance from International Organizations, July 1, 1945–June 30, 1973.*

—, Bureau of Program and Policy Coordination, Office of Planning and Budgeting. *U.S. Overseas Loans and Grants and Assistance from International Organizations, July 1, 1945–September 30, 1982.*

—, Bureau of Program and Policy Coordination, Office of Planning and Budgeting. *U.S. Overseas Loans and Grants and Assistance from International Organizations, July 1, 1945–September 30, 1980.*

—, Office of Programs and Information Analysis Services, Statistics and Research Division. *U.S. Overseas Loans and Grants and Assistance from International Organizations, July 1, 1945–September 30, 1976.*

The American University, Foreign Area Studies. *Nicaragua: A Country Study.* Department of the Army, Washington, D.C.: U.S. Government Printing Office, September 1981.

Binnendikj, Hans, ed. *Authoritarian Regimes in Transition.* Department of State: Foreign Service Institute, June 1987.

Department of Commerce. *Survey of Current Business,* Vol. 61, No. 8, August 1981, Vol. 63, No. 8, August 1983.

—, Bureau of Economic Analysis. *Selected Data on U.S. Investment Abroad, 1950–76.* February 1982.

—, Bureau of International Commerce. *Foreign Economic Trends and their Implications for the United States.* American Embassy, Managua, December 1968, December 1969, December 1973, February 1975, January 1976, March 1977.

—, Domestic and International Business Administration. *United States Foreign Trade Annual 1969–1975* (Overseas Business Reports 76-24). May 1976.

—, Industry and Trade Administration. *United States Foreign Trade Annual 1971–1977* (Overseas Business Reports 78-21). June 1978.

—, International Trade Administration. *United States Foreign Trade Annual 1974–1980* (Overseas Business Reports 81-34) November 1981.

Department of State. *Bureau of Public Affairs Press Releases.*

—, *Foreign Relations of the United States, 1955–1957, Volume VII: American Republics Central and South America.* Washington, D.C.: U.S. Government Printing Office, 1987.

—, *Foreign Relations of the United States, 1958–1960, Volume I: American Republics,* Microfiche Supplement. Washington, D.C.: U.S. Government Printing Office, 1991.

—, *"Revolution Beyond Our Borders": Sandinista Intervention in Central America,* Report No. 132, September 1985.

—, *Soviet Attitudes Towards Aid to and Contacts with Central American Revolutions.* Prepared by C.G. Jacobsen, June 1984.

Foreign Broadcast Information Service. *Daily Report: Latin America.*

General Accounting Office, Report to the Congress. *Nicaragua–An Assessment of Earthquake Relief and Reconstruction Assistance,* ID-77–25, March 17, 1977.

—, *Review of Administration of United States Assistance for Capital Development Projects in Brazil,* B.133283 May 16, 1968.

Matthews, Wade H.B. *Human Rights and the National Interest: Our Policy in Central America and the Philippines.* Executive Seminar in National and International Affairs, Twenty-Second Session, Department of State, June 1980.

Published U.S. government documents: Legislative branch

House, Committee on Appropriations, Subcommittee on Foreign Operations and Related Agencies. *Foreign Assistance and Related Agencies Appropriations for 1978, Part 1,* 95th Congress, 1st Session, March 24, 1977. Washington, D.C.: U.S. Government Printing Office, 1977.

—, Committee on Appropriations, Subcommittee on Foreign Operations and Related Agencies. *Foreign Assistance and Related Agencies Appropriations For 1978, Part 3,* 95th Congress, 1st Session, April 5, 1977. Washington, D.C.: U.S. Government Printing Office, 1977.

—, Committee on Appropriations, Subcommittee on Foreign Operations and Related Programs. *Foreign Assistance and Related Programs Appropriations for 1980, Part 7,* 96th Congress, 1st Session, 1979. Washington, D.C.: U.S. Government Printing Office, 1979.

—, Committee on Appropriations, Subcommittee on Foreign Operations and Related Programs. *Foreign Assistance and Related Programs Appropriations for 1981, Part 1,* 96th Congress, 2nd Session, February 26, 1980. Washington, D.C.: U.S. Government Printing Office, 1980.

—, Committee on Foreign Affairs. *Special Central American Act of 1979,* Report No. 96–713, 96th Congress, 1st Session, December 18, 1979. Washington, D.C.: U.S. Government Printing Office, 1979.

—, Committee on Foreign Affairs, Hearing and Markup. *Special Central American Economic Assistance,* 96th Congress, 1st Session, November 27 and December 11, 1979. Washington, D.C.: U.S. Government Printing Office, 1980.

—, Committee on Foreign Affairs, Subcommittee on Inter-American Affairs. *Assessment of Conditions in Central America,* 96th Congress, 2nd Session, April 29 and May 20, 1980. Washington, D.C.: U.S. Government Printing Office, 1980.

—, Committee on Foreign Affairs, Subcommittee on Inter-American Affairs. *Central America At The Crossroads,* 96th Congress, 1st Session, September 11 and 12, 1979. Washington, D.C.: U.S. Government Printing Office, 1979.

—, Committee on Foreign Affairs, Subcommittee on Inter-American Affairs. *United States Policy Toward Nicaragua,* 96th Congress, 1st Session, June 21 and 26, 1979. Washington, D.C.: U.S. Government Printing Office, 1979.

—, Committee on International Relations, Subcommittee on International Organizations. *Foreign Assistance Legislation for Fiscal Year 1979, Part 4,* 95th Congress, 2nd Session, February 15, 16, 28; March 7 and 8, 1978. Washington, D.C.: U.S. Government Printing Office, 1978.

—, Committee on International Relations, Subcommittee on International Organizations. *Human Rights in Nicaragua, Guatemala, and El Salvador: Implications for*

U.S. Policy, 94th Congress, 2nd Session, June 8 and 9, 1976. Washington, D.C.: U.S. Government Printing Office, 1976.
—, Committee on International Relations, Subcommittee on International Development. *Rethinking United States Foreign Policy Toward the Developing World: Nicaragua, Part II,* 95th Congress, 2nd Session, March 9, 1978. Washington, D.C.: U.S. Government Printing Office, 1978.
—, *Congressional Record*
Senate, Committee on Foreign Relations. *Human Rights and U.S. Foreign Assistance,* Report, Committee Print. 96th Congress, 1st Session, November 1979. Washington, D.C.: U.S. Government Printing Office, 1979.
—, Committee on Foreign Relations. *S.2012.* 96th Congress, 1st Session, December 6 and 7, 1979. Washington, D.C.: U.S. Government Printing Office, 1980.
—, Committee on Foreign Relations, Subcommittee on American Republics Affairs. *Survey of the Alliance for Progress,* 91st Congress, 1st Session, Document No. 91-17, April 29, 1969. Washington, D.C.: U.S. Government Printing Office 1969.
—, Committee on Foreign Relations, Subcommittee on Western Hemisphere Affairs. *Latin America,* 95th Congress, 2nd Session, October 4, 5 and 6, 1978. Washington, D.C.: U.S. Government Printing Office, 1978.
—, *Congressional Record.*
Select Committee on Intelligence. *Covert Action in Chile 1963–1973,* 94th Congress, 1st Session, December 18, 1975. Washington, D.C.: U.S. Government Printing Office 1975.
—, Subcommittee on Oversight and Evaluation. *U.S. Intelligence Performance on Central America: Achievements and Selected Instances of Concern,* Staff Report, Committee Print, 97th Congress, 2nd Session, September 22, 1982. Washington, D.C.: U.S. Government Printing Office, 1982.
Select Committee to Study Governmental Operations. *Alleged Assassination Plots Involving Foreign Leaders,* 94th Congress, 1st Session, Report No. 94-465, November 20, 1975. Washington, D.C.: U.S. Government Printing Office, 1975.

Books and articles

Adelman, Alan, and Reid Reading, eds. *Confrontation in the Caribbean Basis.* University of Pittsburgh: Center for Latin American Studies, 1984.
Adkins, Jason. "Taking Care of Business in Nicaragua," *Multinational Monitor,* Vol. 6, No. 4, April 1985, 3–15.
Ambrose, Stephen E. *Eisenhower, Volume 2: The President.* New York: Simon & Schuster, 1984.
Amnesty International. *The Republic of Nicaragua.* 1976.
Armstrong, Scott, and Malcolm Byrne. *The Chronology: The Documented Day-by-Day Account of the Secret Military Assistance to Iran and the Contras.* New York: Warner Books, 1987.
Arnson, Cynthia J. *Crossroads: Congress, The Reagan Administration, and Central America.* New York: Pantheon Books, 1989.
—, *El Salvador: Revolution Confronts the United States.* Washington, D.C.: Institute for Policy Studies, 1982.
Austin, John E., and John C. Ickis. "Management, Mangers, and Revolution," *World Development,* Vol. 14, No. 7, July 1986, 775–790.

—, "Managing After the Revolutionaries Have Won," *Harvard Business Review*, Vol. 3, May/June 1986, 103–109.

Bahbah, Bishara. *Israel and Latin America: The Military Connection*. New York: St. Martins Press, 1986.

Baloyra, Enrique. *El Salvador in Transition*. Chapel Hill: University of North Carolina Press, 1982.

Barry, Tom, Beth Wood, and Deb Preusch. *Dollars and Dictators*. New York: Grove Press, 1983.

Bell, Peter D. "Brazilian-American Relations," in Riorden Roett, ed. *Brazil in the Sixties*. Nashville: Vanderbilt University Press, 1972, 77–102.

Bermann, Karl. *Under the Big Stick: Nicaragua and the United States Since 1848*. Boston: South End Press, 1986.

Berrios, Ruben. "Relations Between Nicaragua and the Socialist Countries," in Augusto Varas, ed. *Soviet-Latin American Relations in the 1980s*. Boulder: Westview Press, 1987, 144–173.

Biderman, Jaime. "The Development of Capitalism in Nicaragua: A Political Economic History," *Latin American Perspectives*, Vol. X, No. 1, Winter 1983, 7–32.

Blachman, Morris J., William M. LeoGrande, Kenneth E. Sharpe, eds. *Confronting Revolution: Security Through Diplomacy in Central America*. New York: Pantheon Books, 1986.

Black, George. *The Good Neighbor: How the United States Wrote the History of Central America and the Caribbean*. New York: Pantheon Books, 1988.

—, *Triumph of the People: The Sandinista Revolution in Nicaragua*. London: Zed Press, 1981.

Black, Jan Kippers. *United States Penetration of Brazil*. Philadelphia: University of Pennsylvania Press, 1977.

Bonner, Raymond. *Weakness and Deceit: U.S. Policy and El Salvador*. New York: Times Books, 1984.

Booth, John A. *The End and the Beginning: The Nicaraguan Revolution*. Boulder: Westview Press, 1985.

Brzezinski, Zbigniew. *Power and Principle: Memoirs of the National Security Advisor 1977–1981*. London: Wiedenfeld and Nicolson, 1983.

Bulmer-Thomas, Victor. *The Political Economy of Central America Since 1920*. New York: Cambridge University Press, 1987.

Burbach, Roger, and Patricia Flynn, eds. *The Politics of Intervention: The United States in Central America*. New York: Monthly Review Press, 1984.

Carter, Jimmy. *Keeping Faith: Memoirs of a President*. London: William Collins Sons, 1982.

Central American Historical Institute (Georgetown University). *Update*, No. 8, November 5, 1982.

Chace, James. "Dithering in Nicaragua," *New York Review of Books*, August 17, 1989, 46–51.

Chamorro, Edgar. *Packing the Contras: A Case of CIA Disinformation*. New York: Institute for Media Analysis, 1987.

Christian, Shirley. *Nicaragua: Revolution in the Family*. New York: Vintage Books, 1986.

Close, David. *Nicaragua: Politics, Economics and Society*. London: Pinter Publishers, 1988.

Cohen, Stephen B. "Conditioning U.S. Security Assistance on Human Rights Practices," *American Journal of International Law*, Vol. 76, No. 2, April 1982, 246–279.

Conroy, Michael E. "Economic Aggression as an Instrument of Low-Intensity Warfare," in Thomas W. Walker, ed. *Reagan Versus the Sandinistas*. Boulder: Westview Press, 1987, 57–79.

Curry, W. Frick, and Joanne Royce. *Enforcing Human Rights: Congress and the Multilateral Banks*. Washington, D.C.: Center for International Policy, February 1985.

Díaz-Alejandro, Carlos F. "Some Aspects of Brazilian Experience with Foreign Aid," in Jagdish N. Bhagwati et al, eds. *Trade, Balance of Payments and Growth*. New York: American Elsevier, 1971, 443–472.

Dickey, Christopher. *With the Contras: A Reporter in the Wilds of Nicaragua*. New York: Touchstone Books/Simon & Schuster, 1987.

Diederich, Bernard. *Somoza and the Legacy of U.S. Involvement in Central America*. New York: E.P. Dutton, 1981.

Dillon, Sam. *Commandos: The CIA and Nicaragua's Contra Rebels*. New York: Henry Holt, 1991.

Dore, Elizabeth. "Nicaragua: The Experience of the Mixed Economy," in Jonathan Hartlyn and Samuel A. Morley, eds. *Latin American Political Economy*. Boulder: Westview Press, 1986, 319–350.

Downer, Steve. "Nicaragua: The Recovery is Only Just Beginning," *Euromoney*, December 1980, 127–129.

Dunkerly, James. *Power in the Isthmus*. London: Verso Books, 1988.

Etchison, Don L. *The United States and Militarism in Central America*. New York: Praeger Publishers, 1975.

Fagen, Richard R. "Dateline Nicaragua: The End of the Affair," *Foreign Policy*, No. 36, Fall 1979, 178–191.

Feinberg, Richard ed. *Central America: International Dimensions of the Crisis*. New York: Holmes & Meier, 1982.

—, "Central America: No Easy Answers," *Foreign Affairs*, Vol. 59, No. 5, Summer 1981, 1121–1146.

—, "The International Monetary Fund and Basic Needs: The Impact of Stand-by Arrangements," in Margaret E. Crahan, ed. *Human Rights and Basic Needs in the Americas*. Washington, D.C.: Georgetown University Press, 1982, 215–235.

Galloway, K. Bruce, and Robert Bowie, Jr. *West Point: America's Power Fraternity*. New York: Simon & Schuster, 1973.

Garthoff, Raymond L. *Detente and Confrontation: American-Soviet Relations from Nixon to Reagan*. Washington, D.C.: The Brookings Institution, 1985.

Gilbert, Dennis. *Sandinistas*. New York: Basil Blackwell, 1988.

Girling, Robert Henriques. "Nicaragua's Commercial Policy: Building a Socially Responsive Foreign Trade," *Latin American Perspectives*, Vol. X, No. 1, Winter 1983, 33–44.

Gleijeses, Piero. *The Dominican Crisis: The 1965 Constitutionalist Revolt and American Intervention*. Baltimore: The Johns Hopkins University Press, 1978.

Goff, Fred, and Michael Locker. "The Violence of Domination: U.S. Power and the Dominican Republic," in Irving Louis Horowitz et al, eds. *Latin American Radicalism*. New York: Vintage Books, 1969, 249–291.

Gorman, Stephen M. "Nicaragua," in Melvin Gurtov and Ray Maghroori. *Roots of Failure: United States Policy in the Third World*. Westport: Greenwood Press, 1984, 107–164.

—, "Power and Consolidation in the Nicaraguan Revolution," *Journal of Latin American Studies*, Vol. 13, No. 1, 1981, 133–149.

Grabendorff, Wolf, et al., eds. *Political Change in Central America: Internal and External Dimensions.* Boulder: Westview Press, 1984.

"Guerrilla Offensive Sweeps El Salvador as U.S. Renews Aid, Accuses Nicaragua," *Latin American Index*, January 15, 1981, 1.

Gutman, Roy. *Banana Diplomacy: The Making of American Policy in Nicaragua 1981–1987.* New York: Simon & Schuster, 1988.

Hardy, Chandra. "Rescheduling Developing Country Debts," *The Banker*, July 1981, 33–34, 37–38.

Ianni, Octavio. *Crisis in Brazil.* New York: Columbia University Press, 1971.

Immerman, Richard H. *The CIA in Guatemala.* Austin: University of Texas Press, 1982.

Inter-American Development Bank. *Economic and Social Progress in Latin America: 1979 Report.* Washington, D.C., 1979.

—, *Economic and Social Progress in Latin America: 1983 Report.* Washington, D.C., 1983.

"Interview with Ambassador Robert White: El Salvador's Future–and How U.S. Can Influence It," *U.S. News & World Report*, January 26, 1981, 37.

Irvin, George. "Nicaragua: Establishing the State as the Center of Accumulation," *Cambridge Journal of Economics*, Vol. 7, No. 2, June 1983, 125–139.

James, Lewis. "The Truth Behind the Nicaraguan Row with Carter and the IMF," *Euromoney*, January 1979, 109, 111.

Jorden, William J. *Panama Odyssey.* Austin: University of Texas Press, 1984.

Kissinger, Henry. *The White House Years.* London: Weidenfeld and Nicolson and Michael Joseph, 1979.

"The Koch-State Department Correspondence on U.S. Relations with Nicaragua," *Inter-American Economic Affairs*, Vol. XXIX, No. 4, Spring 1976, 85–93.

Kornbluh, Peter. *The Price of Intervention.* Washington, D.C.: Institute for Policy Studies, 1987.

LaFeber, Walter. *Inevitable Revolutions: The United States in Central America.* New York: W.W. Norton, 1983.

Lake, Anthony. *Somoza Falling.* Boston: Houghton Mifflin, 1989.

Leacock, Ruth. *Requiem for Revolution: The United States and Brazil, 1961–1969.* Kent: Kent State University Press, 1990.

Leffler, Melvin P. "From the Truman Doctrine to the Carter Doctrine: Lessons and Dilemmas of the Cold War," *Diplomatic History*, Vol. 7, No. 4, Fall 1983, 245–266.

Leiken, Robert S., and Barry Rubin, eds. *The Central American Crisis Reader.* New York: Summit Books, 1987.

Lenin, V.I. *The National Liberation Movement in the East.* Moscow: Progress Publishers, 1969.

LeoGrande, William M. "Cuba and Nicaragua: From Somozas to the Sandinistas," in Barry B. Levine, ed. *The New Cuban Presence in the Caribbean.* Boulder: Westview Press, 1983, 43–58.

—, "The Revolution in Nicaragua: Another Cuba?," *Foreign Affairs*, Vol. 58, No. 1, Fall 1979, 28–50.

Leonard, Thomas M. *Central America and the United States: The Search for Stability.* Athens: University of Georgia Press, 1991.

—, *The United States and Central America 1944–1949*. Tuscaloosa: University of Alabama Press, 1984.

Lernoux, Penny. *Cry of the People*. New York: Penguin Books, 1986.

Merrit, Jeffrey D. "Unilateral Human Rights Intercession: American Practice Under Nixon, Ford, and Carter," in David Newsom, ed. *The Diplomacy of Human Rights*. Lanham: University Press of America, 1986, 43–59.

Millett, Richard. *Guardians of the Dynasty*. New York: Orbis Books, 1977.

Montgomery, Tommie Sue. *Revolution in El Salvador*. Boulder: Westview Press, 1982.

Morley, Morris H. *Imperial State and Revolution: The United States and Cuba, 1952–1986*. New York: Cambridge University Press, 1987.

Morrell, Jim, and William Jesse Biddle. *Central America: The Financial War*. Washington, D.C.: Center for International Policy, March 1983.

"Multinationals, Development and Democracy: An Interview with Henry Geyelin [President of the Council of the Americas]," *Multinational Monitor*, Vol. 1, No. 2, March 1980, 12–16.

NACLA's Latin America & Empire Report, Vol. X, No. 2, February 1976.

NACLA Report on the Americas, Vol. XII, No. 6, November/December 1978.

—, Vol. XIX, No. 3, May/June 1985.

Organization of American States. *Meeting of Consultation of Ministers of Foreign Affairs*. OEA/Ser.F/11.7, June 23, 1979.

—, Inter-American Commission on Human Rights. *Report on the Situation of Human Rights in Nicaragua*. OEA/Ser. L/V/11.45, November 17, 1978.

Painter, James. *Guatemala: False Hope, False Freedom*. London: Latin American Bureau, 1987.

—, "Guatemala in Civilian Garb," *Third World Quarterly*, Vol. 8. No. 3, July 1986, 818–844.

Parker, Phyllis R. *Brazil and the Quiet Intervention 1964*. Austin: University of Texas Press, 1979.

Pastor, Robert A. *Condemned to Repetition: The United States and Nicaragua*. Princeton: Princeton University Press, 1987.

—, "Continuity and Change in U.S. Foreign Policy: Carter and Reagan on El Salvador," *Journal of Policy Analysis and Management*, Vol. 3, No. 2, Winter 1984, 175–190.

Pearce, Jenny. *Under the Eagle: U.S. Intervention in Central America and the Caribbean*. Boston: South End Press, 1982.

Petras, James F. "President Carter and the 'New Morality,' " *Monthly Review*, Vol. 29, No. 2, June 1977, 42–50.

—, "White Paper on the White Paper," *The Nation*, March 28, 1981, 354, 367–372.

—and Howard Brill. "The IMF, Austerity and the State in Latin America," *Third World Quarterly*, Vol. 8, No. 2, April 1986, 425–448.

—and Fernando Ignacio Leiva. "Chile: The Authoritarian Transition to Electoral Politics," *Latin American Perspectives*, Vol. 15, No. 3, Summer 1988, 97–114.

—and Morris H. Morley. *The United States and Chile: Imperialism and the Overthrow of the Allende Government*. New York: Monthly Review Press, 1975.

—and Morris H. Morley. "The U.S. Imperial State," *Review* (Fernand Braudel Center for the Study of Economies, Historical Systems, and Civilizations), Vol. IV, No. 2, Fall 1980, 171–222.

Poelchau, Warner, ed. *White Paper Whitewash.* New York: Deep Cover Books, 1981.

Rabe, Stephen G. *Eisenhower and Latin America: The Foreign Policy of Anticommunism.* Chapel Hill: University of North Carolina Press, 1988.

Rivas, Donald Castillo. *Acumulación de Capital y Empresas Transnacionales en Centroamérica.* Mexico: Siglo Vientiuno editores, 1980.

Roberts, Charles. "Nicaragua: The Unfolding Scene," *Multinational Monitor,* Vol. 1, No. 2, March 1980, 18–20.

Ropp, Steve C. *Panamanian Politics.* New York: Praeger Publishers, 1982.

Rossiter, Caleb. *Human Rights: The Carter Record, The Reagan Reaction.* Washington, D.C.: Center for International Policy, September 1984.

Rubin, Barry. *Secrets of State: The State Department and The Struggle Over U.S. Foreign Policy.* New York: Oxford University Press, 1987.

Schlesinger, Jr., Arthur M. *A Thousand Days.* Boston: Houghton Mifflin, 1965.

Schlesinger, Stephen, and Stephen Kinzer. *Bitter Fruit.* New York: Doubleday & Co., 1982.

Schoultz, Lars. *Human Rights and United States Policy Toward Latin America.* Princeton: Princeton University Press, 1981.

Sholk, Richard. "The National Bourgeoisie in Post-Revolutionary Nicaragua," *Comparative Politics,* Vol. 16, No. 3, April 1984, 253–276.

Skidmore, Thomas E. *Politics in Brazil 1930–1964.* Oxford: Oxford University Press, 1967.

Smith, Gaddis. *Morality, Reason & Power: American Diplomacy in the Carter Years.* New York: Hill & Wang, 1986.

Somoza, Anastasio. *Nicaragua Betrayed.* Boston and Los Angeles: Western Islands, 1980.

Spalding, Rose J., ed. *The Political Economy of Revolutionary Nicaragua.* Winchester: Allen & Unwin, 1987.

Stafford, Charles. "Somoza Holds a Firm Grip on Nicaragua," *St. Petersburg Times,* October 31, 1977, 1A, 7A.

Stallings, Barbara. "Peru and the U.S. Banks: Privatization of Financial Relations," in Richard R. Fagen, ed. *Capitalism and the State in U.S.-Latin American Relations.* Stanford: Stanford University Press, 1979, 217–253.

United Nations, Economic Commission for Latin America. *Economic Survey of Latin America 1979.* Santiago, Chile, 1981.

"US Pressure on Lenders Blamed for Liquidity Crisis," *Latin American Markets,* No. 63, August 1, 1983, 12.

Vaky, Viron P. "Hemisphere Relations: 'Everything is Part of Everything Else,' " *Foreign Affairs* ("America and the World 1980"), Vol. 59, No. 3, 1981, 615–647.

Vance, Cyrus. *Hard Choices: Critical Years in America's Foreign Policy.* New York: Simon & Schuster, 1983.

Vilas, Carlos M. *The Sandinista Revolution: National Liberation and Social Transformation in Central America.* New York: Monthly Review Press, 1986.

Walker, Thomas W., ed. *Nicaragua in Revolution.* New York: Praeger Publishers, 1982.

—, *Nicaragua: The Land of Sandino.* Boulder: Westview Press, 1986.

Weber, Henri. *Nicaragua: The Sandinista Revolution.* London: New Left Review, 1981.

Weeks, John. *The Economies of Central America.* New York: Holmes & Meier, 1985.

Weinert, Richard. "Nicaragua's Debt Renegotiation," *Cambridge Journal of Economics*, Vol. 5, No. 2, June 1981, 187–194.
Wilkie, James W., ed. *Statistical Abstract of Latin America, Volume 20.* University of California at Los Angeles: Latin American Center, 1980.
Williams, Robert G. *Export Agriculture and the Crisis in Central America.* Chapel Hill: University of North Carolina Press, 1986.
Woodward, Bob. *Veil: The Secret Wars of the CIA 1981–1987.* New York: Simon & Schuster, 1987.
World Bank. *World Development Report 1980.* New York: Oxford University Press, August 1980.
Zeitlin, Maurice, and R.E. Ratcliff. "Research Methods for the Analysis of the Internal Structure of Dominant Classes: The Case of Landlords and Capitalists in Chile," *Latin American Research Review*, Vol. X, No. 3, Winter 1965, 5–61.

Periodicals and Newspapers

Business Latin America
Business Week
Central America Bulletin
Central America Report (Guatemala)
Christian Science Monitor
Congressional Quarterly Weekly Report
Economist Intelligence Unit, *Quarterly Economic Review of Nicaragua* (United Kingdom)
Facts on File
Financial Times (United Kingdom)
Houston Post
Journal of Commerce
Keesings Contemporary Archives
Latin America Economic Report (United Kingdom)
Latin America Political Report (United Kingdom)
Latin America Regional Reports: Mexico and Central America (United Kingdom)
Los Angeles Times
Miami Herald
New York Times
Newsweek
This Week: Central America and Panama (Guatemala)
Wall Street Journal
Washington Post
Washington Report on the Hemisphere
Washington Star

Index